Lecture Notes in Computer Science   11964

More information about this series at http://www.springer.com/series/7407

Nikolaj Bjørner · Irina Virbitskaite ·
Andrei Voronkov (Eds.)

Perspectives of System Informatics

12th International Andrei P. Ershov Informatics Conference, PSI 2019
Novosibirsk, Russia, July 2–5, 2019
Revised Selected Papers

 Springer

Editors
Nikolaj Bjørner
Microsoft Research
Redmond, WA, USA

Irina Virbitskaite
AP Ershov Institute of Informatics Systems
Novosibirsk, Russia

Andrei Voronkov
School of Computer Science
University of Manchester
Manchester, UK

ISSN 0302-9743   ISSN 1611-3349   (electronic)
Lecture Notes in Computer Science
ISBN 978-3-030-37486-0   ISBN 978-3-030-37487-7   (eBook)
https://doi.org/10.1007/978-3-030-37487-7

LNCS Sublibrary: SL1 – Theoretical Computer Science and General Issues

This Springer imprint is published by the registered company Springer Nature Switzerland AG
The registered company address is: Gewerbestrasse 11, 6330 Cham, Switzerland

Preface

PSI is the premier international forum in Russia for academic and industrial researchers, developers, and users working on topics relating to computer, software, and information sciences. The conference serves to bridge the gaps between different communities whose research areas are covered by, but not limited to, foundations of program and system development and analysis, programming methodology and software engineering, and information technologies.

The previous 11 PSI conferences were held in 1991, 1996, 1999, 2001, 2003, 2006, 2009, 2011, 2014, 2015, and 2017, respectively, and proved to be significant international events. Traditionally, PSI offers a program of keynote lectures, presentations of contributed papers and workshops, complemented by a social program reflecting the amazing diversity of Russian culture and history.

The PSI conference series is dedicated to the memory of a pioneer in theoretical and system programming research, academician Andrei Petrovich Ershov (1931–1988). Andrei Ershov graduated from the Moscow State University in 1954. He began his scientific career under the guidance of Professor Lyapunov – the supervisor of his PhD thesis. A.P. Ershov worked at the Institute of Precise Mechanics and Computing Machnery, and later headed the Theoretical Programming Department at the Computing Center of the USSR Academy of Sciences in Moscow. In 1958 the department was reorganized into the Institute of Mathematics of Siberian Branch of the USSR Academy of Sciences, and by the initiative of the academician S.L. Sobolev Ershov, A.P. Ershov was appointed the head of this department, which later became part of the Computing Center in Novosibirsk Akademgorodok. The first significant project of the department was aimed at the development of the ALPHA system, an optimizing compiler for an extension of Algol 60 implemented on a Soviet computer M-20. Later the researchers of the department created the Algibr, Epsilon, Sigma, and Alpha-6 programming systems for the BESM-6 computers. The list of the achievements also includes the first Soviet time-sharing system AIST-0, the multilanguage system BETA, research projects in artificial intelligence and parallel programming, integrated tools for text processing and publishing, and many more. A.P. Ershov was a leader and participant of these projects. In 1974 he was nominated as a Distinguished Fellow of the British Computer Society. In 1981 he received the Silver Core Award for services rendered to IFIP. Andrei Ershov's brilliant speeches were always the focus of public attention. Especially notable was his lecture on "Aesthetic and Human Factor in Programming" presented at the AFIPS Spring Joint Computer Conference in 1972.

This edition of the conference attracted 70 submissions from 15 countries. We wish to thank all their authors for their interest in PSI 2019. Each submission was reviewed by three experts, at least two of them from the same or closely related discipline as the authors. The reviewers generally provided high quality assessment of the papers and often gave extensive comments to the authors for the possible improvement of the contributions. As a result, the Program Committee selected nine high-quality papers as regular talks, nine papers as short talks, three papers as system and experimental talks, and eight poster presers, for presentation at the conference. A range of hot topics in computer science and informatics are covered by five keynote talks given by prominent computer scientists from various countries.

We are glad to express our gratitude to all the persons and organizations who contributed to the conference: the authors of all the papers for their effort in producing the materials included here; the sponsors for their moral, financial, and organizational support; the Steering Committee members for their coordination of the conference, the Program Committee members and the reviewers who did their best to review and select the papers; and the members of the Organizing Committee for their contribution to the success of this event and its great cultural program.

The Program Committee work was done using the EasyChair conference management system.

October 2019

Nikolaj Bjørner
Irina Virbitskaite
Andrei Voronkov

Organization

Program Committee

Farhad Arbab	CWI and Leiden University, The Netherlands
David Aspinall	The University of Edinburgh, UK
Marcello Bersani	Politecnico di Milano, Italy
Leopoldo Bertossi	Universidad Adolfo Ibáñez, Chile, and RelationalAI Inc., USA
Nikolaj Bjørner	Microsoft, USA
Andrea Cali	University of London, Birkbeck College, UK
Marsha Chechik	University of Toronto, Canada
Volker Diekert	University of Stuttgart, Germany
Salvatore Distefano	University of Messina, Italy
Nicola Dragoni	Technical University of Denmark, Denmark
Schahram Dustdar	Vienna University of Technology, Austria
Dieter Fensel	University of Innsbruck, Austria
Carlo Furia	Università della Svizzera Italiana, Italy
Valentin Goranko	Stockholm University, Sweden
Sergei Gorlatch	University of Münster, Germany
Damas Gruska	Comenius University, Slovakia
Arie Gurfinkel	University of Waterloo, Canada
Konstantin Korovin	The University of Manchester, UK
Maciej Koutny	Newcastle University, UK
Laura Kovacs	Vienna University of Technology, Austria
Manuel Mazzara	Innopolis University, Russia
Klaus Meer	BTU Cottbus-Senftenberg, Germany
Torben Ægidius Mogensen	DIKU, Denmark
Peter Mosses	Delft University of Technology, The Netherlands
Jose R. Parama	Universidade da Coruña, Spain
Gennady Pekhimenko	Carnegie Mellon University, USA
Wojciech Penczek	Institute of Computer Science of Polish Academy of Sciences, Poland
Alexander K. Petrenko	Ivannikov Institute for System Programming, Russian Academy of Sciences, Russia
Alberto Pettorossi	Università di Roma Tor Vergata, Italy
Qiang Qu	Shenzhen Institutes of Advanced Technology, China
Wolfgang Reisig	Humboldt-Universitaet zu Berlin, Germany
Andrei Sabelfeld	Chalmers University of Technology, Sweden
Davide Sangiorgi	University of Bologna, Italy
Cristina Seceleanu	Mälardalen University, Sweden
Natalia Sidorova	Technische Universiteit Eindhoven, The Netherlands

Giancarlo Succi	Innopolis University, Russia
Mark Trakhtenbrot	Holon Institute of Technology, Israel
Hans van Ditmarsch	LORIA, CNRS, and University of Lorraine, France
Enrique Herrera Viedma	University of Granada, Spain
Irina Virbitskaite	A.P. Ershov Institute of Informatics Systems, Russia
Andrei Voronkov	The University of Manchester, UK
Matthias Weidlich	Humboldt-Universität zu Berlin, Germany

Additional Reviewers

Angele, Kevin
Beecks, Christian
Blanck, Jens
De Masellis, Riccardo
Di Iorio, Angelo
Enoiu, Eduard Paul
Fey, Florian
Huaman, Elwin
Jaroszewicz, Szymon
Khazeev, Mansur
Knapik, Michał
Kumar, Vivek

Kunnappilly, Ashalatha
Kuznetsov, Sergei O.
Mahmud, Nesredin
Panasiuk, Oleksandra
Robillard, Simon
Silva-Coira, Fernando
Şimşek, Umutcan
Sourdis, Ioannis
Spina, Cinzia Incoronata
Teisseyre, Paweł
Tomak, Juri
Zubair, Adam

Abstracts

Towards Knowledge Graph Based Representation, Augmentation and Exploration of Scholarly Communication

Sören Auer

Leibniz Information Centre for Science and Technology and University Library,
Germany

Abstract. Despite an improved digital access to scientific publications in the last decades, the fundamental principles of scholarly communication remain unchanged and continue to be largely document-based. The document-oriented workflows in science have reached the limits of adequacy as highlighted by recent discussions on the increasing proliferation of scientific literature, the deficiency of peer-review and the reproducibility crisis. We need to represent, analyse, augment and exploit scholarly communication in a knowledge-based way by expressing and linking scientific contributions and related artefacts through semantically rich, interlinked knowledge graphs. This should be based on deep semantic representation of scientific contributions, their manual, crowd-sourced and automatic augmentation and finally the intuitive exploration and interaction employing question answering on the resulting scientific knowledge base. We need to synergistically combine automated extraction and augmentation techniques, with large-scale collaboration to reach an unprecedented level of knowledge graph breadth and depth. As a result, knowledge-based information flows can facilitate completely new ways of search and exploration. The efficiency and effectiveness of scholarly communication will significant increase, since ambiguities are reduced, reproducibility is facilitated, redundancy is avoided, provenance and contributions can be better traced and the interconnections of research contributions are made more explicit and transparent. In this talk we will present first steps in this direction in the context of our Open Research Knowledge Graph initiative and the Science-GRAPH project.

On Termination of Probabilistic Programs

Joost-Pieter Katoen

Aachen University, Germany

Abstract. Program termination is a key question in program verification. This talk considers the termination of probabilistic programs, programs that can describe randomised algorithms and more recently received attention in machine learning. Termination of probabilistic programs has some unexpected effects. Such programs may diverge with zero probability; they almost-surely terminate (AST). Running two AST-programs in sequence that both have a finite expected termination time – so-called positive AST – may yield an AST-program with an infinite termination time (in expectation). Thus positive AST is not compositional with respect to sequential program composition. This talk discusses that proving positive AST (and AST) is harder than the halting problem, shows a powerful proof rule for deciding AST, and sketches a Dijkstra-like weakest precondition calculus for proving positive AST in a fully compositional manner.

Safety Verification for Deep Neural Networks with Provable Guarantees

Marta Kwiatkowska

University of Oxford, UK

Abstract. Deep neural networks have achieved impressive experimental results in image classification, but can surprisingly be unstable with respect to adversarial perturbations, that is, minimal changes to the input image that cause the network to misclassify it. With potential applications including perception modules and end-to-end controllers for self-driving cars, this raises concerns about their safety. This lecture will describe progress with developing automated verification and testing techniques for deep neural networks to ensure safety and security of their classification decisions with respect to input manipulations. The techniques exploit Lipschitz continuity of the networks and aim to approximate, for a given set of inputs, the reachable set of network outputs in terms of lower and upper bounds, in anytime manner, with provable guarantees. We develop novel algorithms based on feature-guided search, games and global optimisation, and evaluate them on state-of-the-art networks. We also develop foundations for probabilistic safety verification for Gaussian processes, with application to neural networks.

The lecture will be based on the following publications:

1. X. Huang, M. Kwiatkowska, S. Wang and M. Wu, Safety Verification of Deep Neural Networks. In *Proc. 29th International Conference on Computer Aided Verification (CAV),* pages 3–29, LNCS, Springer, 2017.
2. W. Ruan, X. Huang, and M. Kwiatkowska. Reachability Analysis of Deep Neural Networks with Provable Guarantees. In *Proc. 27th International Joint Conference on Artificial Intelligence (IJCAI'18),* pages 2651–2659, 2018.
3. M. Wicker, X. Huang, and M. Kwiatkowska. Feature-Guided Black-Box Safety Testing of Deep Neural Networks. In *Proc. 24th International Conference on Tools and Algorithms for the Construction and Analysis of Systems (TACAS 2018),* pages 408–426. Springer, 2018.
4. M. Wu, M. Wicker, W. Ruan, X. Huang and M. Kwiatkowska. A Game-Based Approximate Verification of Deep Neural Networks with Provable Guarantees. Accepted to *Theoretical Computer Science* subject to revisions. CoRR abs/1807.03571 (2018)
5. L. Cardelli, M. Kwiatkowska, L. Laurenti, A. Patane. Robustness Guarantees for Bayesian Inference with Gaussian Processes. In Proc. AAAI 2019. To appear, 2019. CoRR abs/1809.06452 (2018)

Automated-Reasoning Revolution: From Theory to Practice and Back

Moshe Vardi

Rice University, USA

Abstract. For the past 40 years computer scientists generally believed that NP-complete problems are intractable. In particular, Boolean satisfiability (SAT), as a paradigmatic automated-reasoning problem, has been considered to be intractable. Over the past 20 years, however, there has been a quiet, but dramatic, revolution, and very large SAT instances are now being solved routinely as part of software and hardware design. In this talk I will review this amazing development and show how automated reasoning is now an industrial reality.

I will then describe how we can leverage SAT solving to accomplish other automated-reasoning tasks. Sampling uniformly at random satisfying truth assignments of a given Boolean formula or counting the number of such assignments are both fundamental computational problems in computer science with applications in software testing, software synthesis, machine learning, personalized learning, and more. While the theory of these problems has been thoroughly investigated since the 1980s, approximation algorithms developed by theoreticians do not scale up to industrial-sized instances. Algorithms used by the industry offer better scalability, but give up certain correctness guarantees to achieve scalability. We describe a novel approach, based on universal hashing and Satisfiability Modulo Theory, that scales to formulas with hundreds of thousands of variables without giving up correctness guarantees.

The Power of Symbolic Automata and Transducers

Margus Veanes

Microsoft Research, Redmond, USA

Abstract. Symbolic automata and transducers extend finite automata and transducers by allowing transitions to carry predicates and functions over rich alphabet theories, such as linear arithmetic. Therefore, these models extend their classic counterparts to operate over infinite alphabets, such as the set of rational numbers. Due to their expressiveness, symbolic automata and transducers have been used to verify functional programs operating over lists and trees, to prove the correctness of complex implementations of BASE64 and UTF encoders, and to expose data parallelism in computations that may otherwise seem inherently sequential. In this talk, I give an overview of what is currently known about symbolic automata and transducers as well as their variants. We discuss what makes these models different from their finite-alphabet counterparts, what kind of applications symbolic models can enable, and what challenges arise when reasoning about these formalisms. Finally, I present a list of open problems and research directions that relate to both the theory and practice of symbolic automata and transducers.

Contents

Rapid Instruction Decoding for IA-32

Yauhen Klimiankou[✉]

Department of Software for Information Technologies, Belarusian State University
of Informatics and Radioelectronics, 6 P. Brovki Street, 220013 Minsk, Belarus
klimenkov@bsuir.by

Abstract. This paper explains new performance-oriented instruction
decoder for IA-32 ISA. The decoder provides the functionality required
for program analysis and interpretation and exports simple interface for
the conversion of a code byte stream into a stream of generalized instruction descriptions. We report measurements comparing our decoder with
well-known alternative solutions to demonstrate its superior efficiency.

Keywords: IA-32 · Instructions decoding

1 Introduction

This paper attempts to shed light on an essential topic of design and implementation of efficient instruction decoders for CISC-like bytecodes. The fact,
that a wide range of applications including simulators [10], emulators [1], virtual
machines [4], tools for static and dynamic analysis of executables [2,5], disas-
semblers, decompilers [6], and others uses instruction decoders emphasizes their
importance. In the case of its usage in the area of simulators, emulators, and virtual machines, the decoder performance becomes one of the primary contributors
to the efficiency of the entire system.

We draw attention to different approaches used for the design and implementation of software decoders for complex CISC-like ISAs with variable instruction
length. RISC-like ISAs usually assumes fixed instruction length and few easily
parsable and distinguishable instruction formats. That leads to straightforward
decoders both in hardware and in software implementations. Variable instruction length and variety of instruction formats pump significant complexity into
decoder design and implementation in the case of CISC-like ISAs with respective
degradation of performance.

We have developed a new instruction decoder for IA-32 ISA [9] which is a
canonical example of CISC ISA. The decoder design focuses on applications in
a broad range of domains, including such as virtual machines and emulators for
which instruction decoding efficiency is critical. For example, such projects as
IBM PC compatible emulator Bosch [1] and hypervisor QEMU [4] can use it
as front-end. The proposed decoder is well-abstracted from back-end logic, provides a clear interface and preserves universal nature in contrast to the original
instruction decoders used in these projects.

© Springer Nature Switzerland AG 2019
N. Bjørner et al. (Eds.): PSI 2019, LNCS 11964, pp. 1–9, 2019.
https://doi.org/10.1007/978-3-030-37487-7_1

We have explored various techniques and approaches towards optimization of instructions decoding performance. Our experience has shown that Mealy machine-based decoder design leads to pure, flexible, extensible, and efficient implementations. Our decoder demonstrates that there is a significant performance improvement which can be obtained by precaching of decoded instructions not containing the variable part. Such instructions are most frequently faced instructions in industrial applications which amplifies the power of such performance trick.

Finally, we have compared the performance of our decoder implementation for IA-32 ISA with popular and extensively used analogs. We show that our decoder demonstrates its advantage in instructions decoding performance on real industrial quality binary program code.

Our key contributions in this work are:

– To present instruction decoder supporting CISC-like bytecode that reproduces IA-32 ISA.
– To explore design principles and optimization tricks towards efficient decoding of CISC-like bytecodes.
– To present the comparison between different instruction decoders for IA-32 ISA.
– To show that it is practical to use the design based on Mealy machine automata with use of table-guided dispatching, extensive precaching and simplified output interface.

2   IA-32 Instruction Set Architecture

IA-32, also known as *i386*, is a 32-bit version of the *x86* ISA introduced in 1985. Successive generations of microprocessors have extremely complicated *x86* ISA over years. "Manual for Intel 8086" (1979) [7] contains only 43 pages about instruction set. "Programmer's Reference Manual for Intel 80386" [8] (1986) already contains 421 pages. Finally, the current edition of "Intel 64 and IA-32 Architectures Software Developers Manual" (2018) [9] has 2214 pages describing instructions.

Even Intel 8086 was a processor with CISC design and with a set of instructions of variable length (from 1 byte and up to 4 bytes) and with variable execution time. With time going, IA-32 became more and more CISC-like. Currently, it supports a set of more than 200 instructions with lengths varying starting from 1 byte and ending by 15 bytes.

IA-32 supports multiple addressing modes and complex memory access mechanisms. Most of the instructions in that ISA can reference memory directly. In contrast to IA-32, RISC ISAs commonly rely on an especial pair of instructions dedicated to data exchange between memory and registers while rest instructions operate exclusively on registers. Availability of two memory addressing modes and two functioning modes bring additional complexity to IA-32 architecture.

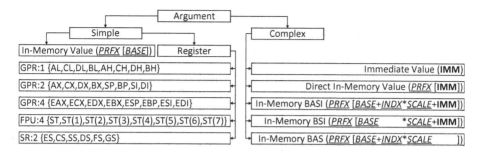

Fig. 1. Instruction argument types supported by the IA-32 instruction set.

2.1 Instructions on IA-32

Instructions in IA-32 consists of three components: opcode, argument types block and immediate values block, where only the opcode is mandatory part while other parts are optional. Opcode bytes not only define instruction behavior but also guides decoder about rest of the instruction bytes.

IA-32 instruction can have from 0 up to 3 either primitive or composite arguments, as shown on Fig. 1. The second ones either comes with immediate value or use multiple registers. *BASE INDX* are one of the registers from the set *GPR:4*. *PRFX* can accompany any memory-referencing argument to specify the size of the referenced value explicitly. The list of prefixes includes byte, word, dword, fword, qword, and tword (1, 2, 4, 6, 8 and 10 bytes respectively). *SCALE* can take only values 1, 2, 4, and 8. *IMM* denotes an immediate value.

From a semantics viewpoint, every instruction in IA-32 consists of a command, three arguments and two immediate values associated with them. First one is the only mandatory component. All other instruction parts are optional and can be void. At the same time, only immediate values explicitly referenced by arguments become meaningful.

2.2 Classification of IA-32 Instructions

In contrast to RISC systems, IA-32 does not have uniform instruction encoding. Besides that, there are few families of instructions. Each instruction from the same family follows the same encoding rules. There are four general families of instructions which are distributed over IA-32 decoding root map as depicted in Fig. 2.

Tiny Instructions. Tiny instructions represent a set of instructions for which one or two bytes define entire semantics of instruction. Almost all commands (instructions which do not have operands) (*std*), frequently used predicates (instructions with only one operand) with in-register arguments (*inc*) and even some operations (instructions with two operands) with in-register only arguments (for example *xchg eax, ecx*) fall into that family.

	0	1	2	3	4	5	6	7	8	9	A	B	C	D	E	F	
0x00	F	F	F	F	S	S	T	T	F	F	F	F	S	S	T	X	0x0F
0x10	F	F	F	F	S	S	T	T	F	F	F	F	S	S	T	T	0x1F
0x20	F	F	F	F	S	S	T	T	F	F	F	F	S	S	T	T	0x2F
0x30	F	F	F	F	S	S	T	T	F	F	F	F	S	S	T	T	0x3F
0x40	T	T	T	T	T	T	T	T	T	T	T	T	T	T	T	T	0x4F
0x50	T	T	T	T	T	T	T	T	T	T	T	T	T	T	T	T	0x5F
0x60	T	T	F	F	T	T	T	T	S	F	S	F	T	T	T	T	0x6F
0x70	S	S	S	S	S	S	S	S	S	S	S	S	S	S	S	S	0x7F
0x80	M	M	M	M	F	F	F	F	F	F	F	F	F	F	F	M	0x8F
0x90	T	T	T	T	T	T	T	T	T	T	S	T	T	T	T	T	0x9F
0xA0	S	S	S	S	T	T	T	T	S	S	T	T	T	T	T	T	0xAF
0xB0	S	S	S	S	S	S	S	S	S	S	S	S	S	S	S	S	0xBF
0xC0	M	M	S	T	F	F	F	F	S	T	S	T	T	S	T	T	0xCF
0xD0	M	M	M	M	S	S	T	T	M	M	M	M	M	M	M	M	0xDF
0xE0	S	S	S	S	S	S	S	S	S	S	S	S	T	T	T	T	0xEF
0xF0	T	T	T	T	T	T	M	M	T	T	T	T	T	T	M	M	0xFF
	0	1	2	3	4	5	6	7	8	9	A	B	C	D	E	F	

Fig. 2. Map of IA-32 decoding tree roots.

Snap Instructions. Snap instructions represent a family of instructions which consist of one command byte and one immediate value following it. There are two subclasses of snap instructions: predicates with an immediate value (*push imm*), and operations with one fixed in-register argument and an immediate value as a second argument (*add eax, imm*). The first byte of the instruction defines its entire semantics, while the immediate value defines its operands.

Instructions with Fixed and Mixed Commands. There is the only difference between these families. In instructions with fixed command, the first byte of instruction explicitly defines command encoded. Instructions with mixed commands use at least two bytes for command encoding. Both families consist of encoding trees each leaf of which contains instructions with particular semantics and encoding.

2.3 Encoding Trees and Instructions Types

IA-32 includes three types of decoding trees:

- Tree of completely manageable register-based operations.
- Tree of semi-manageable register-based operations.
- Tree of operations with an immediate argument.

Each tree contains four leaves on the first level, where first three leaves create three stable triplets that define a type of encoding subtree. The fourth leaf is highly-variable and differs between different decoding trees. Nevertheless, all decoding trees follow the same structure depicted in Fig. 3. All these complexities introduced by encoding trees are a direct consequence of support of multiple addressing modes listed above.

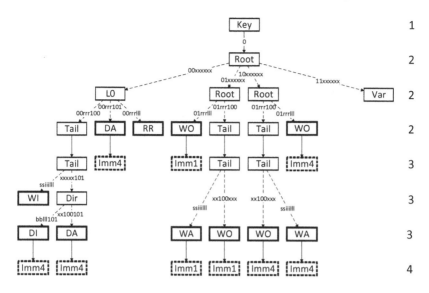

Fig. 3. Structure of IA-32 encoding tree.

3 General Architecture of EIDIA Decoder

The best approach to the feeding of IA-32 instruction decoder is feeding in byte-by-byte fashion. In that case, front-end receives control over decoder and on its input stream of code bytes after processing of each byte of code. Thus, front-end forms the input byte stream, while there is no intermediate buffering. Moreover, this feeding scheme completely releases decoder from feeding management and control tasks. At the same time, the byte-by-byte feeding scheme implies conditional generation of output instruction description. Figure 4 presents the scheme of the interaction of front-end with EIDIA decoder. As can be seen on the figure, the decoder can be in three states: decoding complete, decoding incomplete, and undefined instruction found. When front-end founds decoder in "Decoding incomplete" state, it routes self through a fast path to next feeding round. Otherwise, it captures and processes decoded instruction (in case of "decoding complete" state) or handles the exceptional situation (in case of "undefined instruction" state).

The architecture of interfacing with decoder depicted in Fig. 4 also reflects the fact that it can be beneficial to consider decoder as a state machine in general or as Mealy machine automata in particular and design decoder in the appropriate way. Automata's input is bytes of code. Internal states of decoding can be represented as a graph of handlers, while the internal state of decoder, in that case, will be represented by function pointer defining the current state of decoding. The decoder has an initial state which represents start point in instruction decoding, but it has no distinct finish state. Each time when decoder either have instruction successfully decoded or have undefined opcode detected it reports that decoding was finished and switches self to initial state. Therefore,

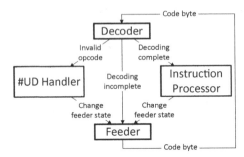

Fig. 4. Scheme of interaction with EIDIA decoder.

each state from which decoder can directly transit into the initial state can be considered finish state.

Mealy machine basis of decoder allows applying extensive table-based dispatching of decoding. Multiple tables are in use. Routing tables switch decoder onto appropriate handler depending on code byte at the input. Additional semantic data table contains a generalized description of the instruction set. Different parts of decoder use this table which increases the uniformity of decoder code, thus, improving the efficiency of CPU cache usage. At the same time, during each decoding step EIDIA accumulates information about instruction decoded, as well as, information which will guide decision making during next decoding steps. Thus, EIDIA does not use instruction bytes as a path to the complete instruction description, but assembles the description in a step-by-step way. Furthermore, EIDIA reconfigures itself during each decoding step.

Following the state machine architecture with byte-by-byte feeding eliminates all external dependencies from EIDIA. For example, EIDIA does not dynamically allocate or manipulate memory and does not use C standard library at all. Furthermore, EIDIA does not involved into the instruction byte stream management which eliminates frequently redundant preparations and checks of the input byte stream.

4   Output Interface of EIDIA

The output interface of decoder should be convenient for use and completely cover general semantic of instruction. EIDIA returns instruction description represented in the form of a pointer to the next data structure:

```
struct Instruction {
    uint32_t command;
    uint32_t args [3];
    uint32_t imms [2];
};
```

The output of the decoder has a size of 24 bytes and can incur significant overhead on memory copying during transfer from the decoder to its front-end. Thus, the efficient decoder should have an internal buffer which it uses for instruction construction during decoding. Decoder exports interface for accessing that buffer to the front-end. Therefore, when the back-end receives status "Decoding complete" that status serves it as a signal that front-end can safely capture instruction from the internal buffer using the provided interface. Furthermore, front-end becomes able to perform access only those components of instruction description which contain actual data. For example, if decoded instruction is a command (have no arguments), then backend can read command opcode, using it determine that there are no arguments and finish work with decoder buffer, hence performing access only to 4 bytes from 24 available bytes of the buffer.

IA-32 has a subset of instructions with a fixed command and which have encoding trees with reverse order of instruction arguments. They have the same encoding as regular instruction. Encoding tree itself and hence first byte of instruction specifies the reverse ordering of arguments. Interface for access to internal buffer allows simplifying decoder internals because it preserves uniformity of decoding algorithms. Such an especial interface can reverse arguments order for backend at access time by logical mapping of the external view of the buffer fields to respective internal implementation.

Especial interface to decoder buffer implements lazy output reset. Lazy reset moves the burden of internal buffer cleanup from the stage of decoding to the results fetching stage, which leads to performance penalty reduction. Decoder front-end can cleanup only those fields of the internal buffer which were set by decoder during assembling of instruction. At the same time, lazy reset can eliminate redundant resetting of those fields which were not modified by the decoder.

Finally, an especial interface provides an opportunity for extensive precaching of ready-to-use generalized instruction descriptions. In case of decoding of tiny instructions, the decoder can point output interface onto appropriate already ready-to-use instruction description instead of filling of the default output buffer.

5   Evaluation

Table 1 presents the specification of CPUs of computer systems which we have used for evaluation.

We have measured the throughput of EIDIA in two scenarios. The first scenario is a pure binary instruction stream decoding. Results achieved for this scenario show throughput in raw instructions decoding. In the second scenario, we have measured the performance of the decoder with the attached back-end. In the role of the back-end, we have used a simple disassembler application that was designed and implemented from scratch.

Finally, we have used two types of workload. The specially generated file containing all variants of IA-32 instructions (2.1152 MB and 445215 instructions) represents a synthetic workload. In the role of real-world workload, we have

Table 1. Hardware used for performance evaluation

	Platform A	Platform B	Platform C
CPU	Intel Core i7-4600U	AMD Phenom FX-8350	Intel Core i7-7500U
Architecture	Haswell	Bulldozer	Kaby Lake
Codename	Haswell-ULT	Piledriver	Kaby Lake-U
Frequency	2100 MHz	4000 MHz	2700 MHz
L1D cache	2 × 32 KB	8 × 16 KB	2 × 32 KB
L1I cache	2 × 32 KB	4 × 64 KB	2 × 32 KB
L2 cache	2 × 256 KB	4 × 2 MB	2 × 256 KB
L3 cache	4 MB	8 MB	4 MB

Table 2. Speedup of the EIDIA decoder in instruction decoding comparing to other instruction decoders for IA-32

Task	Workload	Platform	Udis86	Intel XED
Decoding	Synthetic	A	42,03	4,19
Decoding	Synthetic	B	31,13	3,58
Decoding	Synthetic	C	51,11	4,45
Decoding	Real-World	A	23,08	3,48
Decoding	Real-World	B	21,09	3,83
Decoding	Real-World	C	24,64	3,64
Disassembling	Synthetic	A	12,26	11,15
Disassembling	Synthetic	B	10,95	13,79
Disassembling	Synthetic	C	13,48	10,67
Disassembling	Real-World	A	9,16	6,18
Disassembling	Real-World	B	7,54	7,51
Disassembling	Real-World	C	9,15	5,80

used code sections extracted from Linux kernel file of version *3.13.0-37-generic* (6.7546 MB, 2141376 instructions).

To proof performance benefits of EIDIA, we have compared it with two IA-32 instruction decoders: *Udis86* [6] and *Intel XED* [3]. Both decoders have disassembler capabilities.

It would be interesting to compare EIDIA with decoders used in emulators and virtual machines. However, such decoders are an integral part of VM execution engines, and their extraction is a nontrivial task. Furthermore, they do not have disassembler backends which prevent macrobenchmarking.

The results of the measurements are summarized in Table 2. The numbers in that table show the speedup in processing time achieved by EIDIA in comparison to respective decoder specified in the column header. As can be seen, EIDIA is from 21.09 up to 51.11 times more performant than UDis86 in pure instruction decoding and from 7.54 up to 13.48 times more performant in disassembling tasks. What is more important, the proposed solution provides throughput from 3.48 to 4.45 times better than Intel XED in instruction decoding and from 5.8 to 13.79 times better in disassembling tasks. EIDIA has demonstrated at least 3.48 times better performance in all conducted experiments, and at the same time stays agnostic to the underlying hardware platform and provides pure isolation of decoding from front-end logic.

6 Conclusion

In this paper, we have explored techniques of efficient instruction decoding for IA-32 and have shown that right design decisions in conjunction with multiple optimizations lead to a significant speedup of instruction decoding. Our instructions decoder – EIDIA demonstrates that high-throughput general-purpose decoder based on Mealy machine with byte-by-byte feeding delivers high performance. Our instruction decoder exploits several performance-oriented features including extensive precaching of decoded instructions; multi-level table-guided dispatching; lazy reset of output and compact representation of instruction semantics. This features in the application to the design of state machine make decoder performant while preserving its general-purpose nature. We have compared EIDIA with analogs of industrial quality. The measurements have shown that EIDIA has from 3.5 up to 4.5 times higher throughput than Intel XED in case of pure decoding, and from 5.8 up to 13.8 times better in case of disassembling. At the same time, EIDIA, in contrast to Intel XED, is agnostic to host CPU.

References

1. bochs: The Open Source IA-32 Emulation Project (2017). http://bochs.source forge.net/
2. gem5 (2017). http://gem5.org/Main_Page
3. Intel XED (2017). https://intelxed.github.io/
4. QEMU (2017). https://www.qemu.org/
5. GitHub - dyninst/dyninst: DyninstAPI: tools for binary instrumentation, analysis, and modification (2018). https://github.com/dyninst/dyninst
6. Udis86 Disassembler Library for x86/x86–64 (2018). http://udis86.sourceforge. net/
7. Intel Corporation: The 8086 Family Users Manual. No. 9800722–03, October 1979
8. Intel Corporation: Intel 80386 Programmer's Reference Manual. No. 230985 (1986)
9. Intel Corporation: Intel® 64 and IA-32 Architectures Software Developer's Manual: Instruction Set Reference. No. 325383–066US, March 2018
10. Reshadi, M., Dutt, N.D., Mishra, P.: A retargetable framework for instruction-set architecture simulation. ACM Trans. Embed. Comput. Syst. **5**, 431–452 (2006)

Case-Based Genetic Optimization
of Web User Interfaces

Maxim Bakaev[⊠] ⓘ and Vladimir Khvorostov

Novosibirsk State Technical University, Novosibirsk, Russia
{bakaev,xvorostov}@corp.nstu.ru

Abstract. The combination of case-based approach and genetic optimization can provide significant boost to effectiveness of computer-aided design of web user interfaces (WUIs). However, their integration in web design domain requires certain sophistication, since parts of available solutions cannot be reused directly, due to technical and legal obstacles. This article describes evolutionary algorithm for automatic generation of website designs, which treats parameters of functionality, layout and visual appearance as the variables. The structure of the chromosome is devised, allowing representation of websites' properties in the above three manipulated aspects and facilitating easy application of the genetic operators. We also describe organization and population of repository of filler-up content, which is compulsory for evaluation of WUI fitness with regard to the needs and preferences of users. We demonstrate retrieval of web designs as cases and propose using similarity measure in the fitness function to adapt the generated WUI to these examples. Finally, implementation of the approach is illustrated based on the popular Drupal web framework. The results of the study can empower case-based reuse of existing web designs and therefore be of interest to both AI researchers and software engineers.

Keywords: Web user interface design · Case-based reasoning · Software engineering · Drupal framework

1 Introduction

The continuing exponential growth in the amount of data is accompanied by increase in diversity of data sources and data models. This, together with the forthcoming "Big Interaction", with its multiplicity of user tasks and characteristics, of interface devices and contexts of use, may soon render hand-making of all the necessary human-computer interfaces unfeasible. Discrete optimization methods are seen quite promising for intelligent computer-aided design of interaction, but the combinatorial number of possible solutions is huge even for relatively simple user interface (UI) design problems (Oulasvirta 2017).

Increasingly, genetic algorithms are used as effective tool for solving optimization problems, and there are reports of their successful use for conventional websites designs (Qu 2015), whose UIs are not particularly creative, but mostly provide data I/O. Most types of EAs rely on special data structures that represent properties of a

N. Bjørner et al. (Eds.): PSI 2019, LNCS 11964, pp. 10–25, 2019.
https://doi.org/10.1007/978-3-030-37487-7_2

candidate solution – chromosomes, in which concrete values comprise the solution's genotype. Individual genes that constitute the chromosome may be of different types, depending of a particular problem, and the genetic operators need to take into consideration the types' boundaries and the allowed values – alleles. Hence, just as design of data structures is of crucial importance in software engineering, the choice of the chromosome structure can remarkably affect EA's convergence, speed and the end result's quality (Michalewicz and Hartley 1996).

Another crucial part of EA is fitness function (FF): it must both fully represent the optimization goal and be as easily computable as possible. In domains that deal with human preferences and capacities, such as WUI design, specification of FF is far from trivial, especially given the diversity of user characteristics and tasks. Such customary workarounds as Interactive Evolutionary Computation (delegation of fitness evaluation to humans) and trained user behavior models (simulation of humans' evaluations) have their limitations. We believe that FF evaluation could well exploit operating websites, since "surviving" web projects have presumably adapted to their target users' preferences and needs. The degree of this adaptation's successfulness can be automatically estimated from website's interaction statistics and popularity, representing the dynamic quality-in-use (Bakaev et al. 2017), while the static quality-as-is can be assessed based on static design metrics (Ivory and Hearst 2002).

The number of operational websites accessible on the World Wide Web is currently estimated as 100–250 millions, so there should be no shortage of well-fit design examples for any kind of target users and tasks. The problem is actually the opposite: even despite the recent emergence of design mining field that focuses on extraction of design patterns and trends from large collections of design examples, there is lack of repositories or services capable of finding existing solutions relevant to a new project's UI design context. We believe that the problem could be resolved by supplementing the WUI evolutionary optimization algorithm with case-based reasoning (CBR) approach that has shown successful use in both software and web engineering (Rocha et al. 2014; De Renzis et al. 2016), WUI development (Marir 2012), as well as in many non-IT domains. More detailed justification on CBR applicability for WUI design can be found in one of our previous works (Bakaev 2018a). The classically identified stages in CBR can be summarized as follows (Mantaras et al. 2005):

- Retrieve: describe a new problem and find similar problems with known solutions in a case base (CB);
- Reuse: adapt the solutions of the retrieved problems to the current problem, in an assumption that similar problems have similar solutions;
- Revise: evaluate the new solution and possibly repeat the previous stages;
- Retain: store the results as a new case.

Case thus equals parameterized problem plus one or several solutions, each of which can be supplemented with quality – i.e. how good the solution was in resolving the problem.

The retrieval stage is arguably what most today's CBR-related research focuses on, but the existing infrastructure in WUI design domain remains problematical. For instance, the database of the compelling *design mining* Webzeigeist tool (Kumar et al. 2013) that implemented a kind of design scraping and searching engine, presumably contained millions of web pages at the time of the publication. However, it allows searching by technicalities, such as page aspect ratio or element styles, but not by domain- or user-related aspects. This, effectively, does not allow supporting the CBR approach, as no designs appropriate for a particular problem specification can be retrieved. Moreover, direct employment of retrieved well-fit web design examples as parents in the EA or reuse of their parts within CBR is further restricted due to technical (lack of access to the website's back-office and server-side code) and legal (copyright protection) reasons. Web design frameworks and template libraries do provide rich collections of WUIs and their elements (icons, buttons, form fields, etc.), but cannot aid in adaptation of a chosen design for a particular user group or to resemble exemplary solutions.

Our paper is dedicated to integration of case-based reasoning and evolutionary approaches in web design, which we consider necessary for practical feasibility of UI optimization in this design field. Particularly, we focus on development of the case base and the data structures that the EA relies on. In Sect. 2, we outline the proposed EA for CBR-based web design and justify our approach to genetic representation of the solutions. In Sect. 3, we highlight some particulars of the implementation, specify the concrete chromosome structure, and provide some examples. In the Conclusion, we summarize the contribution of our article and provide final remarks.

2 Methods

2.1 Background and Related Work

Genetic algorithms are based on repeated application of the genetic operators – generally these are selection of candidates for reproduction, crossover (producing child solutions incorporating features of numerous parents) and mutation (introduction of random or directed variations in the features). Their superset is evolutionary algorithms (EAs), which are being successfully used in programming, engineering, website design (Guo et al. 2016), data mining and classification (Freitas 2013), natural language processing, machine learning, intelligent and recommender systems, as well as many other domains (Coello 2015). An archetypal EA incorporates the following stages:

1. Initialization – creation of the first generation (initial population), which can be either random or based on some distinguished existing cases (Kazimipour et al. 2014), for better convergence to global optimum or faster performance.
2. Selection of best-fit individuals for reproduction (parents) based on evaluation of their fitness, which is performed either in real world context or, more commonly, with specially formulated fitness functions.
3. Reproduction of parents to create individuals of the next generation, in which mutation and crossover are used. If the algorithm's termination condition (sufficient quality of the final solution or time limit) is not met, it goes back to the previous step and repeats.

Within CBR approach, Reuse and Revise stages can be naturally implemented as EA, but to the extent of our knowledge there is lack of techniques for adaptation of the retrieved WUI designs. Or rather, due to the technical and legal impediments we've mentioned above, it's the new solution that has to be adapted to the exemplary designs. A measure of genotypic or phenotypic similarity with the example solutions can be included as one of the components in the FF. A notable example of such approach was once implemented in SUPPLE intelligent system for UI automatic generation (Gajos et al. 2005): the optimized goal function could incorporate the metric of similarity with the previous version of UI design – in SUPPLE's case, to maintain familiarity for its users. The metric was linear combination of pairwise similarities between interface widgets, whose features included language, orientation, geometry, etc. Subjective perception of WUI similarity is rather more sophisticated (Bakaev 2018a), but the general approach should be feasible for our CBR and EA integration.

2.2   The Evolutionary Algorithm for WUI Design

The combination of the case-based reasoning approach and the genetic optimization algorithm for WUI design (for detailed description and justification of the algorithm see Bakaev and Gaedke, 2016) can be outlined in the following process:

1. Designer, who initiates the process, creates a new web project (case) in the CB and specifies the problem features and other input information. We will address this in the subsequent sub-section.
2. The CBR algorithm retrieves relevant projects from the CB: based on similarity measures for the cases and the assessed quality of the currently operational solution. We outline the retrieval process based on problem similarity in Sect. 3.
3. The EA (re-)produces new solutions (web designs), dealing with the following major aspects of a web design:

   – Functionality: since the EA is suitable for creating relatively simple websites, we can assume there is no need of generating any new programming code. Instead, we can rely on assembling existing pieces of web functionality, saving their configuration in the chromosome. We justified and detailed the use of functional components through their meta-repository in (Bakaev 2018c). In Sect. 3 of the current paper we demonstrate their specification in the chromosome.
   – Content: by definition, web content is very changing and it does not actually relate to a website's structure, although it may be perceived as related to its design by users. So, it makes little sense to store the content-related properties in the chromosome, they should rather correspond to the phenotype – the individual solutions' properties, which can vary for the same genotype. The content repository is described in Sect. 3.
   – Page structure (layout): in modern websites, pages are composed from elements that are organized hierarchically and consistently ordered within their siblings. This is essential part of the design and its usability, and the corresponding information needs to be saved in the chromosome, which we also describe in the subsequent sub-section.
   – Visual appearance: it is potentially the vastest part of the design space, since the combinatorial number of all possible colors, font styles and sizes, etc. is enough to make every website out of the existing billion unique. The elements do have

constraining relations between them (e.g. font's and background's colors must provide enough contrast), but attempts to specify formal rules for web design have so far been rather fruitless in practice. So, the initial values are quite important for the EA's convergence, and the algorithm should better start from a reasonable visual solution. We representation of the visual appearance in the chromosome is demonstrated in Sect. 3.

4. The EA evaluates fitness functions for the new solutions, based on their similarity with the reference solutions in the retrieved projects and quality assessed with the pre-trained target users' behavior models, and selects the best fit solutions. The corresponding approach was detailed in (Bakaev 2018a).
5. If the EA's finishing conditions aren't met, the algorithm applies the genetic operators and goes again to step 3 to create new generation of solutions, with the new genotypes. We provide an example of applying the mutation genetic operator to website's visual appearance in Sect. 3.
6. The CBR algorithm retains the best solution(s) produced by the EA in the CB, specifying it as prototype. If the web project later goes live, the CB daemons start collecting the quality attributes for the solution (website), e.g. on the basis of the Web Intelligence approach that we previously proposed (Bakaev 2017).

So, in the subsequent sub-section we consider the specificity of the problems and solutions for CBR in the WUI design domain.

2.3   CBR: The Problem Features and the Solutions' Chromosome Structure

Devising the accurate structure to represent the problem's properties is seen as crucial for machine learning and automated reasoning tasks (Anderson et al. 2013). With respect to CBR, this feature engineering also plays important part in shaping the structure of the CB. The process generally includes: forming the excessive list of potential features, implementing all or some of them in a prototype, and selecting relevant features by optimizing the considered subset. In our feature engineering for WUI design problem, we considered web project as corresponding to a case (as design - and goal-wise complete entity) and website to a solution (as several versions of operational and prototype websites are often created in attempts to meet the web project's goals). We relied upon three models selected from the ones prescribed in WUI development: Domain, Tasks, and User (the Platform and Environment models were excluded since they rather relate to website's back-office). The detailed description of the feature engineering for web projects can be found in (Bakaev 2018a).

Unlike reusable programming code, existing website designs differ dramatically in eminence, so the quality aspects must be stored for the solutions, to be considered in the retrieval in addition to similarity. Website quality is best described as collection of attributes, whose relative importance can vary depending of the particular project's goals and context (Glass 2002). Thus, the set of quality-related features must be extendable and provide flexibility for different formulations of the overall quality function. The quality-related values for the cases collected from the WWW (i.e. for someone else's websites) can be obtained e.g. based on the Web Intelligence approach (Bakaev 2017).

As we mentioned before, the key data structure in EA is chromosome, which contains code for the important properties of solutions. Most traditionally, EAs just use linear binary representations for chromosomes, particularly in web design (Qu 2015). However, this implies that knowledge about the design space (the interrelations between the genes) has to be delegated to the procedures responsible for reproduction, crossover, etc.; otherwise the EA may end up trying combinatorial matches and lose in the convergence speed. So it is sensible to separate out this knowledge in an appropriate data structure – domain ontology effectively representing the design space for WUI. Properties (attributes) of the ontology classes thus correspond to genes, while their datatypes and alleles, crucial for the genetic operators' proper application, are defined via the facets' values. WUI design support ontology that we developed in the popular Protégé-Frames editor can be used to represent the functionality, layout and visual appearance. In Fig. 1, we show a fragment of the ontology with some classes related to the genes responsible for web page's visual appearance, relying on the accepted CSS specification.

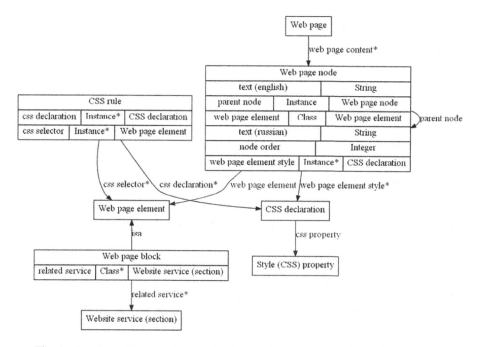

Fig. 1. Ontology classes and properties for a webpage layout and visual appearance.

3   Implementation

In this section we present some highlights of the proposed approach that we implemented (see at our dedicated portal (http://wuikb.info). We used Drupal web content management framework as the platform for the implementation. Despite the usual drawbacks associated with the use of frameworks, such as lower performance and flexibility, the following advantages motivated our choice:

- Drupal has robust architecture that allows handling high number of components.
- Drupal has lots of components (modules) ready for reuse, they are well-organized and centralized in the single repository with API access (http://drupal.org), they have auto-maintained quality attributes (# of downloads, actual installs, open bugs, etc.).
- Drupal has programmable (via command line, API, etc.) support for installment of websites, the layout of interface elements on webpage, handling web forms, menus, content items, adjustment of visual appearance styles, and so on.

A notorious disadvantage of Drupal is high system requirements – particularly, rather complex and costly functionality assembly process. However, its effect in EA can be minimized relatively easily, as there is no need to perform it on each step of the algorithm. Drupal is also renowned for scarcity of high-quality designs in free access, but since our CBR approach retrieves existing web projects, this is a minor concern as well.

3.1   The Case-Based Retrieval

The case base is the registry of projects each of which correspond to a case and can be either automatically scrapped from the web or specially created (Bakaev 2018c). The problem description are Domain, User and Task features, whose values are either directly specified when a new project is created, mined by the supplementary tools, or provided by human annotators. As conventional websites of the same domain have fairly predictable functionality, there was no need to employ full-scale task modeling notations, such as W3C's CTT or HAMSTERS (Martinie et al. 2015). So, the Task model is represented as the structured inventory of website chapters, for which similarity can be calculated fairly easily (see example in Fig. 2). The solutions (websites) have quality attributes, which are either provided by users or experts, or obtained automatically by the supplementary tools in the course of the CB population. So, the CBR algorithm retrieves the cases from the CB based on the following sequence:

1. Pre-selects a set of cases based on the domain similarity
2. For each case in the set it calculates the distance measure that incorporates domain similarity, task similarity and target user similarity (see in Bakaev 2018a).
3. For the most similar cases it calculates the normalized quality values in the range (0; 1) and retrieves similar cases with the highest qualities.

After the retrieval of cases, the "classical" CBR prescribes adapting their solutions, but as we noted above, in web design this process (the Reuse and Revise stages) can't be performed directly due to legal and technical obstacles. Instead, the EA will consider similarity with the retrieved solutions as part of the new solutions' fitness.

3.2   The Chromosome Structure Specification

Our design of the chromosome structure for the EA was based upon the following previously justified theoretical premises and technical considerations:

1. there are three distinct dimensions of a website: functionality, layout (page structure) and visual appearance;
2. representation of design space-related knowledge should be minimized in the code implementing the genetic operators, but moved to the chromosome instead;
3. the chromosome structure design should allow maximal use of the means provided by the framework (without relying on its GUI), particularly Drush project of Drupal.

Based on the above, instead of the classic binary strings we have chosen to rely on the popular "name: value" representation for each of the genes, since it also allows expressing classes and properties from the developed ontology. We subsequently use the Backus-Naur form to describe the parts of the chromosome per the three website dimensions. In one of the following sub-sections we also provide example of using chromosome to specify website features.

web user interaction
knowledgebase

Russian
English

Home   Registry of projects   Registry of recommendations   Repository of components ⌄

Home

Similar projects

Novosibirsk State Technical University

Tasks: About us; Admissions; Faculties and Institutes; Current Students; Conferences, Research and Innovations; International Collaboration; Alumni; Contacts

- Ural Federal University website (**distance:** 0.0267)
- Tomsk Polytechnice University website (**distance:** 0.2113)
- MISiS website (**distance:** 0.3340)

Fig. 2. Retrieved cases based on Task similarity (screenshot from http://wuikb.info)

The representation of website functionality in the chromosome is based on Drush's makefile syntax (http://docs.drush.org/en/8.x/make/) that in turn corresponds to YAML. The website Domain is selected from DMOZ classification. Task names come from the Tasks model, and Drupal modules (themes are not allowed, unlike in the makefile) implement the tasks on a many-to-many relationship basis. Custom configuration for a component can be stored in the string that concatenates the project options from the makefile (by default, most recent production versions of the modules are used). Since the functionality install is the most time-consuming action in the whole EA, the genetic operators are only applied to the modules if the alternatives (alleles) have comparable quality. The resulting data structure in the chromosome can be specified as follows:

```
<functionality_genes> := <domain> | <functionality_item>
| <component_configuration>
<domain> := "domain" ": " <dmoz_domain_name>
<functionality_item> ::= <task_name> ":"
<drupal_module_name> | <functionality_item>
<component_configuration> ::= "_" <drupal_module_name> ":"
<configuration_string> | <component_configuration>
```

Generally, each functionality item implemented for the website's front office has one or several related user interface elements. Correspondingly, in Drupal most front-office modules have blocks (groups of UI elements) placed in one of webpage's regions and ordered within a region by their weight. The currently default list of regions in Drupal (Twig template engine) has 10 items: page.header, page.primary_menu, page.content, etc., which are sufficient for many conventional websites. The names of the blocks are created by Drupal, so they become accessible for the EA after the website functionality is assembled. The part of the chromosome describing the layout can then be specified as follows:

```
<layout_genes> ::= <blocks_placement> | <blocks_order>
<blocks_placement> ::= <region_name> ": " <block_name> |
<blocks_placement>
<blocks_order_in_region> ::= <block_name> ": " <weight> |
<blocks_order_in_region>
<region_name> ::= "page.header" | "page.primary_menu" |
"page.secondary_menu" | "page.highlighted" | "page.help"
| "page.content" | "page.sidebar_first" |
"page.sidebar_second" | "page.footer" | "page.breadcrumb"
```

The genetic operators are applied to the blocks' placement and order, which can be programmatically set via Drush extras commands, such as:

```
drush block-configure --module=block --delta=block_delta
--region=page.header --weight=10
```

In Drupal, themes are responsible for visual appearance of the website, and many of them have adjustable parameters (stored in JSON format) shaping their visual presentation, such as colors, font sizes and families, etc. In the EA, after the website functionality and layout genes are initialized, the algorithm selects the basic theme that has the number of parameters appropriate for the project (more parameters mean more flexibility, but EA's convergence may take much longer time). The visual appearance-related part of the chromosome can be specified as follows:

```
<visual_appearance_configuration> ::= <theme_name>
<theme_parameters>
<theme_name> ::= "theme" ": " <drupal_theme_name>
<theme_parameters> ::= | <parameter_name> ": "
<parameter_value> | <theme_parameters>
```

The genetic operators can be applied to the parameter values, and for each new solution the corresponding sub-theme is created. Although the theme parameters are mechanism very native for Drupal, there's no built-in universal solution for managing the parameters. So, we implemented the dedicated Drush module to adjust themes' parameters from command line (see https://github.com/vkhvorostov/subtheme_color).

3.3   Repository of Content

In the eyes of end users, content is not entirely detachable from design, so auto-assessment of the candidate solutions' quality in the EA's fitness function cannot be performed with wireframe designs, lacking any textual and graphic materials. Obviously, the assessment of the solutions' similarity with the CBR-retrieved designs also calls for filler-up content resembling the one of the reference websites. As we mentioned before, there's barely the need to store content-related properties of solutions in the chromosome (they should rather relate to phenotype). Thus, content items are to be drawn from the respective repository and assigned to the solutions on a stochastic basis. The concrete use cases for such repository are the following:

1. Extracting "original" content items from solutions in projects:
   a. manually by human annotators;
   b. automatically from the solutions' webpage code and screenshot (our corresponding supplementary tool, the visual analyzer, is described in Bakaev et al. 2018b).
2. Creating filler-up content items (linked to the original ones):
   a. manually by human annotators;
   b. automatically using online services for similar images search, text generators, etc.
3. Manual organization and management of the content items.
4. Usage of the content by the EA:
   a. drawing the filler-up content items similar to the original ones in the retrieved projects;
   b. considering the degree of similarity in defining the probability for selecting a particular filler-up content item;
   c. considering the content type and placement in the webpage.

Correspondingly, the Content Item has the following attributes (see in Fig. 3):

- type (text, image, label, header, etc.);
- status (original, filler-up, outdated, etc.);
- content (piece of HTML code);
- links to Projects (mostly for filler-up content) and to their solutions (mostly for original content);
- links to other Content Items (with weights indicating of the degree of similarity).

In Fig. 4 we show (a) part of a reference website's design, (b) an extracted content item – logo; (c) related filler-up content – a similar image collected via Google, with color similarity constraint (red); (d) related filler-up content – a similar image collected via Google, without the color similarity constraint.

Fig. 3. The list of content items in the repository (screenshot from http://wuikb.info)

3.4   Example of the EA Data Structures

In the example we show some data structures from genetic optimization of an educational website project. Extract from the part of chromosome responsible for the functionality generation is presented below (its specification was previously described in The Chromosome Structure sub-section). "Drupal" module name implies that functionality is in Drupal core.

```
domain: "Career and Education"
about_us: drupal
_drupal: "version 7.59"
contact_us: webform
shopping_cart: dc_cart_ajax
...
```

The Component picker also produces the list of alleles for the shopping_cart task (with the quality value being the number of websites using the module) outside of the chromosome:

```
shopping_cart:
  dc_cart_ajax: 1874
  commerce_ajax_cart: 1375
  basic_cart: 1288
  uc_ajax_cart: 1278
...
```

Subsequently, the Website installer additionally installs Drupal's commerce module (as dependency for dc_cart_ajax module).

Fig. 4. The related items in the content repository (Color figure online)

The layout part of the chromosome is naturally created after the functionality part, and we present the extract below:

```
page.header: site-logo
page.header: site-name
site-logo: -10
site-name: 10
page.primary_menu: topbar
page.sidebar_first: content-block-1
page.content: user-login
page.footer: content-block-2
...
```

The number of genes responsible for the visual appearance is potentially unlimited and defined by the theme parameters. An extract of the chromosome's corresponding part is shown below:

```
theme: bartik
top: '#dada4a'
bg: '#ffffff'
footer: '#161617'
text: '#3b3b3b'
link: '#0073b6'
...
```

Our subtheme_color module generated the following command to mutate two of the above genes:

Fig. 5. Theme's mutated visual appearance in generation N (left) vs. N+1 (right).

```
/drush.sh -r projects/test/ stc bartik
'{"top": "#daba4a", "footer": "#361617"}'
```

In Fig. 5 we illustrate the mutation, showing the visual appearance before and after application of the genetic operator.

4 Conclusion

Computer-aided design of user interfaces is increasingly seen as discrete optimization problem, but the design space remains prohibitively large for most tasks of practical importance. Yet the web design domain that our paper specifically considers has the benefits of (a) most web projects having fairly conventional functionality, and (b) the number of accessible cases (the operational websites on the WWW) potentially available for reuse having the order of 10^8. In our work, we proposed combining the time-honored case-based reasoning approach with evolutionary algorithms to generate web user interfaces, and contemplated several domain-specific complicated points:

1. *Currently existing web design repositories are rather poorly organized and do not allow selecting solutions for a particular use context.* Based on the features we engineered for web projects as cases in CB, we proposed mechanism for their retrieval based on domain-, task- and target user similarity. The indexing of cases in the CB can be largely automated using supplementary tools that we developed, but should involve human annotators for the User-related features.
2. *Web designs available from the WWW cannot be reused directly, due to technical and legal obstacles.* So, we suggested instead to adapt the newly generated solution to the retrieved examples, by embracing their alikeness in the EA's fitness function. The similarity measure can be calculated automatically, based on pre-trained user behavior models, as we demonstrated in one of our previous works. Relevant filler-up content can be auto-delivered from the extendable content repository.
3. *Specification of the enormous design space and intertwined constraints for a WUI, so that the genetic operators could be applied, would be a great endeavor.* As a substitute, we proposed relying on pre-existing Drupal framework's data structures, components, and manipulation tools. We specified the structure of the chromosome based on YAML and demonstrated the usage of Drush commands (with some extensions that we programmed) for the purposes of the EA.

In the current paper we only demonstrated operation of some principal parts of the EA: how the WUI functionality, layout, visual appearance and content are created and manipulated. Our further plans include training user behavior models to be employed in the EA's fitness function, performing the genetic optimization to produce the final solutions and assessing their quality with representatives of the target users.

Acknowledgement. The reported study was funded by Russian Ministry of Education and Science, according to the research project No. 2.2327.2017/4.6, and by RFBR according to the research project No. 16-37-60060 mol_a_dk.

References

Anderson, M.R., et al.: Brainwash: a data system for feature engineering. In CIDR (2013)

Bakaev, M.: Assessing similarity for case-based web user interface design. In: Alexandrov, D., Boukhanovsky, A., Chugunov, A., Kabanov, Y., Koltsova, O. (eds.) Digital Transformation and Global Society. DTGS 2018. Communications in Computer and Information Science, vol. 858. Springer, Cham (2018a). https://doi.org/10.1007/978-3-030-02843-5_28

Bakaev, M., Gaedke, M.: Application of evolutionary algorithms in interaction design: from requirements and ontology to optimized web interface. In: IEEE Young Researchers in Electrical and Electronic Engineering Conference (EIConRusNW 2016), pp. 129–134 (2016)

Bakaev, M., Heil, S., Khvorostov, V., Gaedke, M.: HCI vision for automated analysis and mining of web user interfaces. In: Mikkonen, T., Klamma, R., Hernández, J. (eds.) Web Engineering. ICWE 2018. LNCS, vol 10845, pp. 136–144. Springer, Cham (2018b). https://doi.org/10.1007/978-3-319-91662-0_10

Bakaev, M., Khvorostov, V.: Component-based engineering of web user interface designs for evolutionary optimization. In: 19th IEEE/ACIS International Conference on Software Engineering, Artificial Intelligence, Networking and Parallel/Distributed Computing (SNPD), pp. 335–340. IEEE (2018c)

Bakaev, M., Khvorostov, V., Heil, S., Gaedke, M.: Web intelligence linked open data for website design reuse. In: Cabot, J., De Virgilio, R., Torlone, R. (eds.) ICWE 2017. LNCS, vol. 10360, pp. 370–377. Springer, Cham (2017). https://doi.org/10.1007/978-3-319-60131-1_22

Coello, C.A.C.: Multi-objective evolutionary algorithms in real-world applications: some recent results and current challenges. In: Greiner, D., Galván, B., Périaux, J., Gauger, N., Giannakoglou, K., Winter, G. (eds.) Advances in Evolutionary and Deterministic Methods for Design, Optimization and Control in Engineering and Sciences, pp. 3–18. Springer, Cham (2015). https://doi.org/10.1007/978-3-319-11541-2_1

Mantaras, D., et al.: Retrieval, reuse, revision and retention in case-based reasoning. Knowl. Eng. Rev. **20**(3), 215–240 (2005)

De Renzis, A., Garriga, M., Flores, A., Cechich, A., Zunino, A.: Case-based reasoning for web service discovery and selection. Electron. Notes Theoret. Comput. Sci. **321**, 89–112 (2016)

Freitas, A.A.: Data Mining and Knowledge Discovery with Evolutionary Algorithms. Springer, Heidelberg (2013)

Gajos, K., Wu, A., Weld, D.S.: Cross-device consistency in automatically generated user interfaces. In: 2nd Workshop on Multi-User and Ubiquitous User Interfaces, pp. 7–8 (2005)

Glass, R.L.: Facts and Fallacies of Software Engineering. Addison-Wesley Professional, Boston (2002)

Guo, F., Liu, W.L., Cao, Y., Liu, F.T., Li, M.L.: Optimization design of a webpage based on Kansei engineering. Hum. Fact. Ergon. Manuf. Serv. Ind. **26**(1), 110–126 (2016)

Ivory, M.Y., Hearst, M.A.: Statistical profiles of highly-rated web sites. In: ACM SIGCHI Conference on Human Factors in Computing Systems (CHI), pp. 367–374 (2002)

Kazimipour, B., Li, X., Qin, A.K.: A review of population initialization techniques for evolutionary algorithms. In: IEEE Congress on Evolutionary Computation (CEC), pp. 2585–2592 (2014)

Kumar, R., et al.: Webzeitgeist: design mining the web. In: Proceedings of the ACM SIGCHI Conference on Human Factors in Computing Systems (CHI), pp. 3083–3092 (2013)

Marir, F.: Case-based reasoning for an adaptive web user interface. In: The International Conference on Computing, Networking and Digital Technologies (ICCNDT2012), pp. 306–315. The Society of Digital Information and Wireless Communication (2012)

Martinie, C., Navarre, D., Palanque, P., Fayollas, C.: A generic tool-supported framework for coupling task models and interactive applications. In: 7th ACM SIGCHI Symposium on Engineering Interactive Computing Systems (EICS), pp. 244–253 (2015)

Michalewicz, Z., Hartley, S.J.: Genetic algorithms+ data structures= evolution programs. Math. Intell. **18**(3), 71 (1996)

Oulasvirta, A.: User interface design with combinatorial optimization. Computer **50**(1), 40–47 (2017)

Qu, Q.X.: Kansei knowledge extraction based on evolutionary genetic algorithm: an application to E-commerce web appearance design. Theoret. Issues Ergon. Sci. **16**(3), 299–313 (2015)

Rocha, R.G., Azevedo, R.R., Sousa, Y.C., Tavares, E.D.A., Meira, S.: A case-based reasoning system to support the global software development. Procedia Comput. Sci. **35**, 194–202 (2014)

Inter-country Competition and Collaboration in the miRNA Science Field

Artemiy Firsov[1,3](✉) (iD) and Igor Titov[2,3](✉)

[1] Institute of Informatics Systems,
6, Acad. Lavrentjev pr., Novosibirsk 630090, Russia
artemijfirsov@mail.ru
[2] Institute of Cytology and Genetics,
Prospekt Lavrentyeva 10, Novosibirsk 630090, Russia
titov@bionet.nsc.ru
[3] Novosibirsk State University, 1, Pirogova str., Novosibirsk 630090, Russia
https://www.iis.nsk.su, https://nsu.ru/, http://www.bionet.nsc.ru

Abstract. Many digital libraries, such as PubMed, Scopus, appeared with the growth of the Internet: thus, many scientific articles became available in the digital form. We got an opportunity to query articles metadata, gather statistics, build co-authorship graphs, etc. This includes estimating the authors/institutions activity, revealing their interactions and other properties.

In this work we present the analysis of the characteristics of institutions interactions in the miRNA science field using the data from PubMed digital library. To tackle the problem of the institution name writing variability, we proposed the k-mer/n-gram boolean feature vector sorting algorithm -KOFER. We identified the leaders of the field - China, USA -, characterized the interactions and described the country level features of co-authorship. We observed that the USA were leading in the publication activity until China took the lead 4 years ago. However, the USA are the main co-authorship driver in this field.

Keywords: K-Mer · n-gram · DBSCAN · Identification · miRNA · Timsort · KOFER · Digital library · Co-authorship

1 Introduction

Many digital libraries appeared with the growth of the Internet, thus, the format of representation of many scientific articles changed. We got an opportunity to query articles metadata, gather some statistics, etc. This includes understanding the authors/institutions activity, their interactions, and other characteristics. One can also prove that the Paretto rule for the institutions' publication activity

The work of I.T. was supported by the Federal Agency of Scientific Organizations (project #0324-2019-0040).

holds true [2], or that the idea spreads from one author to another like the virus spreads from one person to the others. Having this information, we can further use it to predict the new science field creation, popularity of the particular science field. In general, it can be used in social informatics.

Moreover, right now the new science field is emerging – "science of science" [12]. It is a transdisciplinary field of science that aims to understand the evolution of ideas, choice of a research problem of particular scientist, etc. Without analyzing interactions between authors, institutions, and other, such a field just cannot exist.

However, to do that one should know to which real author/institution the authors name/affiliation from the paper corresponds to. The more precise correspondence we have, the better accuracy of statistics we can get. This disambiguation issue is not that simple considering big datasets, such as PubMed with $2 * 10^7$ articles. It becomes more complicated when you consider errors in the author name/affiliation made either by author, or by editor. Moreover, sometimes author/institution name might be changed, or the affiliation from the papers metadata may have mixed institution names for different authors. E.g. if the Author1 has "Institute of Cytology and Genetics, Novosibirsk, Russia" institution and the Author2 has "Institute of Mathematics, Novosibirsk, Russia" institution, their resulting affiliation for collaborative paper might be "Institute of Cytology and Genetics, Institute of Mathematics, Novosibirsk, Russia". Moreover, affiliation can contain email, postal address and other insertions not related to institution name.

1.1   Author Disambiguation Overview

To disambiguate the authors, many sophisticated algorithms were proposed. Some base on the similarity function [13], others use clustering techniques [14], web information [15], etc. Different approaches are reviewed well in Ferreiras' et al. paper [16].

Although they utilize different algorithms and methods, almost all of them have one thing in common – they use affiliation as the author feature. That means that similarity between two different records of authors from different articles is measured using affiliation also. Moreover, there is no uniform algorithm to process affiliation entry, in different papers researchers use different similarity measures. However, one may think of another use of affiliation.

1.2   Affiliation Disambiguation Problem

We know that the researchers can work in different places, thus, can have multiple affiliations in their papers. We also know that they leave/get fired from/change their institution rarely. By that means, one may identify the author having the knowledge of his affiliations, or at least propose a hypothesis. On the other hand, affiliation is represented by its" authors/workers. That means that having a set of author names, one can deduce, in which institution these authors work, or at least propose a hypothesis. I.e. people are the feature of institution and institutions are the feature of a person. Using this statement, we can think of the author disambiguation issue and the affiliation disambiguation issue as of two separate issues. Moreover, results of one issue solution can be used to enhance the results of the other.

Having this in mind, we in Molecular Genetics Department of Institute of Cytology and Genetics propose an idea that iterative, self-consistent solution of the author disambiguation issue, the affiliation disambiguation, and the paper topic extraction issue can increase the accuracy of all these issues.

In this paper, we aim to provide the solution for Affiliation Disambiguation problem. In addition, the whole self-consistent project is currently under development in the laboratory of molecular genetic systems in the Institute of Cytology and Genetics under I.I. Titov supervision.

The organization name disambiguation problem has already been addressed in several works, in which authors aimed to disambiguate organization names mined in the social web-data. Authors used web data [3], and sophisticated algorithms [4]. However, we are aiming to find the simple and yet precise solution, basing on the simple input data - just affiliations. That way we can get computationally effective algorithm, which can be specified using results of the author name disambiguation problem solution.

2   Methods and Materials

2.1   Prerequisites

The basic idea of the work is to get the groups of organizations mentions, which contain only mentions of one institution. After that we may use that information to build the co-authorship graph of organizations/countries, get static and dynamic characteristics of the science field, etc. So on the first step we solved the clustering problem of institutions names writings:

$$max f(C) \ subject \ to \ C = (C_1, ...C_k), C_1 \cup ... \cup C_k = S, \tag{1}$$

where S - the set of affiliations extracted from the publications, C_i - group of similar affiliations. So we want to assign a label to each of the affiliations in the dataset, so that the final grouping by labels maximizes some function f. This f can be constructed in many ways, however in our case, the closer the grouping is to the ground-truth grouping (i.e. one group contains all and only affiliations that refer to the same institution), the higher the value of the function. So the previous problem statement will transform:

$$max f(C, R) \ subject \ to \ R = (R_1, ...R_k), C = (C_1, ...C_k) \tag{2}$$

$$C_1 \cup ... \cup C_k = S, R_1 \cup ... \cup R_k = S,$$

where R – is the ground-truth grouping of the affiliation set S, labeled by the author, m – the ground-truth number of labels. The function f that provides such characteristics is discussed in the Evaluation Metrics section of this chapter.

2.2 Dataset

To conduct experiments, we have gathered two datasets from PubMed [1] digital library using MEDLINE file format. First one is the Novosibirsk dataset, that consists of the preprocessed affiliations of the Novosibirsk institutions. This dataset was gathered in the Titovs' and Blinovs' work [2] dedicated to the author disambiguation problem. We labeled this dataset to have the ground-truth affiliation clustering to further use it for clustering algorithm hyperparameters fine-tuning. Second one is the miRNA dataset gathered on the following search query on the PubMed website over *Title* and *Abstract* fields:

((((((miRNA) OR mi-RNA) OR microRNA) OR micro-RNA) OR miRNAs)
OR mi-RNAs) OR microRNAs) OR micro-RNAs.

The miRNA dataset contains the publications available on the PubMed digital library as of 11/11/2018 (Table 1).

Table 1. Characteristics of the datasets used in the work

	Novosibirsk dataset	miRNA dataset
# of articles	~6,000	77,800
Year	... - 2014	... - 2018
# of affiliations	951	387,793
# of unique organizations	62	~20,000

2.3 Evaluation Metrics

We used homogeneity (h), completeness (c) and v-measure score (v) [5] to evaluate the clustering results for Novosibirsk dataset.

$$h = 1 - \frac{H(C|K)}{H(C)} \tag{3}$$

$$c = 1 - \frac{H(K|C)}{H(K)} \tag{4}$$

$$v = 2 * \frac{h * c}{h + c}, \tag{5}$$

where $H(C|K) = -\sum_{n=1}^{|C|}\sum_{n=1}^{|K|} \frac{n_{c,k}}{n} * log(\frac{n_{c,k}}{n_k})$, $H(C) = -\sum_{c=1}^{|C|} \frac{n_c}{n} * log(\frac{n_c}{n})$; $H(K|C), H(K)$ are constructed the same way.

These metrics are analogous to precision, recall and f-metric used in supervised learning. Homogeneity equals one if every cluster contains only all data points from one class. Completeness equals one if all data points from one class are assigned to the same cluster for every cluster. In addition, v-measure is derived from homogeneity and completeness. The closer these metrics are to one, the better the solution is.

Although we aimed to increase this parameters, it is pretty hard to have them be near 1 if you work with affiliation entry only. So, we introduced additional metric to choose from different clustering results. As we aim to create an instrument that reveals some statistics of institutions activity basing on their names only, it is reasonable to try to cluster affiliations in the way that final cluster count is equal to ground-truth class count. Thus, we chose those hyperparameters that gave clusters count close to real class count. All the clustering quality metrics were calculated using the most significant clusters (cluster volume ≥ 10), as we want to be aware only on those institutions that are actively publishing in a certain field.

2.4 Data Preprocessing

Pre-processing stage of all algorithms is performed before actual calculations. As discussed in introduction, affiliations have some additional information, which relate to the author, not institution. This leads to the big number of variations of institution name writing. On that stage, we remove emails/zip/phone/numbers from affiliation using regular expressions. We also perform standard operations, like preserving only alphabetical characters, expanding the abbreviations, removing stopwords, etc.

During the research we tried several NLP frameworks hoping they can fix errors described in some points above. These include NLTK [7], language_check [8] and others. We found out that affiliations (or institutions references) cannot be fully considered as manifestations of natural language, and NLP frameworks perform poorly on them, giving a lot of errors on each affiliation. However, they still can be used to fix errors inside words such as "institue" and others.

So far we eliminated explicit artifacts, however, there may be implicit artifacts, like name of the laboratory where the author works. We call this an "implicit" artifact as this name can be different for different institutions and it is hard to provide deterministic algorithm that will work for every situation.

To handle such artifacts, we introduced regular expression based algorithm based on keywords and country names. We provide our algorithm with keywords, such as "center", "institute", etc. We also provided our algorithm with full list of country names. Now, having all that information, we can represent our affiliation as a sequence of numbers. We split affiliation by commas and assign each part 0 number. If any keyword is in a particular part, we assign it number 1. If any country is in a particular part, we assign it number 3. Thus, "Institute of Cytology and Genetics, Novosibirsk, Russia" is represented as "103"; "Institute of Cytology and Genetics, Institute of Mathematics, Novosibirsk, Russia" is represented as "1103". Number of ones represents the number of institution names in the affiliation, which can further be handled with a simple regular expression – "(0?1+0?0*0?3?0?)".

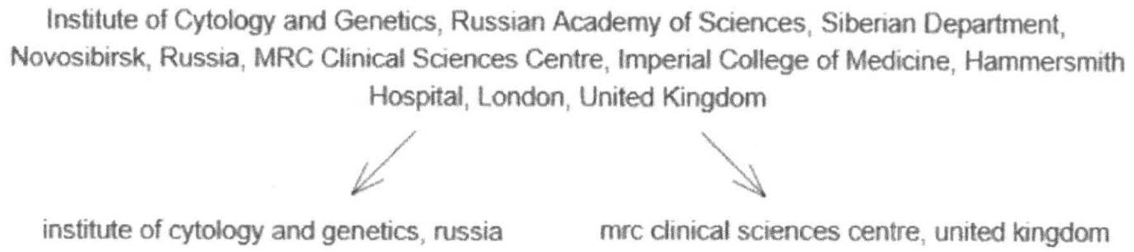

Institute of Cytology and Genetics, Russian Academy of Sciences, Siberian Department, Novosibirsk, Russia, MRC Clinical Sciences Centre, Imperial College of Medicine, Hammersmith Hospital, London, United Kingdom

institute of cytology and genetics, russia   mrc clinical sciences centre, united kingdom

Fig. 1. Example of normalized and split affiliation

The advantage of such approach is that new notions can be introduced into this algorithm, e.g. cities. Moreover, it is extensible and modifiable, as providing new keywords and country/city names, we can wider our algorithm configuration to work with bigger domain of affiliations.

2.5   Clustering and Similarity

After the pre-processing stage, the clustering stage is performed. We tried different techniques for the clustering – K-Means and DBSCAN [10] – and different popular similarity functions – Levenshtein, Jaccard, Smith-Waterman. We used scikit-learn [9] implementation of those.

We also tried using K-Mers feature vectors to find similarity between affiliations. K-Mer is a notion that came from genetics. It is a substring of a certain string of length K. Geneticists use it to analyze DNA/RNA sequences. In Natural Language Processing there is a similar notion – n-gram. Building K-Mer feature vector is described below and in section K-Mers Boolean Feature Vector Sorting (KOFER) based Clustering. However, it is important to notice that we used letter K-Mers, not word K-Mers in the work.

Similarity functions were used to create the distance matrix, and also K-Mers were used to create features of a certain affiliation. As K-Mer is a substring of a string of length K, one can assign the Boolean vector to the affiliation. In this vector each bit represents the presence of a certain K-Mer in the affiliation. As K-Mer dictionary power exponentially grows with the K number, this dictionary upon K-Mers consists only of K-Mers present in the certain dataset that is being processed in the experiment.

Basically, similarity function for strings is a function that takes as an input two terms and outputs the value between 0 and 1:

$$f(x,y) = z, \tag{6}$$

where $z \in [0,1], x, y \in V^*, V$ - alphabet. However, for Boolean vectors - $x, y \in B^m$, m - the size of the K-Mer dictionary.

During experiments we found out that KMeans and DBSCAN perform poorly on affiliations data, so we proposed another method based on the K-Mer boolean feature vectors clustering.

The idea of the method is based on the consistency of affiliation writing. E.g. if an author works in "Institute of Cytology and Genetics", it is highly likely that this particular words with some additional information will be present as affiliation in his work. Moreover, we can assume that these words should usually be placed in the "first position" of affiliation, like in "Novosibirsk Institute of Cytology and Genetics, Novosibirsk, Russia".

The naive idea would be to sort affiliations strings, find distance between current and next neighbors, and then set a threshold for the distance. If the distance exceeds the threshold, we can consider this pair to belong to different clusters, e.g. Table 2.

Table 2. 10 affiliation entries sorted by name. $d(i, i+1)$ is the demonstrative distance. 5th line has high distance as affiliations refer to different organizations. The last row is automatically assigned to the latest cluster as there is no next row to calculate similarity with.

i	Affiliation	$d(i, i+1)$
1	Institute of cytology and genetics	0.1
2	Institute of cytologyand genetics	0.2
3	Institute of cytology and gnetics	0.3
4	Instiute of cytologyand genetics	0.2
5	Institute of cytology and genetics	**0.8**
6	Institue of bioorganic chemistry	0.1
7	Institue of biorganic chemistry	0.2
8	Institue of bioorganicchemistry	0.1
9	Institue of bioorganic chemistry	0
10	Institue of bioorganic chemistry	

Such an approach benefits in performance time. DBSCAN complexity is $O(n^2)$ in the worst case (running ahead, we note that we observed such situation running experiments), as well as sorting (however we did not observe that problem during experiments). Distance calculation time grows linearly with increasing number of records, as well as comparison time. Thus, performance complexity would be $O(nlog(n))$ ideally. However, the naive approach performs badly in the following situations:

1. There exists preceding part in affiliation name – "Institute of Cytology and Genetics" vs "Novosibirsk Institute of Cytology and Genetics".
2. There is an error in the beginning of the affiliation – "Lnstitute of Cytology and Genetics".

In both cases, entries are assigned into different clusters, as they start with different characters.

2.6   K-Mer Boolean Vector Sorting

To tackle the problems pointed above, we decided to perform sorting on K-Mers vector instead of plain text. Here and further, we mean letter K-Mer when mention K-Mer, not word K-Mer. K-Mer vector can be constructed in different ways, but firstly, one should calculate K-Mer dictionary:

1. Take the dataset with affiliations
2. Calculate K-Mers for each string
3. Take only unique K-Mers and reorder them from frequent to rare

We need reordering to provide each K-Mer with its place and to provide position invariance.

Having this done, we then proceed to feature vector calculation, which can be done using one of the following approaches:

1. Create the binary vector, that represents the presence of all K-Mers in the affiliation
2. Create natural vector, that represents the number of occurrences of all K-Mers in the affiliation

Further, we discuss the first approach and provide the results of clustering using binary K-Mer features. Then, we can lexicographically sort these vectors so that affiliations with similar contents will be aligned together in the array of all affiliations. And moreover, this procedure can restore the conformity between affiliation substrings, as we can see from the Table 4.

E.g., assume that the dataset contains only two words – "institute" and "institue". We use the simple example here for the ease of understanding. Then the K-Mer dictionary and K-Mer Boolean feature vectors would look like this:

Table 3. K-Mers dictionary and K-Mers boolean feature vectors for the simple case

Dictionary	K-Mer occurrences	in	ns	st	ti	it	tu	ut	tu	ue
		2	2	2	2	2	2	1	1	1
For the word "institute"		1	1	1	1	1	1	1	1	0
For the word "institue"		1	1	1	1	1	1	0	0	1

Having this done, we can further lexicographically sort the K-Mer Boolean feature vectors and find the distance between two neighboring vectors using Boolean distance metrics, as we did in the Results chapter, for the use in clustering by the threshold. For example, below is the table showing words sorted by their K-Mer Boolean feature vectors representation. Here, we use five words to show how we reach the threshold of the distance in the sorted list of vectors – "institute", "institute", "institute", "center", "centre". We also eliminate the explanation of the K-Mers dictionary construction, as it was explained before. The distance was calculated using Dice distance [11].

We can see that similar words grouped and the distance reaches its peak when there is a change from the word "institue" to the word "center". If we

Table 4. Affiliations sorted lexicographically by the K-Mer boolean feature vectors with distances between neighboring records calculated with Dice distance

Word	K-Mer Boolean feature vector	Distance between current and next
Institute	1111111100000000	0.2
Institute	1111100100001000	0.43
Institute	1111011000010000	**0.83**
Center	0000100011100100	0.4
Centre	0000000011100011	0.2

than say that the distance threshold should be bigger than 0.43 to consider previous and further records to belong to different clusters, we than can validly assign different words to different clusters.

2.7   Country Identification

To identify countries in affiliations we used the open data [17] with the list of countries and cities provided. If the country or city was present in the affiliation, than the affiliation was assigned the corresponding country

3   Results

In this paper, we present the results for country level co-authorship in the miRNA field. Using the K-Mer Boolean vector sorting algorithm we were able to cluster the miRNA affiliations data. From the 387,793 affiliations we got 23,655 clusters. i.e. institutions.

3.1   PubMed Statistics

To have the properties to compare with, we got the statistics from the PubMed website in Fig. 2. All the plots were generated using the matplotlib software [19]. The growth of the articles available in the PubMed is different from the ones foe the miRNA science field - for all the publications in the miRNA field the linear model does not fit. The beginning of the growth is different from the remainder part.

The logistic function estimation on the remainder part gives

$$\frac{a}{1 + b * \exp^{-c*x}} = \frac{19603.09}{1 + 31.09 * \exp^{-0.42*x}} \tag{7}$$

parameter values. And the exponential estimation at the beginning

$$\exp^{a*x+b} = \exp^{3.62*x+0.74} \tag{8}$$

In these formulae the $x \in \mathbb{N}$ represents the offset between the first publication year and others, i.e. $x \in 0, 1, ...$ This shows that likely the miRNA field is in the saturation state. All the graphs are built using the 2003–2016 data, because the 2017, 2018 years are the years when the field reaches it's plateau.

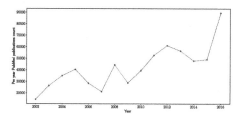

(a) Number of publications added to the PubMed digital library per year

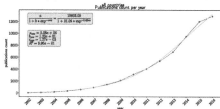
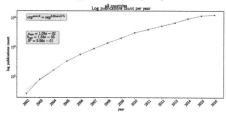

(b) Number of publications per year in the miRNA science field

(c) Log number of publications per year in the miRNA science field

Fig. 2. Publications activity of PubMed. Lines are built using approximation functions in the boxes starting at $x = 0, x \in 0, 1, ...$

3.2 Countries Publication Activity

It would be interesting now to see per country publication activity (Fig. 3). We may see that the USA had the rapid start of publication in this field, reaching 100 publications in 2004. However, the growth started to reduce over time, whereas China had higher growth, which led to China becoming the new leader in 2013. The numeric growth estimations for separate countries are available in Fig. 4 and Table 5.

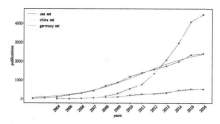

Fig. 3. Number of publications of USA, China, Germany in the miRNA science field added to the PubMed per year

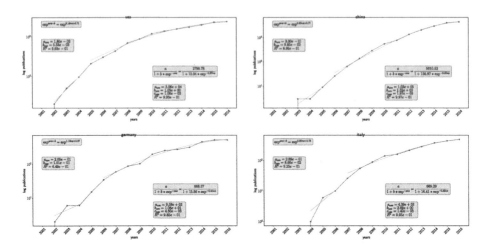

Fig. 4. Log number of publications of USA, China, Germany, Italy in the miRNA science field added to the PubMed per year. Left-upper corner contains exponential estimation of the first 3 years of publication activity. Right-bottom corner contains logistic estimation of the rest of the years of publication activity

The logistic parameters estimations for publication activity of different countries is presented in the table below:

3.3 Countries Interaction Graph

To see how countries interact, we have built the graph using the gephi software [18]. We used only those countries that have published more than 500 articles to reduce the noisiness of the graph in Fig. 5.

The graph shows that the USA and China are the leaders in this field, as well as they publish together a lot. Although connections are quite dense, and there are many joint publications between different country pairs, the number of joint publications seems to be quite low, and it is not clear whether some country is the driver of joint publications, or it is the common practice in the field to publish together. This problem will be addressed in the Sect. 3.4.

3.4 Joint Publications

During the 2002–2016 period, there were 52,407 publications, 5,412 of which were international, i.e. joint. The field until some time did not have much joint publications, however things changed in 2013. That year USA and China started actively publish together (Fig. 6).

However, the main driver for joint publications is the USA, as it has more publications with different countries than China (Table 6). Also, it is interesting to notice that major part of all USA joint publications appeared after the 2013, when it started actively publishing with China.

Table 5. Parameter of the logistic function estimation for publication activity of different countries

Country	a	b	c
Australia	397,04	44,51	0.49
Canada	396,36	36,44	0.42
China	5,610.52	156,97	0.65
France	270,78	56,34	0.42
Germany	668,37	15,56	0,41
India	300,92	93,69	0.61
Italy	669,29	16,41	0,42
Japan	400,22	25,3.1	0.54
Korea	277,04	150,24	0,68
Netherlands	237,04	10,57	0.38
Spain	268,22	47,5	0.47
Switzerland	193,1	14.26	0.38
UK	961,07	29.11	0.36
USA	2798,78	10,04	0.37

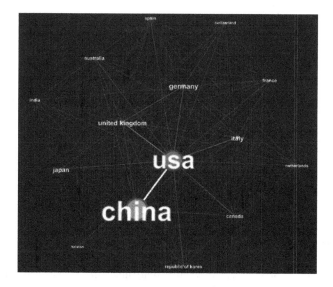

Fig. 5. Co-authorship of countries in the miRNA field. The label text, as well as the size of the point reflects the number of published articles, edges thickness shows the number of articles published together. If there were more than 2 countries in the publication, each pair of countries is considered to have had the joint publication.

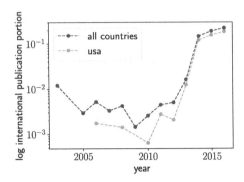

Fig. 6. The log portion of international publications relative to overall number of publications. Blue color - within all countries. Red color - within USA only (Color figure online)

Table 6. Most active countries pairs sorted by the number of joint publications

Country 1	Country 2	Joint publications
USA	China	1,084
USA	UK	324
USA	Italy	227
USA	Germany	223
USA	Canada	190
UK	Germany	182
USA	Korea	165
USA	Japan	145
USA	Australia	131
China	Canada	110
UK	Italy	103
China	UK	101
USA	France	100

4   Discussion

Getting the implicit properties of science field has major research interest as it reveals the current state of the field, provides the opportunity to compare different science fields with uniform instrument and gives the possibility to predict the creation of new fields or the future of the particular one.

And although metrics are the subject of the disputes - whether they are needed or not, useful or harmful - they are still of peoples interest. Whether government or companies support the research, they also rely on information environment surrounding the science field, which is often quantified to, e.g. number of publications within a science field, the impact of the research on the market, etc. Having more possibilities to reveal the "true" state of the science field would help researchers to show the importance of their field, as well as the funding organizations to distribute their funds efficiently. Thus, this work aims to reveal the quantitative metrics of the science field.

In our worked we used K-Mer Boolean feature vector sorting algorithm, which performed fast, however it still has the drawback of splitting the cluster into 2 separate cluster if there appears the different affiliation with common k-mer/n-gram inside the cluster. This problem can be tackled using the numeric feature vector, which will consider not only the presence of the k-mer/n-gram, but also the count of them present in the affiliation.

This work yet does not cover the affiliation level properties of the miRNA science field. It would be interesting to see the leaders of the field, track their history and also get the properties of the co-authorship graph.

The points mentioned above will be considered in the upcoming paper.

5   Conclusion

In this work we have implemented the algorithm for fast institution name clustering based on the K-Mer Boolean feature vector sorting - KOFER. Using that algorithm we managed to cluster the miRNA science field affiliations data.

Using the clustering results, we were able to get properties of country level interactions, see that China is currently the leading country in this field, however the USA is the biggest driver of joint publications.

The linear growth model does not fit the publication activity of countries - the relaxation should be taken into account. That tells us that the field is currently reaching it's peak.

References

1. Ncbi.nlm.nih.gov. Home - PubMed - NCBI (2019). https://www.ncbi.nlm.nih.gov/pubmed/. Accessed 17 Jan 2019
2. Titov, I., Blinov, A., Research of the structure and evolution of scientific co-authorship based on the analysis of Novosibirsk institutes publications in the biology and medicine science field. Vavilov J. Genet. Sel. **18** (2014)
3. Zhang, S., Wu, J., Zheng, D., Meng, Y., Yu, H.: An adaptive method for organization name disambiguation with feature reinforcing. In: 26th Pacific Asia Conference on Language, Information and Computation, pp. 237–245 (2012)
4. Polat, N.: Experiments on company name disambiguation with supervised classification techniques. In: 2013 International Conference on Electronics, Computer and Computation (ICECCO) (2013). https://doi.org/10.1109/ICECCO.2013.6718248
5. Bell Hirschberg, J., Rosenberg, A.: V-Measure: a conditional entropy-based external cluster evaluation. In: EMNLP, Prague (2007)
6. Rajaraman, A., Ulman, J.: Data mining. In: I.stanford.edu (2011). http://i.stanford.edu/ullman/mmds/ch1.pdf. Accessed 20 Jan 2019
7. Natural Language Toolkit - NLTK 3.4 documentation. In: Nltk.org. https://www.nltk.org/. Accessed 20 Jan 2019

8. Language-check. In: PyPI. https://pypi.org/project/language-check/. Accessed 20 Jan 2019
9. Scikit-learn: machine learning in Python - scikit-learn 0.20.2 documentation. In: Scikit-learn.org. https://scikit-learn.org/stable/. Accessed 20 Jan 2019
10. Ester, M., Kriegel, H., Sander, J., Xu, X.: A density-based algorithm for discovering clusters in large spatial databases with noise. AAAI Press (1996)
11. Dice, L.R.: Measures of the Amount of Ecologic Association Between Species (1945)
12. Fortunato, S., et al.: Science of science. Science (2018). https://doi.org/10.1126/science.aao0185
13. Cohen, W.W., Ravikumar, P.D., Fienberg, S.E.: A comparison of string distance metrics for name-matching tasks. IIWeb (2003)
14. Kamber, H.J.: Data Mining: Concepts and Technique. Morgan Kauffman, Burlington (2005)
15. Jain, A.K., Murty, M.N., Flynn, P.J.: Data clustering: a review. ACM Comput. Surv. **31**, 264–323 (1999)
16. Ferreira, A.A., Gonçalves, M.A., Laender, A.H.F.: A brief survey of automatic methods for author name. SIGMOD Rec. **41**, 15–26 (2012)
17. Usoltcev, E.: meMo-Minsk - Overview. In: GitHub (2016). https://github.com/meMo-Minsk. Accessed 25 Jan 2019
18. Gephi - The Open Graph Viz Platform. In: Gephi.org. https://gephi.org/. Accessed 25 Jan 2019
19. Matplotlib: Python plotting - Matplotlib 3.0.2 documentation. In: Matplotlib.org. https://matplotlib.org/. Accessed 25 Jan 2019

Archival Information Systems: New Opportunities for Historians

Irina Krayneva and Sergey Troshkov[✉]

A.P. Ershov Institute of Informatics Systems,
Lavrentiev ave. 6, 630090 Novosibirsk, Russia
cora@iis.nsk.su, kamronis@xtech.ru

Abstract. This paper presents a brief summary of the twenty years of research carried out at the A. P. Ershov Institute of Informatics Systems SB RAS in the area of developing electronic archives for heterogeneous documents. The phenomenon of electronic archives emerged and has been developing as part of the Novosibirsk school of informatics, which has always been oriented towards the contracting of social services. In the 1970s, the first social service projects launched by the Institute were educational initiatives for school education, accordant with the well-known thesis of Andrey Ershov: "Programming is the second literacy". Over the years, the IIS SB RAS has completed a range of projects on digitizing historical and cultural heritage of the Siberian Branch of the Russian Academy of Sciences: the Academician A. P. Ershov Electronic Archive, SB RAS Photo Archive and the SB RAS Open Archive. This work has become especially relevant in view of the ongoing restructuring of the Russian academic science.

Keywords: A.P. Ershov · Digital archives · Digital historical factography · Drupal

1 Introduction

The current information boom has brought up a number of challenges dealing with the problem of relevance of the information produced by a researcher; providing quality information to the scientific community has become a cornerstone task. James Nicolas Gray, an American researcher in computational systems and a Turing Award holder, suggested the concept of the fourth paradigm of research, a grid-technology based science that uses big data. Even though Gray and his followers stress the importance of systematization and free access to scientific archives (including experimental data and modeling results), the notion of a big virtual archive for humanities studies is no less relevant [1]. This highlights the relevance of free access to information since scientific workers are known to benefit from information and communication technologies (ICT) [2].

The demand for novelty and relevance of scientific research as a socio-cognitive institute stresses the need for a better and quicker access to archives,

© Springer Nature Switzerland AG 2019
N. Bjørner et al. (Eds.): PSI 2019, LNCS 11964, pp. 41–49, 2019.
https://doi.org/10.1007/978-3-030-37487-7_4

libraries, museums and other types of heritage content. Informatization as well as commercialization of state-run archives in Russia was propelled even further by the emergence of the Internet in the 1990s. Evidently, there should be alternative options of free access to information as well. The IIS SB RAS research team was among the first to complete several projects on the creation, scientific interpretation, organization and development of the methodology of digitizing scientific heritage; our experience can be viewed as technology-intensive, scientifically based, successfully tested and implemented [3].

Interdisciplinary collaboration of specialists in human studies and IT at the dawn of the Internet relied predominantly on the concept of open scientific communications. In essence, this is a cluster of civil society supported by professionals. Museums, libraries, universities and research institutions getting access to the Internet boosted user experience and the emergence of Internet-oriented resources: published museum collections, online library systems and catalogs, archival tools for research and reference, and select collections. For instance, in the Novosibirsk Scientific Center, projects on the creation of electronic archives of different types of documents became possible as part of the project called "The Internet of Novosibirsk Scientific Center" in 1994–1998, funded by the Soros Foundation, Russian Foundation of Basic Research, and INTAS. As result, research institutions and other organizations of the NSC got free access to the Internet.

2 Tools

The emergence and distribution of special tools – information systems (IS) – facilitates the development and systematization of information in professional communities, including those engaged in humanities studies [4]. Electronic catalogs and knowledge bases became an integral part of scientific community processes by the end of the 20th century. Specialized information systems appeared aimed at presenting, storing and organizing historical sources and texts, i.e. history-oriented IS's. We understand information systems as a complex of technical, program, organizational and financial utilities as well as the personnel capable of working with this complex and complete the project [5]. The minimal staffing of such projects, based on the experience of the IIS SB RAS, is about 10 people, including programmers, historians, information specialists (operators) and translators.

Specialists from Perm State University whose interest is the application of the IT in humanities suggested a specification of history-oriented systems [6]. Of special interest are systems containing, in addition to historical information, a set of research tools (search, analytics, text recognition, etc.). We see two approaches to creating the IS's: history-oriented, when a system is based on an array of documents from a single source, and the system is modeled according to the structure of this source, and problem-oriented, when a model is built based on the structure of the studied field of knowledge. According to this classification, the systems created in the IIS SB RAS are history-oriented. The SB RAS Photo

Archive integrates two sources on its platform: scans of photographic documents and archives of the *Nauka v Sibiri* (*Science in Siberia*) newspaper. There is an organic and thematic connection between the two sources, because the newspaper staff reporters took many of the photos. In addition to documents, the A. P. Ershov's Electronic Archive and the SB RAS Open Archive contain photographs and research papers. We consider our IS's source-oriented for another reason, too: the archives contain images (scans) of original documents with transcriptions supplied as an additional feature allowing to read compromised and poorly legible scans. Finally, our IS's support remote workspaces for document description.

3   Analogies and Problems

Currently there are many resources created for the accumulation of historical and cultural heritage in a digital format. Millions of photographs from the LIFE photo archive, stretching from the 1750s to today, are now available for the first time through the joint work of LIFE and Google (2008). Digital collections of the Science History Institute (https://digital.sciencehistory.org/) includes 6,508 digitized items: artifacts, photographs, advertisements, letters, rare books. Library of Congress (https://www.loc.gov/) and digital collections of UNESCO (https://digital.archives.unesco.org/en/collection) are the most impressive ones. Though, they have no available catalogue to help determine the connections between documents.

One of the main problems faced by the creators of these projects was financing. In 2015, UNESCO launched a fundraising project to digitize the archives of the Organization belonging to its predecessors, including the League of Nations International Institute for Intellectual Cooperation. Two years later, thanks to the generous support of the Japanese government, UNESCO launched a major two-year initiative. In partnership with the digitization company Picturae BV, a laboratory was established at the site of UNESCO Headquarters in Paris in February 2018.

Financing a project is a painful question for us as well. Russian foundatians are willingly provide finance for the launch of the project but not for its support and development. At present, the attraction of sponsor funds has not been undertaken, since the project A. P. Ershov's Archive has been practically completed. The remaining digital projects of the Institute of Informatics Systems of the SB RAS are carried out within the framework of the government assignment to the Institute on the theme "Research of the fundamentals of data structuring, information resources management, creation of information and computing systems and environments for science and education" The purpose of this study is the development of automated support methods for ontology design. The bottleneck in this direction so far is the creation of more accurate search tools, text recognition tools, involving qualified personnel.

4   Technology and Method of Digital Historical Factography

As part of Internet-oriented professional IS's, the IIS SB RAS team has developed a technology and method of electronic historical factography, which allows working with arrays of heterogeneous documents and their further structuring by establishing connections between the entities reflected in the documents. The Internet resources developed at the IIS focus on the materials on the history of science and technology in Siberia – the Siberian Branch of the Russian (formerly Soviet) Academy of Sciences. Electronic historical factography dates back to 1999, when the IIS team began working on an automated information system for the creation and support of the Academician Andrey P. Ershov digital archive.

The method of electronic, or digital, historical factography consists in the publication of historical sources in Internet-oriented information systems according to the rules of working with conventional archival documents: properties such as the document source, type, author, addressee (either a person or an organization), dates, geographic data, etc., must be provided. The IS makes use of the technology allowing to establish connections between these entities of the subject field. Document quoting s from a digital archive is possible by means of web links as well as by indicating a specific volume and page of the archive (this is the case with the A. P. Ershov Electronic Archive and with other archives of the SB RAS where documents originate from the state-run storages).

While working on the first academic project of an Internet-oriented IS referred to as the A. P. Ershov Electronic Archive (http://ershov.iis.nsk.su), the IIS SB RAS team developed original software tools based on the client-server technology using predominantly Microsoft solutions. The archivist's workspace is written in Perl [7]. The specialized IS was created not only as a means of making a body of documents available to science, but also as a tool allowing a historian of science to perform a range of research tasks, such as organizing historical documents, providing remote access to these documents, keyword-based queries search, accumulating thematically connected sources from different storages, scientific description, etc. Almost all the documents from the Ershov's archive were digitalized with the exception of some personal letters.

The software tools created at the IIS SB RAS ensure stable functioning and continuous maintenance of virtual content. The developers wanted the visual archive in the public interface to correspond to the physical archive created by A. P. Ershov. He formed the cases on the thematic-chronological and thematic principles. His approach remained almost unchanged. Some corrections were made in order to remove duplicates, build chronology, establish authorship and dating of documents. The archive, formed by A. P. Ershov, was supplemented by some new documents received from the state archives. The electronic version supports two types of systematization: on the basis of cases and on the basis of thematic-chronological approach in the form of a corresponding catalog.

Document types that were digitalized included letters, drafts of scientific articles, photos, reports, diaries, paperwork documents, reviews on scientific works, etc.

The Electronic Archive framework also contains documents on the history of IIS SB RAS, VTNK "Start" (Temporary scientific and technical team "Start") and the A.P. Ershov Informatics Conference (PSI'). The pupils of the corresponding member of the USSR Ac. of Sci. S. S. Lavrov (1923-2004, St. Petersburg), transferred his archive to Novosibirsk. It is also presented on the platform of Ershov's archive.

The use of digitized documents is of communicational as well as of ergonomical importance, since many researchers with year of hands-on experience with archives suffer from the chronic disease caused by long-term contact with old paper, glue and dust, which at times prevents them from working directly in the archives. From this point of view, digital archives are safe and convenient to use. During the existence of the archive in the public domain, we did not receive objections to the publication of any documents.

5 Expansion of Project Activities

Upon the completion of the A. P. Ershov Electronic Archive project, in the run-up to the 50th Anniversary of the Siberian Branch of the RAS, an initiative group from the IIS SB RAS led by Dr. Alexander Marchuk began working on a new project – the SB RAS Electronic Photo Archive (http://www.soran1957.ru) (2005–2009). The project united a large number of separate photograph collections on the history of science in Siberia into a single volume of documents, which came from photoreporters, organizations (such as the SB RAS Museum, SB RAS Expo Center, SB RAS Press Center as well as a number of research institutes), and private collections. A landmark event in the history of Novosibirsk of the 20th century was setting up a town of science: Akademgorodok of Novosibirsk. We owe the existence photographic records of Akademgorodok from the moment of searching for a location for the new town to the foresight of Mikhail Lavrentiev, its founding father, who ordered that a cinema and photo-laboratory be organized and invited Rashid Akhmerov (1926–2017) to be the staff photographer.

Especially for the Photo Archive a new IS was created– the SORAN1957 system [8]. It supports collecting, structuring and digital publication of historical data and documents using specially developed software and organizational mechanisms. The SORAN1957 includes a system of structured data reflecting real-world entities and their relationships. Methodologically, the system is based on the ideology of Semantic Web. This approach allows structuring data according to an ontology. An ontology is a formal specification of a shared conceptual model – an abstract model of the subject area describing a system of its concepts. A shared model is a conventional understanding of a conceptual model by a certain community (a group of people). "Specification" is an explicit description of the system of concepts, and "formal" means that the conceptual model is machine-readable. An ontology consists of classes of entities of a subject area, properties of these classes, connections between these classes and statements made up of classes, their properties and connections. The resulting software tools enable input and editing of data as well as import of data from other sources, such as newspapers.

The SORAN1957 system features a public interface to the database and to the photographic documents. Users can study photographs, documents and database facts and their interconnections. For instance, by using text search the user can find a person of interest and their personal data, linked photographs, organizations (for instance, where that person worked), titles, etc. A nonspecific information ontology is used here, which allows avoiding the duplication of information contents in general-purpose and specialized information systems. The system is based on the Semantic Web concept and .NET technologies and can be installed on a server or an end user machine.

Our experience with the projects described above allowed us to cover a broader range of historical sources. In 2012, an integrative project of the SB RAS Presidium Fundamental Research, "The SB RAS Open Archive as a system of presenting, accumulation and systematization of scientific heritage" began (2012–2014, http://odasib.ru/). In this project, IIS SB RAS collaborated with a number of research institutes of the Siberian Branch specializing in humanities. Currently the SB RAS Open Archive contains 17 collections with 54,362 document scans (as of March 28, 2018). Documents added to each collections are systematized based on the internal logics of the content type. The system allows the creation of topic-based collections and sub-collections containing linked sources.

6 "Migration" Policy

It follows from the above descriptions of the projects that for each of them an original information system was developed, supported by grants from funds and sponsors (proprietary software). Some experts predicted over a dozen years ago that "in the future applied programs might not be developed but 'assembled' from ready-made components, a job that will not require a programmer but a qualified user who can formulate what he/she wants to receive at the output in the terms understood by the component management system. The center of gravity will shift from programming to design" [9]. Real life, however, has turned out to be much more complicated, and the key word here is a "qualified user."

In 2001, the open-source software expanded with the Drupal content management system (https://www.drupal.org/), developed and supported by programmers from all over the world [10]. The Drupal architecture allows for the construction of various web-applications like blogs, news sites, archives and social nets. Drupal contains over 40,000 modules that can be used to create an application necessary for solving the developers' problems. To achieve this, however, the developers need to learn how to find and install the necessary modules and how to write their own modules to solve highly specialized tasks. This means that using information technologies by humanities-minded people is not a trivial task, and help from programmers is welcome if not a must.

In 2016, the A.P. Ershov Electronic Archive was migrated to the Drupal platform (the graduate project of Sergey N. Troshkov, Mechanics and Mathematics Department, Novosibirsk State University, supervised by Doctor of Physics and Mathematics Alexander G. Marchuk and programmer Marina Ya. Philippova) [11,12]. Parenthetically, following the migration of the Electronic Archive was the migration of the Library system developed by Ya. M. Kourliandchik for the A.P. Ershov Programming Department in the mid-1980s. Until recently, the latter system had been used by the IIS SB RAS but as it was not written in the client-server architecture and both the database and application were on installed the same computer, it could not be accessed from another computer [13].

The experience of developing the IS has revealed two approaches to project work. The approach to the creation of the A. P. Ershov's Electronic Archive is engineering: its creators used quite complex tools. Nevertheless, they have created a convenient and multifunctional system in the service and user interfaces. Achieving a workable version was a one-step process and did not require significant additions to the working tools. Changes and additions to the system architecture were made imperceptibly for operators and users, eliminating the loss or duplication of data. The tools were improved in the direction of increasing the speed of access to the database. All the developers of this system are currently the leading specialists of foreign software companies.

The approach of the creators of IS SORAN1957 and Open archive SB RAS can be called as researching. The system was developed with the help of complex Semantic Web tools. At the same time there was a search for the most optimal solutions in the creation of software. Variants of platform solutions have repeatedly changed, which sometimes led to duplication and loss of information, slowed down the work of operators, for some time stopped the filling of IS. The creators of the IS "Open archive SB RAS" did not provide short links to scans of documents.

7   Conclusion

An important scientific problem of electronic archives is the reliability of content. Professional historians believe that the researcher needs to see the original document in order to get the most complete picture of it. But the existing archiving system cannot provide a wide coverage of valuable archives. The creation of professional IS involves the responsibility of its developers for the quality of reproduction of documents. Modern means of representation allow the researcher to get enough information about the source. It is no coincidence that facsimiles and scans of rare books are being actively published.

Since the mid-1980s, the European community has launched projects supporting specialists engaged in the preservation, conservation and dissemination of knowledge about the heritage with the help of digital reality: Framework Programme for Research & Technological Development FR1, 1984–1987, continued until 2013, and then HORIZON 2020 became its successor [14]. In addition to the programmes supporting appropriate research, special-purpose centers were set up in some countries like the U.K. and France to provide the long-term storage of software and access to it [15,16]. Moreover, the European Commission is planning to launch a single European Open Science Cloud for storing, exchanging and reusing research data in a variety of areas and support its infrastructure. In Russia, apparently, the critical mass required for making such decisions at the national level has yet to be achieved. The Russian State Archives have begun publicizing their meetings and reference apparatus fairly recently, later than other institutions keeping historical sources. The Archive of the Russian Academy of Sciences (RAS) is the umbrella association for launching a universal corporate resource (http://www.isaran.ru). The Science Archive of the Siberian Branch, RAS, however, neither digitizes its collections nor is represented in the Internet. This is an urgent issue of the SB RAS and Russian Ministry for Science and Education.

The structural changes undergoing in the RAS Siberian Branch in connection with reforming the Russian Academy of Sciences have so far ignored the SB RAS archival activity. Therefore, the future of the SB RAS Science Archive is uncertain. This most valuable collection of documents on the development of Siberian science is in danger of neglect because the SB RAS Presidium has no funds to maintain or, more importantly, to develop it. The SB RAS Science Archive established simultaneously with the RAS Siberian Branch in 1958 possesses a richest array of representative sources on the history of science in Siberia. It includes 86 library collections and 52,219 files including 9,356 personal files. Until now, the Archive's library collections have not been digitized for professional or public purposes, and the Archive has no electronic resources of its own (even though the SB RAS State Public Scientific-Technical Library has the Internet connection). With a view to preserving the unique historical documents, we need to digitize them and establish permanent repositories of datasets using cloud technologies. Within the framework of the project SB RAS Open Archive, which is in line with the all-Russia trend for the extensive use of information and communication technologies in the cultural and scientific spheres, the IIS has pioneered the organization of archival work in the RAS Siberian Branch. We expect that our experience will be in demand.

Acknowledgements. Natalia Cheremnykh, Alexander Marchuk, Vladimir Philippov, Marina Philippova, Mikhail Bulyonkov, Andrey Nemov, Sergey Antuyfeev, Konstantin Fedorov, Irina Pavlovskaya, Alexander Rar, Natalia Poluydova, Igor Agamirzian, Ivan Golosov, Irina Adrianova. The study was carried out with the financial support of the Russian Foundation for Basic Research and the Novosibirsk Region, project №19-49-540001.

References

1. Lynch, C.: Jim Gray's fourth paradigm and the construction of the scientific record. In: Hey, T., Tansley, S., Tolle, K. (eds.) The Fourth Paradigm: Data-Intensive Scientific Discovery, pp. 175–182. Microsoft Research, Redmond (2009)

2. Mirskaya, E.Z. : New information technologies in Russian science: history, results, problems and prospects. In: Rakhitov, A.I. (ed.) Science Research: Coll. Proceedings, pp. 174–200. INION RAN, Moscow (2011)

3. Krayneva, I.A.: Electronic archives on the history of science. Vestnik NSU Ser.: Hist. Philol. **12**(1), 76–83 (2013)

4. Chrictofer, J.D.: An Introduction to Database System. Dialektika, Moscow (1998). 1070 p

5. ISO/IEC 2382:2015 Information technology - Vocabulary: Information system - An information processing system, together with associated organizational resources such as human, technical, and financial resources, that provides and distributes information. http://www.morepc.ru/informatisation/iso2381-1.html#s

6. Gagarina, D.A., Kiryanov, I.K., Kornienko, S.I.: History-oriented information systems: "perm" project experience. Perm University Herald. History **16**, 35 (2011)

7. Srinivasan, S.: Advanced Perl Programming. O'Reily Media Inc., Newton (1997). 404 p

8. Marchuk, A.G., Marchuk, P.A. : Archival factographic system. Digital libraries: advanced methods and technologies, digital collections. In: Proceedings of the XI All-Russian Scientific Conference (RCDL-2009), pp. 177–185 (2009)

9. Evtushkin, A.: Dialectics and life of information technology. Computerra, **21**, 31 (2001). http://old.computerra.ru/197835/

10. Mercer, D.: Drupal 7, p. 403. Packt Publishing, Birmingham-Mumbai (2010)

11. James, T.: Migration to Drupal 7, p. 145. Packt Publishing, Birmingham-Mumbai (2012)

12. Troshkov, S.N. : Migrating web applications to the freely distributable open source software. Bachelor's final qualifying work. Novosibirsk, NSU, 25 p. Scientific adviser M.Y. Fillipova, programmer IIS SB RAS. Authors archive (2016)

13. Troshkov, S.N.: On expirience in migrating applications to the freely distributable open source software. Vestnik NSU Seri.: Inform. Technol. **16**(2), 86–94 (2018)

14. Ioannides, M., et al. (eds.): Digital Heritage: Progress in Cultural Heritage: Documentation, preservation and protection. 6th International Conference, EuroMed 2016, Nicosia, Cyprus, October 31 – November 5, 2016, Proceedings, Part II. LNCS, vol. 10058, pp. V–VII. Springer, Heidelberg (2016). https://doi.org/10.1007/978-3-319-48974-2d

15. Doorn-Moiseenko, T.L.: Electronic archives and their role in the development of the information infrastructure of historical science. In: Vorontsova, E.A., Aiani, V.Y., Petrov, Y.A. (eds.) Role of Archives in Information Support of Historical Science: A Collection of Articles, pp. 101–117. ETERNA, Moscow (2017)

16. Schurer, K., Anderson, S.J., Duncan, J.A.: A Guide to Hictorical Datafiles Held in Machine-Readable Form, 339 p. Assocoation for History and Computing, Cambridge (1992). http://www.aik-sng.ru/text/bullet/8/89-95.pdf

Two-Step Deductive Verification
of Control Software Using Reflex

Igor Anureev[1,3(✉)], Natalia Garanina[1,2,3], Tatiana Liakh[2,3], Andrei Rozov[2,3],
Vladimir Zyubin[2,3], and Sergei Gorlatch[4]

[1] A. P. Ershov Institute of Informatics Systems,
Acad. Lavrentieva prosp. 6, 630090 Novosibirsk, Russia
`anureev@gmail.com, garanina@iis.nsk.su`
[2] Novosibirsk State University, Pirogova str. 2, 630090 Novosibirsk, Russia
[3] Institute of Automation and Electrometry,
Acad. Koptyuga prosp. 1, 630090 Novosibirsk, Russia
`{rozov,zyubin}@iae.nsk.su`
[4] University of Muenster, Einsteinstr. 62, 48149 Münster, Germany
`gorlatch@uni-muenster.de`

Abstract. In this paper, we introduce a new verification method for
control software. The novelty of the method consists in reducing the verification of temporal properties of a control software algorithm to the
Hoare-like deductive verification of an imperative program that explicitly models time and the history of the execution of the algorithm. The
method is applied to control software specified in Reflex—a domain-
specific extension of the C language developed as an alternative to IEC
61131-3 languages. As a process-oriented language, Reflex enables control software description in terms of interacting processes, event-driven
operations, and operations with discrete time intervals. The first step
of our method rewrites an annotated Reflex program into an equivalent
annotated C program. The second step is deductive verification of this
C program. We illustrate our method with deductive verification of a
Reflex program for a hand dryer device: we provide the source Reflex
program, the set of requirements, the resulting annotated C program,
the generated verification conditions, and the results of proving these
conditions in Z3py – a Python-based front-end to the SMT solver Z3.

Keywords: Control software · Process-oriented languages · Deductive
verification · SMT solver · Reflex language · Z3

1 Introduction

The increasing complexity of control systems used in our everyday life requires a
reassessment of the design and development tools. Most challenging are safety-
critical systems, where incorrect behavior and/or lack of robustness may lead
to an unacceptable loss of funds or even human life. Such systems are widely

© Springer Nature Switzerland AG 2019
N. Bjørner et al. (Eds.): PSI 2019, LNCS 11964, pp. 50–63, 2019.
https://doi.org/10.1007/978-3-030-37487-7_5

spread in industry, especially, in chemical and metallurgical plants. Since behavior of control systems is specified in software, the study of control software is of great interest. Correct behavior under various environmental conditions must be ensured. In case of a hardware failure, e.g. plant damage or actuator fault, the control system must automatically react to prevent dangerous consequences. This is commonly referred to as fault tolerant behavior [1]. Because of the domain specificity, control systems are usually based on industrial controllers, also known as programmable logic controllers (PLCs), and specialized languages are used for designing control software.

PLCs are inherently open (i.e. communicate with external environment via sensors and actuators), reactive (have event-driven behaviour) and concurrent (have to process multiple asynchronous events). These features lead to special languages being used in the development of control software, e.g. the IEC 61131-3 languages [2] which are the most popular in the PLC domain. However, as the complexity of control software increases and quality is of higher priority, the 35 years old technology based on the IEC 61131-3 approach is not always able to address the present-day requirements [3]. This motivates enriching the IEC 61131-3 development model with object-oriented concepts [4], or developing alternative approaches, e.g. [5–8].

To address the restrictions and challenges in developing present-day complex control software, the concept of process-oriented programming (POP) was suggested in [9]. POP involves expressing control software as a set of interacting processes, where processes are finite state automata enhanced with inactive states and special operators that implement concurrent control flows and time-interval handling. Compared to well-known FSA modifications, e.g. Communicating Sequential Processes [10], Harel's Statecharts [11], Input/Output Automata [12], Esterel [13], Hybrid Automata [14], Calculus of Communicating Systems [15], and their timed extensions [16,17], this technique both provides means to specify concurrency and preserves the linearity of the control flow at the process level. Therefore, it provides a conceptual framework for developing process-oriented languages suitable to design PLC software. The process-oriented approach was implemented in domain-specific programming languages, such as SPARM [18], Reflex [19], and IndustrialC [20]. These languages are C-like and, therefore, easy to learn. Translators of these languages produce C-code, which provides cross-platform portability. With their native support for state machines and floating point operations, these languages allow PLC software to be conveniently expressed.

The SPARM language is a predecessor of the Reflex language and is now out of use. IndustrialC targets strict utilization of microcontroller peripherals (registers, timers, PWM, etc.) and extends Reflex with means for handling interrupt. A Reflex program is specified as a set of communicating concurrent processes. Specialized constructs are introduced for controlling processes and handling time intervals. Reflex also provides constructs for linking its variables to physical I/O signals. Procedures for reading/writing data through registers and their mapping to the variables are generated automatically by the translator.

Reflex assumes scan-based execution, i.e. a time-triggered control loop, and strict encapsulation of platform-dependent I/O subroutines into a library, which is a widely applied technique in IEC 6113-3 based systems. To provide both ease of support and cross-platform portability, the generation of executable code is implemented in two stages: the Reflex translator generates C-code and then a C-compiler produces executable code for the target platform. Reflex has no pointers, arrays or loops. Despite its very simple syntax, the language has been successfully used for several safety-critical control systems, e.g., control software for a silicon single-crystal growth furnace [21]. Semantic simplicity of the language together with the continuing practical applicability makes Reflex attractive for theoretical studies.

Currently, the Reflex project is focused on design and development tools for safety-critical systems. Because of its system independence Reflex easily integrates with LabVIEW [22]. This allows to develop software combining event-driven behavior with advanced graphic user interface, remote sensors and actuators, LabVIEW-supported devices, etc. Using the flexibility of LabVIEW, a set of plant simulators was designed for learning purposes [23]. The LabVIEW-based simulators include 2D animation, tools for debugging, and language support for learning of control software design. One of the results obtained in this direction is a LabVIEW-based dynamic verification toolset for Reflex programs. Dynamic verification treats the software as a black-box, and checks its compliance with the requirements by observing run-time behavior of the software on a set of test-cases. While such a procedure can help detect the presence of bugs in the software, it cannot guarantee their absence [24].

Unlike dynamic verification, static methods are based on source code analysis and are commonly recognized as the only way to ensure required properties of the software. It is therefore very important to adopt static verification methods for Reflex programs.

In this paper, we propose a method of deductive verification of Reflex programs. The original two-step scheme of the method allows us to reduce the verification of temporal properties of a control algorithm written in Reflex to the Hoare-like deductive verification of a C program that explicitly models time and the history of the execution of the algorithm.

The paper has the following structure. In Sect. 2, we describe the language for specifying of temporal properties of Reflex programs and an example of a Reflex program controlling a hand dryer with its properties. Section 3 presents the algorithm of transforming an annotated Reflex programs into a very restricted subset of annotated C programs called C-projections of Reflex programs. We illustrate this algorithm by the example of the C-projection of the dryer-controlling program. Rewriting an annotated Reflex program into its C-projection is the first step of our deductive verification method. The second step—generation of verification conditions for C-projection programs of this subset—is defined in Sect. 4. Examples of verification conditions for the C-projection of the dryer-controlling program illustrate the rules of this generation. In the concluding Sect. 5, we discuss the features of our method and future work.

2   Specification of Properties of Reflex Programs

Our verification method reduces the verification of Reflex programs to the verification of C-projection programs. A Reflex program, together with its requirements for verification, is translated into an equivalent C-projection program and a corresponding set of properties. In this section, we define the specification method for the properties of Reflex programs. This method is illustrated with an example Reflex program for a hand dryer controller.

We specify properties of Reflex programs using two kind of languages: an annotation language and an annotating language. The *annotation language* is a language of logic formulas that describe program properties. These formulas are called *annotations*. The *annotating language* is a markup language for attributing annotations to a program. Constructs of this language are called *annotators*. A program extended with annotators is an *annotated program*.

Annotations of Reflex programs are formulas of a many-sorted first-order logic. The specific formula syntax in the example uses the language of the python-based front-end Z3py [25] to the SMT solver Z3 [26] used in deductive verification of the resulting C-projection programs.

Temporal properties of Reflex programs can be expressed in the annotations. The discrete-time model used in the annotations is based on the periodicity of interaction between a Reflex program and its object under control. A Reflex program and its controlled object interact via input and output ports associated with the program variables. Every time-triggered control loop the program reads input ports and then writes the values to the corresponding variables. Changing a variable value as a result of writing to an input port is called its *external update*. At the end of control loop, the program writes new values to output ports. Writing values from input ports to variables and reading values from variables to output ports occur periodically with a fixed period (program cycle) specified in milliseconds. Time in the annotations is modeled by the implicit variable *tick* (which is not used in Reflex programs explicitly) specifying the number of program cycles. Thus, *tick* is an analogue of the global clock, counting the number of interactions of the Reflex program with its controlled object. One tick of the clock corresponds to one program cycle.

Each program variable x is interpreted in the annotations as an array in which indexes are values of *tick*, and elements are values of x associated with *tick*. Thus, in the annotation context, x stores a history of its changes. We denote a set of annotations by F, such that $f \in F$ is an annotation specifying some Reflex program property.

The annotating language for Reflex programs includes three kinds of annotators. *The invariant annotator* INV f; specifies that the property f must be true before each program cycle. *The initial condition annotator* ICON f; specifies that the property f must be true before the first program cycle. *The external condition annotator* ECON f; constrains external updates: the property f must be true after each external update.

Let us illustrate our approach by using a simple example of a program controlling a hand dryer like those often found in public restrooms (Fig. 1, Listing 1).

controller

dryer   hands

Fig. 1. Hand dryer

Here, the program uses the input from an infrared sensor, indicating presence of hands under the dryer and it controls the fan and heater with a joint output signal. The first basic requirement is that the dryer is on while hands are present and it turns off automatically otherwise. Trivial at first sight, the task becomes complicated because of discontinuity of the input signal caused by the users rubbing and turning their hands under the dryer. To avoid erratic toggling of the dryer heater and fan, the program should not react to brief interruptions in the signal, and the actuators should only be turned off once the sensor reading is a steady "off". The control algorithm can only meet this requirement by measuring the duration of the off state of the sensor. In this case, a continuous "off" signal longer than a certain given time (for example, 1s) would be regarded as a "hands removed" event. The second requirement is more simple and formulated as 'dryer never turns on spontaneously'. These two requirements (specified by the formulas p_1 and p_2 below) we will verify to demonstrate the proposed approach.

```
    PROGR HandDryerController {
/* ============================ */
/* == ANNOTATIONS:             */
/* INV inv;                    */
/* ICON icon;                  */
/* ECON econ;                  */
/* == END OF ANNOTATIONS       */
      TACT 100;
      CONST ON 1;
      CONST OFF 0;
   /*==============================*/
   /* I/O ports specification     */
   /* direction, name, address,   */
   /* offset, size of the port    */
   /*==============================*/
      INPUT   SENSOR_PORT  0 0 8;
      OUTPUT ACTUATOR_PORT 1 0 8;

   /*==============================*/
   /* processes definition         */
   /*==============================*/
      PROC Ctrl {
   /*====== VARIABLES ============*/
      BOOL hands = {SENSOR_PORT[1]} FOR ALL;
      BOOL dryer = {ACTUATOR_PORT[1]} FOR ALL;

   /*====== STATES ===============*/
      STATE Waiting {
        IF (hands == ON) {
          dryer = ON;
          SET NEXT;
        } ELSE dryer = OFF;
      }
      STATE Drying {
        IF (hands == ON)
          RESET TIMEOUT;
          TIMEOUT 10
```

```
                    SET STATE Waiting;
        }
    } /* \PROC */
}   /* \PROGRAM */
```

Listing 1. Hand dryer example in Reflex

In Reflex programs, the `PROGR` construct specifies the name and body of the program. The annotators are added at the beginning of the program body as the special kind of comments. In our case the annotators are `INV inv;`, `ICON icon;`, and `ECON econ;`, where `inv`, `icon`, and `econ` are annotations defined below. The `TACT` construct specifies the number of milliseconds corresponding to one program cycle. The `CONST` construct is used to specify program constants. Constructs `INPUT` and `OUTPUT` describe the input and output ports, respectively. Program variables are specified by variable declarations. For example, the variable declaration `BOOL hands = SENSOR_PORT[1] FOR ALL;` associates the boolean variable `hands` with the first bit of the port `SENSOR_PORT` and specifies that all processes can use this variable. The `PROC` construct is used to describe processes of the program. Our example program has one process `Ctrl` (controller) that controls a hand dryer, i.e. its fun and heater. The `STATE` construct specifies process states. Process `Ctrl` can be in two states `WAITING` and `DRYING`. Actions executed by the process in a state are described in the body of that state by statements and operators. In addition to C-statements and operators, there are Reflex-specific ones. Each process has its own time counter (local clock), which is also counted in ticks (the number of program cycles). Statement `RESET TIMEOUT;` resets the local clock of the process. Statement `TIMEOUT x stm;` launches the execution of statement stm when the local clock is equal to x. Statement `SET NEXT;` moves the process to the next state in the text of the program, and statement `SET STATE s;` sets the process to the state s. These two statements also reset the local clock of the process.

The initial condition `icon` of the form (in the format of formulas in Z3py [25])

$$And(Or(dryer[0] == 0, dryer[0] == 1), Or(hands[0] == 0, hands[0] == 1))$$

specifies that variables $dryer$ and $hands$ can only have values 0 or 1. The external condition `econ` of the form

$$Or(hands[tick] == 0, hands[tick] == 1)$$

expresses the fact that external updates of $hands$ return 0 or 1.

Invariant `inv` of the form $And(p_1, p_2, ap)$ includes properties p_1 and p_2 which specify the desirable behaviour of the program and the conjunction ap of auxiliary properties necessary to verify them. These auxiliary properties are as follows: (1) the values of the program constants are equal to their predefined values, (2) counter $tick$ is non-negative, (3) all previous and current values of variables $hands$ and $dryer$ are 0 or 1, (4) the current values of the latter variables are the same as their previous values (since they have not yet been modified by external updates), (5) the dryer can only be in two states `WAITING` and `DRYING`, and 6) the dryer in state DRYING is always on. We omit the notation for ap because it is rather cumbersome.

Property p_1 of the form

$$For All(i, Implies(And(0 <= i, i < tick),$$
$$Implies(And(Implies(i > 0, hands[i-1] == 0), hands[i] == 1),$$
$$dryer[i] == 1)))$$

refines the first hand-dryer requirement that the dryer is turned on ($dryer[i] = 1$) no later than 100 ms (1 tick) after the appearance of hands.

Property p_2 of the form

$$For All(i, Implies(And(0 <= i, i < tick - 1),$$
$$Implies(And(dryer[i] == 0, hands[i+1] == 0), dryer[i+1] == 0)))$$

corresponds to the second requirement that the dryer never turns on spontaneously.

In the next section, we present the method of rewriting an annotated Reflex program to the annotated C-projection to generate the verification conditions and subsequently check them with a theorem proving tool which can handle the many-sorted first-order logic. We apply this method to the Reflex program describing the hand dryer controller.

3   Rewriting Annotated Reflex Programs into C-Projections

Reflex programs and their C-like projections share the same annotation language. The annotating language for C-projections of Reflex programs includes four annotators. *The assume annotator* ASSUME f; specifies that f is supposed to be true at the location of this annotator in the program. *The assert annotator* ASSERT f; states that f must be true at the location of this annotator in the program. *The invariant annotator* INV l f; is a special variant of the named assert annotator with the name l which is processed by our verification condition generator in a special way. *The function annotator* REQUIRES P_f; ENSURES Q_f; must be placed directly after the function prototype $t\ f\ (t_1\ x_1,\ \ldots,\ t_n x_n)$. The function prototypes are used to call functions written in other programming languages in Reflex programs. This annotator specifies the precondition P_f and postcondition Q_f of the function f. Formulae P_f and Q_f depend on $x_1, \ldots, x_n$. Postcondition Q_f also depends on the special variable ret_f which stores the value returned by f. The variables $x_1, \ldots, x_n$ and ret_f are considered to be global variables of the C-projection program.

The C-projection of the Reflex program for a hand dryer controller reads as follows:

```
#define TACT 100
#define ON 1
#define OFF 0
#define STOP_STATE 0
```

```
#define ERROR_STATE 1
#define Ctrl_Waiting 2
#define Ctrl_Drying 3

int Ctrl_state;
int Ctrl_clock;
int tick;
int hands[];
int dryer[];

inline void init() {
  tick = 0;
  Ctrl_state = Ctrl_Waiting;
  Ctrl_clock = 0;
  ASSUME icon;
}

inline void Ctrl_exec() {
  switch (Ctrl_state) {
    case Ctrl_Waiting:
      if (hands[tick] == ON) {
        dryer[tick] = ON;
        Ctrl_clock = 0;
        Ctrl_state = Ctrl_Drying;
      }
      else
        dryer[tick] = OFF;
      break;
    case Ctrl_Drying:
      if (hands[tick] == ON) {
        Ctrl_clock = 0;
        Ctrl_state = Ctrl_Drying;
      }
      if (Ctrl_clock >= 10) {
        Ctrl_clock = 0;
        Ctrl_state = Ctrl_Waiting;
      }
      break;
  }
}

void main() {
  init();
  for (;;) {
    INV lab inv;
    havoc hands[tick];
    ASSUME econ;
    Ctrl_exec();
    Ctrl_clock = Ctrl_clock + 1;
    tick = tick + 1;
    hands[tick] = hands[tick-1];
    dryer[tick] = dryer[tick-1];
  }
}
```

Listing 2. Hand dryer example in C-projection

This program is the result of applying program transformation rules that are used for generating an equivalent program that must include the following constructs which replace the source Reflex constructs.

The macro constant TACT specifying the time of the program cycle replaces the TACT construct. Reflex constants (for example, ON and OFF) are replaced by macro constants as well. The macro constants STOP_STATE and ERROR_STATE encode the stop state (specifying that the program terminates normally) and the error state (specifying that the program terminates with an error). For each program process p and for each state s of this process, the macro constant s_p encodes this state. The variable tick specifies the global clock. For each program process p, the variables p_state and p_clock specify the current state and the current value of the local clock of the process p. Like tick, these variables are also implicit variables of the Reflex program, and so they can be found in its annotations. The type t of each Reflex variable x is replaced by the dynamic array type t[].

Function init() initializes the program processes. It sets the global clock and all local clocks to 0, sets all processes to their initial states and imposes restrictions on the initial values of Reflex variables, using the assume annotator ASSUME f (for the hand-dryer program ASSUME icon).

For each program process p, function p_exec specifies the actions of the process p during the program cycle. The body of function p_exec represents the switch statement where labels are macro constants coding states of the process p_exec. All Reflex-specific statements and operators in bodies of process states are replaced by C constructs in accordance with their semantics.

The infinite loop for(;;) specifying the actions of all processes during the program cycle is the last statement of the resulting program. Its body starts with the invariant annotator INV lab inv; specifying the invariant inv of the Reflex program. The next fragment havoc hands[tick]; ASSUME econ; specifies external updates of Reflex variables (in our case, hands) and the constraint econ for them. We add the special statement havoc x; [27] to the standard C language in order to model assigning an arbitrary value to the variable x. The third fragment is a sequence of calls of the functions p_exec() for each program process p. The next fragment increments the values of global clock and all local clocks. The last fragment specifies that values of Reflex variables are preserved after incrementing the global time and before executing external updates. For the hand-dryer program, this fragment is hands[tick] = hands[tick-1]; dryer[tick] = dryer[tick-1];.

The definition of the transformational semantics of a Reflex program (the rules for its transformation into C projection) and proving transformation correctness (equivalence of the Reflex program and its C projection) are beyond the scope of this paper. The equivalence means functional equivalence of the Reflex program and its C projection, where the inputs of both programs are the external updates vector for each Reflex variable, and the outputs are the vector of values for each Reflex variable, as well as the current process states and the values of global clock and local clocks. It is based on the operational semantics of Reflex programs, their C projections, and annotators of both annotation languages.

Thus, we reduce the verification of Reflex programs to the verification of programs of a very restricted subset of C extended by the havoc statement. Next we describe the rules of generating the verification conditions for programs of this subset. These verification conditions can further be checked by some theorem proving tool that can handle many-sorted first-order logic.

4 Generating Verification Conditions for C-Projections of Reflex Programs

Like many other deductive verification engines, such as FramaC [28], Spark [29], KeY [30], Dafny [31], etc., our algorithm for generating verification conditions implements a predicate transformer. We use Z3 to prove such verification conditions. Let us consider the features of its implementation especially taking into account the fact that it is applied to a program which is an infinite loop and some variables of this program are externally changed at each iteration of the loop. The algorithm $sp(A, P)$ recursively calculates the strongest postcondition [32] expressed in the many-sorted first-order logic for program fragment A and precondition P. It starts with the entire program and the precondition $True$. Its output is the set of verification conditions saved in the variable vcs. The algorithm uses service variables $vars$ and $reached$. Variable $vars$ stores information about variables and their types as a set of pairs of the form $x : t$, where x is a variable, and t is its type. Variable $reached$ stores the set of names of invariant annotators that have been reached by the algorithm. It is used to ensure termination of the algorithm. The initial values of these variables are empty sets.

We define the generation algorithm sp as the ordered set of equalities of the form $sp(A, P) = [a_1; \ldots; a_n; e]$. This notation means that the actions $a_1, \ldots, a_n$ are sequentially executed before the expression e is computed. Every action a_i of the form $v + = S$ adds the elements of the set S to the set v. The equality $sp(A, P) = e$ is an abridgement for $sp(A, P) = [e]$.

We use the following notation in the algorithm definition. Let $array(t)$ denote the array type with the elements of type t. Let expression e have type t, $\{x : t, y : array(t)\} \subseteq vars$, $\{z : t, v : t\} \cap vars = \emptyset$ for each t, and e' be the result of conversion of C expression e to a Z3py expression. Function $Store(a, i, v)$ is the array update function from Z3 language.

Since the syntax of C-projections of annotated Reflex programs is very restricted, algorithm sp has the following compact form:

1. $sp(t\ f(t_1\ x_1,\ \ldots,\ t_n\ x_n);,\ P) =$
$$[vars + = \{x_1 : t_1, \ldots, x_n : t_n, ret\_f : t\};\ P];$$
2. $sp(t\ x;,\ P) = [vars + = \{x : t\};\ P];$
3. $sp(\#define\ c\ e;,\ P) = [vars + = \{c : t\};\ And(P, c == e')];$
4. $sp(havoc\ y[i];,\ P) =$
$$[vars + = \{z : t, v : t\};\ And(P(y \leftarrow z), y == Store(z, i, v))];$$
5. $sp(havoc\ x;,\ P) = [vars + = \{z : t\};\ And(P(x \leftarrow z), x == z)];$
6. $sp(x[i]\ =\ e;,\ P) =$
$$[vars + = \{z : array(t)\};\ And(P(y \leftarrow z), y == Store(z, i, e'(y \leftarrow z)))];$$
7. $sp(x\ =\ e;,\ P) = [vars + = \{z : t\};\ And(P(x \leftarrow z), x == e'(x \leftarrow z))];$
8. $sp(\{B\},\ P) = sp(B,\ P);$
9. $sp(if\ (e)\ B\ else\ C,\ P) =$
$$Or(sp(B, And(P, econv(e))), sp(C, And(P, Not(econv(e)))));$$

10. $sp(switch\ (e)\ l_1 :\ B_1\ break;\ \ldots\ l_n :\ B_n\ break;,\ P) =$
$$Or(sp(B_1, And(P, e' == l_1)), \ldots, sp(B_n, And(P, e' == l_n)),$$
$$And(P, e'! = l_1, \ldots, e'! = l_n));$$

11. $sp(for(;;)\ B,\ P) = sp(B\ for(;;)\ B,\ P);$

12. $sp(x\ =\ f(e_1,\ \ldots,\ e_n);,\ P) =$
$$sp(x_1\ =\ e_1;\ \ldots\ x_n\ =\ e_n;\ ASSERT\ P_f;\ havoc\ ret\_f;$$
$$ASSUME\ Q_f;\ x\ =\ ret\_f;,\ P);$$

13. $sp(ASSUME\ e;,\ P) = And(P,\ e);$

14. $sp(ASSERT\ e;,\ P) = [vcs+ = \{Implies(P, e)\};\ And(P, e)];$

15. if $l \notin reached, sp(INV\ l\ e;\ A,\ P) =$
$$[reached + = \{l\};\ vcs + =\ Implies(P, e);\ sp(A, e)];$$

16. if $l \in reached, sp(INV\ l\ e;\ A,\ P) = [vcs + =\ Implies(P, e);\ e];$

17. $sp(s\ A,\ P) = sp(A,\ sp(s,\ P)).$

This algorithm terminates because sp recursively reduces the input program in all cases except $for(;;)$ (case 11), and due to case 16 the algorithm can pass the invariant annotator at the begin of body of $for(;;)$ only once.

The computation of verification conditions for the trace of the annotated hand dryer program (Listing 2) starting at the point #define TACT 100 and ending at the point INV lab inv; results in

- $vcs = \{Implies(And(true, TACT == 100, ON == 1, OFF == 0,$
$$STOP\_STATE == 0, ERROR\_STATE == 1, Ctrl\_WAITING == 2,$$
$$Ctrl\_DRYING == 3, tick == 0, init\_state == INIT\_WAITING,$$
$$init\_clock == 0, dryer[0] == 0, icon), inv)\};$$
- $vars = \{TACT : int, ON : int, OFF : int, STOP\_STATE : int,$
$$ERROR\_STATE : int,\ Ctrl\_WAITING : int,\ Ctrl\_DRYING : int,$$
$$Ctrl\_state : int, Ctrl\_clock : int, dryer : array(int), hands : array(int),$$
$$tick : int, tick\_1 : int, Ctrl\_state\_1 : int, Ctrl\_clock\_1 : int\};$$
- $reached = \{lab\}.$

Here x_i, where i is a natural number, is a fresh variable generated by algorithm sp in the case of the assignment of the form $x = \ldots$ or $x[\ldots] = \ldots$.

Other seven verification conditions starting at the point INV lab inv; and ending at the same point and corresponding to different branches of the switch statement and if statements are generated likewise. All generated verification conditions are successfully proved in Z3py.

The generation of verification conditions for C-projections of annotated Reflex programs and proving them complete the description of our two-step method of deductive verification for Reflex programs.

Currently, we prepare for publication a description of the transformational semantics of Reflex programs (including a formal proof of its correctness) and a formal proof of the soundness of the axiomatic semantics of C projections w.r.t. their operational semantics. Software tools automating the steps of the method are being developed on their basis.

5   Discussion and Conclusion

In this paper we propose a two-step method of deductive verification of Reflex programs. This method includes the annotation and annotating languages for Reflex programs, the algorithm for transforming an annotated Reflex program into the annotated program written in restricted C (the C-projection of the Reflex program), the annotating language, and the algorithm of generating verification conditions for C-projections of Reflex programs. Our method can be applied to the so-called pure Reflex programs that do not contain definitions of functions written in other languages.

In practice, Reflex programs often include definitions and calls of C functions. We can extend our method to this more general case of Reflex, because such programs must also include a prototype for each C function. Verification of such Reflex programs is reduced to separate verification of definitions of C functions and a pure Reflex program extended by calls of functions. These functions are considered black boxes and their prototypes are annotated with preconditions and postconditions treated as specifications of these black boxes. The definitions of C functions can be verified by any C program verification method or tool. For verification of Reflex programs with function calls, we use our two-step method.

Our verification method has several remarkable properties. Firstly, it models the interaction between a Reflex program and its controlled object through the input and output ports associated with the program variables. The havoc statement in the C-projection of the Reflex program allows to represent writing values from input ports to variables. These external variable updates are constrained by the assume annotator. Checking values read from variables to output ports is specified by the assert and invariant annotators. Secondly, this method reduces the verification of some time properties of Reflex programs to Hoare-like deductive verification by explicitly modeling time in C-projections of Reflex programs with variables which specify the global clock, local clocks of program processes and history of values of Reflex variables. Thirdly, our verification conditions generation algorithm can handle infinite loops intrinsic to control systems.

There are several directions for further development of the method. We plan to extend it to the textual languages of the IEC 61131-3 family. Like Reflex, these languages are used for programs that interact with the controlled object only between program cycles. The other research direction is to investigate new temporal properties for which verification can also be reduced to Hoare-like deductive verification. Especially, we are interested in temporal aspects associated with the histories of values of process states and process clocks, which would allow to evaluate the performance of control sofware algorithms. Explicit time modeling in Reflex annotations is not a very natural way to represent the time properties of Reflex programs. We plan to use temporal logics (LTL, CTL and MTL) and their extensions to describe these properties and develop an algorithm for translating such descriptions into formulas with explicit time modeling. To make this task feasible, we plan to use specialized ontological patterns [33] instead of arbitrary formulas of these logics. In addition to Z3 solver, we intend to use in our method other provers and solvers in order to extend the class of verifiable properties. In particular, Z3 solver cannot prove that dryer will work for at least 10 seconds after hands have been removed because this property requires advanced induction. The interactive theorem prover ACL2 [34] with advanced induction schemes is a good candidate to solve this problem. Finally, we plan to consider new case studies on control software algorithms.

Acknowledgement. The reported study was funded by the Russian Ministry of Education and Science; RFBR, project number 17-07-01600; RFBR, project number 20-01-00541; and RFBR, project number 20-07-00927.

References

1. Blanke, M., Kinnaert, M., Lunze, J., Staroswiecki, M.: Diagnosis and Fault-Tolerant Control, 2nd edn. Springer, Heidelberg (2006). https://doi.org/10.1007/978-3-540-35653-0
2. IEC 61131–3: Programmable controllers Part 3: Programming languages. Rev. 2.0. International Electrotechnical Commission Standard (2003)
3. Basile, F., Chiacchio, P., Gerbasio, D.: On the Implementation of industrial automation systems based on PLC. IEEE Trans. Autom. Sci. Eng. **4**(10), 990–1003 (2013)
4. Thramboulidis, K., Frey, G.: An MDD process for IEC 61131-based industrial automation systems. In: 16th IEEE International Conference on Emerging Technologies and Factory Automation (ETFA11), Toulouse, France, pp. 1–8 (2011)
5. IEC 61499: Function Blocks for Industrial Process Measurement andControl Systems. Parts 1–4. Rev. 1.0. International Electrotechnical Commission Standard (2004/2005)
6. Wagner, F., Schmuki, R., Wagner, T., Wolstenholme, P.: Modeling Software with Finite State Machines. Auerbach Publications, Boston (2006)
7. Samek, M.: Practical UML Statecharts in C/C++: Event-driven Programming for Embedded Systems, 2nd edn. Newnes, Oxford (2009)
8. Control Technology Corporation. QuickBuilder^{TM}Reference Guide (2018). https://controltechnologycorp.com/docs/QuickBuilder_Ref.pdf. Accessed 20 Jan 2019
9. Zyubin, V.E.: Hyper-automaton: a model of control algorithms. In: Proceedings of the IEEE International Siberian Conference on Control and Communications (SIBCON-2007), pp. 51–57. The Tomsk IEEE Chapter & Student Branch, Tomsk (2007)
10. Hoare, C.A.R.: Communicating Sequential Processes. Prentice-Hall Int., Upper Saddle River (1985)
11. Harel, D.: Statecharts: a visual formalism for complex systems. Sci. Comput. Program. **8**(3), 231–274 (1987)
12. Lynch, N., Tuttle, M.: An introduction to input/output automata. CWI Q. **2**(3), 219–246 (1989)
13. Berry, G.: The foundations of Esterel. In: Proof, Language and Interaction: Essays in Honour of Robin Milner. Foundations of Computing Series, pp. 425–454. MIT Press (2000)
14. Henzinger, T.A.: The theory of hybrid automata. In: Inan, M.K., Kurshan, R.P. (eds.) Verification of Digital and Hybrid Systems. NATO ASI Series (Series F: Computer and Systems Sciences), vol. 170, pp. 265–292. Springer, Heidelberg (2000). https://doi.org/10.1007/978-3-642-59615-5_13

15. Milner, R.: Communication and Concurrency. Series in Computer Science. Prentice Hall, New Jersey (1989)
16. Kaynar, D.K., Lynch, N., Segala, R., Vaandrager, F.: Timed I/O automata: a mathematical framework for modeling and analyzing real-time systems. In: 24th IEEE International Real-Time Systems Symposium (RTSS 2003), pp. 166–177. IEEE Computer Society Cancun, Mexico (2003)
17. Kof, L., Schätz, B.: Combining aspects of reactive systems. In: Broy, M., Zamulin, A.V. (eds.) PSI 2003. LNCS, vol. 2890, pp. 344–349. Springer, Heidelberg (2004). https://doi.org/10.1007/978-3-540-39866-0_34
18. Zyubin, V.: SPARM language as a means for programming microcontrollers. Optoelectron. Instr. Data Process. **2**(7), 36–44 (1996)
19. Liakh, T.V., Rozov, A.S., Zyubin, V.E.: Reflex language: a practical notation for cyber-physical systems. Syst. Inform. **12**(6), 85–104 (2018)
20. Rozov A.S., Zyubin V.E.: Process-oriented programming language for MCU-based automation. In: Proceedings of the IEEE International Siberian Conference on Control and Communications, pp. 1–4. The Tomsk IEEE Chapter Student Branch, Tomsk (2013)
21. Bulavskij, D., Zyubin, V., Karlson, N., Krivoruchko, V., Mironov, V.: An automated control system for a silicon single-crystal growth furnace. Optoelectron. Instr. Data Process. **2**(5), 25–30 (1996)
22. Travis, J., Kring, J.: LabVIEW for Everyone: Graphical Programming Made Easy and Fun, 3rd edn. Prentice Hall PTR, Upper Saddle River (2006)
23. Zyubin, V.: Using process-oriented programming in LabVIEW. In: Proceedings of the Second IASTED Intern. Multi-Conference on "Automation, control, and information technology": Control, Diagnostics, and Automation, Novosibirsk, pp. 35–41 (2010)
24. Randell, B.: Software engineering techniques. Report on a conference sponsored by the NATO Science Committee, p. 16. Brussels, Scientific Affairs Division, NATO, Rome, Italy (1970)
25. Z3 API in Python. https://ericpony.github.io/z3py-tutorial/guide-examples.htm. Accessed 20 Jan 2019
26. de Moura, L., Bjørner, N.: Z3: an efficient SMT solver. In: Ramakrishnan, C.R., Rehof, J. (eds.) TACAS 2008. LNCS, vol. 4963, pp. 337–340. Springer, Heidelberg (2008). https://doi.org/10.1007/978-3-540-78800-3_24
27. Barnett, M., Chang, B.-Y.E., DeLine, R., Jacobs, B., Leino, K.R.M.: Boogie: a modular reusable verifier for object-oriented programs. In: de Boer, F.S., Bonsangue, M.M., Graf, S., de Roever, W.-P. (eds.) FMCO 2005. LNCS, vol. 4111, pp. 364–387. Springer, Heidelberg (2006). https://doi.org/10.1007/11804192_17
28. FramaC Homepage. https://frama-c.com/
29. Spark Pro Homepage. https://www.adacore.com/sparkpro
30. The KeY project Homepage https://www.key-project.org/
31. Dafny Homepage. https://www.microsoft.com/en-us/research/project/dafny-a-language-and-program-verifier-for-functional-correctness/
32. Dijkstra, E.W., Scholten, C.S.: Predicate Calculus and Program Semantics. Springer, Heidelberg (1990). https://doi.org/10.1007/978-1-4612-3228-5
33. Garanina, N., Zyubin, V., Lyakh, V., Gorlatch, S.: An ontology of specification patterns for verification of concurrent systems. In: New Trends in Intelligent Software Methodologies, Tools and Techniques. Proceedings of the 17th International Conference on SoMeT-18. Series: Frontiers in Artificial Intelligence and Applications, pp. 515–528. IOS Press, Amsterdam (2018)
34. ACL2 Homepage. http://www.cs.utexas.edu/users/moore/acl2/

Distributed Representation of n-gram Statistics for Boosting Self-organizing Maps with Hyperdimensional Computing

Denis Kleyko[1(✉)], Evgeny Osipov[1], Daswin De Silva[2], Urban Wiklund[3], Valeriy Vyatkin[1], and Damminda Alahakoon[2]

[1] Luleå University of Technology, Luleå, Sweden
{denis.kleyko,evgeny.osipov,valeriy.vyatkin}@ltu.se
[2] La Trobe University, Melbourne, Australia
{d.desilva,d.alahakoon}@latrobe.edu.au
[3] Umeå University, Umeå, Sweden
urban.wiklund@umu.se

Abstract. This paper presents an approach for substantial reduction of the training and operating phases of Self-Organizing Maps in tasks of 2-D projection of multi-dimensional symbolic data for natural language processing such as language classification, topic extraction, and ontology development. The conventional approach for this type of problem is to use n-gram statistics as a fixed size representation for input of Self-Organizing Maps. The performance bottleneck with n-gram statistics is that the size of representation and as a result the computation time of Self-Organizing Maps grows exponentially with the size of n-grams. The presented approach is based on distributed representations of structured data using principles of hyperdimensional computing. The experiments performed on the European languages recognition task demonstrate that Self-Organizing Maps trained with distributed representations require less computations than the conventional n-gram statistics while well preserving the overall performance of Self-Organizing Maps.

Keywords: Self-organizing maps · n-gram statistics · Hyperdimensional computing · Symbol strings

1 Introduction

The Self-Organizing Map (SOM) algorithm [25,41] has been proven to be an effective technique for unsupervised machine learning and dimension reduction

This work was supported by the Swedish Research Council (VR, grant 2015-04677) and the Swedish Foundation for International Cooperation in Research and Higher Education (grant IB2018-7482) for its Initiation Grant for Internationalisation, which allowed conducting the study.

N. Bjørner et al. (Eds.): PSI 2019, LNCS 11964, pp. 64–79, 2019.
https://doi.org/10.1007/978-3-030-37487-7_6

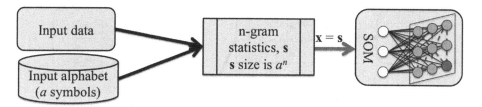

Fig. 1. Outline of the conventional approach.

of multi-dimensional data. A broad range of applications ranging from its conventional use in 2-D visualization of multi-dimensional data to more recent developments such as analysis of energy consumption patterns in urban environments [6,8], autonomous video surveillance [29], multimodal data fusion [14], incremental change detection [28], learning models from spiking neurons [12], and identification of social media trends [3,7]. The latter use-case is an example of an entire application domain of SOMs for learning on symbolic data. This type of data is typically present in various tasks of natural language processing.

As the SOM uses weight vectors of fixed dimensionality, this dimensionality must be equal to the dimensionality of the input data. A conventional approach for feeding variable length symbolic data into the SOM is to obtain a fixed length representation through n-gram statistics (e.g., bigrams when $n = 2$ or trigrams when $n = 3$). The n-gram statistics, which is a vector of all possible combinations of n symbols of the data alphabet, is calculated during a pre-processing routine, which populates the vector with occurrences of each n-gram in the symbolic data. An obvious computational bottleneck of such approach is due to the length of n-gram statistics, which grows exponentially with n. Since the vector is typically sparse some memory optimization is possible on the data input side. For example, only the indices of non-zero positions can be presented to the SOM. This, however, does not help with the distance calculation, which is the major operation of the SOM. Since weight vectors are dense, for computing the distances the input vectors must be unrolled to their original dimensionality. In this paper, we present an approach where the SOM uses mappings of n-gram statistics instead of the conventional n-gram statistics. Mappings are vectors of fixed arbitrary dimensionality, where the dimensionality can be substantially lower than the number of all possible n-grams.

Outline of the Proposed Approach

The core of the proposed approach is in the use of hyperdimensional computing and distributed data representation. Hyperdimensional computing is a bio-inspired computational paradigm in which all computations are done with randomly generated vectors of high dimensionality. Figure 1 outlines the conventional approach of using n-gram statistics with SOMs. First, for the input symbolic data we calculate n-gram statistics. The size of the vector $\mathbf{s}$, which contains the n-gram statistics, will be determined by the size of the data's alphabet

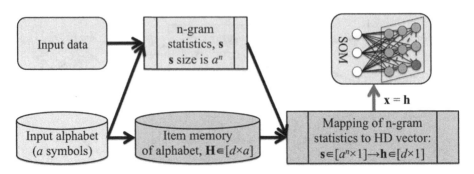

Fig. 2. Outline of the proposed approach.

a and the chosen n. Next, the conventional approach will be to use **s** as an input **x** to either train or test the SOM (the red vertical line in Fig. 1). The approach proposed in this paper modifies the conventional approach by introducing an additional step, as outlined in Fig. 2. The blocks in green denote the elements of the introduced additional step. For example, the item memory stores the distributed representations of the alphabet. In the proposed approach, before providing **s** to the SOM, **s** is mapped to a distributed representation **h**, which is then used as an input to the SOM (the red vertical line in Fig. 2).

The paper is structured as follows. Section 2 describes the related work. Section 3 presents the methods used in this paper. Section 4 reports the results of the experiments. The conclusions follow in Sect. 5.

2   Related Work

The SOM algorithm [25] was originally designed for metric vector spaces. It develops a non-linear mapping of a high-dimensional input space to a two-dimensional map of nodes using competitive, unsupervised learning. The output of the algorithm, the SOM represents an ordered topology of complex entities [26], which is then used for visualization, clustering, classification, profiling, or prediction. Multiple variants of the SOM algorithm that overcome structural, functional and application-focused limitations have been proposed. Among the key developments are the Generative Topographic Mapping based on non-linear latent variable modeling [4], the Growing SOM (GSOM) that addresses the pre-determined size constraints [1], the TASOM based on adaptive learning rates and neighborhood sizes [40], the WEBSOM for text analysis [17], and the IKASL algorithm [5] that addresses challenges in incremental unsupervised learning. Moreover, recently an important direction is the simplification of the SOM algorithm [2,19,39] for improving its speed and power-efficiency.

However, only a limited body of work has explored the plausibility of the SOM beyond its original metric vector space. In contrast to a metric vector space, a symbolic data space is a non-vectorial representation that possesses an

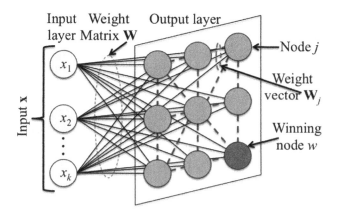

Fig. 3. Illustration of a self-organizing map with nine nodes organized according to the grid topology.

internal variation and structure which must be taken into account in computations. Records in a symbolic dataset are not limited to a single value, for instance, each data point can be a hypercube in p-dimensional space or Cartesian product of distribution. In [26], authors make the first effort to apply SOM algorithm to symbol strings, the primary challenges were the discrete nature of data points and adjustments required for the learning rule, addressed using the generalized means/medians and batch map principle. Research reported in [42] takes a more direct approach to n-gram modeling of HTTP requests from network logs. Feature matrices are formed by counting the occurrences of n-characters corresponding to each array in the HTTP request, generating a memory-intensive feature vector of length 256^n. Feature matrices are fed into a variant of the SOM, Growing Hierarchical SOMs [9] to detect anomalous requests. Authors report both accuracy and precision of 99.9% on average, when using bigrams and trigrams. Given the limited awareness and availability of research into unsupervised machine learning on symbolic data, coupled with the increasing complexity of raw data [27], it is pertinent to investigate the functional synergies between hyperdimensional computing and the principles of SOMs.

3   Methods

This section presents the methods used in this paper. We describe: the basics of the SOM algorithm; the process of collecting n-gram statistics; the basics of hyperdimensional computing; and the mapping of n-gram statistics to the distributed representation using hyperdimensional computing.

3.1   Self-organizing Maps

A SOM [25] (see Fig. 3) consists of a set of nodes arranged in a certain topology (e.g., a rectangular or a hexagonal grid or even a straight line). Each node j is characterized by a weight vector of dimensionality equal the dimensionality of an input vector (denoted as $\mathbf{x}$). The weight vectors are typically initialized at random. Denote a $u \times k$ matrix of k-dimensional weight vectors of u nodes in a SOM as $\mathbf{W}$. Also denote a weight vector of node j as $\mathbf{W}_j$ and i'th positions of this vector as $\mathbf{W}_{ji}$. One of the main steps in the SOM algorithm is for a given input vector $\mathbf{x}$ to identify the winning node, which has the closest weight vector to $\mathbf{x}$. Computation of a distance between the input $\mathbf{x}$ and the weight vectors in $\mathbf{W}$, the winner takes all procedure as well as the weight update rule are the main components of SOM logic. They are outlined in the text below.

In order to compare $\mathbf{x}$ and $\mathbf{W}_j$, a similarity measure is needed. The SOM uses Euclidian distance:

$$D(\mathbf{x}, \mathbf{W}_j) = \sqrt{\sum_{i=1}^{i=k} (\mathbf{x}_i - \mathbf{W}_{ji})^2}, \tag{1}$$

where $\mathbf{x}_i$ and $\mathbf{W}_{ji}$ are the corresponding values of ith positions. The winning node (denoted as w) is defined as a node with the lowest Euclidian distance to the input $\mathbf{x}$.

In the SOM, a neighborhood $\mathcal{M}$ of nodes around the winning node w is selected and updated; the size of the neighborhood progressively decreases:

$$\gamma(j, w, t) = e^{-l(j,w)/2\sigma(t)^2}, \tag{2}$$

where $l(j, w)$ is the lateral distance between a node j and the winning node w on the SOM's topology; $\sigma(t)$ is the decreasing function, which depends of the current training iteration t. If a node j is within the neighborhood $\mathcal{M}$ of w then the weight vector $\mathbf{W}_j$ is updated with:

$$\triangle \mathbf{W}_j = \eta(t)\gamma(j, w, t)(\mathbf{x} - \mathbf{W}_j), \tag{3}$$

where $\eta(t)$ denotes the learning rate decreasing with increasing t. During an iteration t, the weights are updated for all available training inputs $\mathbf{x}$. The training process usually runs for T iterations.

Once the SOM has been trained it could be used in the operating phase. The operating phase is very similar to that of the training one except that the weights stored in $\mathbf{W}$ are kept fixed. For a given input $\mathbf{x}$, the SOM identifies the winning node w. This information is used depending on the task at hand. For example, in clustering tasks, a node could be associated with a certain region. In this paper, we consider the classification task, and therefore, each node would have an assigned classification label.

3.2   n-gram Statistics

In order to calculate n-gram statistics for the input symbolic data $\mathcal{D}$, which is described by the alphabet of size a, we first initialize an empty vector $\mathbf{s}$. This vector will store the n-gram statistics for $\mathcal{D}$, where the ith position in $\mathbf{s}$ corresponds to an n-gram $\mathcal{N}_i = \langle \mathcal{S}_1, \mathcal{S}_2, \ldots, \mathcal{S}_n, \rangle$ from the set $\mathcal{N}$ of all unique n-grams; $\mathcal{S}_j$ corresponds to a symbol in jth position of $\mathcal{N}_i$. The value s_i indicates the number of times $\mathcal{N}_i$ was observed in the input symbolic data $\mathcal{D}$. The dimensionality of $\mathbf{s}$ is equal to the total number of n-grams in $\mathcal{N}$, which in turn depends on a and n (size of n-grams) and is calculated as a^n (i.e., $\mathbf{s} \in [a^n \times 1]$). The n-gram statistics $\mathbf{s}$ is calculated via a single pass through $\mathcal{D}$ using the overlapping sliding window of size n, where for an n-gram observed in the current window the value of its corresponding position in $\mathbf{s}$ (i.e., counter) is incremented by one. Thus, $\mathbf{s}$ characterizes how many times each n-gram in $\mathcal{N}$ was observed in $\mathcal{D}$.

3.3   Hyperdimensional Computing

Hyperdimensional computing [16,31,33,34] also known as Vector Symbolic Architectures is a family of bio-inspired methods of representing and manipulating concepts and their meanings in a high-dimensional space. Hyperdimensional computing finds its applications in, for example, cognitive architectures [10], natural language processing [20,38], biomedical signal processing [22,35], approximation of conventional data structures [23,30], and for classification tasks [18], such as gesture recognition [24], physical activity recognition [37], fault isolation [21]. Vectors of high (but fixed) dimensionality (denoted as d) are the basis for representing information in hyperdimensional computing. These vectors are often referred to as high-dimensional vectors or HD vectors. The information is distributed across HD vector's positions, therefore, HD vectors use distributed representations. Distributed representations [13] are contrary to the localist representations (which are used in the conventional n-gram statistics) since any subset of the positions can be interpreted. In other words, a particular position of an HD vector does not have any interpretable meaning – only the whole HD vector can be interpreted as a holistic representation of some entity, which in turn bears some information load. In the scope of this paper, symbols of the alphabet are the most basic components of a system and their atomic HD vectors are generated randomly. Atomic HD vectors are stored in the so-called item memory, which in its simplest form is a matrix. Denote the item memory as $\mathbf{H}$, where $\mathbf{H} \in [d \times a]$. For a given symbol $\mathcal{S}$ its corresponding HD vector from $\mathbf{H}$ is denoted as $\mathbf{H}_\mathcal{S}$. Atomic HD vectors in $\mathbf{H}$ are bipolar ($\mathbf{H}_\mathcal{S} \in \{-1, +1\}^{[d \times 1]}$) and random with equal probabilities for $+1$ and -1. It is worth noting that an important property of high-dimensional spaces is that with an extremely high probability all random HD vectors are dissimilar to each other (quasi orthogonal).

In order to manipulate atomic HD vectors hyperdimensional computing defines operations and a similarity measure on HD vectors. In this paper, we use the cosine similarity for characterizing the similarity. Three key operations for computing with HD vectors are bundling, binding, and permutation.

The binding operation is used to bind two HD vectors together. The result of binding is another HD vector. For example, for two symbols $\mathcal{S}_1$ and $\mathcal{S}_2$ the result of binding of their HD vectors (denotes as $\mathbf{b}$) is calculated as follows:

$$\mathbf{b} = \mathbf{H}_{\mathcal{S}_1} \odot \mathbf{H}_{\mathcal{S}_2}, \tag{4}$$

where the notation $\odot$ for the Hadamard product is used to denote the binding operation since this paper uses positionwise multiplication for binding. An important property of the binding operation is that the resultant HD vector $\mathbf{b}$ is dissimilar to the HD vectors being bound, i.e., the cosine similarity between $\mathbf{b}$ and $\mathbf{H}_{\mathcal{S}_1}$ or $\mathbf{H}_{\mathcal{S}_2}$ is approximately 0.

An alternative approach to binding when there is only one HD vector is to permute (rotate) the positions of the HD vector. It is convenient to use a fixed permutation (denoted as ρ) to bind a position of a symbol in a sequence to an HD vector representing the symbol in that position. Thus, for a symbol $\mathcal{S}_1$ the result of permutation of its HD vector (denotes as $\mathbf{r}$) is calculated as follows:

$$\mathbf{r} = \rho(\mathbf{H}_{\mathcal{S}_1}). \tag{5}$$

Similar to the binding operation, the resultant HD vector $\mathbf{r}$ is dissimilar to $\mathbf{H}_{\mathcal{S}_1}$.

The last operation is called bundling. It is denoted with $+$ and implemented via positionwise addition. The bundling operation combines several HD vectors into a single HD vector. For example, for $\mathcal{S}_1$ and $\mathcal{S}_2$ the result of bundling of their HD vectors (denotes as $\mathbf{a}$) is simply:

$$\mathbf{a} = \mathbf{H}_{\mathcal{S}_1} + \mathbf{H}_{\mathcal{S}_2}. \tag{6}$$

In contrast to the binding and permutation operations, the resultant HD vector $\mathbf{a}$ is similar to all bundled HD vectors, i.e., the cosine similarity between $\mathbf{b}$ and $\mathbf{H}_{\mathcal{S}_1}$ or $\mathbf{H}_{\mathcal{S}_1}$ is more than 0. Thus, the bundling operation allows storing information in HD vectors [11]. Moreover if several copies of any HD vector are included (e.g., $\mathbf{a} = 3\mathbf{H}_{\mathcal{S}_1} + \mathbf{H}_{\mathcal{S}_2}$), the resultant HD vector is more similar to the dominating HD vector than to other components.

3.4 Mapping of n-gram Statistics with Hyperdimensional Computing

The mapping of n-gram statistics into distributed representation using hyperdimensional computing was first shown in [15]. At the initialization phase, the random item memory $\mathbf{H}$ is generated for the alphabet. A position of symbol $\mathcal{S}_j$ in $\mathcal{N}_i$ is represented by applying the fixed permutation ρ to the corresponding atomic HD vector $\mathbf{H}_{\mathcal{S}_j}$ j times, which is denoted as $\rho^j(\mathbf{H}_{\mathcal{S}_j})$. Next, a single HD vector for $\mathcal{N}_i$ (denoted as $\mathbf{m}_{\mathcal{N}_i}$) is formed via the consecutive binding of permuted HD vectors $\rho^j(\mathbf{H}_{\mathcal{S}_j})$ representing symbols in each position j of $\mathcal{N}_i$. For example, for the trigram 'cba' will be mapped to its HD vector as follows: $\rho^1(\mathbf{H}_c) \odot \rho^2(\mathbf{H}_b) \odot \rho^3(\mathbf{H}_a)$. In general, the process of forming HD vector of an n-gram can be formalized as follows:

$$\mathbf{m}_{\mathcal{N}_i} = \prod_{j=1}^{n} \rho^j(\mathbf{H}_{\mathcal{S}_j}), \tag{7}$$

where $\prod$ denotes the binding operation (positionwise multiplication) when applied to n HD vectors.

Once it is known how to map a particular n-gram to an HD vector, mapping the whole n-gram statistics **s** is straightforward. HD vector **h** corresponding to **s** is created by bundling together all n-grams observed in the data, which is expressed as follows:

$$\mathbf{h} = \sum_{i=1}^{a^n} \mathbf{s}_i \mathbf{m}_{\mathcal{N}_i} = \sum_{i=1}^{a^n} \mathbf{s}_i \prod_{j=1}^{n} \rho^j(\mathbf{H}_{\mathcal{S}_j}), \tag{8}$$

where $\sum$ denotes the bundling operation when applied to several HD vectors. Note that **h** is not bipolar, therefore, in the experiments below we normalized it by its ℓ_2 norm.

4   Experimental Results

This section describes the experimental results studying several configurations of the proposed approach and comparing it with the results obtained for the conventional n-gram statistics. We slightly modified the experimental setup from that used in [15], where the task was to identify a language of a given text sample (i.e., for a string of symbols). The language recognition was done for 21 European languages. The list of languages is as follows: Bulgarian, Czech, Danish, German, Greek, English, Estonian, Finnish, French, Hungarian, Italian, Latvian, Lithuanian, Dutch, Polish, Portuguese, Romanian, Slovak, Slovene, Spanish, Swedish. The training data is based on the Wortschatz Corpora [32]. The average size of a language's corpus in the training data was $1,085,637.3 \pm 121,904.1$ symbols. It is worth noting, that in the experiments reported in [15] the whole training corpus of a particular language was used to estimate the corresponding n-grams statistics. While in this study, in order to enable training of SOMs, each language corpus was divided into samples where the length of each sample was set to $1,000$ symbols. The total number of samples in the training data was $22,791$. The test data is based on the Europarl Parallel Corpus[1]. The test data also represent 21 European languages. The total number of samples in the test data was $21,000$, where each language was represented with $1,000$ samples. Each sample in the test data corresponds to a single sentence. The average size of a sample in the test data was 150.3 ± 89.5 symbols.

The data for each language was preprocessed such that the text included only lower case letters and spaces. All punctuation was removed. Lastly, all text used the 26-letter ISO basic Latin alphabet, i.e., the alphabet for both training and test data was the same and it included 27 symbols. For each text sample the n-gram statistics (either conventional or mapped to the distributed representation) was obtained, which was then used as input **x** when training or testing SOMs. Since each sample was preprocessed to use the alphabet of only $a = 27$ symbols, the conventional n-gram statistics input is 27^n dimensional (e.g., $k = 729$ when $n = 2$) while the dimensionality of the mapped n-gram statistics depends on the

---

[1] Available online at http://www.statmt.org/europarl/.

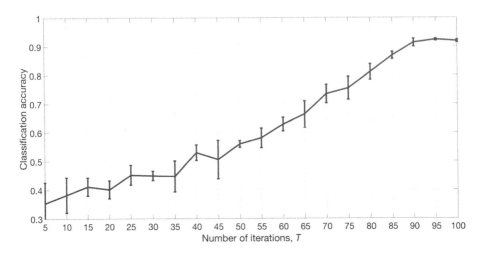

Fig. 4. The classification accuracy of the SOM trained on the conventional bigram statistics ($n = 2$; $k = 729$) against the number of training iterations T. The grid size was set to ten ($u = 100$). T varied in the range $[5, 100]$ with step 5.

dimensionality of HD vectors d (i.e., $k = d$). In all experiments reported in this paper, we used the standard SOMs implementation, which is a part of the Deep Learning Toolbox in MATLAB R2018B (Mathworks Inc, Natick, Ma).

During the experiments, certain parameters SOM were fixed. In particular, the topology of SOMs was set to the standard grid topology. The initial size of the neighborhood was always fixed to ten. The size of the neighborhood and the learning rate were decreasing progressively with training according to the default rules of the used implementation. In all simulations, a SOM was trained for a given number of iterations T, which was set according to an experiment reported in Fig. 4. All reported results were averaged across five independent simulations. The bars in the figure show standard deviations.

Recall that SOMs are suited for the unsupervised training, therefore, an extra mechanism is needed to use them in supervised tasks such as the considered language recognition task, i.e., once the SOM is trained there is still a need to assign a label to each trained node. After training a SOM for T iterations using all $22,791$ training samples, the whole training data were presented to the trained SOM one more time without modifying **W**. Labels for the training data were used to collect the statistics for the winning nodes. The nodes were assigned the labels of the languages dominating in the collected statistics. If a node in the trained SOM was never chosen as the winning node for the training samples (i.e., its statistics information is empty) then this node was ignored during the testing phase. During the testing phase, $21,000$ samples of the test data were used to assess the trained SOM. For each sample in the test data, the winning node was determined. The test sample then was assigned the language label corresponding to its winning node. The classification accuracy was calculated using the SOM

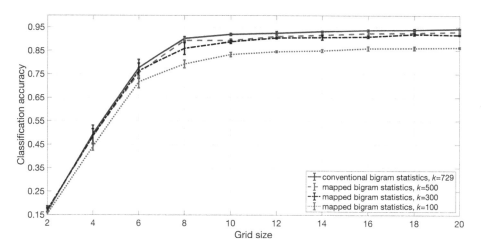

Fig. 5. The classification accuracy of the SOM against the grid size for the case of bigram statistics. The grid size varied in the range $[2, 20]$ with step 2.

predictions and the ground truth of the test data. The accuracy was used as the main performance metric for evaluation and comparison of different SOMs. It is worth emphasizing that the focus of experiments is not on achieving the highest possible accuracy but on a comparative analysis of SOMs with the conventional n-gram statistics versus SOMs with the mapped n-gram statistics with varying d. However, it is worth noting that the accuracy, obtained when collecting an n-gram statistics profile for each language [15,36] for $n = 2$ and $n = 3$ and using the nearest neighbor classifier, was 0.945 and 0.977 respectively. Thus, the results presented below for SOMs match the ones obtained with the supervised learning on bigrams when the number of nodes is sufficiently high. In the case of trigrams, the highest accuracy obtained with SOMs was slightly (about 0.02) lower. While SOMs not necessarily achieve the highest accuracy compared to the supervised methods, their important advantage is data visualization. For example, in the considered task one could imagine using the trained SOM for identifying the clusters typical for each language and even reflecting on their relative locations on the map.

The experiment in Fig. 4 presents the classification accuracy of the SOM trained on the conventional bigram statistics against T. The results demonstrated that the accuracy increased with the increased number T. Moreover, for higher values of T the predictions are more stable. The performance started to saturate at T more than 90, therefore, in the other experiments the value of T was fixed to 100.

The grid size varied in the range $[2, 20]$ with step 2, i.e, the number of nodes u varied between 4 and 400. In Fig. 5 the solid curve corresponds to the SOM trained on the conventional bigram statistics. The dashed, dash-dot, and dotted curves correspond to the SOMs trained on the mapped bigram statistics with $k = d = 500$, $k = d = 300$, and $k = d = 100$ respectively.

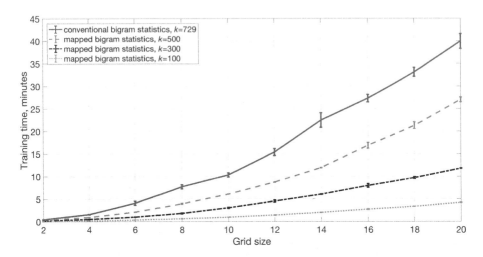

Fig. 6. The training time of the SOM against the grid size for the case of bigram statistics. The grid size varied in the range $[2, 20]$ with step 2.

The experiment presented in Fig. 5 studied the classification accuracy of the SOM against the grid size for the case of bigram statistics. Note that the number of nodes u in the SOM is proportional to the square of the grid size. For example, when the gris size equals 2 the SOM has $u = 4$ nodes while when it equals 20 the SOM has $u = 400$ nodes. The results in Fig. 5 demonstrated that the accuracy of all considered SOMs improves with the increased grid size. It is intuitive that all SOMs with grid sizes less than five performed poorly since the number of nodes in SOMs was lower than the number of different languages in the task. Nevertheless, the performance of all SOMs was constantly improving with the increased grid size, but the accuracy started to saturate at about 100 nodes. Moreover, increasing the dimensionality of HD vectors d was improving the accuracy. Note, however, that there was a better improvement when going from $d = 100$ to $d = 300$ compared to increasing d from 300 to 500. The performance of the conventional bigram statistics was already approximated well even when $d = 300$; for $d = 500$ the accuracy was just slightly worse than that of the conventional bigram statistics.

It is important to mention that the usage of the mapped n-grams statistics allows decreasing the size of $\mathbf{W}$ in proportion to d/a^n. Moreover, it allows decreasing the training time of SOMs. The experiment in Fig. 6 presents the training time of the SOM against the grid size for the case of bigram statistics. Figure 6 corresponds to that of Fig. 5. The number of training iterations was fixed to $T = 100$. For example, for grid size 16 the average training time on a laptop for $k = d = 100$ was 2.7 min (accuracy 0.86); for $k = d = 300$ it was 8.0 min (accuracy 0.91); for $k = d = 500$ it was 16.9 min (accuracy 0.92); and for $k = a^n = 729$ it was 27.3 min (accuracy 0.93). Thus, the usage of the

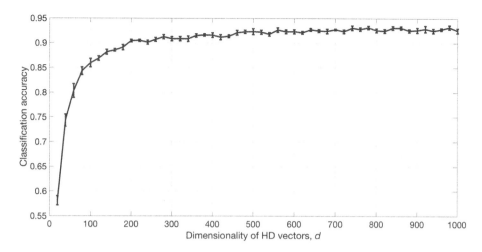

Fig. 7. The classification accuracy of the SOM trained on the mapped bigram statistics ($n = 2$) against the dimensionality of HD vectors d ($k = d$). The grid size was set to 16 ($u = 256$). The number of training iterations T was fixed to 100.

mapping allows the trade-off between the obtained accuracy and the required computational resources.

In order to observe a more detailed dependency between the classification accuracy and the dimensionality of distributed representations d of the mapped n-gram statistics, an additional experiment was done. Figure 7 depicts the results. The dimensionality of distributed representations d varied in the range $[20, 1000]$ with step 20. It is worth mentioning that even for small dimensionalities ($d < 100$), the accuracy is far beyond random. The results in Fig. 7 are consistent with the observations in Fig. 5 in a way that the accuracy was increasing with the increased d. The performance saturation begins for the values above 200 and the improvements beyond $d = 500$ look marginal. Thus, we experimentally observed that the quality of mappings grows with d, however, after a certain saturation point increasing d further becomes impractical.

The last experiment in Fig. 8 is similar to Fig. 5 but it studied the classification accuracy for the case of trigram statistics ($n = 3$). The grid size varied in the range $[2, 20]$ with step 2. The solid curve corresponds to the SOM trained on the conventional trigram statistics ($k = 27^3 = 19,683$). The dashed and dash-dot curves correspond to the SOMs trained on the mapped trigram statistics with $k = d = 5,000$ and $k = d = 1,000$ respectively. The results in Fig. 8 are consistent with the case of bigrams. The classification of SOMs was better for higher d and even when $d < a^n$ the accuracy was approximated well.

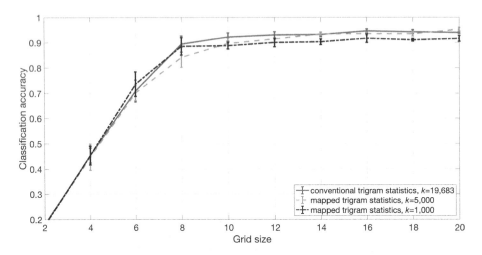

Fig. 8. The classification accuracy of the SOM against the grid size for the case of trigram statistics ($n = 3$). The number of training iterations T was fixed to 100.

5 Conclusions

This paper presented an approach for the mapping of n-gram statistics into vectors of fixed arbitrary dimensionality, which does not depend on the size of n-grams n. The mapping is aided by hyperdimensional computing a bio-inspired approach for computing with large random vectors. Mapped in this way n-gram statistics is used as the input to Self-Organized Maps. This novel for Self-Organized Maps step allows removing the computational bottleneck caused by the exponentially growing dimensionality of n-gram statistics with increased n. While preserving the performance of the trained Self-Organized Maps (as demonstrated in the languages recognition task) the presented approach results in reduced memory consumption due to smaller weight matrix (proportional to d and u) and shorter training times. The main limitation of this study is that we have validated the proposed approach only on a single task when using the conventional Self-Organized Maps. However, it is worth noting that the proposed approach could be easily used for other modifications of the conventional Self-Organizing Maps such as Growing Self-Organizing Maps [1], where dynamic topology preservation facilitates unconstrained learning. This is in contrast to a fixed-structure feature map as the map itself is defined by the unsupervised learning process of the feature vectors. We intend to investigate distributed representation of n-gram statistics in structure-adapting feature maps in future work.

References

1. Alahakoon, D., Halgamuge, S., Srinivasan, B.: Dynamic self-organizing maps with controlled growth for knowledge discovery. IEEE Trans. Neural Netw. **11**(3), 601–614 (2000)
2. Appiah, K., Hunter, A., Dickinson, P., Meng, H.: Implementation and applications of tri-state self-organizing maps on FPGA. IEEE Trans. Circ. Syst. Video Technol. **22**(8), 1150–1160 (2012)
3. Bandaragoda, T.R., De Silva, D., Alahakoon, D.: Automatic event detection in microblogs using incremental machine learning. J. Assoc. Inform. Sci. Technol. **68**(10), 2394–2411 (2017)
4. Bishop, C.M., Svensén, M., Williams, C.K.: GTM: the generative topographic mapping. Neural Comput. **10**(1), 215–234 (1998)
5. De Silva, D., Alahakoon, D.: Incremental knowledge acquisition and self learning from text. In: International Joint Conference on Neural Networks (IJCNN), pp. 1–8. IEEE (2010)
6. De Silva, D., Alahakoon, D., Yu, X.: A data fusion technique for smart home energy management and analysis. In: Annual Conference of the IEEE Industrial Electronics Society (IECON), pp. 4594–4600 (2016)
7. De Silva, D., et al.: Machine learning to support social media empowered patients in cancer care and cancer treatment decisions. PLoS One **13**(10), 1–10 (2018)
8. De Silva, D., Yu, X., Alahakoon, D., Holmes, G.: A data mining framework for electricity consumption analysis from meter data. IEEE Trans. Industr. Inf. **7**(3), 399–407 (2011)
9. Dittenbach, M., Merkl, D., Rauber, A.: The growing hierarchical self-organizing map. In: International Joint Conference on Neural Networks (IJCNN), vol. 6, pp. 15–19 (2000)
10. Eliasmith, C.: How to Build a Brain. Oxford University Press, Oxford (2013)
11. Frady, E.P., Kleyko, D., Sommer, F.T.: A theory of sequence indexing and working memory in recurrent neural networks. Neural Comput. **30**, 1449–1513 (2018)
12. Hazan, H., Saunders, D.J., Sanghavi, D.T., Siegelmann, H.T., Kozma, R.: Unsupervised learning with self-organizing spiking neural networks. In: International Joint Conference on Neural Networks (IJCNN), pp. 1–6 (2018)
13. Hinton, G., McClelland, J., Rumelhart, D.: Distributed representations. In: Rumelhart, D., McClelland, J. (eds.) Parallel Distributed Processing. Explorations in the Microstructure of Cognition - Volume 1 Foundations, pp. 77–109. MIT Press, Cambridge (1986)
14. Jayaratne, M., Alahakoon, D., De Silva, D., Yu, X.: Bio-inspired multisensory fusion for autonomous robots. In: Annual Conference of the IEEE Industrial Electronics Society (IECON), pp. 3090–3095 (2018)
15. Joshi, A., Halseth, J.T., Kanerva, P.: Language geometry using random indexing. In: de Barros, J.A., Coecke, B., Pothos, E. (eds.) QI 2016. LNCS, vol. 10106, pp. 265–274. Springer, Cham (2017). https://doi.org/10.1007/978-3-319-52289-0_21
16. Kanerva, P.: Hyperdimensional computing: an introduction to computing in distributed representation with high-dimensional random vectors. Cogn. Comput. **1**(2), 139–159 (2009)
17. Kaski, S., Honkela, T., Lagus, K., Kohonen, T.: WEBSOM-self-organizing maps of document collections1. Neurocomputing **21**(1–3), 101–117 (1998)
18. Kleyko, D., Osipov, E.: Brain-like classifier of temporal patterns. In: International Conference on Computer and Information Sciences (ICCOINS), pp. 104–113 (2014)

19. Kleyko, D., Osipov, E., De Silva, D., Wiklund, U., Alahakoon, D.: Integer self-organizing maps for digital hardware. In: International Joint Conference on Neural Networks (IJCNN), pp. 1–8 (2019)

20. Kleyko, D., Osipov, E., Gayler, R.: Recognizing permuted words with vector symbolic architectures: a cambridge test for machines. Proc. Comput. Sci. **88**, 169–175 (2016)

21. Kleyko, D., Osipov, E., Papakonstantinou, N., Vyatkin, V.: Hyperdimensional computing in industrial systems: the use-case of distributed fault isolation in a power plant. IEEE Access **6**, 30766–30777 (2018)

22. Kleyko, D., Osipov, E., Wiklund, U.: A hyperdimensional computing framework for analysis of cardiorespiratory synchronization during paced deep breathing. IEEE Access **7**, 34403–34415 (2019)

23. Kleyko, D., Rahimi, A., Gayler, R., Osipov, E.: Autoscaling bloom filter: controlling trade-off between true and false positives. Neural Comput. Appl. 1–10 (2019)

24. Kleyko, D., Rahimi, A., Rachkovskij, D., Osipov, E., Rabaey, J.: Classification and recall with binary hyperdimensional computing: trade-offs in choice of density and mapping characteristic. IEEE Trans. Neural Netw. Learn. Syst. **29**(12), 5880–5898 (2018)

25. Kohonen, T.: Self-Organizing Maps. Springer Series in Information Sciences. Springer, Heidelberg (2001). https://doi.org/10.1007/978-3-642-56927-2

26. Kohonen, T., Somervuo, P.: Self-organizing maps of symbol strings. Neurocomputing **21**(1–3), 19–30 (1998)

27. Kusiak, A.: Smart manufacturing must embrace big data. Nat. News **544**(7648), 23 (2017)

28. Nallaperuma, D., De Silva, D., Alahakoon, D., Yu, X.: Intelligent detection of driver behavior changes for effective coordination between autonomous and human driven vehicles. In: Annual Conference of the IEEE Industrial Electronics Society (IECON), pp. 3120–3125 (2018)

29. Nawaratne, R., Bandaragoda, T., Adikari, A., Alahakoon, D., De Silva, D., Yu, X.: Incremental knowledge acquisition and self-learning for autonomous video surveillance. In: Annual Conference of the IEEE Industrial Electronics Society (IECON), pp. 4790–4795 (2017)

30. Osipov, E., Kleyko, D., Legalov, A.: Associative synthesis of finite state automata model of a controlled object with hyperdimensional computing. In: Annual Conference of the IEEE Industrial Electronics Society (IECON), pp. 3276–3281 (2017)

31. Plate, T.A.: Holographic Reduced Representations: Distributed Representation for Cognitive Structures. Center for the Study of Language and Information (CSLI), Stanford (2003)

32. Quasto, U., Richter, M., Biemann, C.: Corpus portal for search in monolingual corpora. In: Fifth International Conference on Language Resources and Evaluation (LREC), pp. 1799–1802 (2006)

33. Rachkovskij, D.A.: Representation and processing of structures with binary sparse distributed codes. IEEE Trans. Knowl. Data Eng. **3**(2), 261–276 (2001)

34. Rahimi, A., et al.: High-dimensional Computing as a Nanoscalable Paradigm. IEEE Trans. Circ. Syst. I: Regul. Pap. **64**(9), 2508–2521 (2017)

35. Rahimi, A., Kanerva, P., Benini, L., Rabaey, J.M.: Efficient biosignal processing using hyperdimensional computing: network templates for combined learning and classification of ExG signals. Proc. IEEE **107**(1), 123–143 (2019)

36. Rahimi, A., Kanerva, P., Rabaey, J.: A robust and energy efficient classifier using brain-inspired hyperdimensional computing. In: IEEE/ACM International Symposium on Low Power Electronics and Design (ISLPED), pp. 64–69 (2016)

37. Rasanen, O., Kakouros, S.: Modeling dependencies in multiple parallel data streams with hyperdimensional computing. IEEE Signal Process. Lett. **21**(7), 899–903 (2014)
38. Recchia, G., Sahlgren, M., Kanerva, P., Jones, M.: Encoding sequential information in semantic space models: comparing holographic reduced representation and random permutation. Computat. Intell. Neurosci. 1–18 (2015)
39. Santana, A., Morais, A., Quiles, M.: An alternative approach for binary and categorical self-organizing maps. In: International Joint Conference on Neural Networks (IJCNN), pp. 2604–2610 (2017)
40. Shah-Hosseini, H., Safabakhsh, R.: TASOM: a new time adaptive self-organizing map. IEEE Trans. Syst. Man Cybern. Part B (Cybern.) **33**(2), 271–282 (2003)
41. Vesanto, J., Alhoniemi, E.: Clustering of the self-organizing map. IEEE Trans. Neural Netw. **11**(3), 586–600 (2000)
42. Zolotukhin, M., Hamalainen, T., Juvonen, A.: Online anomaly detection by using n-gram model and growing hierarchical self-organizing maps. In: International Wireless Communications and Mobile Computing Conference (IWCMC), pp. 47–52 (2012)

Parallel Factorization of Boolean Polynomials

Vadiraj Kulkarni[1]([✉]), Pavel Emelyanov[2,3], Denis Ponomaryov[2,3],
Madhava Krishna[1,4], Soumyendu Raha[1], and S. K. Nandy[1]

[1] Computer Aided Design Laboratory, Indian Institute of Science,
Bangalore 560012, India
{vadirajk,madhava,raha,nandy}@iisc.ac.in
[2] Ershov Institute of Informatics Systems,
Lavrentiev av. 6, 630090 Novosibirsk, Russia
{emelyanov,ponom}@iis.nsk.su
[3] Novosibirsk State University, Pirogova st. 1, 630090 Novosibirsk, Russia
[4] Morphing Machines Pvt. Ltd., Bangalore, India

Abstract. Polynomial factorization is a classical algorithmic problem in algebra, which has a wide range of applications. Of special interest is factorization over finite fields, among which the field of order two is probably the most important one due to the relationship to Boolean functions. In particular, factorization of Boolean polynomials corresponds to decomposition of Boolean functions given in the Algebraic Normal Form. It has been also shown that factorization provides a solution to decomposition of functions given in the full DNF (i.e., by a truth table), for positive DNFs, and for cartesian decomposition of relational datatables. These applications show the importance of developing fast and practical factorization algorithms. In the paper, we consider some recently proposed polynomial time factorization algorithms for Boolean polynomials and describe a parallel MIMD implementation thereof, which exploits both the task and data level parallelism. We report on an experimental evaluation, which has been conducted on logic circuit synthesis benchmarks and synthetic polynomials, and show that our implementation significantly improves the efficiency of factorization. Finally, we report on the performance benefits obtained from a parallel algorithm when executed on a massively parallel many core architecture (Redefine).

Keywords: Boolean polynomials · Factorization · Reconfigurable computing

1 Introduction

Polynomial factorization is a classical algorithmic problem in algebra, [8], which has numerous important applications. An instance of this problem, which

This work was supported by the grant of Russian Foundation for Basic Research No. 17-51-45125 and by the Ministry of Science and Education of the Russian Federation under the 5–100 Excellence Program.

© Springer Nature Switzerland AG 2019
N. Bjørner et al. (Eds.): PSI 2019, LNCS 11964, pp. 80–94, 2019.
https://doi.org/10.1007/978-3-030-37487-7_7

deserves a particular attention, is factorization of Boolean polynomials, i.e., multilinear polynomials over the finite field of order 2. A Boolean polynomial is one of the well-known sum-of-product representations of Boolean functions known as Zhegalkine polynomials [14] in the mathematical logic or the Reed–Muller canonical form [10] in the circuit synthesis. The advantage of this form that has recently made it popular again is a more natural and compact representation of some classes of Boolean functions (e.g., arithmetical functions, coders/cyphers, etc.), a more natural mapping to some circuit technologies (FPGA–based and nanostructure–based electronics), and good testability properties.

Factorization of Boolean polynomials is a particular case of decomposition (so–called disjoint conjunctive or AND–decomposition) of Boolean functions. Indeed, in a Boolean polynomial each variable has degree at most 1, which makes the factors have disjoint variables: $F(X,Y) = F_1(X) \cdot F_2(Y)$, $X \cap Y = \varnothing$.

It has been recently shown [4,5] that factorizaton of Boolean polynomials provides a solution to conjunctive decomposition of functions given in the full DNF (i.e., by a truth table) and for positive DNFs without the need of (inefficient) transformation between the representations. Besides, it provides a method for Cartesian decomposition of relational datatables [3,6], i.e., finding tables such that their unordered Cartesian product gives the source table. We give some illustrating examples below.

Consider the following DNF

$$\varphi = (x \wedge u) \ \vee \ (x \wedge v) \ \vee \ (y \wedge u) \ \vee \ (y \wedge v) \vee (x \wedge u \wedge v)$$

It is equivalent to

$$\psi = (x \wedge u) \ \vee \ (x \wedge v) \ \vee \ (y \wedge u) \ \vee \ (y \wedge v)$$

since the last term in φ is redundant. One can see that

$$\psi \equiv (x \vee y) \wedge (u \vee v)$$

and the decomposition components $x \vee y$ and $u \vee v$ can be recovered from the factors of the polynomial

$$F_\psi = xu + xv + yu + yv = (x + y) \cdot (u + v)$$

constructed for ψ.

The following full DNF

$$\varphi = (x \wedge \neg y \wedge u \wedge \neg v) \vee (x \wedge \neg y \wedge \neg u \wedge v) \vee$$
$$\vee (\neg x \wedge y \wedge u \wedge \neg v) \vee (\neg x \wedge y \wedge \neg u \wedge v)$$

is equivalent to

$$(x \wedge \neg y) \vee (\neg x \wedge y) \bigwedge (u \wedge \neg v) \vee (\neg u \wedge v)$$

and the decomposition components of φ can be recovered from the factors of the polynomial

$$F_\varphi = x\bar{y}u\bar{v} + x\bar{y}\bar{u}v + \bar{x}yu\bar{v} + \bar{x}y\bar{u}v = (x\bar{y} + \bar{x}y) \cdot (u\bar{v} + \bar{u}v) \tag{1}$$

constructed for φ.

Finally, Cartesian decomposition of the following table

B	E	D	A	C
z	q	u	x	y
y	q	u	x	y
y	r	v	x	z
z	r	v	x	z
y	p	u	x	x
z	p	u	x	x

$=$

A	B
x	y
x	z

$\times$

C	D	E
x	u	p
y	u	q
z	v	r

can be obtained from the factors of the polynomial

$$z_B \cdot q \cdot u \cdot x_A \cdot y_C + y_B \cdot q \cdot u \cdot x_A \cdot y_C +$$
$$y_B \cdot r \cdot v \cdot x_A \cdot z_C + z_B \cdot r \cdot v \cdot x_A \cdot z_C +$$
$$y_B \cdot p \cdot u \cdot x_A \cdot x_C + z_B \cdot p \cdot u \cdot x_A \cdot x_C =$$
$$= (x_A \cdot y_B + x_A \cdot z_B) \cdot (q \cdot u \cdot y_C + r \cdot v \cdot z_C + p \cdot u \cdot x_C)$$

constructed for the table's content.

Decomposition facilitates finding a more compact representation of Boolean functions and data tables, which is applied in the scope of the Logic Circuit Synthesis, self-organizing databases, and dependency mining, respectively. Due to the typically large inputs in these tasks, it is important to develop efficient and practical factorization algorithms for Boolean polynomials.

In [13], Shpilka and Volkovich showed a connection between polynomial factorization and identity testing. It follows from their results that a Boolean polynomial can be factored in time $O(l^3)$, where l is the size of the polynomial given as a symbol sequence. The approach employs multiplication of polynomials obtained from the input one, which is a costly operation in case of large inputs. In [4], Emelyanov and Ponomaryov proposed an alternative approach to factorization and showed that it can be done without explicit multiplication of Boolean polynomials. The approach has been further discussed in [7].

In this paper, we propose a parallel version of the decomposition algorithm from [4,7]. In Sect. 2, we revisit the sequential factorization algorithm from these papers. In Sect. 3, we describe a parallel MIMD implementation of the algorithm and further in Sect. 4 we perform a quantitative analysis of the parallel algorithm versus the sequential one. Finally, in Sect. 5 we evaluate our algorithm on a massively parallel many core architecture (Redefine) and outline the results.

2   Background

In this section we reproduce the sequential algorithm from [4,7] for the ease of exposition. Let us first introduce basic definitions and notations.

A polynomial $F \in \mathbb{F}_2[x_1, \ldots, x_n]$ is called *factorable* if $F = F_1 \cdot \ldots \cdot F_k$, where $k \geq 2$ and $F_1, \ldots, F_k$ are non-constant polynomials. The polynomials $F_1, \ldots, F_k$ are called *factors* of F. It is important to realize that since we consider multilinear polynomials (every variable can occur only in the power of ≤ 1), the factors are polynomials *over disjoint sets of variables*. In the following sections, we assume that the polynomial F does not have *trivial divisors*, i.e., neither x, nor $x + 1$ divides F. Clearly, trivial divisors can easily be recognized.

For a polynomial F, a variable x from the set of variables $Var(F)$ of F, and a value $a \in \{0, 1\}$, we denote by $F_{x=a}$ the polynomial obtained from F by substituting x with a. $\frac{\partial F}{\partial x}$ denotes a *formal derivative* of F wrt x. Given a variable z, we write $z|F$ if z divides F, i.e., z is present in every monomial of F (note that this is equivalent to the condition $\frac{\partial F}{\partial z} = F_{z=1}$). Given a set of variables Σ and a monomial m, the *projection* of m onto Σ is 1 if m does not contain any variable from Σ, or is equal to the monomial obtained from m by removing all the variables not contained in Σ, otherwise. The *projection* of a polynomial F onto Σ, denoted by $F|_\Sigma$, is the polynomial obtained as the sum of monomials from the set S projected onto Σ, with duplicate monomials removed.

2.1 Factorization Algorithm

Algorithm 1 describes the sequential version of the factorization algorithm. As already mentioned, the factors of a Boolean polynomial have disjoint sets of variables. This property is employed in the algorithm, which tries to compute a variable partition. Once it is computed, the corresponding factors can be easily obtained as projections of the input polynomial onto the sets from the partition.

The algorithm chooses a variable randomly from the variable set of F. Assuming the polynomial F contains at least two variables the algorithm partitions the variable set of F into two sets with respect to the chosen variable:

- the first set Σ_{same} contains the selected variable and corresponds to an irreducible polynomial;
- the second set Σ_{other} corresponds to the second polynomial which can admit further factorization.

The factors of F, F_{same} and F_{other} are obtained as the projections of the input polynomial onto Σ_{same} and Σ_{other}, respectively.

In lines 1–3, we select an arbitrary variable x from the variable set of F and compute the polynomials A and B. A is the derivative of F wrt x and B is the polynomial obtained by setting x to zero in F. In lines 4–10, we loop through the variable set of F excluding x, calculate the polynomials C and D, and check if the product AD is equal to BC. C is the derivative of polynomial A and D is the derivative of polynomial B. To check whether AD is equal to BC we invoke the **IsEqual** procedure in line 6. We describe the **IsEqual** procedure in detail in the next subsection.

2.2   IsEqual Procedure

Algorithm 2 describes the sequential version of the IsEqual procedure.

Algorithm 1. Sequential Factorization Algorithm

    Input Boolean polynomial to be factored F

    Output F_{same} and F_{other} which are the factors of the input polynomial F

1: Take an arbitrary variable x occurring in F

2: Let $A = \frac{\partial F}{\partial x}, B = F_{x=0}$

3: Let $\Sigma_{same} = x, \Sigma_{other} = \emptyset, F_{same} = 0, F_{other} = 0$

4: **for each** $y \in var(F) \setminus \{x\}$ **do**

5:      Let $C = \frac{\partial A}{\partial y}, D = \frac{\partial B}{\partial y}$

6:      **if** IsEqual(A, D, B, C) **then**

7:         $\Sigma_{other} = \Sigma_{other} \cup \{y\}$

8:      **else**

9:         $\Sigma_{same} = \Sigma_{same} \cup \{y\}$

10:     **end if**

11: **end for**

12: If $\Sigma_{other} = \emptyset$ then F is non-factorable

13: Return polynomials F_{same} and F_{other} obtained as projections onto Σ_{same} and Σ_{other} respectively.

- The procedure takes input polynomials A, B, C, D and computes whether $AD = BC$ by employing recursion.
- Lines 1–2, 7–16 implement the base cases when $AD = BC$ can be determined trivially.
- In Line 3–5, we check whether a variable z divides the polynomials A, B, C, D such that the condition in Line 4 holds. If this is not the case, then we can eliminate z from A, B, C, D and check if the products of the resulting polynomials are equal.
- In Lines 17–25, we recursively invoke **IsEqual** procedure on polynomials, whose sizes are smaller than the size of the original ones.

2.3   Scope for Parallelism

The crux of Algorithm 1 is the loop in Lines 4–11. We observe that the different iterations of the loop are independent of each other. Hence the loop exhibits thread level parallelism which can be exploited for performance gain. The conditional block inside the loop in Lines 6–10 can be used to exploit the task level parallelism between the multiple threads.

    Multiple sections of Algorithm 2 are amenable for parallelization. Checking the divisibility of the polynomials A, B, C, D in Lines 3–6 of **IsEqual** procedure can be performed independently. In Lines 16–23, the recursive calls to **IsEqual** procedure are independent of each other and exhibit thread level parallelism.

    In the next section we propose a parallel algorithm using the above observations.

Algorithm 2. Sequential IsEqual Procedure

    Input Boolean polynomials A,B,C,D
    Output TRUE if AD is equal to BC and FALSE otherwise.

1: If A=0 or D=0 then return (B=0 or C=0)
2: If B=0 or C=0 then return FALSE
3: **for each** z occurring in at least one of A,B,C,D **do**
4:     **if** $z|A$ or $z|D$ xor $z|B$ or $z|C$ **then**
5:         return FALSE
6:     **end if**
7: Replace every $X \in \{A, B, C, D\}$ with $\frac{\partial X}{\partial z}$, provided $z|X$
8: **end for**
9: **if** A=1 and D=1 **then** return (B=1 and C=1)
10: **end if**
11: **if** B=1 and C=1 **then** return FALSE
12: **end if**
13: **if** A=1 and B=1 **then** return (D=C)
14: **end if**
15: **if** D=1 and C=1 **then** return (A=B)
16: **end if**
17: Pick a variable z
18: **if** not(IsEqual($A_{z=0}, D_{z=0}, B_{z=0}, C_{z=0}$)) **then** return FALSE
19: **end if**
20: **if** not(IsEqual($\frac{\partial A}{\partial z}, \frac{\partial D}{\partial z}, \frac{\partial B}{\partial z}, \frac{\partial C}{\partial z}$)) **then** return FALSE
21: **end if**
22: **if** IsEqual($\frac{\partial A}{\partial z}, B_{z=0}, A_{z=0}, \frac{\partial B}{\partial z}$) **then** return TRUE
23: **end if**
24: **if** IsEqual($\frac{\partial A}{\partial z}, C_{z=0}, A_{z=0}, \frac{\partial C}{\partial z}$) **then** return TRUE
25: **else** return FALSE
26: **end if**

---

3 Proposed Approach

3.1 Parallel Factorization Algorithm

Algorithm 3 describes the parallel version of the factorization algorithm. In Lines 1–3, we select an arbitrary variable x from the variable set of F and compute the polynomials A and B. In Lines 4–11, we perform multiple loop iterations independently in parallel by spawning multiple threads. Each thread will return two sets Σ_{same}^{tid} and Σ_{other}^{tid} specific to the scope of the thread designated by thread identifier tid. In Lines 12–13, the variable sets Σ_{same} and Σ_{other} are computed as the union of the thread specific instances, respectively. Note that Lines 12–13 perform barrier synchronization of all the parallel threads.

3.2 Parallel IsEqual Procedure

Algorithm 4 describes the parallel version of the IsEqual procedure. This algorithm takes as input four polynomials A, D, B, C and checks whether the product

---

Algorithm 3. Parallel Decomposition Algorithm

Input Boolean polynomial to be factored F
Output F_{same} and F_{other} which are the factors of the input polynomial F

1: Take an arbitrary variable x occurring in F
2: Let $A = \frac{\partial F}{\partial z}, B = F_{z=0}$
3: Let $\Sigma_{same} = x, \Sigma_{other} = \emptyset, F_{same} = 0, F_{other} = 0$
4: **for each** $y \in var(F) \setminus \{x\}$ **do in parallel**
5:     Let $C = \frac{\partial A}{\partial y}$ $D = \frac{\partial B}{\partial y}$
6:     **if** IsEqual(A, D, B, C) **then**
7:         $\Sigma_{other}^{tid} = \Sigma_{other}^{tid} \cup \{y\}$
8:     **else**
9:         $\Sigma_{same}^{tid} = \Sigma_{same}^{tid} \cup \{y\}$
10:     **end if**
11: **end for Wait for all the parallel threads to finish**
12: $\Sigma_{other} = \bigcup_{tid} \Sigma_{other}^{tid}$
13: $\Sigma_{same} = \bigcup_{tid} \Sigma_{same}^{tid}$
14: If $\Sigma_{other} = \emptyset$ then F is non-factorable; stop
15: Return polynomials F_{same} and F_{other} obtained as projections onto Σ_{same} and Σ_{other}, respectively.

AD is equal to the product BC. Lines 1–2 and lines 14–21 describe the cases when determining $AD = BC$ is trivial. In lines 3–9, we check whether a variable z divides the input polynomials A, D, B, C such that the condition in Line 5 holds. If this is not the case, we divide them by z to obtain the reduced polynomials. The above operations are performed for each variable independently in parallel by spawning multiple threads. In Line 8 each thread checks whether a variable z^{tid} (tid denotes the thread id) is a divisor of any of A, B, C, D. If z^{tid} divides any of A, B, C, D it computes the corresponding reduced polynomials $A^{tid}, D^{tid}, B^{tid}, C^{tid}$ obtained by dividing any of A, D, B, C by z^{tid}, respectively. In line 10 we wait for all the threads to finish. In Line 13 we take pairwise intersection of the corresponding monomials of thread specific polynomials $A^{tid}, D^{tid}, B^{tid}, C^{tid}$ to form polynomials which are free of trivial divisors. Intersection of two monomials m_1, m_2 is 1 if m_1, m_2 do not contain common variables and otherwise it is the monomial, which consists of the variables present in both m_1 and m_2. In Lines 23–27, we perform four recursive calls to the IsEqual function independently in parallel by spawning multiple threads. In Line 28–37, we wait for all the threads to finish and compare the outputs of each threads to form the final output. Note that lines 10 and 28 perform barrier synchronization of all the parallel threads.

Algorithm 4. Parallel IsEqual Function

Input Boolean polynomials A,B,C,D

Output TRUE if AD is equal to BC and FALSE otherwise.

1: If A=0 or D=0 then return (B=0 or C=0)
2: If B=0 or C=0 then return FALSE
3: **for each** z occurring in at least one of A,B,C,D **do in parallel**
4:     set $flag^{tid}$= True
5:     **if** $z|A$ or $z|D$ xor $z|B$ or $z|C$ **then**
6:         set $flag^{tid}$= FALSE
7:     **end if**
8:     Replace every $X^{tid} \in \{A, B, C, D\}$ with $\frac{\partial X^{tid}}{\partial z}$, provided $z|X^{tid}$
9: **end for**
10: **Wait for all threads to finish**
11: **if** $\bigwedge_{tid} flag^{tid} = FALSE$ **then** return FALSE
12: **end if**
13: $X = \bigcap_{tid} X^{tid}$, for $X \in \{A, B, C, D\}$
14: **if** A=1 and D=1 **then** return (B=1 and C=1)
15: **end if**
16: **if** B=1 and C=1 **then** return FALSE
17: **end if**
18: **if** A=1 and B=1 **then** return (D=C)
19: **end if**
20: **if** D=1 and C=1 **then** return (A=B)
21: **end if**
22: Pick a variable z
23:   **Do the next 4 lines in parallel**
24: x = not(IsEqual($A_{z=0}, D_{z=0}, B_{z=0}, C_{z=0}$))
25: y = not(IsEqual($\frac{\partial A}{\partial z}, \frac{\partial D}{\partial z}, \frac{\partial B}{\partial z}, \frac{\partial C}{\partial z}$))
26: z = IsEqual($\frac{\partial A}{\partial z}, B_{z=0}, A_{z=0}, \frac{\partial B}{\partial z}$)
27: w = IsEqual($\frac{\partial A}{\partial z}, C_{z=0}, A_{z=0}, \frac{\partial C}{\partial z}$)
28: **Wait for all threads to finish**
29: **if** not(x) **then** return FALSE
30: **end if**
31: **if** not(y) **then** return FALSE
32: **end if**
33: **if** z **then** return TRUE
34: **end if**
35: **if** w **then** return TRUE
36: **else** return FALSE
37: **end if**

4 Experiments and Results

Experimental evaluation of the sequential and parallel algorithms was made on Logic circuit synthesis benchmarks and synthetic Boolean polynomials.

4.1   Logic Circuit Synthesis Benchmarks

We used ITC'99 [2], Iscas'85 [9], and n-bit ripple carry adder [12] benchmarks. RTL designs of the digital logic circuits were converted from Verilog to the full disjunctive normal form to obtain the corresponding Boolean polynomial. The sequential and parallel algorithms were evaluated on the obtained Boolean polynomials. Table 1 shows the execution time of sequential and parallel algorithms executed on Xeon processor running at 2.8 GHz with 4 threads averaged over 5 runs. One can observe a considerable performance speedup of the parallel algorithm over the sequential one.

Table 1. Results on Xeon processor at 2.8 GHz using 4 threads

Benchmark	Sequential	Multi-threaded	Speedup
ITC'99	4324 (s)	1441 (s)	3.01
Iscas'85	7181 (s)	2633 (s)	2.73
EPFL adder	1381 (s)	374 (s)	3.69

4.2   Synthetic Polynomials

Synthetic polynomials of varying complexities were generated at random and sequential and parallel algorithms were evaluated on them. Table 2 shows execution times for the sequential and parallel algorithms executed on Xeon processor running at 2.8 GHz with 4 threads averaged over 5 runs. We observe that the execution time of both sequential and multithreaded algorithm increases drastically with the increase in the complexity of Boolean polynomials. We also observe that the speedup due to parallelization decreases with the increase in the complexity of Boolean polynomials.

4.3   Scaling Results

Figure 1a shows the speedup of the parallel decomposition algorithm over the sequential one wrt the number of threads. Here, the problem size is fixed to examine the strong scaling behaviour of the parallel decomposition algorithm. We observe that the parallel speedup is decreased as the size (complexity) of the problem increases. As the problem size increases, so does the call to the sequential bottleneck of the algorithm (simplification of Boolean polynomials), which causes the speedup to reduce.

Figure 1b shows the speedup of the parallel decomposition algorithm over the sequential algorithm wrt the number of threads. Here, the problem size per thread is fixed to examine the weak scaling behaviour of the parallel algorithm. The increase in the parallel speedup with the increase in the number of threads is less than the ideal linear speedup. This is due to the sequential bottlenecks in the decomposition algorithm (simplification of Boolean polynomials) and the communication bottleneck among multiple threads. Note that in these tests number of variables ranges from tens to two hundreds.

Table 2. Execution time of factoring synthetic polynomials on Xeon processor at 2.8 GHz using 4 threads

Number of monomials	Sequential	Multi-threaded	Speedup
10	0.023 (s)	0.0074 (s)	3.12
50	16.29 (s)	5.07 (s)	3.21
100	103.5 (s)	30.44 (s)	3.4
500	483.6 (s)	178.1 (s)	2.7
1000	1165 (s)	520.9 (s)	2.2
5000	1430 (s)	735.11 (s)	1.91
10000	12614 (s)	8034 (s)	1.57

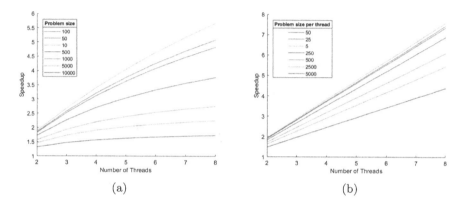

(a)   (b)

Fig. 1. (a) Parallel speedup vs number of threads with fixed problem size (b) Parallel speedup vs number of threads with fixed problem size per thread

5 Implementation on Redefine

The REDEFINE architecture [1] comprises Compute Resources (CRs) connected through a Network-on-Chip (NoC) (see Fig. 2a). REDEFINE is an application accelerator, which can be customized for a specific application domain through reconfiguration. Reconfiguration in REDEFINE can be performed primarily at two levels, viz. the level of aggregation of CRs to serve as processing cores for coarse grain multi-input, multi-output macro operations, and at the level of Custom Function Units (CFU) presented at the Hardware Abstraction Layer (HAL) as Instruction Extensions. Unlike traditional architectures, Instructions Extensions in REDEFINE can be defined post-silicon. Post-silicon definition of Instruction Extensions in REDEFINE is a unique feature of REDEFINE that sets it aside from other commercial multicores by allowing customization of REDEFINE for different application domains.

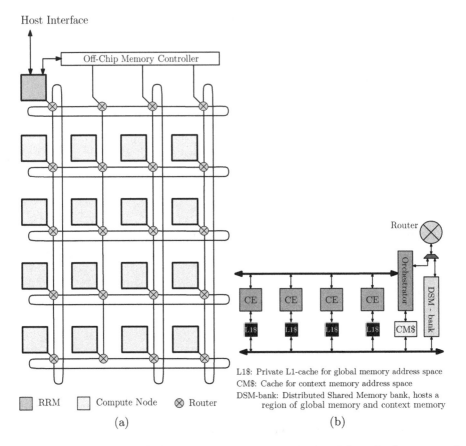

Fig. 2. (a) A 16 node REDEFINE comprising of a 4 × 4 toriodal mesh of routers and a redefine resource manager (RRM) for interfacing with the host (b) Composition of a compute Node

REDEFINE execution model is inspired by the macro-dataflow model. In this model, an application is described as a hierarchical dataflow graph, as shown in Fig. 3, in which the vertices are called hyperOps, and the edges represent explicit data transfer or execution order requirements among hyperOps. A hyperOp is a multiple-input and multiple-output (MIMO) macro operation. A hyperOp is ready for execution as soon as all its operands are available and all its execution order or synchronization dependencies are satisfied. Apart from the arithmetic, control, and memory load and store instructions, the REDEFINE execution model includes primitives for explicit data transfers and synchronization among hyperOps and primitives for adding new nodes (hyperOps) and edges to the application graph during execution. Thus, the execution model supports dynamic (data-dependent) parallelism. The execution model follows non-preemptive scheduling of hyperOps; therefore cyclic dependencies are forbidden among hyperOps. The runtime unit named Orchestrator schedules ready hyperOps onto CRs. A CR comprises four Compute Elements (CEs). Each CE executes a hyperOp (see Fig. 2b). All communications among hyperOps are unidirectional i.e., only producer hyperOp initiates and completes a communication. Thus with sufficient parallelism, all communications can overlap with computations. Compared to other hybrid dataflow/control-flow execution models, REDEFINE execution model simplifies the resource management and the memory model required to support arbitrary parallelism.

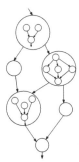

Fig. 3. Macro-dataflow execution model. An application described as a hierarchical dataflow graph, in which vertices represent hyperOps and edges represent explicit data transfer or execution order requirements between the connected hyperOps.

5.1   Decomposition Algorithm Using HyperOps

Algorithm 5 describes in pseudo-code the decomposition algorithm when written using "C with HyperOps". The code snippet, corresponding to Algorithm 5 is presented in the listing below. In the code snippet the terms __CMAddr, __Sync, __kernel, __WriteCM, CMADDR are REDEFINE specific annotations. Lines 2–8 and 12–13 of Algorithm 5 are the same as Lines 5–10 and 1–3 of Algorithm 1, respectively. In Lines 15–17 of Algorithm 5, for each variable y in the variable set of F (excluding x) we spawn HyperOps in parallel to calculate whether y belongs to Σ_{same} or Σ_{other}. In Lines 1–10, we define the HyperOp. It takes as input Boolean polynomials A, B and a variable y and adds y to Σ_{same} or Σ_{other}. In Lines 18–20, we wait for the all the HyperOps to finish and output F_{same} and F_{other}.

Algorithm 5. Decomposition Algorithm using HyperOps

> **Input** Boolean polynomial to be factored F
> **Output** F_{same} and F_{other} which are the factors of the input polynomial F
> **Global variables** $\Sigma_{same}, \Sigma_{other}$

1: **Begin HyperOp**
2: Inputs: A, B, variable y
3: Calculate $C = \frac{\partial A}{\partial y}, D = \frac{\partial B}{\partial y}$
4: **if** IsEqual(A,D,B,C) **then**
5:     $\Sigma_{other} = \Sigma_{other} \cup \{y\}$
6: **else**
7:     $\Sigma_{same} = \Sigma_{same} \cup \{y\}$
8: **end if**
9: Call Sync HyperOp
10: **End HyperOp**
11: Take an arbitrary variable x occurring in F
12: Let $A = \frac{\partial F}{\partial z}, B = F_{z=0}$
13: Let $\Sigma_{same} = x, \Sigma_{other} = \emptyset, F_{same} = 0, F_{other} = 0$
14: **for each** $y \in var(F) \setminus \{x\}$ **do in parallel**
15:     Spawn HyperOp with inputs A, B, y
16: **end for**
17: Wait for the Sync HyperOp to return
18: If $\Sigma_{other} = \emptyset$ then F is non-factorable; stop
19: Return polynomials F_{same} and F_{other} obtained as projections onto Σ_{same} and Σ_{other}, respectively.

Table 3. Parallel factoring of synthetic boolean polynomials using REDEFINE emulation running on Intel Xeon processor at 2.8 GHz

Number of monomials	Sequential (cpu cycles)	Multi-threaded (cpu cycles)	Redefine (cpu cycles)
30	17192×10^3	7896×10^3	6837×10^3
50	45612×10^3	14196×10^3	12320×10^3

Listing 1.1 below shows the decomposition algorithm written in C with HyperOps. The proposed algorithm with HyperOps was evaluated using REDEFINE emulator executed on Intel Xeon processor. Table 3 shows the execution time of the decomposition algorithm executed on Redefine emulator on synthetic Boolean polynomials. The Redefine implementation has the lowest CPU cycles.

```
 1  __hyperOp__ void decompose(__CMAddr selfId , __Op32 a, __Op32 b,__Op32 p_s ,__Op32
        p_o , __Op32 m,__Op32 n, __Op32 i , __Op32 consumerFrId ){
 2
 3      int *A    = a.ptr ;
 4      int *B    = b.ptr ;
 5      int *partition_same = p_s.ptr ;
 6      int *partition_other = p_o.ptr ;
 7      int I = i.i32 ;
 8      int n = n.i32 ;
 9      int m = m.i32 ;
10      int I=0,J = 0;
11      int *C, *D;
12
13      __CMAddr confrId = consumerFrId.cmAddr ;
14      for (I = 0; I<n; I++){
15          *(partition_same+J) = 0;
16          *(partition_other+J) = 0;
17      }
18
19      for (I = 0; I<m; I++){
20          for(J=0;J<n;j++){
21              *(C+I*columns+J) = 0;
22              *(D+I*columns+J) = 0;
23          }
24      }
25      derivative(A,B,C,i );
26      derviative(A,B,D,i );
27      if(IsEqual(A,D,B,C)){
28          *(partition_other+i ) =1;
29      }
30      else{
31          *(partition_same+i ) =1;
32      }
33      __Sync( confrId , −1);
34  }
35
36
37  __kernel int decompose_start (int *A, int *B,int *partition_same , int *
        partition_other , int N){
38
39      int i = 0, j = 0;
40      static int counter = 0;
41      __CMAddr decomposeFr ;
42      __CMAddr syncFr = __CreateInst(&smd_Sync );
43      __WriteCM( CMADDR(syncFr , 15), N−1);
44
45      for (i = 1; i<N; i++){
46          decomposeFr = __CreateInst(&smd_decompose );
47          __WriteCM( CMADDR(decomposeFr , 0), (void *)(A));
48          __WriteCM( CMADDR(decomposeFr , 1), (void *)(B));
49          __WriteCM( CMADDR(decomposeFr , 2), (void *)(partition_same));
50          __WriteCM( CMADDR(decomposeFr , 3), (void *)(partition_other));
51          __WriteCM( CMADDR(decomposeFr , 4), M);
52          __WriteCM( CMADDR(decomposeFr , 5), N);
53          __WriteCM( CMADDR(decomposeFr , 6), i );
54          __WriteCM( CMADDR(decomposeFr , 7), CMADDR(syncFr ,15));
55      }
56      return 0;
57  }
```

Listing 1.1. Snippet of decomposition algorithm using Hyperops

6 Conclusions and Future Work

In this paper, we have reviewed the factorization problem for Boolean polynomials. Factorization provides the basis for decomposition of Boolean functions in DNF and for decomposition of data tables. Hence, it is important to develop efficient factorization procedures. We have considered the approach from [4] for factoring Boolean polynomials and presented a MIMD implementation thereof, which exploits task and data level parallelism to achieve better performance. Evaluation of the sequential and parallel algorithms on logic circuit synthesis benchmarks and synthetic Boolean polynomials showed a considerable speedup obtained by parallelization. The implementation of the parallel algorithm on a REDEFINE emulator outlined the performance benefits under execution on a massively parallel many core architecture. REDEFINE execution model is based on data flow principles and hence, the need for explicit barrier synchronization is obviated. This results in better performance of MIMD applications (Ex:Boolean factorization) on the REDEFINE architecture. In the future work we are going to benchmark the proposed parallel algorithm on REDEFINE hardware. We also plan to use REDEFINE for an efficient hardware implementation of Boolean functions given as Boolean polynomials and DNFs in order to efficiently implement decomposition algorithms for these representations. Finally, we are going to use these implementations for non-disjoint decomposition of DNFs [11] and data tables [3], which is based on massive computation of disjoint decompositions as a subtask.

References

1. Redefine - reconfigurable silicon core description. http://morphing.in/redefine. Accessed 07 Dec 2018
2. Corno, F., Reorda, M., Squillero, G.: RT-level ITC'99 benchmarks and first atpg results. IEEE Design Test Comput. **17**(3), 44–53 (2000). https://doi.org/10.1109/54.867894
3. Emelyanov, P.: On two kinds of dataset decomposition. In: Shi, Y., et al. (eds.) ICCS 2018. LNCS, vol. 10861, pp. 171–183. Springer, Cham (2018). https://doi.org/10.1007/978-3-319-93701-4_13
4. Emelyanov, P., Ponomaryov, D.: Algorithmic issues of AND-decomposition of boolean formulas. Programm. Comput. Softw. **41**(3), 162–169 (2015)
5. Emelyanov, P., Ponomaryov, D.: On tractability of disjoint and-decomposition of boolean formulas. In: Voronkov, A., Virbitskaite, I. (eds.) PSI 2014. LNCS, vol. 8974, pp. 92–101. Springer, Heidelberg (2015). https://doi.org/10.1007/978-3-662-46823-4_8
6. Emelyanov, P., Ponomaryov, D.: Cartesian decomposition in data analysis. In: Siberian Symposium on Data Science and Engineering (SSDSE) (2017)
7. Emelyanov, P., Ponomaryov, D.: On a polytime factorization algorithm for multi-linear polynomials over $\mathbb{F}_2$. In: Gerdt, V.P., Koepf, W., Seiler, W.M., Vorozhtsov, E.V. (eds.) CASC 2018. LNCS, vol. 11077, pp. 164–176. Springer, Cham (2018). https://doi.org/10.1007/978-3-319-99639-4_11
8. von zur Gathen, J., Gerhard, J.: Modern Computer Algebra, 3rd edn. Cambridge University Press, New York (2013)
9. Hansen, M.C., Yalcin, H., Hayes, J.P.: Unveiling the ISCAS-85 benchmarks: a case study in reverse engineering. IEEE Des. Test **16**(3), 72–80 (1999). https://doi.org/10.1109/54.785838
10. Muller, D.E.: Application of boolean algebra to switching circuit design and to error detection. IRE Trans. Electron. Comput. **EC–3**, 6–12 (1954)
11. Ponomaryov, D.: A polynomial time delta-decomposition algorithm for positive DNFs. In: van Bevern, R., Kucherov, G. (eds.) CSR 2019. LNCS, vol. 11532, pp. 325–336. Springer, Cham (2019). https://doi.org/10.1007/978-3-030-19955-5_28
12. Schmidt, J., Fišer, P.: A prudent approach to benchmark collection
13. Shpilka, A., Volkovich, I.: On the relation between polynomial identity testing and finding variable disjoint factors. In: Abramsky, S., Gavoille, C., Kirchner, C., Meyer auf der Heide, F., Spirakis, P.G. (eds.) ICALP 2010. LNCS, vol. 6198, pp. 408–419. Springer, Heidelberg (2010). https://doi.org/10.1007/978-3-642-14165-2_35
14. Zhegalkin, I.: Arithmetization of symbolic logics. Sbornik Math. **35**(1), 311–377 (1928). (in Russian)

Providing the Sharing of Heterogeneous Ontology Design Patterns in the Development of the Ontologies of Scientific Subject Domains

Yury Zagorulko[(⊠)] and Olesya Borovikova

A.P. Ershov Institute of Informatics Systems,
Lavrent'ev av., 6, Novosibirsk 630090, Russia
{zagor,olesya}@iis.nsk.su

Abstract. The paper describes an approach to solving the problems of using ontology design patterns (ODPs) for the development of the ontologies of scientific subject domains (SSDs). This approach offers a system of the heterogeneous ODPs, including both universal patterns and patterns oriented to the presentation of scientific knowledge, as well as methods of their joint use for building ontologies of SSDs. The use of this approach allows us to save resources spent on the development of ontologies, avoid errors common in ontological modeling, as well as ensure a consistent presentation of all the entities of the ontologies of scientific subject domains.

Keywords: Ontology · Scientific subject domain · Ontology design pattern · Structural pattern · Content pattern

1 Introduction

Currently, ontologies are the main means of formalization and systematization of knowledge in various subject areas including scientific subject domains (SSDs). (Note that by "scientific subject domain" we mean a subject area that encompasses a branch of science or field of scientific knowledge in all its aspects).

The development of ontology is a very complicated and time-consuming process. To simplify and facilitate it, various methods of and approaches to ontology development [1–4] have been proposed. Recently, an approach based on ontology design patterns (ODPs) [5–7] has gained popularity. According to this approach, ODPs are documented descriptions of proven solutions to typical problems of ontological modeling. Despite the fact that the use of ODPs allows us to greatly simplify the process of building ontologies and improves their quality, ontology

The work is financially supported by the Russian Foundation for Basic Research (Grant No. 19-07-00762) and by grant funding for scientific and (or) scientific and technical research for 2018–2020 MES RK (No. AP 05133546).

© Springer Nature Switzerland AG 2019
N. Bjørner et al. (Eds.): PSI 2019, LNCS 11964, pp. 95–105, 2019.
https://doi.org/10.1007/978-3-030-37487-7_8

design patterns have not yet found wide practical application due to a number of problems arising from their use.

One of the widespread problems of pattern reuse is their complexity: it is often difficult for the developer of a new ontology to understand the semantics the authors have laid down in the pattern. Another common problem is that the patterns are described and used separately and do not constitute a single system. In the development of ontologies of SSDs, there is yet another important problem, which is the absence of patterns designed to present scientific knowledge.

The paper presents the approach to the construction of ontologies of scientific subject domains based on the ODPs. The approach complements and develops the ontology development methodology proposed by the authors and used in development of intelligent scientific internet resources [8]. The ODPs used in this approach emerged as a result of solving the problems of ontological modeling, which the authors of the paper encountered in the process of developing ontologies for various scientific subject domains [9, 10].

This paper is organized as follows. The second section contains a short review of the ontology design patterns; the third section analyzes the problems of their use. The proposed approach to the development of ontologies of scientific subject domains is described in detail in the fourth section. The main advantages and practical benefits of this approach, as well as plans for the near future, are discussed in the Conclusion.

2   A Short Review of Ontology Design Patterns

The progenitors of ontology design patterns are design patterns, widely used in software development [11]. Similar to this design patterns, ODPs are employed to describe solutions of typical problems arising in the development of ontologies [7].

Depending on the problems for solution of which the ODPs are created, we distinguish between structural patterns, correspondence patterns, content patterns, reasoning patterns, presentation patterns and lexico-syntactic patterns. (Note that this typology of patterns was proposed in the framework of the NeOn project [12]).

From all types of patterns listed above only structural patterns, patterns of content and presentation are used in the development of ontologies.

The structural patterns either fix the ways to solve problems caused by the limitations of the expressive capabilities of ontology description languages or specify the general (modular) structure of an ontology. Patterns of the first type are called logical patterns, and patterns of the second type are called architectural patterns.

The content patterns define the ways of representing typical ontology fragments, on the basis of which ontologies of a whole class of subject domains can be built.

The presentation patterns actually represent the rules (recommendations) for naming and annotating elements of ontology. The application of these rules should increase the readability of the ontology, as well as the convenience and ease of its use.

Currently, several catalogs of ODPs have been created and are developing [13–15]. The most complete of them is posted on the ODPA (Association for Ontology Design & Patterns) portal [13], created as part of the NeOn project [12].

ODPs are most often described in the format proposed on the ODPA association portal [13]. According to it, the description of the pattern includes information about its author and scope, its graphical representation, text description, a set of scenarios and examples of usages, and links to other patterns. Content patterns can also be supplied with a set of competency questions [6,7], which can be used both in the development of patterns and in the search for the desired patterns in the development of a specific ontology.

3   Problems of Using Ontology Design Patterns

The first problem of pattern reuse is due to their complexity: it is often difficult for the developer of a new ontology to understand the semantics that the authors have laid down in the pattern. Recently there has been a tendency to simplify patterns [16]. Even so-called meta-patterns, describing very simple entities, were suggested [17]. However, such simple patterns cannot significantly facilitate the construction of SSD ontologies.

Another problem is caused by the lack of convenient ontology development tools supporting the use of ODPs. Here we can note the plugins for the ontology development tool of the project NeOn [18] and the ontology editor WebProtégé [19]. However, the first plugin is available only to the participants of the NeOn project, and the second can be used only in the WebProtégé editor, which is not yet popular enough among ontology developers due to its limited functionality (in comparison with the desktop version).

The third problem is that the patterns are described and applied separately and do not constitute a single system. One more problem associated with this problem is the lack of systematized sets of patterns targeted at subject matter experts. Existing catalogs of ontology design patterns do not meet this requirement.

In our opinion, the OTTR library (Reasonable Ontology Templates) [20] is the closest to solving the latter problem. This library provides a language for the representation of ontology design patterns and software supporting it. The OTTR library supplies ontology developers with patterns in the form of high-level OWL macros [21], which makes possible their use by subject matter experts.

As for the availability of patterns that can be used in the development of SSD ontologies, the catalogs mentioned above do not even partially cover the needs of building ontologies of scientific fields since they do not contain patterns designed to represent scientific knowledge.

4   Approach to the Development of Ontologies of Scientific Subject Domains

This section describes an approach to solving the problem of reusing ODPs in the development of ontologies of scientific subject domains. This approach offers a system of heterogeneous ODPs and methods for their sharing (joint use) for building SSD ontology. At the moment, there are three types of patterns in the system: structural logical patterns, content patterns and presentation patterns. One part of these patterns is universal, and the other part is focused on the presentation of scientific knowledge.

An important feature of this approach is the use of base (core) ontologies, which include only the most general entities that are not dependent on a particular SSD. These ontologies were previously developed for the technology for building subject-based intelligent scientific internet resources [8] and are now represented by content patterns which were developed for all main entities of base ontologies. In this regard, the construction of SSD ontology using the base ontologies is reduced to their specialization and expansion. In particular, the content patterns presented in the base ontologies are tuned (specialized) to a specific SSD. As for the population of SSD ontology with actual data, it is performed by instantiation of content patterns. This process is supported by a data editor developed in the frameworks of this approach.

4.1   An SSD Ontology and Base Ontologies

Usually the ontology of any SSD contains not only descriptions of its inherent system of concepts and methods for processing and analyzing information, but also descriptions of relevant information resources. In this regard, an SSD ontology can be represented as a system of interrelated ontologies responsible for representing the above three components of knowledge, namely, the ontology of the knowledge domain, the ontology of tasks and methods, and the ontology of scientific Internet resources.

The ontology of the knowledge domain defines the system of concepts and relations intended for a detailed description of a modeled SSD and its scientific and research activities. The ontology of tasks and methods describes the tasks solved in a given SSD and the methods for their solution. The ontology of scientific Internet resources is used to describe the information resources available on the Internet relevant to this SSD.

Since the development of an ontology of an SSD from scratch is not an easy task, we have proposed a method for its construction based on a small but representative set of base ontologies that include only the most general entities not dependent on a particular SSD. This set includes: (1) the ontology of scientific knowledge, (2) the ontology of scientific activity, (3) the base ontology of tasks and methods, (4) the base ontology of information resources.

All base ontologies have specifications in the OWL language [21].

The ontology of scientific knowledge contains classes that define structures for describing concepts included in any SSD. Such concepts are *Division of science, Object of research, Subject of research, Method of research, Scientific result*, etc.

The ontology of scientific activity includes classes of concepts related to the organization of research activities, such as *Person, Organization, Event, Activity (Scientific activity), Project, Publication*, etc.

The base ontology of information resources includes the class *Information resource* as the main class. The set of properties (attributes and relationships) of this class is based on the Dublin core standard [22].

Concepts and relations of base ontology of tasks and methods are used to describe tasks to be solved in a given SSD, methods for their solution and software components and algorithms implementing them.

4.2 A System of Ontology Design Patterns

To support the considered approach, a set of ODPs [23] was developed and implemented in the OWL language. This set includes various types of patterns: structural logical patterns, content patterns and presentation patterns. All these patterns are combined into a single system.

Note that in this approach the presentation patterns define the rules for naming and annotating elements of ontology, which are close to the generally accepted ones [24].

The need to use structural logical patterns was attributed to the absence in OWL of expressive means for representing complex entities and structures required for building SSD ontologies, in particular, the ranges of admissible values, and n-ary and attributed relations (a binary relation with attributes).

The pattern of representation of the range of admissible values is intended to specify such structures that are called domains in the relational data model and are characterized by a name and a set of elementary values. Domains are convenient to use for describing possible values of class properties when the entire set of such values is known in advance. In this pattern, the domain is defined by an enumerated class, which is the successor of the specially introduced service class called the Domain class and consists of a finite set of different individuals (objects) determining the possible values of a certain property (see Fig. 1).

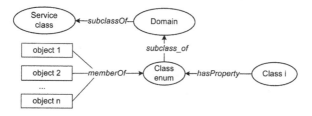

Fig. 1. Structural pattern of representation of the range of admissible values.

Examples of such domains are "Geographic type", "Position", "Type of organization", "Type of publication", which include, respectively, types of localities, types of positions in organization, types of organizations and publications.

Note that in the figures of the patterns presented in the paper, classes are shown in the form of ellipses, individuals and attributes are in the form of rectangles. An *ObjectProperty* type connection (a relation) is shown by a solid straight line, and a *DataProperty* type connection (an attribute), by a dash line. At the same time, classes, attributes and individuals, which must necessarily be present in the pattern, are represented by figures surrounded by a thick line.

To represent an attributed relation, a structural pattern is proposed. It is shown in the left side of Fig. 2.

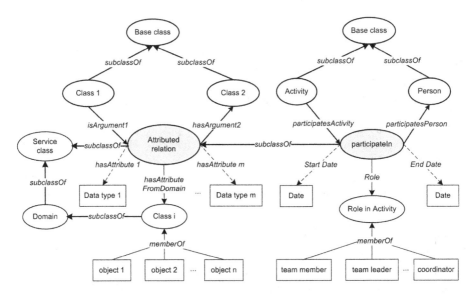

Fig. 2. Structural pattern of the binary attributed relation and an example of its specialization.

The central place in this pattern is occupied by the service class *Attributed relation* with which the base classes of an ontology modeling the arguments of the binary relation are connected by the links *isArgument1* and *hasArgument2*. At the same time, the attributes of a binary relation are modeled by the properties of this class (in OWL notation, either *DataProperty* or *ObjectProperty*) *hasAttribute* and *hasAttributeFromDomain*. For this pattern, it is required to set constraints on the obligatoriness and uniqueness of the arguments of the attributed relation (*Class 1* and *Class 2*).

To represent a specific type of the attributed relation, a new class, which is its successor, can be defined.

The right side of Fig. 2 shows an example of a structural pattern for describing a person's participation in scientific activities (the attributed relation *partic-*

ipateIn). Here, the *Person* class serves as the first argument, the *Activity* class is the second argument. The pattern also allows us to specify the start and end dates of the person's participation in an activity, as well as his/her role in it.

Similarly, we can build a pattern for an n-ary relation. Note that for this pattern we must also specify the order of the arguments.

For a uniform and consistent presentation of the concepts used in SSD and their properties, content patterns were constructed for the main concepts of base ontologies using the structural patterns proposed. Due to this, the development of an ontology of a specific SSD mainly consists in the specialization of content patterns and the construction of fragments of a target ontology based on them.

As an example, we give a pattern intended for the description of applied tasks solved within the framework of a scientific subject domain (see Fig. 3).

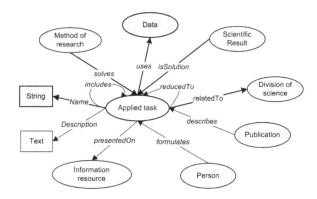

Fig. 3. Pattern for describing the applied task.

The following set of competency questions represents the content of this pattern:

What methods solve the applied task?

What data is used for solving the applied task?

What is the result of solving the applied task?

Who formulates the task?

and etc.

It should be noted that the content patterns included in the proposed set are interrelated through common concepts and relationships and thus form a single network of patterns. For example, presented in Fig. 4 content patterns, describing the concepts of *Activity* and *Person*, are interconnected not only by the attributed relation *participateIn*, but also through the concepts of *Scientific result*, *Method of research*, *Publication*, and *Organization*.

Note that in the Fig. 4 the attributed relations *participateIn* and *workIn* are shown by a dotted line.

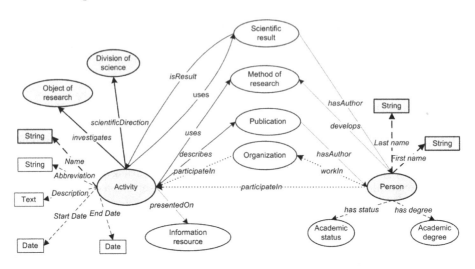

Fig. 4. Fragment of a network of patterns.

4.3 Methods of Building Ontologies of SSDs

Building an SSD ontology involves two main steps:

1. Construction of the components of SSD ontology using the base ontologies through their specialization and expansion.
2. Population of SSD ontology with actual data by instantiation of content patterns presented in base ontologies and specialized at step 1.

Note that in this approach the ontology of the knowledge domain is built on the basis of ontologies of scientific knowledge and scientific activity; ontology of tasks and methods, on the basis of base ontology of tasks and methods; and ontology of scientific Internet resources, on the basis of base ontology of Internet resources.

The use of content patterns is supported by a special editor, which allows specialists in the subject area to populate the ontology with actual data, i.e. objects of classes and their properties. When populating an ontology with the help of the editor, the user selects the required class from the class hierarchy presented to him, and the editor uses the class name to find the corresponding pattern. After that, the editor, using the information from the pattern, builds a form containing the fields for filling in all the properties of the object of this class. At the same time, the editor can interpret the relations with attributes described by the patterns. Thanks to this, the user can work with the properties of the created object that are set by such relations as with "ordinary" object properties. The difference consists only in the need to specify the values of the attributes in a separate window.

5   Conclusion and Future Work

The paper discusses the problems of applying ontological design patterns for the development of ontologies of scientific subject domains. An approach to the development of SSD ontologies that solves most of these problems is presented. This approach is supported by a system of heterogeneous ontology design patterns, describing the main structures and entities necessary for describing scientific domains, and the data editor, which makes it possible to populate the ontology with actual data by instantiation of content patterns. Due to the simplicity and clarity of the pattern system and the data editor, this approach can be used not only by knowledge engineers, but also by specialists in the modeled area of knowledge.

This approach has shown its practical utility in the development of ontologies of various scientific subject domains ("Decision Support" [25], "Active Seismology" [26], etc.).

In the near future, it is planned to expand this approach in such a way that it provides automated population of ontology. For this, the pattern system will be expanded with lexico-syntactic patterns [27], which will be used to facilitate the population (completion) of ontologies based on texts in the natural language. Lexico-syntactic patterns are supposed to be automatically generated based on the existing content and structural patterns using the synonyms dictionary and subject area thesaurus.

References

1. Fernández-López, M., Gómez-Pérez, A., Pazos, A., Pazos, J.: Building a chemical ontology using methontology and the ontology design environment. IEEE Intell. Syst. Appl. 4(1), 37–46 (1999)
2. Sure, Y., Staab, S., Studer, R.: Ontology engineering methodology. In: Staab, S., Studer, R. (eds.) Handbook on Ontologies. IHIS, pp. 135–152. Springer, Heidelberg (2009). https://doi.org/10.1007/978-3-540-92673-3_6
3. Pinto, H., Staab, S., Tempich, C.: DILIGENT: towards a fine-grained methodology for DIstributed, loosely-controlled and evolvInG Engineering of oNTologies. In: The Proceedings of the 16th European Conference on Artificial Intelligence. Frontiers in Artificial Intelligence and Applications, vol. 110, pp. 393–397. IOS Press, Amsterdam (2004)
4. De Nicola, A., Missikoff, M., Navigli, R.: A proposal for a unified process for ontology building: UPON. In: Andersen, K.V., Debenham, J., Wagner, R. (eds.) DEXA 2005. LNCS, vol. 3588, pp. 655–664. Springer, Heidelberg (2005). https://doi.org/10.1007/11546924_64
5. Gangemi, A., Presutti, V.: Ontology design patterns. In: Staab, S., Studer, R. (eds.) Handbook on Ontologies. IHIS, pp. 221–243. Springer, Heidelberg (2009). https://doi.org/10.1007/978-3-540-92673-3_10
6. Blomqvist, E., Hammar, K., Presutti, V.: Engineering ontologies with patterns: the eXtreme design methodology. In: Hitzler, P., Gangemi, A., Janowicz, K., Krisnadhi, A., Presutti, V. (eds.) Ontology Engineering with Ontology Design Patterns, Studies on the Semantic Web, vol. 25, pp. 23–50. IOS Press, Amsterdam (2016)

7. Karima, N., Hammar, K., Hitzler, P.: How to document ontology design patterns. In: Hammar, K., Hitzler, P., Krisnadhi, A., Lawrynowicz, A., Nuzzolese, A., Solanki, M. (eds.) Advances in Ontology Design and Patterns, Studies on the Semantic Web, vol. 32, pp. 15–28. IOS Press/AKA Verlag, Amsterdam/Berlin (2017)

8. Zagorulko, Y., Zagorulko, G.: Ontology-based technology for development of intelligent scientific internet resources. In: Fujita, H., Guizzi, G. (eds.) SoMeT 2015. CCIS, vol. 532, pp. 227–241. Springer, Cham (2015). https://doi.org/10.1007/978-3-319-22689-7_17

9. Zagorulko, Y., Borovikova, O.: Technology of ontology building for knowledge portals on humanities. In: Wolff, K.E., Palchunov, D.E., Zagoruiko, N.G., Andelfinger, U. (eds.) KONT/KPP -2007. LNCS (LNAI), vol. 6581, pp. 203–216. Springer, Heidelberg (2011). https://doi.org/10.1007/978-3-642-22140-8_13

10. Borovikova, O., Globa, L., Novogrudska, R., Ternovoy, M., Zagorulko, G., Zagorulko, Y.: Methodology for knowledge portals development: background, foundations, experience of application, problems and prospects. Joint NCC IIS Bull. Ser. Comput. Sci. **34**, 73–92 (2012)

11. Johnson, R., Vlissides, J., Helm, R.: Design Patterns: Elements of Reusable Object-Oriented Software by Erich Gamma. Addison-Wesley Professional, Boston (1994)

12. NeOn Project. http://www.neon-project.org. Accessed 2 Feb 2019

13. Association for Ontology Design & Patterns. http://ontologydesignpatterns.org. Accessed 2 Feb 2019

14. Ontology Design Patterns (ODPs) Public Catalog. http://odps.sourceforge.net. Accessed 2 Feb 2019

15. Dodds, L., Davis, I.: Linked data patterns (2012). http://patterns.dataincubator.org/book. Accessed 2 Feb 2019

16. Krisnadhi, A., Hitzler, P.: A core pattern for events. In: Hammar, K., Hitzler, P., Krisnadhi, A. (eds.) Advances in Ontology Design and Patterns, vol. 32, pp. 29–37. IOS Press, Kobe (2017)

17. Krisnadhi, A., Hitzler, P.: The stub metapattern. A core pattern for events. In: Hammar, K., Hitzler, P., Krisnadhi, A. (eds.) Advances in Ontology Design and Patterns, vol. 32, pp. 29–45. IOS Press, Kobe (2017)

18. Blomqvist, E., Presutti, V., Daga, E., Gangemi, A.: Experimenting with eXtreme design. In: Cimiano, P., Pinto, H.S. (eds.) EKAW 2010. LNCS (LNAI), vol. 6317, pp. 120–134. Springer, Heidelberg (2010). https://doi.org/10.1007/978-3-642-16438-5_9

19. Hammar, K.: Ontology design patterns in WebProtégé. In: The Proceedings of 14th International Semantic Web Conference (ISWC-2015). Posters & Demonstrations Track, p. 1486. CEUR Workshop Proceedings (2015). http://ceur-ws.org/Vol-1486/paper_50.pdf. Accessed 2 Feb 2019

20. Skjæveland, M.G., Forssell, H., Klüwer, J.W., Lupp, D., Thorstensen, E., Waaler, A.: Pattern-based ontology design and instantiation with reasonable ontology templates. In: The Proceedings of the 8th Workshop on Ontology Design and Patterns (WOP 2017), Vienna, Austria, 21 October, p. 2043. CEUR Workshop Proceedings (2017). http://ceur-ws.org/Vol-2043/paper-04.pdf. Accessed 2 Feb 2019

21. Antoniou, G., Harmelen, F.: Web ontology language: OWL. In: Staab, S., Studer, R. (eds.) Handbook on Ontologies, pp. 91–110. Springer, Berlin (2009). https://doi.org/10.1007/978-3-540-24750-0_4

22. DCMI Metadata Terms. http://dublincore.org/documents/dcmi-terms. Accessed 2 Feb 2019

23. Zagorulko, Y., Borovikova, O., Zagorulko, G.: Development of ontologies of scientific subject domains using ontology design patterns. In: Kalinichenko, L., Manolopoulos, Y., Malkov, O., Skvortsov, N., Stupnikov, S., Sukhomlin, V. (eds.) DAMDID/RCDL 2017. CCIS, vol. 822, pp. 141–156. Springer, Cham (2018). https://doi.org/10.1007/978-3-319-96553-6_11

24. Noy, N., McGuinness, D.: Ontology development 101: a guide to creating your first ontology. Stanford Knowledge Systems Laboratory Technical Report KSL-01-05 and Stanford Medical Informatics Technical Report SMI-2001-0880, March 2001, Stanford (2001)

25. Zagorulko, Y., Zagorulko, G.: Features of development of internet resource for supporting developers of intelligent decision support systems. In: The Proceedings of Eight International conference "Open Semantic Technologies for Intelligent Systems", Belarus, Minsk, pp. 63–66 (2018)

26. Braginskaya, L., Kovalevsky, V., Grigoryuk, A., Zagorulko, G.: Ontological approach to information support of investigations in active seismology. In: The Proceedings of the 2nd Russian-Pacific Conference on Computer Technology and Applications (RPC), Vladivostok, Russky Island, Russia, 25–29 September, pp. 27–29. IEEE Xplore digital library (2017). http://ieeexplore.ieee.org/document/8168060. Accessed 2 Feb 2019

27. Maynard, D., Funk, A., Peters, W.: Using lexico-syntactic ontology design patterns for ontology creation and population. In: Proceedings of WOP2009 Collocated with ISWC2009, vol. 516, pp. 39–52. CEUR-WS.org (2009). http://ceur-ws.org/Vol-516/pap08.pdf. Accessed 2 Feb 2019

The Analytical Object Model as a Base of Heterogeneous Data Integration

Anna Korobko[✉] and Anna Metus

Institute of Computational Modeling of the SB RAS, Krasnoyarsk, Russia
`lynx@icm.krasn.ru`

Abstract. When viewed the issue of analytical integration of heterogeneous data without warehouse building the unified model of diverse data sources has to be suggested. The desired model has to take into account analytical features of original file formats, to provide a construction of the integral analytical model and to attend to unlimited user data queries. This paper proposes the analytical object model in terms of a formal specification as the unified model and presents the mapping of an XSD schema and a relational database to this model. The model has been applied to analyze the All-Russia website of procurement that uses XML and The Local System of procurement that uses relation DB. The model instances obtained for each format are partly represented in this paper in the form of JSON.

Keywords: OLAP · Integral analytic model · Analytical integration of heterogeneous data · MDA · XML

1 Introduction

One of the most important aspects of the evolution of On-Line Analytical Processing (OLAP) is developing theoretical approaches to simultaneous analysis of heterogeneous data. OLAP tools are extensively used in decision support systems assisting managers of large companies with advanced analysis and reporting. As usual, a lot of business information flows from internal sources, that provides an accumulation of the great amount of operational data [1]. In some sources [2], the internal data that are owned by the decision-maker and can be directly incorporated into the decisional process are called stationary. Each source is a special-purpose data store associated with its data format. Joined internal sources represent a model for heterogeneous data. However, with significant growth of the number of open-access databases, it becomes possible to involve external data in the decision-making process for extra benefits. Valuable external data which may be related, for instance, to the market, to competitors, or potential customers, are called situational data [3]. Well-informed and effective decisions often require a tight relationship between stationary and situational data [2].

© Springer Nature Switzerland AG 2019
N. Bjørner et al. (Eds.): PSI 2019, LNCS 11964, pp. 106–115, 2019.
https://doi.org/10.1007/978-3-030-37487-7_9

Analysis of municipal procurement is the task demanding simultaneous analysis of heterogeneous data. According to the Federal Law N 44-FZ "Contract system in the procurement of goods, works and services for state and municipal needs" the Official All-Russia website of procurement (zakupki.gov.ru) has been developed. It consolidates municipal demands, ongoing purchases and contracts all over the country. It sends and receives data in XML format according to system pre-defined XSD schemas. Otherwise, the Local System of procurement forms municipal demand orders and scheduled plan of purchases. The Local System has a bidirectional link with the All-Russia website of procurement. Also, the Local System uses Oracle DBMS to store data and metadata. From the regional government perspective, the Local System data is an internal data source and the All-Russia website data is an external one. An analyst, who wants to trace some purchase from a demand order to a contract, or to analyze some supplier activity, needs to integrate these heterogeneous data.

Complex analysis of internal and external data together concerns reconciling (merging) diverse data sources. Often this step is performed by data warehouse building or integration of separate analysis results while representing. This process requires highly qualified analysts to intent and extra time for data actualization and preparation.

We can consider related works from different points of view. Nowadays, the complex analysis of heterogeneous data is actively discussed by researchers [4–11]. In speaking about ideology, there are several conceptual foundations for OLAP technology development which have been suggested by modern leading researchers. Thus, the concept of self-service Business Intelligence [2,12] reduces the requirements for user skills. On the other hand, the concept of exploratory OLAP supports ad-hoc arbitrary query execution [1,13]. The conceptual description of these approaches shows further researches a way forward, leaving them a wide discretion for realization. From the logical viewpoint, modern researches unanimously recognize the need for constructing a global (or a mediated) schema that enables uniform access to the data [14]. The particular realizations of the approaches are rather different. They fall somewhere on the spectrum between warehousing and virtual integration [15]. Approaches to extraction, transformation and loading data to a centralized warehouse are proposed in [16,17]. But it requires highly experienced modelers and designers to compare a wide variety of domain concepts. Standards of heterogeneous data interchange have been already developed that provide creating an unified format of data exchange [18]. However, there aren't common algorithms for transforming miscellaneous data into this specific standard. As a virtual global schema, ontology is proposed [15] for information disclosure from integrated data. This approach isn't aimed for analytical processing notwithstanding its grace and feasibility. The analytical model of data source [19] has been suggested under the "virtual schema" approach. Moreover, it allows us to reduce the requirements to user-analysts skills so that analytical concepts (measures and dimensions) can be arranged according to their analytical features that mean grouped into the same request allowed by data consistency. The model serves to view all available data in a multidimensional form and provides unlimited querying without knowledge specified about database structure, functional dependencies and SQL. Another technology concept of operational analysis of heterogeneous data was suggested to avoid warehouse building. This technology constructs the integral analytical model by comparing and integrating of original data sources automatically. This integral model supports the design and performance of random user data query straight to an original data store and delineates author vision of implementation of heterogeneous data analysis.

Analytical integration of heterogeneous data without warehouse building requires the unified model of diverse data sources has to be suggested. The desired model has to take into account the analytical features of original file formats, to provide a construction of the integral analytical model and to attend to unlimited user data queries.

This paper proposes the analytical object model (AOM) as the unified model. The AOM is a metamodel describing the structure for model instances of original data sources regardless of its format. Mapping of an XSD schema and a relational database to this model is presented. Matching of source structure items for model items in municipal procurement analysis is presented.

2   The Formal Specification of the Analytical Object Model

Development of the analytical object model accords with the model-driven development (MDD) of information systems, based on 4 level modeling [18]. The highest level (M3) describes a modeling specification and the lowest one (M0) describes program system data. To develop the analytical object model model-driven approach allows creating metamodel (M2) for describing the model instance structure of the original data source regardless of its format. During system lifecycle this model services to sources metadata store, sources link details and instances production and maintain order. At the abstract layer, the analytical object model is a base of heterogeneous system integration and unifies data format particularities.

Furthermore, the analytical object model has to take into account the analytical features of original file formats to provide a multidimensional form for OLAP. Consortium OMG specifies open standard Common Warehouse Metamodel to combine multidimensional modeling and model-driven approach for data warehouses. The standard consists of the set of metamodels for data interchange within the conceptual layer and assumes data moving to a warehouse manually. Model instances production taking into account implementation requirements are beyond the standard scope, so it needs to be produced additionally. Automatical source integration without warehouse building requires the standard extension by adding analytical object metamodel. Suggested metamodel determinates the unified structure of a source regardless of its format and consists of analytical classes such as "AssociationClass", "DAttribute", "FAttribute" "Hierarchy". "AssociationClass" is a container class for other items. It matches the

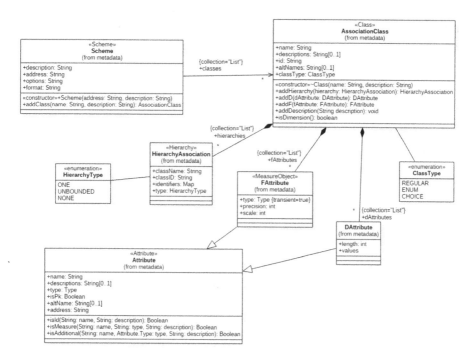

Fig. 1. The class diagram for the analytical object model for integrating sources.

source items of a top level. The model has been applied to analyze municipal procurement. There are XML and relational data formats in this task.

So, integration of these two sources model instances is produced from XML Schema Definition and Oracle database. The class diagram of the analytical object model is shown in Fig. 1 using UML.

"AssociationClass" instances are created for each table in relation source and each complex type in XSD. Inner simple types and relation table column relates "DAttribute" class (descriptive attribute) or "FAttribute" class (fact attribute) depending on its analytical features and links "AssociationClass" with the composite association. "Hierarchy" class instances describe analytical relations between source items, it matches foreign keys in a relational data source and parent-child relations in XSD. Full rules to produce analytical model instances for relation DB and XSD metadata are shown in Table 1.

The unified representation of diverse data sources in the form of the analytical object model allows producing a single algorithm of multidimensional form constructing and merging structures of heterogeneous data sources into an integral analytical model. Like traditional multidimensional approach numerical data produces measures, descriptive attribute forms dimensions and "Hierarchy" instances arrange dimensions hierarchically. Every model class has features to facilitate both multidimensional modeling and user query support. "Scheme" class has the connection properties of physical data sources.

Table 1. Matching of XSD and relation DB metadata and analytical object model items

Analytical object model	Relation DB metadata	XSD metadata
class "AssociationClass"	a table	- a complexType
		- a simpleType (enumeration restricted)
		- a choice
		*elements with the same name (type, if exist) and inner elements relate the same AssociationClass
+name: String	a table name	value of a element name attribute
+descriptions: String [0..*]	- a table description or a table name in Russian;	value of a documentation element
	- a description of foreign keys to this table	
+id	an auto increment identifier	
+altNames: String [0..*]	a foreign key name to this table	value of a complexType name attribute
+classType: [REGULAR, ENUM, CHOICE]	REGULAR (fixed value)	REGULAR - if an element type is a complexType;
		ENUM - if an element is a restricted by enumeration one;
		CHOICE - if it is a choice element
class "DAttribute"	a column, if it's of string, boolean or primary key types	an element based on a simpleType (String, Boolean Integer type)
+name: String	a column name value of	an element name attribute
+descriptions: String [0..*]	a column description	- value of a documentation element;
		- value of a simpleType name attribute
+type: [BOOLEAN, DATE, DATETIME, INTEGER, NUMERIC, STRING]	system data types	
+isPK: Boolean	TRUE – if the column contains a primary key, otherwise FALSE	TRUE – if an element is required, otherwise FALSE
+altName	no value	value of an simpleType name attribute if a type of the element relates the one
+values	no value	enumeration values for restricted simpleType
+address	no value	a specified wildcard (@) - if an element is an attribute, otherwise - no value
+length	a data type length	a data type length, according to restrictions:
		- facets maxLength, maxExclusive-1, maxInclusive;
		- pattern value
		- 0 – unrestricted length

(continued)

Table 1. (*continued*)

Analytical object model	Relation DB metadata	XSD metadata
class "FAttribute"	a column, if it's of decimal type	an element based on a simpleType (Double, Decimal)
+name: String	a column name	value of an element name attribute
+descriptions: String [0..*]	a column description	- value of a documentation element; - value of a simpleType name attribute
+type	system data types	NUMERIC − fixed for "xs:double", "xs:decimal"
+isPK	FALSE − fixed	FALSE − fixed
+altName	no value	value of an simpleType name attribute if a type of the element relates the one
+address	no value	a specified wildcard (@) - if an element is an attribute, otherwise - no value
+precision	count of numbers	according to facets totalDigits, pattern. otherwise 0 − unrestricted
+scale	count of digits following the decimal point	according to facets ractionDigits, pattern. otherwise 0 − unrestricted
class "Hierarchy Association"	a foreign key	parent-child relation
+className	a name of the table related by the foreign key	a name of an inner complexType element
+classID	an unique id of the table related by the foreign key	an unique id of the inner complexType element related by the foreign key
+identifiers	pairs of foreign key - primary key	no value
+type: [ONE, UNBOUNDED]	ONE - fixed	ONE - if maxOccures attribute value of the child element equals one UNBOUNDED - if maxOccures attribute value of the child element more than one

Having produced the AOM, an analyst is able to select objects for analysis regardless of which source owns them. After the objects are selected, the AOM maintains the query construction process due to preserving structure peculiarities of the data source format.

3 An Example of Analytical Object Model Instance Producing

According to the approach a program system was developed to produce an instance of an analytical object model for a source to be integrated automatically. The program system has services specified for XML and relational data format. Each service is capable to construct AOM for one of the format types

```
{ ▼ 5 properties, 366 bytes
  "name": "OKEI",
  "description": "Reference to OKEI",
  "hierarchies": [],
  "dAttributes": [ ▼ 3 items, 260 bytes
    { ▶ 5 properties, 84 bytes "name": "code", "description": "Cod", "ty…},
    { ▶ 4 properties, 89 bytes "name": "nationalCode", "description": "N…},
    { ▶ 4 properties, 79 bytes "name": "fullName", "description": "Full …}
  ],
  "fAttributes": []
},
{ ▼ 5 properties, 1015 bytes
  "name": "product",
  "description": "The object of the procurement",
  "hierarchies": [ ▼ 2 items, 117 bytes
    { ▶ 2 properties, 58 bytes "className": "OKPD", "identifiers": { 1 p…},
    { ▼ 2 properties, 55 bytes
      "className": "OKEI",
      "identifiers": { ▼ 1 property, 20 bytes
        "OKEI_code": "code"
      }
    }
  ],
  "dAttributes": [ ▼ 3 items, 284 bytes
    { ▶ 4 properties, 84 bytes "name": "sid", "description": "Unique ide…},
    { ▶ 4 properties, 108 bytes "name": "externalSid", "description": "Ex…},
    { ▶ 4 properties, 88 bytes "name": "name", "description": "Product n…}
  ],
  "fAttributes": [ ▼ 5 items, 502 bytes
    { ▼ 4 properties, 93 bytes
      "name": "price",
      "description": "Unit price in the contract currency",
      "precision": 10,
      "scale": 0
    },
    { ▶ 4 properties, 91 bytes "name": "priceRUR", "description": "Unit …},
    { ▶ 4 properties, 81 bytes "name": "sum", "description": "Cost in co…},
    { ▶ 4 properties, 83 bytes "name": "sumRUR", "description": "Cost in…},
    { ▶ 4 properties, 142 bytes "name": "quantity", "description": "Quant…}
  ]
}
```

Fig. 2. A part of the analytical object model instance for fcsExtegration.xsd

and to send it to a server in the form of JSON. The server is capable to construct a multidimensional model and subsequently to produce the integral analytical model. The AOM instance obtained for XSD format when analyzed the All-Russia website of procurement (zakupki.gov.ru) is partly shown in Fig. 2 in the form of JSON.

The hierarchies elements of "product" class accord with the relation between "Hierarchy" and "AssociationClass". Particularly according to this instance a product relates the All-Russian Classifier of Products (OKPD) and the All-Russia Classifier of Measurement Units (OKEI). The analytical object model takes into account both XML peculiarities and relational database ones. Another

AOM instance obtained for relation format when analyzed the Local System of procurement is partly shown in Fig. 3 in the form of JSON. This part of the AOM instance presents the All-Russia Classifier of Measurement Units (OKEI) and its descriptive attributes.

```
{ ▼ 5 properties, 951 bytes
  "name": "FOKEI",
  "description": "Russian classifier of measurement units",
  "hierarchies": [],
  "dAttributes": [ ▼ 9 items, 822 bytes
    { ▶ 4 properties, 78 bytes "name": "FOKEI", "description": "Name title… },
    { ▶ 4 properties, 89 bytes "name": "RUSSIAN", "description": "Symbol c… },
    { ▶ 4 properties, 94 bytes "name": "ENGLISH", "description": "Symbol c… },
    { ▶ 4 properties, 82 bytes "name": "COD_3", "description": "Three-digi… },
    { ▶ 5 properties, 94 bytes "name": "IDFOKEI", "description": "Identifi… },
    { ▶ 4 properties, 89 bytes "name": "SECT", "description": "Classifier … },
    { ▶ 4 properties, 95 bytes "name": "GRUPA", "description": "Code group… },
    { ▶ 4 properties, 74 bytes "name": "COD", "description": "OKEI code", … },
    { ▶ 3 properties, 107 bytes "name": "RU", "description": "The basis of … }
  ],
  "fAttributes": []
}
```

Fig. 3. A part of the analytical object model instance for the Local System of procurement

The popularity of relational and XML data formats allows involving additional information concerning the business environment from a large number of open data sources in the analysis. So, XML format is used by Federal State Statistics Service for social and macroeconomics statistics [19], by the Central Bank of Russia for financial market indicators [20], by Federal Tax Service for open governmental data [21]. Also, a large number of research and academic institutions across the world create relational databases in various fields of science and technology, which are available free through web portals [22,23].

Complete deployment of the program system based on the suggested model and its successful beta testing on analyzing municipal procurement data verify the approach. Further developing of the technology of integral analytical modeling concern producing and testing of the algorithm of multidimensional view forming based on AOM.

4 Conclusion

The analytical object model has been suggested. The model formally describes the analytical and structural peculiarities of heterogeneous data sources to overcome their diversity and to allow them to be integrated automatically. Possibility to include some source to the integral model without warehouse building is provided with analyzing of analytical features and relations of a source format. Retaining a format metadata arrangement contributes to supporting unlimited user data queries.

References

1. Ibragimov, D., Hose, K., Pedersen, T.B., Zimányi, E.: Towards exploratory OLAP over linked open data – a case study. In: Castellanos, M., Dayal, U., Pedersen, T.B., Tatbul, N. (eds.) BIRTE 2013-2014. LNBIP, vol. 206, pp. 114–132. Springer, Heidelberg (2015). https://doi.org/10.1007/978-3-662-46839-5_8
2. Abelló, A., et al.: Fusion cubes: towards self-service business intelligence. Int. J. Data Warehous. Min. **9**, 66–88 (2013)
3. Löser, A., Hueske, F., Markl, V.: Situational business intelligence. In: Castellanos, M., Dayal, U., Sellis, T. (eds.) BIRTE 2008. LNBIP, vol. 27, pp. 1–11. Springer, Heidelberg (2009). https://doi.org/10.1007/978-3-642-03422-0_1
4. Gallinucci, E., Golfarelli, M., Rizzi, S., Abelló, A., Romero, O.: Interactive multidimensional modeling of linked data for exploratory OLAP. Inf. Syst. **77**, 86–104 (2018)
5. Alpar, P., Schulz, M.: Self-Service business intelligence. Bus. Inf. Syst. Eng. **58**, 151–155 (2016)
6. Chen, H., Chiang, R.H., Storey, V.C.: Business intelligence and analytics: from big data to big impact. MIS Q. **36**, 1165–1188 (2012)
7. Singh, R., Yoon, V.Y., Redmond, R.T.: Integrating data mining and on-line analytical processing for intelligent decision systems. J. Decis. Syst. **11**, 185–204 (2002)
8. Baranović, M., Kalpić, D., Brkić, L.: Application of semantic and structural similarity for schema reuse in conceptual database design. In: Proceedings 6th WSEAS European Computing Conference (ECC 2012), pp. 368–373 (2012)
9. Cuzzocrea, A., Bellatreche, L., Song, I.-Y.: Data warehousing and OLAP over big data: current challenges and future research directions. In: Proceedings of the Sixteenth International Workshop on Data Warehousing and OLAP - DOLAP 2013, pp. 67–70 (2013)
10. Pe, J.M., Rafael, B., Aramburu, M.J., Pederson, T.B.: Integrating data warehouses with web data: a survey. IEEE Trans. Knowl. Data Eng. **20**, 940–955 (2008)
11. Salem, R., Boussaïd, O., Darmont, J.: Active XML-based web data integration. Inf. Syst. Front. **15**, 371–398 (2013)
12. Varga, J., Romero, O., Pedersen, T.B., Thomsen, C.: Analytical metadata modeling for next generation BI systems. J. Syst. Softw. **144**, 240–254 (2018)
13. Rizzi, S., Gallinucci, E., Golfarelli, M., Romero, O., Abelló, A.: Towards exploratory OLAP on linked data. In: In: 24th Italian Symposium on Advanced Database Systems, SEBD 2016, pp. 86–93 (2016)
14. Benedikt, M., Cuenca Grau, B., Kostylev, E.V.: Logical foundations of information disclosure in ontology-based data integration. Artif. Intell. **262**, 52–95 (2018)
15. Doan, A.H., Alon, H., Zachary, I.: Principles of Data Integration. Elsevier, Amsterdam (2012)
16. Luján-Mora, S., Vassiliadis, P., Trujillo, J.: Data mapping diagrams for data warehouse design with UML. In: Atzeni, P., Chu, W., Lu, H., Zhou, S., Ling, T.-W. (eds.) ER 2004. LNCS, vol. 3288, pp. 191–204. Springer, Heidelberg (2004). https://doi.org/10.1007/978-3-540-30464-7_16
17. Kimball, R., Ross, M.: The Data Warehouse Toolkit, The Definitive Guide to Dimensional Modeling. Wiley, Hoboken (2013)
18. OMG, Object Management Group: Object Management Group, Model Driven Architecture (MDA), pp. 1–15. OMG Doc. ormsc/2014-06-01. 2.0 (2014)
19. Korobko, A.V., Penkova, T.G.: On-line analytical processing based on formal concept analysis. Procedia Comput. Sci. **1**, 2311–2317 (2010)

20. Federal State Statistics Service. http://www.gks.ru/wps/wcm/connect/rosstat_main/rosstat/ru/statistics/accounts/
21. Central Bank of Russia for financial market indicators. http://www.cbr.ru/development/DWS/
22. Federal Tax Service for open governmental data. https://www.nalog.ru/opendata/
23. Listing of Open Access Databases - LOADB. http://www.loadb.org/Control.do?_brse

Prediction of RNA Secondary Structure Based on Optimization in the Space of Its Descriptors by the Simulated Annealing Algorithm

Nikolay Kobalo[1]([✉]), Alexander Kulikov[1], and Igor Titov[2]

[1] Institute of Computational Mathematics and Mathematical Geophysics
SB RAS, Novosibirsk, Russia
rerf2010rerf@yandex.ru, kulikovail2@gmail.com
[2] Institute of Cytology and Genetics SB RAS, Novosibirsk, Russia
titov@bionet.nsc.ru

Abstract. The proportion of genome coding proteins is only a small part of a whole genome (for example, about 5% in human's genome). Among other things the remaining part contains regulatory RNAs whose function depends on their three-dimensional structure. Secondary structure is the first level of RNA structure description (three-dimensional structure is approximated by secondary structure).

Therefore the problem of determining the common secondary structure of isofunctional RNA sequences (i.e., a set having similar functionality) is an important and longstanding problem of bioinformatics. In this paper we present the program which builds the secondary structure model for a such set of non-homologous RNA sequences.

Secondary structure is described by directed acyclic graph i.e. multitree. The problem of determining the model of secondary structure is reduced to the discrete optimization task in the space of structure multitrees. The optimizable function depends on the energy of the referenced sequences being folded into this structure.

The optimization task is solved by simulated annealing algorithm. We developed the program for building a common secondary structure model of RNA and compared it with the existing solutions on the set of mobile group II introns.

Keywords: RNA · Secondary structure prediction · Mobile group II intron · Optimization · Simulated annealing · Software

1 Introduction

The task of determining the common secondary structure of a set of RNA sequences with the same functionality is an important task of bioinformatics. However, currently existing methods make it possible to effectively build models of secondary structures only for small sets of sequences. In addition, they do not work well with sets of low-homologous sequences and do not allow to take into account *a priori* information about the structure of sequences.

© Springer Nature Switzerland AG 2019
N. Bjørner et al. (Eds.): PSI 2019, LNCS 11964, pp. 116–124, 2019.
https://doi.org/10.1007/978-3-030-37487-7_10

This paper presents a new method for constructing a secondary structure model for a variety of sequences. This method is based on reducing the problem of constructing a model to the problem of discrete optimization in the space of all possible models, and the optimized parameter is the energy of the resulting structure [1].

In Fig. 1 shows an example of a tRNA secondary structure and shows the elements of which it is composed. As it can be seen, the secondary structure consists of stems formed by paired nucleotide bases and loops - free RNA segments.

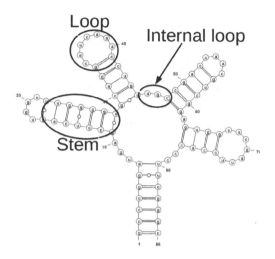

Fig. 1. An example of the secondary structure of RNA

2 Basic Requirements for the Secondary Structure Prediction Method

The following requirements are imposed on our method.

- Ability to build models for sets of sequences of any size. At the same time, it should detect and correctly handle the situation when the set is a mixture of sequences that actually have different secondary structure.
- Ability to build models for sets of low homologous sequences.
- There are cases when some general information about the structure of RNA sequences belonging to a given set is known in advance. The method should allow to set this *a priori* information and take it into account when building a model.
- After setting the initial parameters and *a priori* information about the structure, the system should work in automatic mode and not require manual intervention.
- The system must provide a practically acceptable speed of building a model.

3   Review of Existing Software for Predicting the Secondary Structure of RNA

Consider a few common methods and software that implements them that meet the requirements - the ability to work with sets of low homologous sequences and the ability to set *a priori* information about the structure.

- RNAStructure Multialign - predicts the secondary structure of a set of three or more RNA sequences using the minimum energy estimate [2].
- RNAStructure TurboFold - predicts the secondary structure of two or more sequences. It generates pairwise alignments for the set using a hidden markov model, which supplies extrinsic information to one of three selectable folding modes [3].
- PFold - this algorithm allows to specify some *a priori* information about the secondary structure, such as the exact position of the nucleotides that should be paired in the resulting structure or, in contrast, free [4].

4   Used Programs and Real Data

- Our method uses the RScan program [5] to determine the correspondence of the constructed model of the secondary structure to specific sequences and calculate its energy.
- To test the program, a set of 40 sequences was used, each 72 nucleotides in length, with the same secondary structure shown in Fig. 4. These sequences were taken from rfam [6]. For this set, the value of the optimal secondary structure energy was calculated [7].
- The sequences of the first domain of the following mobile introns of group II [8, 9] were used: Pylaiella littoralis cox1.I3 and 8 other introns, with the first domain similar to it in its secondary structure: Thalassiosira pseudooana cox1.I2, Allomyces macrogynus cox1.I3, Podaspora anserina cox1.I1, Podaspora anserina cox1.I4, Podaspora comata cox1.I1, Kluyveromyces lactis cox1.I1, Saccharomyces cerevisiae cox1.I2 and Schizosaccharomyces pombe cox1.I1. The average length of these sequences is 405 nucleotides.
- To compare programs, a set of 10 tRNA sequences from rfam tRNA-Sec RF01852 [10] were also used. The average length of the sequences of this set is 89 nucleotides.

5   Method Description

5.1   Data Representation

The model of the secondary structure of RNA is represented as an oriented acyclic graph—a multi-tree. In this case, the stems are represented by the edges of a multi-tree, and the loops – by the vertices.

Each element of the tree has a set of attributes that define restrictions on the elements of the secondary structure. The following attributes are supported:

- Permitted length range of elements (loops and stems).
- The sequence of nucleotides, which must necessarily be present on this element and its position relative to the beginning of the element.

For example, in Fig. 2b shows an example of a secondary structure model, and Fig. 2a - its representation in the form of a multi-tree.

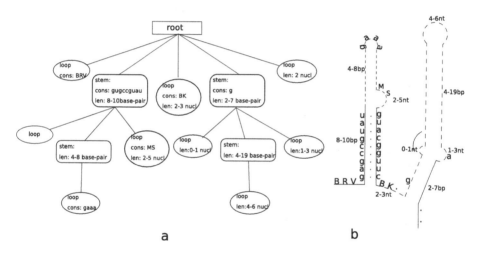

Fig. 2. a: Multi-tree modeling the secondary structure of RNA; b: The corresponding secondary structure of RNA

5.2   Reducing to Discrete Optimization Task

The problem of building a model of the secondary structure of a set of RNA sequences is reduced to the discrete optimization task as follows:

Let be:

- T - is the set of all admissible multi-trees representing the secondary structure.
- $S = \{s | s \in n^*, n \in \{a, u, g, c\}\}$ - is the finite set of words in the alphabet a, u, g, c, representing the set of RNA nucleotide sequences for which the secondary structure model is built.

- $R(t, s) : T \times S \rightarrow \mathbb{R}$ - is a function that calculates for a given multi-tree and sequence the value of the energy of a given sequence, folded into a given structure. $R(t, s) = \infty$, if the sequence s cannot be folded into the structure t.
- $C(t, S)$ - is the number of sequences $s \in S$, such that $R(t, s) < \infty$.
- $E(t, S)$ - is the average energy for all sequences $s \in S$, such that $R(t, s) < \infty$.
- $T(t, S)$ - is the average computation time for $R(t, S)$.

Then the expression $F(x) = -k_1 E(t, S) + k_2 T(t, S) - k_3 C(t, S)$ defines the objective function for the problem of discrete optimization in the multi-tree space T. Coefficients k_1, k_2, k_3 are selected in each specific case manually and set when the program is started.

In this expression, the first term takes into account the energy of the secondary structure, which is a measure of its stability and should be minimized. The second term allows to take into account the calculation time of the objective function using the RScan program. The inclusion of this term in the objective function is important from a practical point of view, because it allows to speed up the calculation. The third term of the expression allows to build a model for as many sequences as possible from the original set. At the same time, it allows the algorithm to correctly handle the situation when the set of sequences is an actual mixture of sets with different secondary structure.

6   Solution of the Optimization Task

To solve the optimization task described above, an annealing simulation algorithm was applied. To start the computation, you must specify some initial model of the secondary structure. At each iteration, the annealing simulation algorithm applies one or more of the following mutation operators to a multi-tree:

- Changing the value of a numeric attribute of a multi-tree element (for example, the range of lengths or the position of the consensus sequence, if specified).
- Adding a leaf to the tree, or deleting an existing one.
- Adding a vertex to an arbitrary multi-tree location, or deleting an existing one.

All the described operators select a part of the tree for modification at random. The last two operators correspond to the addition or removal from the tree of a random element of the secondary structure - a stem or loop, as shown in Fig. 3a and b.

The described algorithm was implemented in java and is available on github [11]. To calculate the value of the function $R(t, s)$, the RScan program is used.

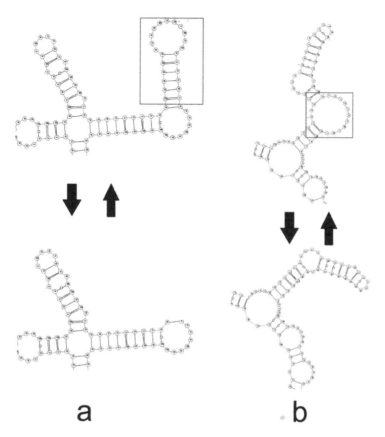

Fig. 3. a: Modification of the secondary structure by adding or removing a multi-tree leaf; b: Modification of the secondary structure by adding or removing the inner vertex of a multi-tree.

7   Testing

7.1   Evaluation of the Accuracy of the Solution

To verify the accuracy of solving the optimization task found by the implemented algorithm, a set of 40 sequences with the same optimal secondary structure was formed and the implemented program was launched on it. The following parameters were used: $k_1 = 10$, $k_2 = 1$, $k_3 = 10$.

Table 1 shows the optimal and program-determined values of each term of the objective function.

Table 1. Comparison of optimal and predicted secondary structure models

Structure	Time of computation	Optimal energy	Number of sequences	Cost function
Optimal	40	144	40	−1800
Predicted	169	126	40	−1491

The sensitivity and F-measure were also calculated [12]:

- Sensetivity = 0.9
- F-Measure = 0.95.

In Fig. 4b shows the optimal secondary structure of the considered set of sequences, and Fig. 4a - predicted by the program.

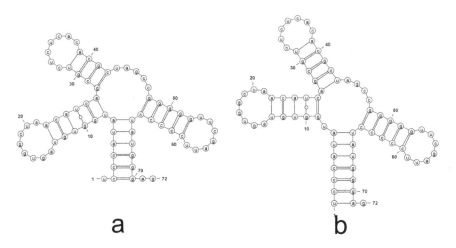

a   b

Fig. 4. a: Predicted secondary structure for test set; b: Optimal secondary structure of the test set.

7.2   Comparison of Programs

The program was also tested on a sample of the rfam family tRNA-Sec sequences. For each predicted structure, the number of erroneously predicted paired bases was calculated. Then, sensitivity and F-measure were calculated for all sequences. The results obtained for all compared programs are shown in Table 2.

Table 2. Comparison of programs on a sample of transport RNA sequences

Program	Sensetivity	F-measure	Time of computation
Simulated annealing	0.79	0.8	13 min
PFold	0.42	0.5	2 s
RNAStructure multialign	0.8	0.82	7 min
RNAStructure TurboFold	0.79	0.82	40 s

Also, the programs were launched on a set of 9 group II introns. We took introns, the secondary structure of which best corresponds to the generalized structure of intron data [13].

Table 3 shows the program comparison

Table 3. Comparison of programs on a sample of group II introns

Program	Sensitivity	F-measure	Time of computation
Simulated annealing	0.51	0.53	~112 h
PFold	0.06	0.07	6 s
RNAStructure multialign	0.38	0.4	~21 h
RNAStructure TurboFold	0.46	0.47	320 s

As one can see from the Tables 2 and 3, on the set of small sequences of tRNA with an average length of 89 nucleotides, the proposed method gives the results comparable with other existing methods. However, for large sequences of group II introns with an average length of 405 nucleotides and complex secondary structure, the developed method gives more accurate results.

Acknowledgements. The work of I.T. was supported by the Federal Agency of Scientific Organizations (project #0324-2019-0040).

References

1. Skiena, S.: The Algorithm Design Manual, 2nd edn. Springer, Heidelberg (2010). https://doi.org/10.1007/978-1-84800-070-4
2. Reuter, J., Mathews, D.H.: RNAstructure: software for RNA secondary structure prediction and analysis. J. Biomol. Struct. Dyn. **26**, 831–832 (2009)
3. Harmanci, A.O., Sharma, G., Mathews, D.H.: TurboFold: iterative probabilistic estimation of secondary structures for multiple RNA sequences. BMC Bioinform. **12**, 108 (2011). https://doi.org/10.1186/1471-2105-12-108
4. Sukosd, Z., Knudsen, B., Kjems, J., Pedersen, C.N.S.: PPfold 3.0: fast RNA secondary structure prediction using phylogeny and auxiliary data. Bioinformatics **28**(16), 2012. https://doi.org/10.1093/bioinformatics/bts488
5. http://www.softberry.com/freedownloadhelp/rna/rscan/rscan.all.html
6. Rfam family of tRNA. http://rfam.xfam.org/family/RF00005
7. Jaeger, J.A., Turner, D.H., Zuker, M.: Improved predictions of secondary structures for RNA. Proc. Natl. Acad. Sci. U.S.A. **86**, 7706–7710 (1989)
8. Candales, M.A., et al.: Database for bacterial group II introns. Nucleic Acids Res. 187–190 (2012). https://doi.org/10.1093/nar/gkr1043
9. Fontaine, J.M., Goux, D., Kloareg, B., Loiseaux-de Goer, S.: The reverse-transcriptase-like proteins encoded by group II introns in the mitochondrial genome of the brown alga pylaiella littoralis belong to two different lineages which apparently coevolved with the group II ribosyme lineages. J. Mol. Evol. **44**, 33–42 (1997). https://doi.org/10.1007/PL00006119

10. Rfam family of selenocysteine transfer RNA http://rfam.xfam.org/family/RF01852
11. https://github.com/rerf2010rerf/RNAStructBuilder
12. Powers, D.M.W.: Evaluation: from precision, recall and F-Measure to ROC, informedness, markedness & correlation (PDF). J. Mach. Learn. Technol. **2**(1), 37–63 (2011)
13. Zimmerly, S., Semper, C.: Evolution of group II introns. Mob. DNA **6**, 7 (2015). https://doi.org/10.1186/s13100-015-0037-5

A Metamodel-Based Approach for Adding Modularization to KeYmaera's Input Syntax

Thomas Baar$^{(\boxtimes)}$ (iD)

Department of Engineering I, Hochschule für Technik und Wirtschaft (HTW) Berlin,
Wilhelminenhofstraße 75A, 12459 Berlin, Germany
`thomas.baar@htw-berlin.de`

Abstract. The theorem prover KeYmaera allows (1) to describe Cyber-Physical Systems (CPSs) in terms of a Hybrid Program (HP), (2) to specify properties for the defined system, and (3) to formally verify these properties using a tailored logic called Differential Dynamic Logic (DDL).

The syntax of Hybrid Programs is rather poor and covers only the most basic program statements, such as assignment, test, sequential execution, and iteration. The decision to keep the syntax of HPs very simple has different consequences: An advantage is that also the verification calculus can be kept relatively simple. On the downside we have that even small programs are hard to understand and that the programmer is forced to program using a copy-and-paste style, which obviously hampers maintenance. The most significant drawback, however, is the absence of modularization and a library concept; making the development and verification of bigger systems a huge burden.

In this paper, we identify several problems of KeYmaera's input syntax and illustrate them with examples. To overcome these problems, we first describe the original syntax in form of a metamodel. Then, we propose to extend this metamodel with established programming concepts such as subprogram and abrupt termination. We illustrate our extensions by using a new graphical concrete syntax. Examples from a recent KeYmaera tutorial serve for our paper as illustration examples.

Keywords: Cyber-Physical System (CPS) · Safety property verification · Theorem proving · Language design · Domain-Specific Language (DSL) · Metamodel

1 Motivation

A Cyber-Physical System (CPS) is a system existing in the real world, which usually consists of both cyber and physical components. The behaviour of a cyber component is determined by the (computer) program, which is executed

This work was supported in part by the Deutsche Forschungsgemeinschaft (DFG, German Research Foundation) - project number 415309034.

N. Bjørner et al. (Eds.): PSI 2019, LNCS 11964, pp. 125–139, 2019.
https://doi.org/10.1007/978-3-030-37487-7_11

on this component while the behaviour of a physical component follows laws from physics, e.g. for torque, acceleration, velocity, etc. An important subset of CPSs are control systems consisting of sensors, processors, and actuators, whose correct functioning is of upmost importance and should be assured by formal verification techniques.

A hybrid system is a formal model of a CPS. To capture the behaviour of cyber components, the hybrid system needs the notion of programs. The behaviour of physical components are modelled by law in physics, which are formulated in terms of ordinary differential equations (ODEs). The theorem prover KeYmaera is able to formally verify properties of hybrid systems formulated in differential dynamic logic (DDL) [13, 18]. In this paper, we analyse DDL as used by KeYmaera as input format. We point out some obstacles of the chosen input syntax and make proposals to overcome them.

One of the main problems of the used DDL is, that this single formalism is used for three different purposes, namely, to (i) describe the system to be analysed (*system description*), to (ii) formulate the properties to be hold for the system (*system specification*), and (iii) formulate proofs (*system verification*). Note that a proof is a tree of DDL-formulas where each connection between nodes of the proof tree must be justified by one rule of the used proof calculus.

Thus, the very same DDL formalism serves quite different purposes and there are some cases, in which it is hard to say, which purpose a given DDL artefact actually serves. For example, the user of KeYmaera is sometimes forced to reformulate a system description in a non-intuitive way, just to make a property of this system verifiable. In other words, the property *about* the system one would like to prove has a strong influence on the way one describes the system itself! Note that - ideally - one should be able to formulate the system description fully independent from the properties one would like to prove - usually later - about the system. As we illustrate with a model of the very simple bouncing ball example, this independence is sometimes not possible. This makes the usage of KeYmaera rather an art than an engineering discipline.

The input syntax for KeYmaera is very rudimentary and forces the user to describe a system is a Big Blob, since modularization, e.g. by subsystems or subprograms, is simply syntactically not possible. In our analysis, we identify also other weaknesses, for example that the correct function of evolutional states rely on executing the right statement before entering the state or that evolutional states usually share a high portion of ODEs. Unfortunately, the current syntax makes it impossible to let an evolutional state 'inherit' from an already defined evolutional state to prevent a copy-paste style in the system description.

In addition to identifying problems of KeYmaera's input syntax, we also make proposals to overcome these problems. In order to describe our solutions at the right level of abstraction, our solution proposal will address the abstract syntax - which we define in form of a metamodel - instead of the textual concrete syntax. In order to stress the independence of our solution proposals from the concrete syntax, we will employ also a graphical syntax, which is close to the Abstract Syntax Tree (AST).

2   Background

We first review the logical basis of the prover KeYmaera.

2.1   Dynamic Logic (DL)

The term Dynamic Logic (DL) was coined for the first time by Harel et al. in [7], which is based on the work of Pratt [16] and Hoare/Floyd [4,8]. A recent review on the history of Dynamic Logic is given by Pratt in [17].

Dynamic Logic has a long tradition in analysing *programs running on a machine*. (First-Order) Dynamic Logic allows for a program α to formulate properties for the pre- and post-state of the program's execution. Syntactically, DL formulas are built on top of arithmetic terms and arithmetic atomic formulas, such as $x < 5 + 3$. The set of DL formulas is closed under the logical junctors $\land, \lor, \to, \leftrightarrow$, under the quantifiers $\forall \; \exists$, and under the parametrized modalities $[\alpha]$ (*box*), $<\alpha>$ (*diamond*), where α is a program. A program is syntactically defined as a tree of statements. We have *assignment* ($:=$), *test* ($?$), *skip* (*skip*[1]) as atomic statements and *nondeterministic choice* ($\cup$), *sequential composition* ($;$), and *iteration* ($*$) as composed statements. Furthermore, some derived statements (known as *syntactic sugar*) are allowed. For example, the program *if c then s1 else s2 endif* is defined as an abbreviation for $(?c; s1) \cup (?\neg c; s2)$. In the version of DL supported by KeYmaera, all terms (e.g. $3 + 8$) including variables are of type Real, so there is no support for a sophisticated type system. For a thorough introduction to Dynamic Logic in syntax and semantics, the reader is referred to [6].

Semantically, a formula of form $\phi \to [\alpha]\psi$ claims that program α, when started in a state in which ϕ holds, might not terminate or, in case it actually terminates, will result always in a state, in which ψ holds. The second modality $<>$ (diamond), which can occur in DL-formulas as well, has a different semantics: $<\alpha> \psi$ claims that program α terminates and that for at least one post-state the formula ψ holds (note, that α can behave non-deterministically).

As a concrete example, let us consider the formula

$$x > 0 \to [\textit{if } x > 0 \textit{ then } x := x - 1 \textit{ else } x := -25 \textit{ endif}; x := x + 1] \; x > 0 \quad (1)$$

The program α within the box modality is the sequential composition (operator $;$) of an if-statement and an assignment (operator $:=$). The claim, formulated by (1) about program α reads as follows: Whenever α is started in a state, in which $x > 0$ holds, then $x > 0$ must also hold once α has terminated (note, that termination of α is not part of the claim). Formula (1) is actually valid, i.e. under all circumstances the formula is evaluated to true (see [6] for a formal definition of validity).

It is rather easy to argue informally on the validity of (1): This implication evaluates only to false, when its premise evaluates to true and its conclusion to

---

[1] Since *skip* can be simulated by *? true* it is not supported by all versions of KeYmaera.

false. The premise is $x > 0$. Under this assumption, when executing program α, the then-branch of the first statement (if-statement) is always taken and decreases variable x by one. In the second statement, the value of x is again increased by one, so the value of x in the post-state – let us denote it by x_{post} – is $x_{post} = x_{pre} - 1 + 1$, while x_{pre} denotes the value of variable x in the pre-state. The conclusion of (1) can thus be reduced to the proof obligation $x_{pre} - 1 + 1 > 0$, which can never evaluate to false if we assume $x_{pre} > 0$. Fortunately, we do not have to rely on informal argumentation for showing the validity of (1) but can also use the theorem prover KeYmaera, which proves (1) fully automatically.

Please note that the formulas of DL do not make any claim about the execution time of program α, but only formulate properties on the relationship of α's pre- and post-states. You might just think all statements within program α being executed instantaneously, i.e. their execution does not take any time. This is an important difference to the extension of DL, called Differential Dynamic Logic (DDL), we consider next.

2.2 Differential Dynamic Logic (DDL)

DDL [12] is an extension of DL, which means that every DL formula is also a DDL formula. The same way as DL formulas, a DDL formula usually makes a claim about a program α. However, since DDL formulas are mainly used to describe the behaviour of Cyber-Physical Systems, we rather say that program α *encodes the behaviour of the CPS* instead of α *is executed on a machine*, as we do for programs α of pure DL formulas.

The only difference between DL and DDL is a new kind of statement called *continuous evolution statement* (or simply *evolution statement*), which is allowed to occur in programs α. When during the execution of α a continuous evolution statement is reached, then the execution of this statement *takes time* and the system will stay in the corresponding *evolution state* for a while. Note that this is a new semantic concept of DDL and marks an important difference to pure DL!

Executing the evolution statement means for the modelled CPS to stay in the evolution state as long as it wishes (the time to stay is - in general - chosen non-deterministically). However, the modeller has two possibilities to restrict the time period the system stays in the evolution state: The first possibility is to add a so-called *domain constraint* to the evolution statement, which is a first-order formula and which is separated from the rest of the statement by & (ampersand). The domain constraint semantically means that the system cannot stay longer in the evolution state than the time at which the constraint is evaluated to *true*. In other words: at latest when the evaluation of the domain constraint switches from *true* to *false*, the system has to leave the evolution state.

The second possibility to restrict the time period is to have a sequential composition of an evolution statement followed by a test statement. Theoretically, the machine can leave the evolution state at any time, but if the following test evaluates to *false*, then this branch of execution is dismissed for the logical analysis of the system behaviour. Thus, an evolution statement immediately followed by a test statement is a general technique to force the system to remain in the evolution state as long as the test condition is evaluated to *false*.

Bouncing Ball as a Simple CPS. We illustrate both the usage of an evolution statement as well as the two mentioned techniques to control the time the system will stay in the evolution state by the following bouncing ball example:

$$\alpha_{BB} \equiv (\{x' = v, v' = -g \ \& \ x \geq 0\}; ?x = 0; v := -cv)* \tag{2}$$

The behaviour of the bouncing ball is described with the help of a new kind of variables, called *continuous variables*. For example, variable x is always a non-negative number and encodes the ball's position and variable v encodes velocity, which can be both positive (going up) or negative (going down). The constant g is the gravitation acceleration and greater 0. The constant c is the damping coefficient, a number between 0 and 1.

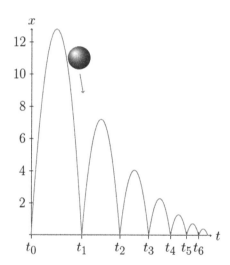

Fig. 1. Sample trajectory of a bouncing ball (Source: [13, p. 98])

The structure of α_{BB} is that of an iteration (operator *) over a sequence (operator ;) of an evolution statement (enclosed by the curly braces), followed by a test (operator ?), followed by an assignment (operator :=). The program α_{BB} is read as follows: The systems starts in a state with given values for variables x and v. These values are not specified yet, but later, we will force the start position x_0 to be a positive number while the start velocity v_0 is allowed to be positive, zero, or negative. As long as the system stays in the first evolution state, the values of x, v will change continuously over time according to physical laws. Thus, the continuous variables x, v represent rather functions $x(t), v(t)$ over time t. The relevant physical laws for x, v are expressed by the two differential equations: $x' = v, v' = -g$.

The latter means that the velocity decreases constantly over time due to the gravitational force of the earth. Fortunately, this ODE has a simple polynomial solution, which facilitates the analysis of the whole system considerably: $v(t) = v_0 + -g * t$. Analogously, depending on the changing velocity v, the position x of the bouncing ball changes with $x(t) = x_0 + v_0 * t + \frac{-g}{2}t^2$.

The domain constraint $x \geq 0$ mentioned in the evolution statement allows the system to remain in the evolution state only as long as x is non-negative. Theoretically, the system can leave at any time the evolution state, but the next statement is the test $?x = 0$. Thus, if the system leaves the evolution state with $x > 0$, then this computational branch will be discarded. Thus, when verifying properties of the system we can rely on the system leaving the evolution state only when $x = 0$, meaning when the ball touches the ground. The following assignment $v := -cv$ encodes that the ball goes up again: The negative value v due to the ball falling down will change instantaneously to a positive value (multiplication with $-c$) but the absolute value of v decreases since the ball loses energy when touching the ground and changing the move direction. Figure 1 shows how the position x of a bouncing ball might change over time (sample trajectory).

3   Problems in Using KeYmaera's Input Syntax

Differential Dynamic Logic as introduced above is supported by KeYmaera and allows to verify formally important properties of technical system as demonstrated in numerous case studies from different domains, e.g. aircrafts [9,14], trains [15], and robots [11].

However, the used input syntax to formulate properties in form of DDL formulas suffers from numerous problems that are described in the following. The solutions we propose to overcome these problems are discussed in Sect. 4.

(1) **Invariant specification is not directly supported in DDL.** Besides describing the behaviour of hybrid systems as done with program α_{BB} for the bouncing ball, the main purpose of DDL is to specify also properties of such systems. Typical and in practice very important properties are so-called *safety properties*, saying that the system never runs into a 'bad situation'. Let's encode a 'bad situation' with $\neg\psi$. We can show the absence of $\neg\psi$ by proving that in all reachable system states formula ψ holds, i.e. ψ is an invariant. If we assume all statements except the evolution state are executed instantaneously, then showing invariant ψ actually means to show that ψ holds while the system stays in any of its evolution states. However, the modality operators provided by DDL allow only to describe the state *after* the program has terminated. For example, for the bouncing ball system α_{BB} defined in (2) we can prove very easily

$$x = 0 \rightarrow [\alpha_{BB}]x = 0 \tag{3}$$

Note, however, that $x = 0$ has not been proven to be an invariant! If we want to express the interesting invariant, that position x remains all the time within the interval $[0, H]$, while H encodes the system's initial position and if velocity v is initially 0, we have to admit that the formula

$$H > 0 \wedge v = 0 \wedge x = H \wedge 0 < c \wedge c < 1 \rightarrow [\alpha_{BB}]x \leq H \qquad (4)$$

is provable, but does NOT encode $x \leq H$ being an invariant because this formula does not say anything about x and H *while* the system stays in the evolution state $\{x' = v, v' = -g \ \& \ x \geq 0\}$, which is part of α_{BB}. In order to prove $x \leq H$ being an invariant the user is forced to reformulate α_{BB} to

$$\alpha'_{BB} \equiv (\{x' = v, v' = -g \ \& \ x \geq 0\}; (skip \cup (?x = 0; v := -cv))* \qquad (5)$$

This, however, would be an example for choosing the system description depending on the property we would like to prove! We consider this as bad style.

(2) **Evolution state definition cannot be reused.** Evolution statements have to contain all ODEs that should hold in the corresponding states. If a program contains multiple evolution statements, then all ODEs usually have to be copied for all these statements, since an ODE normally encodes a physical law that holds in each of the evolution states. Currently, the syntax of KeYmaera does not allow to define all ODEs once and then to reuse this definition for all occurring evolution statements. This lack of reuse results in a copy-and-paste style for describing a system. As an example, we refer to Example 3a from the KeYmaera-tutorial [18], page 10, Eq. (20): $\{p' = v, v' = -a \ \& \ v \geq 0 \wedge p + \frac{v^2}{2B} \leq S\} \cup \{p' = v, v' = -a \ \& \ v \geq 0 \wedge p + \frac{v^2}{2B} \geq S\}$ Here, the definition of the two evolution states (in curly braces) are very similar and defined by copy-and-paste.

(3) **Evolution state definition is not encapsulated.** In the KeYmaera-tutorials [12,18], there is a frequently applied pattern to ensure that the system stays in an evolution state $ev \equiv \{\ldots \& \ldots\}$ for at most time ϵ. This is achieved by extending the definition of ev to $ev' \equiv \{\ldots, t' = 1\& \ldots \wedge t \leq \epsilon\}$ while t is a fresh continuous variable. Together with the ODE $t' = 1$, the additional domain constraint $t \leq \epsilon$ forces the system to leave ev' at latest after time ϵ has elapsed. However, this refined definition of ev works only, if the value of t has been set beforehand to 0. In order to achieve this, the statement ev is usually substituted by $t := 0; ev'$. While this pattern works basically in practice, the definition of ev' is not encapsulated and prevents compositionality of programs.

(4) **Missing notion of subprogram (or function call in general).** Once the examples in the KeYmaera-tutorials [12,18] become a little bit more complicate, they are given in a composed form, e.g. Example 3a from [18, p. 10]: $init \rightarrow [(ctrl; plant)*]req$ where $init \equiv \ldots$, $ctrl \equiv \ldots$, $plant \equiv \ldots$, $req \equiv \ldots$ Presenting a DDL problem in such a composed form highly improves readability. However, the usage of such a composed notation is impossible for the input file of KeYmaera. While one could imagine to

introduce new relational symbols *init, req* and to constrain their interpretation by subformulas *init* ↔ ..., *req* ↔ ..., it is currently impossible to define subprograms *ctrl* and *plant* and to compose the resulting program from these subprograms.

4   A Metamodel-Based Approach to Solve Identified Problems

The problems identified above can be overcome by incorporating language concepts from object-oriented programming languages and statecharts into the input syntax of KeYmaera. In order to discuss the incorporated new language concepts at the right level of abstraction, we formulate our proposal in form of a changed metamodel for KeYmaera's input syntax. As a starting point, we present the metamodel of the current syntax.

4.1   Metamodel of Current KeYmaera Syntax

Metamodeling [5] is a widely adopted technique to specify the abstract syntax of modelling and programming languages. One well-known language definition is that of the Unified Modeling Language (UML) [19].

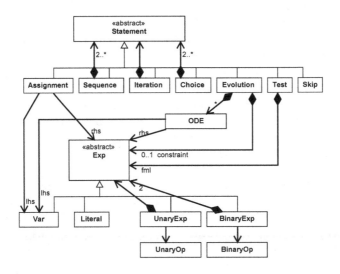

Fig. 2. Metamodel of KeYmaera's input syntax

Figure 2 shows a sketch of the metamodel of KeYmaera's current input syntax with focus on statements within a program. All meta-associations with multiplicity greater than 1 are assumed to be ordered. If the multiplicity on a meta-association is missing, then 1 is the default value. The metaclass Exp represents expressions of both type *Real* (e.g. 5 + x) and of type *Boolean* (e.g. x < 10).

A concrete program α for KeYmaera can be represented by an instance of the metamodel. This instance is equivalent to the result obtained by parsing this program, i.e. the abstract syntax tree (AST).

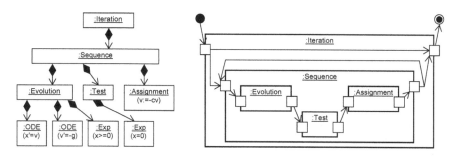

Fig. 3. Instance of the metamodel (left) and control-flow inspired graphical syntax (right) for bouncing ball program (α_{BB})

The left part of Fig. 3 shows the metamodel instance for the bouncing ball program $\alpha_{BB} \equiv (\{x' = v, v' = -g \ \& \ x \geq 0\}; ?x = 0; v := -cv)*$ as defined in (2). In the right part we see an AST-aligned graphical representation of the same program: Each kind of statement is represented by a block with input and output pins. The control flow is visualized by directed edges connecting two pins. The pre-/post-states of the program execution are represented by the symbol for start/final state known from UML's statemachine [19].

4.2   Solutions for Identified Problems

Based of the graphical notation introduced above we discuss now solutions for the problems listed in Sect. 3.

(1) Invariant specification is not directly supported in DDL. As described in Sect. 3, the modal operator [α] refers always to the post-state represented by the final state node in Fig. 3, right part. However, for checking an invariant we need a reference to the state after each evolution statement has been finished. This moment in the execution is represented by the output-pin of the Evolution state. What is needed in the program semantics is a direct edge from each output-pin of each Evolution state to the final state, as shown in Fig. 4 by the green edge. This concept is known as *abrupt termination*.

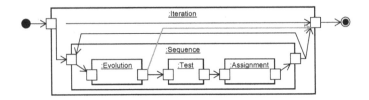

Fig. 4. Solution for invariant specification problem

Note that abrupt termination could be realized without any change of the input syntax of KeYmaera since it requires merely a changed control-flow for the existing statements.

(2) Evolution state definition cannot be reused. Often, the very same ODEs and constraints occur again and again in multiple evolution statements, which hampers readability. To prevent this, our proposal is to introduce the *declaration of* named evolution statements which can be referenced by other evolution statement to - for example - inherit from them ODEs and constraints. The relevant change of the metamodel is shown in Fig. 5.

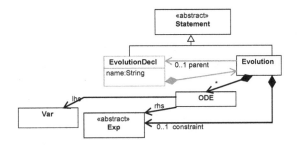

Fig. 5. Solution for evolution state reuse problem

One problem still to be discussed is, whether the declaration of an evolution state can occur at an arbitrary location in the program or should be rather done prior to the program as a global declaration. This question refers to the important issue of which scope the identifier introduced by the declaration (see metaattribute **name**) should actually have. Since resolving the scope of an identifier is rather a problem when parsing a program, this issue is out of scope for this paper.

(3) Evolution state definition is not encapsulated. As demonstrated in the problem definition, an evolution statement sometimes works only as intended when a variable has been set beforehand to the right value. Practically this means, the evolution state EV is always prepended by an assignment $ASGN$, so $(ASGN; EV)$ has to occur always for correctness. In order to get rid of dependencies of evolution state to assignments from the context (which prevents a simple reuse of *EV* within a different context), we propose to extend the evolution state with optional additional statements that are always executed when entering or leaving the state. This state extension is well-known as entry-/exit-actions from UML statemachines. The relevant change of the metamodel is shown in Fig. 6.

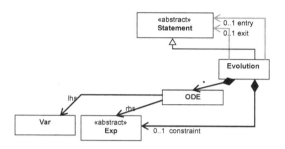

Fig. 6. Solution for evolution state encapsulation problem

(4) **Missing notion of subprogram.** One of the most basic concepts in programming is the possibility to encapsulate (a block of) statements with a given name and to reuse these statements at various locations of the program. This concept is usually called *subprogram*, *procedure*, or *method*; depending whether parameters are used or not. In general, this is a very old, proven and well understood concept, so that we introduce only the most simple variant in our solution proposal here (cmp. Fig. 7).

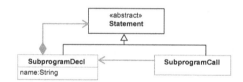

Fig. 7. Solution for missing subprogram problem

5   Towards the Realization of Solution Proposals

In this section we review possible realization options for the proposed solution. Finally, we give a recommendation for one realization option.

5.1   Realization by Extending the Prover KeYmaera

The prover KeYmaera mainly consists of a parser for the input syntax and a calculus in form of proof rules, which even can be changed by the user. In addition, there are some technical components such as (i) a prover engine for applying proof rules to create a formal proof, (ii) adapters to incorporate external proof systems such as *Z3* or *Mathematica*, and (iii) a GUI to control the proof editing process. However, all these technical components are out of scope for this paper.

For our proposals it is worth to distinguish pure syntactic changes from those, that have an impact on the calculus used by KeYmaera. To the latter belong the support of abrupt termination (problem (1)) and the possibility to invoke subprograms (problem (4)). These changes would require to considerably extend KeYmaera's calculus. While such an extension requires intimate knowledge of the underlying proof engine, it is nevertheless possible, as the prover KeY [1][2] demonstrates. KeY is an interactive verification tool for programs implemented in the language Java and its calculus covers all the subtleties of a real world programming language, including *function calls, call stack, variable scope, abrupt termination* by throwing an exception, *heap analysis*, etc.

Pure syntactic changes among our proposals, i.e. addressing problems (2), (3), could be realized in KeYmaera just by extending the parser. Note that the creation of an alternative concrete input syntax is also topic of the ongoing project called Sphinx [10] carried out by the authors of KeYmaera. Sphinx aims to add a graphical frontend to the prover and will allow the user to specify a program in a pure graphical syntax (similar to our graphical notation proposed in Fig. 3, right part).

The general problem with any deep change of the prover KeYmaera is the technical knowledge it requires. Furthermore, there are good reasons to keep a version of the tool with the original syntax due to its simplicity, what makes it much simpler to use KeYmaera for teaching than, for example, its predecessor KeY. However, a new version of KeYmaera with deep changes is hard to maintain as the original KeYmaera might evolve in future. For these reasons, deep changes can hardly be done by others than the original authors of KeYmaera themselves.

5.2   Realization by Creating a Frontend-DSL

An alternative and flexible approach is the development of a frontend-DSL to incorporate the new language concepts introduced in Sect. 4.2. The main idea is to develop a new Domain-Specific Language according to the given metamodel. Note that the metamodel covers merely the abstract syntax and keeps some flexibility for the concrete syntax. Modern frameworks for defining DSLs such as Xtext and Sirius even allow to have for one DSL *multiple* representations (i.e. *concrete syntaxes*) supported by corresponding editors, e.g. a textual syntax and a graphical syntax. Figure 8 shows the general architecture of such a tool. Note that the new tool will allow the user to interact synchronously with both a textual and a graphical editor to create a model. However, the new models cannot be simply transformed to input files for the original KeYmaera, because the new syntax supports some semantically new concepts such as abrupt termination or subprogram invocation stack. It is the task of the ProofManagement component

---

[2] Historically, the prover KeY is the predecessor of KeYmaera.

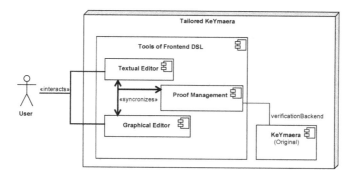

Fig. 8. Architecture of solution using a frontend-DSL

to split tasks - for instance to prove an invariant - into smaller proof obligations, which can be formulated as formulas of differential dynamic logic (DDL) and to pass these obligations to the original KeYmaera tool as verification backend. How an invariant task can be split into smaller proof obligations is demonstrated based on a concrete example in [2].

6   Related Work

The definition of DSLs can be done with numerous technologies, e.g. Xtext, Spoofax, Metaedit, MPS. For realizing a DSL with both a textual and a graphical concrete syntax, the combination Xtext and Sirius is very attractive.

Enriching the prover KeYmaera with a graphical syntax for DDL programs is done in the project Sphinx [10]. The architecture of this tool is pretty similar to our proposal in Fig. 8, but the focus is - in difference to our approach - not the improvement of readability and modularization by making the input syntax richer, but to enable the user to graphically construct a program for DDL.

While enriching a plain, imperative language with concepts from object-oriented programming has been done many times in computing science's history (take the transition from C to C++ or from Modula to Oberon as examples), it is still considered as a challenge. There is an excellent tutorial by Bettini in [3] on how to incorporate into a plain sequential language based on simple expressions additional concepts from object-oriented programming (e.g. *class, attribute, method, visibility*). The resulting language in this tutorial is called *SmallJava* and illustrates almost all technical difficulties when realizing a Java-like programming language in form of a DSL.

7   Conclusion and Future Work

The syntax of programs of differential dynamic logic as supported by the theorem prover KeYmaera have been kept very simple and low level. An advantage of this decision is that also the calculus for proving such programs being correct could be kept relatively simple and that proofs can be constructed and understood easily. At the downside we have that - once the examples become a little bit more complicate - programs are hard to read, poorly structured, and are impossible to reuse within a different context.

In this paper, we identified four general problems when applying the current program syntax in practice. Furthermore, we made proposals to overcome the identified problems by incorporating proven language concepts from programming languages and from UML's statemachines into KeYmaera's input syntax. These concepts have the potential to make programs scalable and easier to be understood since they foster readability and modularization.

Our proposals have been formulated in form of a changed metamodel representing the abstract syntax of programs. The chosen form for formulating the proposal has the advantage of being very precise while leaving it open, how the changes should actually be realized in a given concrete syntax. Currently, the implementation of a frontend DSL being the main constituent of a *Tailored KeYmaera* tool set is under construction, but not finished yet.

References

1. Ahrendt, W., Beckert, B., Bubel, R., Hähnle, R., Schmitt, P.H., Ulbrich, M. (eds.): Deductive Software Verification - The KeY Book - From Theory to Practice. LNCS, vol. 10001. Springer, Heidelberg (2016). https://doi.org/10.1007/978-3-319-49812-6
2. Baar, T., Staroletov, S.: A control flow graph based approach to make the verification of cyber-physical systems using KeYmaera easier. Model. Anal. Inf. Syst. **25**(5), 465–480 (2018)
3. Bettini, L.: Implementing Domain-Specific Languages with Xtext and Xtend, 2nd edn. Packt Publisher, Birmingham (2016)
4. Floyd, R.W.: Assigning meanings to programs. In: Schwartz, J.T. (ed.) Proceedings of Symposium on Applied Mathematics, pp. 19–32. Mathematical Aspects of Computer Science, American Mathematical Society (1967)
5. Gonzalez-Perez, C., Henderson-Sellers, B.: Metamodelling for Software Engineering. Wiley, Hoboken (2008)
6. Harel, D., Kozen, D., Tiuryn, J.: Dynamic Logic. Foundation of Computing. MIT Press, Cambridge (2000)
7. Harel, D., Meyer, A.R., Pratt, V.R.: Computability and completeness in logics of programs (preliminary report). In: Hopcroft, J.E., Friedman, E.P., Harrison, M.A. (eds.) Proceedings of the 9th Annual ACM Symposium on Theory of Computing, 4–6 May 1977, Boulder, Colorado, USA, pp. 261–268. ACM (1977)
8. Hoare, C.A.R.: An axiomatic basis for computer programming. Commun. ACM **12**(10), 576–580 (1969)
9. Jeannin, J.-B., et al.: A formally verified hybrid system for the next-generation airborne collision avoidance system. In: Baier, C., Tinelli, C. (eds.) TACAS 2015. LNCS, vol. 9035, pp. 21–36. Springer, Heidelberg (2015). https://doi.org/10.1007/978-3-662-46681-0_2
10. Mitsch, S.: Modeling and Analyzing Hybrid Systems with Sphinx - A User Manual. Carnegie Mellon University and Johannes Kepler University, Pittsburgh and Linz (2013). http://www.cs.cmu.edu/afs/cs/Web/People/smitsch/pdf/userdoc.pdf

11. Mitsch, S., Ghorbal, K., Platzer, A.: On provably safe obstacle avoidance for autonomous robotic ground vehicles. In: Newman, P., Fox, D., Hsu, D. (eds.) Robotics: Science and Systems IX, 24–28 June 2013. Technische Universität Berlin, Berlin (2013)

12. Platzer, A.: Logical Analysis of Hybrid Systems: Proving Theorems for Complex Dynamics. Springer, Heidelberg (2010). https://doi.org/10.1007/978-3-642-14509-4

13. Platzer, A.: Logical Foundations of Cyber-Physical Systems. Springer, Heidelberg (2018). https://doi.org/10.1007/978-3-319-63588-0

14. Platzer, A., Clarke, E.M.: Formal verification of curved flight collision avoidance maneuvers: a case study. In: Cavalcanti, A., Dams, D.R. (eds.) FM 2009. LNCS, vol. 5850, pp. 547–562. Springer, Heidelberg (2009). https://doi.org/10.1007/978-3-642-05089-3_35

15. Platzer, A., Quesel, J.-D.: European train control system: a case study in formal verification. In: Breitman, K., Cavalcanti, A. (eds.) ICFEM 2009. LNCS, vol. 5885, pp. 246–265. Springer, Heidelberg (2009). https://doi.org/10.1007/978-3-642-10373-5_13

16. Pratt, V.R.: Semantical considerations on Floyd-Hoare logic. In: 17th Annual Symposium on Foundations of Computer Science, Houston, Texas, USA, 25–27 October 1976, pp. 109–121. IEEE Computer Society (1976)

17. Pratt, V.: Dynamic logic: a personal perspective. In: Madeira, A., Benevides, M. (eds.) DALI 2017. LNCS, vol. 10669, pp. 153–170. Springer, Cham (2018). https://doi.org/10.1007/978-3-319-73579-5_10

18. Quesel, J.D., Mitsch, S., Loos, S., Aréchiga, N., Platzer, A.: How to model and prove hybrid systems with KeYmaera: a tutorial on safety. STTT **18**(1), 67–91 (2016)

19. Rumbaugh, J.E., Jacobson, I., Booch, G.: The Unified Modeling Language Reference Manuel - Covers UML 2.0. Addison Wesley Object Technology Series, 2nd edn. Addison-Wesley, Boston (2005)

Nobrainer: An Example-Driven Framework for C/C++ Code Transformations

Valeriy Savchenko[1(✉)], Konstantin Sorokin[1(✉)], Georgiy Pankratenko[1(✉)],
Sergey Markov[1(✉)], Alexander Spiridonov[1(✉)], Ilia Alexandrov[1(✉)],
Alexander Volkov[2(✉)], and Kwangwon Sun[3(✉)]

[1] Ivannikov Institute for System Programming of the Russian Academy of Sciences,
25, Alexander Solzhenitsyn st., Moscow 109004, Russian Federation
{vsavchenko,ksorokin,gpankratenko,markov,
aspiridonov,ialexandrov}@ispras.ru
[2] Lomonosov Moscow State University,
GSP-1, Leninskie Gory, Moscow 119991, Russian Federation
asvolkov@ispras.ru
[3] Samsung Electronics,
Samsung GEC, 26, Sangil-ro 6-gil, Gangdong-gu, Seoul, South Korea
kwangwon.sun@samsung.com

Abstract. Refactoring is a standard part of any modern development cycle. It helps to reduce technical debt and keep software projects healthy. However, in many cases refactoring requires that transformations are applied globally across multiple files. Applying them manually involves large amounts of monotonous work. Nevertheless, automatic tools are severely underused because users find them unreliable, difficult to adopt, and not customizable enough.

This paper presents a new code transformation framework. It delivers an intuitive way to specify the expected outcome of a transformation applied within the whole project. The user provides simple C/C++ code snippets that serve as examples of what the code should look like before and after the transformation. Due to the absence of any additional abstractions (such as domain-specific languages), we believe this approach flattens the learning curve, making adoption easier.

Besides using the source code of the provided snippets, the framework also operates at the AST level. This gives it a deeper understanding of the program, which allows it to validate the correctness of the transformation and match the exact cases required by the user.

Keywords: Code transformation · Global refactoring · C/C++

1 Introduction

The lifecycle of any software project is a constant evolution. Not only does it mean writing new code while adding new features, but it also includes continuously modifying the existing code. Excessive focus on extending the system's

© Springer Nature Switzerland AG 2019
N. Bjørner et al. (Eds.): PSI 2019, LNCS 11964, pp. 140–155, 2019.
https://doi.org/10.1007/978-3-030-37487-7_12

functionality can lead to a rapid accumulation of the project's technical debt. The concept of *technical debt* is a widespread metaphor for design-wise imperfection that boosts initial product development and deployment. With time, however, the debt grows larger and can potentially stall the whole organization [3].

A common way to mitigate this problem is *refactoring* [2,12], which is a modification of the system's internal structure that does not change its external behavior [4]. It helps to eliminate existing architectural flaws and ease further code maintenance. Murphy-Hill et al. [9] have estimated that 41% of all programming activities involve refactoring. The same study also concluded that developers underuse automatic tools and perform code transformations manually despite the fact that a manual approach is more error-prone. Research performed on StackOverflow website data [10] found that corresponding tools can be too difficult and unreliable, as well as require too much human interaction. This reveals a few natural requirements for a beneficial refactoring tool—it should be easy to use, ask a minimal number of questions from the end user, and rely on syntactic and semantic information in order to ensure the correctness of the performed transformations.

Highly customizable refactoring tools typically utilize additional domain-specific languages (DSL) for describing user-defined transformation rules [5,7, 14]. Such languages need to express both the intended refactoring and the different syntactical and semantical structures of the target programming language. Adopting a DSL can be too overwhelming in the case of C/C++ languages because the language itself is already complex. Studies show that C and C++ take longer to learn [8], and projects in these languages are more error-prone [11] compared to other popular languages.

This insight further qualifies the ease-of-use requirement: the tool should not introduce another level of sophistication on top of C/C++ nor expect additional knowledge from its user.

This study presents the Clang-based transformation framework **nobrainer**, which is built on such principles. The expression *a no-brainer* refers to something so simple or obvious that you do not need to think much about it.[1,2] This concept reflects the core idea behind **nobrainer**, the idea of providing an easy-to-use framework for implementing and applying a user's own code transformations.

Individual **nobrainer** rules are written in C/C++ without any DSLs. Each rule is a group of examples that represents situations that should be refactored and illustrates the way they should be refactored. They look exactly like developer's code, thus flattening the learning curve of the instrument.

In this paper, we describe the main principles behind **nobrainer**, illustrate the most interesting design and implementation solutions, and demonstrate the tool's application in real-world scenarios.

---

[1] https://www.merriam-webster.com/dictionary/no-brainer.
[2] https://dictionary.cambridge.org/dictionary/english/no-brainer.

2   Related Work

This section covers the various approaches on code transformation and automatic refactoring presented in the literature. We distinguish two key points in the current review. The first point is the form, in which the transformations are described. The second point is the way these transformations are performed. There are a few similar approaches that can be combined and compared.

Most of the tools reviewed here rely on a separate syntax for describing transformation or refactoring rules. For example, Waddington et al. [5] introduce their language YATL; whereas, Lahoda et al. [7] extend the Java language to simplify rule descriptions. We believe that various types of DSLs can confuse the user and introduce another layer of complexity. Wright and Jasper [14] describe a different approach. Their tool `ClangMR` adopts Clang AST matchers [1] as a mechanism for describing the parts of the user's code that should be transformed. The user must define replacements in terms of AST nodes. The authors imply that the user is familiar with the principles of syntax trees and how it is built for C/C++ programming languages. We believe that this requirement is rarely met, and that is why the adoption of `ClangMR` can be challenging for a regular user.

Wasserman [13], on the other hand, introduces a tool (`Refaster`) that does not involve any DSLs. He suggests using the target project's programming language for describing transformations. This allows the user to embed transformation rules into the project's code base, which leads to simpler syntax checks and symbol availability validations. Transformation rules are written in the form of classes and methods with either `@BeforeTemplate` or `@AfterTemplate` annotations. Each class represents a transformation and should contain one or more `@BeforeTemplate` methods and a single `@AfterTemplate` method. Then the tool treats the transformation as follows: match the code that is written in `@BeforeTemplate` method and replace it with the code written in `@AfterTemplate` method.

We consider Wasserman's tool design to be clear and user-friendly because it uses the language of the project's code base to define transformations. We use a similar approach in `nobrainer`.

We decided that the best method for matching the C/C++ source code is the approach used in `ClangMR`. However, because using Clang AST matchers directly can be challenging, we provide a higher level framework that utilizes AST matchers internally.

Regarding the code transformation, a common solution is to generate an AST, transform it, and restore the source code in the end. This kind of approach is used by `Proteus` [5], `Jackpot` [7] and Eclipse C++ Tooling Plugin [6]. The main problem of implementing such an approach is code generation. We should remember all the nuances of the original source code in order to replicate them when restoring the resulting code. This includes preserving comments, redundant spaces, etc. On the other hand, in `ClangMR` [14], the authors suggest using the Clang[3] framework for code transformation because it allows developers to directly modify the source code token wise. We also use the Clang framework because we believe it is the best solution to transform C/C++ source code.

3   Design

In this section, we describe the overall design and the user's workflow. Running the tool on a real project involves the following list of actions:

- writing transformation rules as part of the target project
- providing compilation commands for the target project (the currently supported format is the Clang compilation database[4])

Nobrainer either applies all the replacements or generates a YAML file containing these replacements. In the latter case, replacements can be applied later with the clang-apply-replacements tool (part of the Clang Extra Tools[5]).

Figure 1 provides an insight into the internal nobrainer structure. Each numbered block represents a work phase of the tool. Boxes at the bottom correspond to each phase's output.

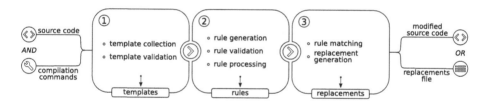

Fig. 1. Nobrainer workflow

During the first phase, the tool analyzes all of the translation units that are extracted from the given compilation commands. For each translation unit, it searches for and collects templates that represent our transformation examples. Then nobrainer filters invalid templates. The result of the first phase is a list of valid templates.

In the second phase, we group conforming templates into rules. Nobrainer also checks each rule for consistency and then processes each rule to generate internal template representation.

In the third phase, we work with the list of preprocessed rules. Nobrainer tries to match each rule against the project's source code. For each match, we construct a special data structure, which we use to generate a replacement. As a result, we obtain a set of replacements.

For more details on each phase, see Sect. 4.

---

[3] https://clang.llvm.org/.
[4] https://clang.llvm.org/docs/JSONCompilationDatabase.html.
[5] https://clang.llvm.org/extra/index.html.

4   Detailed Description

The core idea of **nobrainer** is the use of **examples**, which are code snippets written in C/C++ languages. Because each snippet may represent a whole family of cases, we call them *templates*. The user submits the situations she wants to change in the **Before** templates and the substituting code in the **After** templates. These templates can be defined anywhere in the project.

Nobrainer offers a special API for writing such examples, which is subdivided into C and C++ APIs. Both provide the ability to write **expression** and **statement** templates to match C/C++ expressions or statements respectively.

For a clearer explanation of what a template is, let us proceed with an example. Suppose the user wants to find all calls to function **foo** with an arbitrary **int** expression as the first argument and global variable **globalVar** as the second argument and replace the function with **bar**, while keeping all the same arguments. Listing 1 demonstrates how such a rule can be specified (using **nobrainer** C API).

```
int NOB_BEFORE_EXPR(ruleId)(int a) {
  return foo(a, globalVar);
}

int NOB_AFTER_EXPR(ruleId)(int a) {
  return bar(a, globalVar);
}
```

Listing 1: Expression template example

Expressions for matching and substitution reside inside of **return** statements. We force this limitation intentionally because it allows us to delegate the type compatibility check of **Before** and **After** expressions to the compiler.

Nobrainer's transformations are based on the concept that two valid expressions of the same type are syntactically interchangeable. This statement is correct with the exception of parenthesis placement. In certain contexts, some expressions must be surrounded with parentheses. However, we introduce a simple set of rules that solve this issue and are not covered in this paper.

In order to properly define the term *template*, we first need to introduce the following notations (with respect to the given program):

- Θ is a finite set of all types defined
- Σ is a finite set of all defined symbols (functions, variables, types)
- $\mathcal{A}$ is a finite set of all AST nodes representing the program
- $\mathcal{C}$ is a finite set of characters allowed for C/C++ identifiers
- $\mathcal{P}$ is a finite set of all function parameters $p = \langle n_p, t_p \rangle$ where $n_p \in \mathcal{C}^*$ is the parameter's name and $t_p \in \Theta$ is its type.

An expression template can be formally defined as a 6-tuple

$$T_{expr} = \langle k, n, r, P, B, S \rangle \tag{1}$$

where

- $k \in \{\texttt{before}, \texttt{after}\}$ is the template's kind
- $n \in \mathcal{C}^*$ is the rule's identifier, it is used for pairing corresponding `before`/`after` templates
- $r \in \Theta$ is the return type
- $B \subset \mathcal{A}$ is the body
- $P \subseteq \mathcal{P}$ is the set of parameters
- $S \subseteq \Sigma$ is the set of symbols used in B.

The last two elements of the tuple require additional commentary.

Template parameters P represent generic placeholders for different situations encountered in the real source code. Nobrainer reads these parameters as arbitrary expressions of the corresponding type. For example, parameter **a** from Listing 1 corresponds to **any** expression of type `int`.

The set of symbols S is important for the correctness affirmation (see Sects. 4.4 and 4.6).

$$
\begin{array}{cccc}
r & k & n & P = \{\bullet\} \\
\overbrace{\texttt{int}} & \overbrace{\texttt{NOB\_BEFORE\_EXPR}}(\overbrace{\texttt{ruleId}})(\overbrace{\texttt{int a}}) \texttt{ \{} \\
& \texttt{return } \texttt{foo(a, globalVar)}; \\
\texttt{\}} & B & S = \{\bullet, \bullet\}
\end{array}
$$

Fig. 2. `Before` template deconstruction

Figure 2 dissects the `Before` template from Listing 1.

The following subsections cover **nobrainer**'s phases in more detail.

4.1 Template Collection

The first phase is to collect all the templates from the project. **Nobrainer** scans each file and tries to find functions that were declared using the API. This can only be done for parsed source files. Doing so for the whole project can have a drastic impact on the tool's performance. In order to avoid checking all the files, we only process files that contain inclusion directives of **nobrainer** API header files.

As the output, this phase has a set of all templates defined by the user. We denote it as $\mathcal{T}$.

4.2 Template Validation

After the template collection phase, we validate each template individually. We need to check that the collected templates in $\mathcal{T}$ are structurally valid. First it is important to note that the syntactic correctness of a template is guaranteed by the compilation process. Templates are implemented as the part of the existing code base, which implies that they are actually parsed and checked during the collection phase. This includes checks for the availability of all symbols, type checks, etc.

In every separate case, nobrainer replaces a single expression with another single expression. Considering this fact, each template T_{expr} should define *exactly one* expression. This requirement is transformed into a syntax form as: a template's body B should consist of a single return statement with a non-empty return expression. During the template validation stage, we check this constraint. Thus, nobrainer filters out templates without a body (i.e. declarations), templates with an empty body, and templates with a single statement return;.

Currently there are some limitations regarding the usage of functional style macros and the usage of C++ lambda expressions in template bodies. For this reason, we validate the absence of either of these language features.

Thus, if nobrainer encounters invalid templates, it filters them out and proceeds to the next phase with the set of valid ones T_+.

4.3   Rule Generation

For an arbitrary $id \in C^*$, we define two sets of templates B_{id} and A_{id} as follows:

$$B_{id} = \{T \in T_+ | n_T = id, k_T = \texttt{before}\} \tag{2}$$

$$A_{id} = \{T \in T_+ | n_T = id, k_T = \texttt{after}\} \tag{3}$$

These two groups describe exactly one user-defined transformation scenario because they include all of the *Before* and *After* examples under the same name. However, in order for B_{id} and A_{id} to form a transformation rule, the following additional conditions must be met:

$$\begin{cases} |B_{id}| \geq 1 \\ A_{id} = \{a_{id}\} \text{ (i.e. } |A_{id}| = 1) \\ \forall b \in B_{id} \rightarrow a_{id} \prec b \end{cases} \tag{4}$$

where

$$\forall x, y \in T_+ \rightarrow x \prec y \Leftrightarrow \begin{cases} P_x \subseteq P_y \\ r_x = r_y \end{cases} \tag{5}$$

We refer to operator $\prec$ as the *compatibility operator*. It indicates that the snippet defined in x can safely replace the code matching y. The equality of return types r ensures that the substituting expression has the same type as the original one, while condition $P_x \subseteq P_y$ guarantees that nobrainer will have enough expressions to fill all of the x's placeholders.

As a result, we define *transformation rule* as a pair $R_{id} = \langle B_{id}, A_{id} \rangle$ where B_{id} and A_{id} meet conditions (4). Additionally we denote the set of all project rules as $\mathcal{R}$.

4.4   Rule Processing

Before Template Processing. As mentioned before, we convert `Before` templates to Clang AST matchers. These provide a convenient way to search for sub-trees that fit the given conditions. They describe each node, its properties, and the properties of its children. Thus, this structure resembles the structure of the AST itself. In order to generate matchers programmatically, we exploit this fact. Each node of the template's sub-tree is recursively traversed and paired with a matcher. As a result, we encapsulate the logic related to different AST nodes and avoid the necessity of supporting an exponential number of possible node combinations.

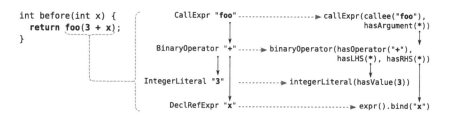

Fig. 3. Recursive AST matcher generation

Figure 3 demonstrates a simplified example of such a conversion. It depicts three stages of `Before` template processing: source code, AST, and AST matchers. Bold arrows reflect parent-child relationships, while dashed arrows stand for node-matcher correspondence. Because matchers are represented by a series of nested function calls, we construct the innermost matchers first, traversing the tree in a depth-first fashion.

Matching Identical Sub-Trees. Consider the `Before` template from Listing 2. It is unlikely that the user expects the system to match two arbitrary expressions as `foo`'s arguments. In fact, the most intuitive interpretation of this template is matching calls to function `foo` with identical arguments only.

```
int before(int x) {
    return foo(x, x);
}
```

Listing 2: An example of reusing a template parameter

Clang does not provide a matcher that can do the job. However, `nobrainer` already has a mechanism to find identical sub-trees for `Before` templates without parameters. During the matching process, we reuse this mechanism to dynamically generate a matcher. Thus, for the given example, we bind the first argument to `x`, generate a matcher, and check if the second argument fits.

After Template Processing. Our goal is to construct a text that represents the result of a replacement. Therefore, we convert *After* templates into plain strings. However, there are some parts of the *After* template's body that cannot be taken as is and placed into the desired location. We call such parts *mutable*. During the traversal of the *After* template's body, we extract the ranges that represent mutable parts. Each range consists of the start and the end locations of the certain AST node. There are two cases of *mutable* parts.

The first case is the use of a template parameter inside of an *After* template's body. We treat each template parameter as a placeholder that we fill during replacement generation (see Sect. 4.6).

The second case is the use of a symbol. Inserting symbols in arbitrary places in the source code can be syntactically incorrect. Indeed, in the location of insertion, the symbol may not yet have been declared. Thus, we collect symbol information that is used during replacement generation (see Sect. 4.6).

Given these points, for the *After* template from Listing 3, we construct the following format string: `"#{bar}(${x}) + 42"`. In this example, `nobrainer` distinguishes the symbol `bar` and the template parameter `x`, and handles them accordingly. The tool treats all the remaining parts of the string as immutable, and, with this in mind, constructs the resulting format string.

```
int after(int x) {
    return bar(x) + 42;
}
```

Listing 3: An example of an *After* template

4.5 Rule Application

The next step is to identify all situations, in which to apply rules $\mathcal{R}$. In order to do this across the whole project, `nobrainer` independently parses all the source files. After that, the tool applies AST matchers generated for each rule.

Each time a match is found, `nobrainer` obtains a top-level expression that should be replaced and a list of AST sub-trees bound to parameters from the corresponding *Before* template. Using this information and the *After* template, `nobrainer` generates an actual code change called a *replacement*.

4.6 Replacement Generation

Replacement is a sufficient specification for a complete textual transformation. It consists of four components:

- the file where current replacement is applied
- the byte offset where the replaced text starts
- the length of the replaced text
- the replacement text

Nobrainer extracts the first three components from the expression marked for substitution. The replacing text is composed from the *After* template and AST nodes bound to parameters. For each node, **nobrainer** gathers the corresponding source code and fills placeholders from the *After* template. This operation results in plain text for the substitution. Figure 4 demonstrates this procedure using a real code snippet.

```
int before(int x, char y) {          match
    return foo(y, x, y);            foo('a', 10 * 42, 'a')
}
                                                        result
                                                      "bar('a') + 10 * 42"
int after(int x, char y) {
    return bar(y) + x;           "bar(${y}) + ${x}"
}                                      format string
```

Fig. 4. Replacement generation

Such a transformation may nevertheless cause compilation errors due to symbol availability. **Nobrainer** should check that each symbol that comes with a substitution is declared and has all required name qualifiers. In order to ensure this, we:

– add inclusion directives for the corresponding header files
– add namespace specifiers.

The resulting code incorporates only the pieces of real source code that have been checked by Clang at different stages of the analysis.

4.7   Type Parameters

Parametrization with arbitrary expressions provides a flexible instrument for generic rule definition. However, this may not be enough. Exact type specification can significantly limit the rule's expressiveness and reduce the number of potential use cases.

In order to combat this shortcoming, we introduce a set of type parameters $\Phi \subset C^*$ to a template syntax. This extends the template definition (1) to

$$T_{expr} = \langle k, n, r, P, B, S, \Phi \rangle \tag{6}$$

and compatibility operator $\prec$ (5) to

$$\forall x, y \in T_+ \rightarrow x \prec y \Leftrightarrow \begin{cases} \Phi_x \subseteq \Phi_y \\ P_x \subseteq P_y \\ r_x = r_y \end{cases} \tag{7}$$

Note that type parameters Φ are fully symmetrical to parameters P.

```
template <class T> T *before() {
  return (T *)malloc(sizeof(T));
}

template <class T> T *after() {
  return new T;
}
```

Listing 4: An example of a type-parametrized rule

Listing 4 demonstrates a rule parametrized with type.

5   Results

In this section, we describe how we test **nobrainer**, provide some transformation rule examples and present the performance results.

5.1   Testing

Our tests can be divided into two main groups. First, we have a group of unit- and integration-tests for each phase described in Sect. 3. These are mainly used to check the correctness of AST matcher generation (Sect. 4.4) and format string generation (Sect. 4.4) for various AST nodes.

Second, we have a group of regression tests consisting of several open source projects.

For each project, we have created files with predefined **nobrainer** templates. Our testing framework runs the tool, measures the execution time, checks that all the predefined transformations have been performed as expected, and verifies that the project can be compiled afterwards.

5.2   Examples

In this section, we present three notable transformation rules that are supported by **nobrainer**.

The first example (Listing 5) shows the transformation rule that changes the order of arguments inside of the **compose** method call. Specifically, **nobrainer** will replace each call of the **compose** method of the **Agent** class **a.compose(x, y)** with the call **a.compose(y, x)**.

Thus, we demonstrate how to perform an argument swap automatically when method's signature changes.

```
int NOB_BEFORE_EXPR(ChangeOrder)(Agent a, char *x, char *y) {
  return a.compose(x, y);
}

int NOB_AFTER_EXPR(ChangeOrder)(Agent a, char *x, char *y) {
  return a.compose(y, x);
}
```

Listing 5: An example template for the argument swap

The second example (Listing 6) shows that nobrainer can be used to perform simplifying code transformations.

```
class EmptyCheckRefactoring : public nobrainer::ExprTemplate {
public:
  bool beforeSize(const std::string x) {
    return x.size() == 0;
  }

  bool beforeLength(const std::string x) {
    return x.length() == 0;
  }

  bool after(const std::string x) {
    return x.empty();
  }
};
```

Listing 6: An example template for a string emptiness check

Recall that each rule can have an arbitrary number of *before* templates, but only one *after* template. Writing several *before* expressions helps to group common transformations.

The third example contains type and expression parameters. Listing 7 shows the corresponding rule.

```
class ConstCastRefactoring : public nobrainer::ExprTemplate {
public:
  template <class T>
  T *before(const T *x) { return (T *)x; }

  template <class T>
  T *after(const T *x) { return const_cast<T *>(x); }
};
```

Listing 7: An example template for const casts

It detects the C-style cast that "drops" the const qualifier from the pointed type and replaces it with an equivalent C++-style cast. Parameter x should be of any pointer-to-const type and should be cast to exactly this type, but without a `const` qualifier. `Nobrainer` captures all of these connections and processes them as expected.

5.3   Performance

To measure the performance we run our regression tests five times on a machine with Intel(R) Core(TM) i7-7700K CPU @ 4.20 GHz CPU, and 64 GB of RAM. The machine runs on Ubuntu 16.04 LTS. We perform the execution in eight threads.

Table 1 contains the results. For each project, we list its size in *lines of code*, the number of replacements `nobrainer` applies during the test, and our time measurements. We distinguish two stages of `nobrainer`'s workflow and measure them separately. The first stage incorporates the project's source code parsing. The second stage contains all the remaining computations up to replacement generation. We divide the whole process this way because the parsing process is performed by the *Clang* framework. For this reason, we can only minimize the time `nobrainer` spends in the second stage.

Table 1. Performance results

Project	KLOC	Replacements	Parsing time (s)	Remaining operation time (s)
CMake	493	24	31.36	7.13
curl	129	7	3.17	2.01
json	70	7	13.99	1.34
mysql	1170	10	9.54	3.12
protobuf	264	8	16.62	2.97
v8	3055	6	281.57	28.52
xgboost	43	14	6.75	1.18

It should be noted that the execution time does not directly correlate with the project's size. Other factors, such as translation unit sizes may also influence the overall performance.

As can be seen in Table 1, the elapsed time varies significantly between projects. In particular, this behavior applies both to the parsing time and to remaining processing time. Therefore, comparing the elapsed time of different projects offers few insights. Thus, in our evaluations, we consider the percentage of time that the file parsing takes from the whole process. Then, we compare this proportion among different projects. Figure 5 demonstrates the corresponding rates for the regression projects. Our results show that parsing takes up more than 81% of the whole execution time on average. For a global refactoring, all files must be parsed. The fact that the remaining procedure takes less than 20% of the execution time means that `nobrainer` has reached near-optimal performance.

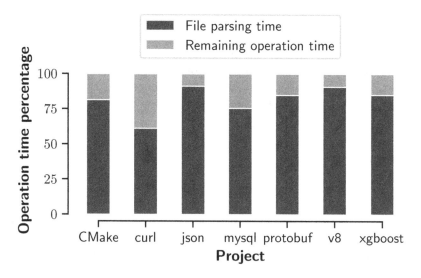

Fig. 5. File parsing percentage in **nobrainer** operation

Nevertheless, in certain cases, it is possible to avoid parsing files when it is sure that the file contains nothing to transform. The next section explains this and other directions in our future work.

6   Limitations and Future Work

Currently **nobrainer** supports expression templates and type parameterization. It can be used to perform transformations in continuous integration environments (CI). However, the execution time is still unsuitable for running it on large projects as a background task in IDE. There is still room for improvement. Thus, we consider three main directions for future work:

1. Full statement support
2. Performance improvements
3. Usability improvements

At the moment, we have already designed infrastructure for statement support. This includes API, validation and stubs for processing **Before** and **After** templates. We have also added support for **if** statements, **compound** statements, and variable declaration nodes. Our next task is to implement processing for each remaining statement node.

Regarding performance, we plan to research methods for reducing the parsing time. We are considering two directions. Firstly, we would like to improve the matching phase by skipping files that do not contain symbols used in **Before** templates. Secondly, we will explore automatic precompiled header (PCH) creation, which is expected to speed up the process of parsing the project's header files.

Further, the usability of our tool can be improved in two ways. Currently nobrainer performs found transformations only for the whole code base. We would like to add support for executing on user-defined parts of the project. We are also considering integrating with other developer tools. For example, nobrainer can be used as an IDE plugin to enhance user experience and the convenience of usage. Another possible scenario is to use nobrainer to assist static analyzers for fixing errors or defects.

7   Conclusion

In this paper, we presented nobrainer—a transformation and refactoring framework for C and C++ languages based on the Clang infrastructure. Its design is built on two main principles: ease-of-use and the extensive validation of transformation rules. A substantial part of this article includes describing its design and implementation, accompanied with examples and results.

Our results showed that nobrainer already supports real-world transformation examples and can be successfully applied to large C/C++ projects in continuous integration environments. We also highlighted the current limitations of the tool and some directions for later improvements. In the future, we plan to enhance the usability of nobrainer and integrate with other developer tools.

Acknowledgments. This work resulted from a joint project with Samsung Research. The authors of this paper are grateful to the colleagues from Samsung for their valuable ideas and feedback.

References

1. Clang documentation: Matching the clang AST. https://clang.llvm.org/docs/LibASTMatchers.html
2. Brown, N., et al.: Managing technical debt in software-reliant systems. In: Proceedings of the FSE/SDP Workshop on Future of Software Engineering Research, FoSER 2010, pp. 47–52. ACM, New York (2010). https://doi.org/10.1145/1882362.1882373, http://doi.acm.org/10.1145/1882362.1882373
3. Cunningham, W.: The WyCash portfolio management system. SIGPLAN OOPS Mess. 4(2), 29–30 (1992). https://doi.org/10.1145/157710.157715. http://doi.acm.org/10.1145/157710.157715
4. Fowler, M., Beck, K., Brant, J., Opdyke, W., Roberts, D.: Refactoring: Improving the Design of Existing Code. Addison-Wesley Professional, Boston (1999)
5. Waddington, D.G., Yao, B.: High-fidelity C/C++ code transformation. Electron. Notes Theoret. Comput. Sci. **141**, 35–56 (2007). https://doi.org/10.1016/j.entcs.2005.04.037
6. Graf, E., Zgraggen, G., Sommerlad, P.: Refactoring support for the C++ development tooling. In: OOPSLA Companion (2007)
7. Lahoda, J., Bečička, J., Ruijs, R.B.: Custom declarative refactoring in NetBeans: tool demonstration. In: Proceedings of the Fifth Workshop on Refactoring Tools, WRT 2012, pp. 63–64. ACM, New York (2012). https://doi.org/10.1145/2328876.2328886, http://doi.acm.org/10.1145/2328876.2328886

8. Meyerovich, L.A., Rabkin, A.S.: Empirical analysis of programming language adoption. SIGPLAN Not. **48**(10), 1–18 (2013). https://doi.org/10.1145/2544173. 2509515. http://doi.acm.org/10.1145/2544173.2509515

9. Murphy-Hill, E.R., Parnin, C., Black, A.P.: How we refactor, and how we know it. In: ICSE, pp. 287–297. IEEE (2009). http://dblp.uni-trier.de/db/conf/icse/ icse2009.html#Murphy-HillPB09

10. Pinto, G.H., Kamei, F.: What programmers say about refactoring tools?: An empirical investigation of stack overflow. In: Proceedings of the 2013 ACM Workshop on Workshop on Refactoring Tools. WRT 2013, pp. 33–36. ACM, New York (2013). https://doi.org/10.1145/2541348.2541357, http://doi.acm.org/10.1145/2541348.2 541357

11. Ray, B., Posnett, D., Devanbu, P., Filkov, V.: A large-scale study of programming languages and code quality in github. Commun. ACM **60**(10), 91–100 (2017). https://doi.org/10.1145/3126905. http://doi.acm.org/10.1145/3126905

12. Tracz, W.: Refactoring for software design smells: managing technical debt by Girish Suryanarayana, Ganesh Samarthyam, and Tushar Sharma. ACM SIGSOFT Softw. Eng. Notes **40**(6), 36 (2015). http://dblp.uni-trier.de/db/journals/ sigsoft/sigsoft40.html#Tracz15a

13. Wasserman, L.: Scalable, example-based refactorings with refaster. In: Proceedings of the 2013 ACM Workshop on Workshop on Refactoring Tools, pp. 25–28. ACM (2013)

14. Wright, H., Jasper, D., Klimek, M., Carruth, C., Wan, Z.: Large-scale automated refactoring using ClangMR. In: Proceedings of the 29th International Conference on Software Maintenance (2013)

A Logical Approach to the Analysis of Aerospace Images

Valeriy Kuchuganov, Denis Kasimov$^{(\boxtimes)}$, and Aleksandr Kuchuganov

Kalashnikov Izhevsk State Technical University, Izhevsk, Russian Federation
kuchuganov@istu.ru, kasden@mail.ru, Aleks_KAV@udm.ru

Abstract. The paper proposes algorithms and software tools for the automatic interpretation and classification of objects and situations on aerospace images by structural-spatial analysis and iterative reasoning based on fuzzy logic and expert rules of inference. During iterations, the decision tree is built, the transition to local rules and additional features is carried out, and the ranges of acceptable values are adjusted. Particular attention is paid to geometric features of objects. Quantitative attributes are converted to qualitative ones for ease of perception of results and forming decision rules. The results of the experiment on the automatic identification of objects in the aerial image of an urban area are given. The system is useful for automating the process of labeling images for supervised learning and testing programs that recognize objects in aerospace images.

Keywords: Image analysis · Object detection · Object features · Decision rule · Decision tree · Ground truth · Image labeling

1 Introduction

Due to the rapid growth in the volume of aerospace monitoring data, there is an urgent need for the tools that automate the extraction of knowledge from images, the identification and structured description of image objects.

Currently, the GEOBIA (Geographic Object-Based Image Analysis) approach [1] is actively being developed in the field of aerospace image analysis. Within this approach, the processing of areas obtained as a result of automatic color segmentation and their classification based on rules set by an expert is implemented. There is an extensive experience of using the object-oriented approach for solving various tasks: analysis of changes in territories [2], classification of urban garden surfaces [3], automatic detection of built-up areas [4], estimation of crop residues [5], etc.

The work [6] is interesting by the proposed method of obtaining the object classification rules. The rules are formed on the basis of supervised learning: using manually prepared training examples, an automatic synthesis of a decision tree is performed, from which the most reliable classification rules are then manually extracted. The process of classifying objects in the image includes color image segmentation, calculation of spectral and geometric characteristics of the obtained segments, and classifying the segments into the target object categories by checking the rules that test feature values. In general, the considered work is aimed at maximizing the effectiveness of the final stage of image analysis, which is associated with decision

© Springer Nature Switzerland AG 2019
N. Bjørner et al. (Eds.): PSI 2019, LNCS 11964, pp. 156–166, 2019.
https://doi.org/10.1007/978-3-030-37487-7_13

making. It should be noted that the overall effectiveness of the analyzing system is determined not only by this factor, but also largely depends on the quality of image segmentation, the completeness of the set of analyzed features and the degree of consideration of the environment of objects.

In [7], an ontological approach to representing the knowledge of GEOBIA-systems is proposed. Based on the formalism of description logics, the relationships between the target categories of objects and their patterns in images are described. From these logical descriptions, it is then easy to extract the rules for assigning image objects provided by the segmentation procedure to the desired categories. The advantage of this approach is that the knowledge of experts is transferred to the analyzing system in a more systematic way, the subjectivity of the decision rules is leveled, and the possibility of using automatic means for checking the consistency of the knowledge base appears. Unfortunately, the approach does not specify any form of contextual analysis of objects. Identification relies entirely on spectral and geometric characteristics of individual objects (NDVI, squareness, etc.). The authors noted that automatic segmentation did not always perfectly delineate the boundaries of objects, especially in the case of shadows and trees. In this regard, the existing free database of cartographic data was used to refine the results of segmentation.

In existing implementations of the GEOBIA approach, relatively simple classification rules are applied that do not take into account the context of an object. The decision making mechanism is built on the production knowledge model. A significant drawback is the lack of tools for complex analysis of the shape of objects. Under conditions of imperfection of automatic image segmentation, it is not always possible to achieve high identification rates.

The purpose of this work is to develop mechanisms for the automatic interpretation and classification of objects and situations on aerospace images by structural-spatial analysis and iterative reasoning based on fuzzy logic and expert rules of inference. During iterations, the decision tree is built, the transition to local rules and additional features is carried out, and the ranges of acceptable values are adjusted. Particular attention is paid to geometric features of objects. Quantitative attributes are converted to qualitative ones for ease of perception of results and forming decision rules.

2 Formation of a Set of Features

At the stage of image preprocessing, color segmentation and approximation of the edges of regions by circular arcs and straight line segments are performed. The algorithms of image approximation and extraction of basic features used by us are discussed in detail in [8]. The result of the stage is the set of **color regions** represented as the cyclic lists of straight line segments and circular arcs:

$REGIONS = \{R_1, \ldots, R_n\}$, $n \in N$, $R_i = (Color_i, Edge_i)$, $Edge_i = (e_{i1}, \ldots, e_{ik})$, $k \in N$, $\forall j \in [1..k]\, LineSegment(e_{ij}) \lor CircularArc(e_{ij})$, $Connected(e_{ik}, e_{i1})$, $\forall j \in [1..k-1]$ $Connected(e_{ij}, e_{ij+1})$, where $Color_i$ is the region's average color; $LineSegment(e)$ is true if e is a straight line segment; $CircularArc(e)$ is true if e is a circular arc; $Connected(e_1, e_2)$ is true if any endpoints of e_1 and e_2 are the same.

Many of the obtained regions correspond unequivocally to the target objects of the image or their structural fragments (a typical example is a roof slope of a building). On the other hand, it is not possible to avoid regions that are incorrect to some degree: a very tortuous border, the capture of a part of a neighboring object, etc. In a number of researches [9, 10], it is noted that the inaccuracy, insufficiency or excessiveness of automatically obtained color segments is a serious problem for object-oriented approaches, preventing them from achieving a high level of recognition. In view of this, the subsequent stages of processing and analysis have been designed in such a way as to minimize the influence of this negative factor.

Next, **the adjacency graph** of the regions and sections of their edges is constructed. Each node of the graph corresponds to a certain region of the image. Arcs of the graph represent relationships between the regions:

$$(BegNode, EndNode, R, V, AdjChains),$$

where *BegNode* is the number of the node from which the arc exits; *EndNode* is the number of the node to which the arc enters; R is the type of relationship between the regions: *IsNeighbourOf, Contains, IsInsideOf*; V is the vector that connects the regions' centroids, showing relative orientation and distance; *AdjChains* is the set of adjacent chains of the regions' edges.

To describe the image regions, the following **features** are calculated:

1. Significant elements of the region's edge:

$$SignifEls_i = \{e \mid e \in Edge_i \wedge L(e)/P(Edge_i) \geq \delta\},$$

where L is the length calculation function, $L(e) \in \mathbf{R}^+$, P is the perimeter calculation function, $P(Edge_i) \in \mathbf{R}^+$, δ is a threshold, $\delta \in [0, 1]$.

2. Significant line segments: $SL_i = \{e \mid e \in SignifEls_i \wedge LineSegment(e)\}$.
3. Straightness of the region's edge:

$$Straightness(R_i) = \frac{\sum\limits_{e \in SL_i} L(e)}{P(Edge_i)}.$$

4. The presence of three sides of a rectangle:

$$\exists a, b, c \in SL_i(a \tilde{\perp} b, b \tilde{\perp} c, a \tilde{\|} c, Near(a, b), Near(b, c)) \rightarrow Has3RectSides(Edge_i)$$

where *Near* is true if the elements are located relatively close to each other; $\tilde{\perp}$ and $\tilde{\|}$ are the relations of fuzzy perpendicularity and parallelism that allow a slight deviation of the angle from $90°$ and $0°$, respectively.

5. The presence of significant perpendicular line segments (*Has2PerpLines*).
6. *Area*, converted to a relative form through clustering.

7. Average width (*AvgWidth*), calculated on the basis of creating cross sections and clustering their lengths. The calculated absolute value is converted to a relative form, namely, it is considered depending on the size of the region.

8. Elongation of the region: $Elongation(R_i) = \min(a, b)/\max(a, b)$,
   where a and b are the lengths of the sides of $MinBoundRect(R_i)$ – the minimum rectangle that covers the region R_i.

9. Squareness of the region: $Squareness(R_i) = Area(R_i)/Area(MinBoundRect(R_i))$,
   where *Area* is the area calculation function, $Area(R_i) \in \mathbf{R}^+$.

10. *Circleness* – the ratio of the region's area to the area of a circle of the corresponding radius.

11. Tortuosity of the region's edge:

$$Tortuosity(R_i) = SignChangeCount(Edge_i)/P(Edge_i),$$

where *SignChangeCount* is the number of changes of the sign of the element inclination angle when traversing the edge.

12. Density of contour points: $ContourPointDensity(R_i) = |ContourPoints(R_i)|/Area(R_i)$,
   where *ContourPoints* is the function that detects contour points in the given region of the image.

The last feature characterizes the texture of the region: if the value is small, then the region is homogeneous and smooth, otherwise it has a complex texture.

Quantitative values of the features are translated into qualitative form in order to simplify the process of forming decision rules and perception of the analysis results. Conversion can be based on a simple partition of a value range into several subranges. However, a more flexible approach is to assign membership functions in accordance with the principles of fuzzy sets [11]. The second method is more laborious and time-consuming to set up, but the costs pay off to some extent, since some of classification errors associated with a slight violation of range boundaries are eliminated. At present, approaches are being developed [12, 13], aimed at simplifying the fuzzification process, seeking to eliminate subjectivity and reduce the share of manual labor in the creation of membership functions.

To facilitate the user's process of determining the ranges of qualitative values, the system has a tool for constructing histograms of the distribution of numerical values of the features. Figure 1 shows a program window in which the *Straightness* feature is examined. Initially, the histogram is built with a large number of equal ranges (Fig. 1a) to give the user a general idea of the shape of the distribution. The task of the user is to reduce the number of ranges to the required number of qualitative values of the feature. For example, in Fig. 1b, the user has defined ranges of four qualitative straightness values that he considers sufficient for classification.

By clicking on any bar of the histogram, the system highlights all the color areas in the image for which the feature value falls within the range corresponding to this bar. This feature helps the user to evaluate the correctness of the resulting ranges.

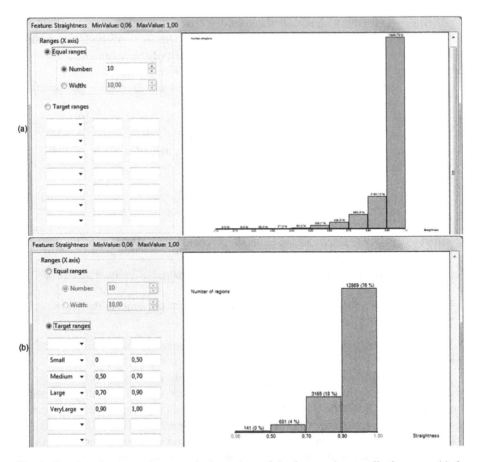

Fig. 1. Interface for converting quantitative values of the features into qualitative ones: (a) the initial equal ranges; (b) the target ranges *Small*, *Medium*, *Large*, and *VeryLarge*

During the interpretation of decision rules, the quantitative values are fuzzified using simple built-in trapezoidal functions, which are automatically scaled to the width of the user-defined ranges.

3 Formation of Decision Rules

Decision rules are divided into the following types:

– rules that analyze image regions in isolation from other regions, classifying the most reliable objects;
– rules that consider aggregates of adjacent regions, classifying less reliable objects and refining previously detected objects.

Consider some rules of the first type, applied at the beginning of the object classification stage:

Object Category: Building
General requirements: $(Color(R) \neq Green) \wedge (Color(R) \neq VeryDark) \wedge (Area(R) \geq Medium) \wedge (Elongation(R) \leq Medium) \wedge (AvgWidth(R) \geq VeryLarge) \wedge (ContourPointDensity(R) \leq Medium) \wedge (\neg \exists R_2 (Color(R_2) = Green \wedge Contains(R, R_2)))$.
 Variants:

- **IF** $(Straightness(R) \geq VeryLarge)$ **THEN** $Building(R, 1.0)$.
- **IF** $(Squareness(R) \geq Large) \wedge (Has3RectSides(R) \vee Has2PerpLines(R))$ **THEN** $Building(R, 1.0)$.
- **IF** $(Straightness(R) \geq Large) \wedge (Has3RectSides(R) \vee Has2PerpLines(R)) \wedge (Squareness(R) \geq Medium) \wedge (Tortuosity(R) \leq Medium)$ **THEN** $Building(R, 1.0)$.
- **IF** $(Straightness(R) \geq Large) \wedge (Has3RectSides(R) \vee Has2PerpLines(R)) \wedge (Tortuosity(R) \leq Medium)$ **THEN** $Building(R, 0.7)$.
- **IF** $(Squareness(R) \geq Large)$ **THEN** $Building(R, 0.5)$.
- **IF** $(\exists e \in R.Edge\ L(e) \geq VeryLarge)$ **THEN** $Building(R, 0.5)$.

Object Category: Shadow of Building
General requirements: $(Color(R) = VeryDark)$.
 Variants:

- **IF** $(Straightness(R) \geq VeryLarge)$ **THEN** $ShadowOfBuilding(R, 1.0)$.
- **IF** $(Straightness(R) \geq Large)$ **THEN** $ShadowOfBuilding(R, 0.8)$.
- **IF** $(Straightness(R) \geq Medium) \wedge (Tortuosity(R) \leq Large)$ **THEN** $ShadowOfBuilding(R, 0.6)$.

When a rule is triggered, the image region obtains a classification variant with the degree of reliability specified in the rule's consequent. The reliability value is set by the expert.

The rules of the second type are repeatedly applied to the results of the previous classification steps, while new information is added. Below is an example of one of these rules:

Object Category: Building near ShadowOfBuilding
IF $ShadowOfBuilding(R_2, m), Adjacent(R, R_2) \wedge (Straightness(CommonEdge(R, R_2)) \geq Large) \wedge (Orientation(R_2, R) \cong SolarAngle) \wedge \ldots$ **THEN** $Building(R, m), ShadowOfBuilding(R_2, m + 0.2)$,

where m is the reliability of classification of the region R_2 before executing the rule.

The classification stage has an iterative principle of organization. Different sets of rules can be used at different iterations. Namely, when setting rules, the expert can specify on which iterations they can be applied. This principle makes it possible to implement various image analysis strategies. For example, the rules used in the i-th iteration can serve the purpose of detecting all potential objects, ensuring maximum recall rate and not worrying much about the precision. Then the elimination of false objects can be made on the $i + 1$ iteration by specifying additional features, checking the contextual rules and adjusting the ranges of acceptable values.

In our experiments, iterations were used as follows: (1) detection of the most reliable objects; (2) classification of less reliable objects with the condition that they are adjacent to reliable objects; (3) identifying buildings near shadows the source of which has not yet determined; (4) detection of buildings and roads among the remaining regions on the basis of weakened requirements; (5) classifying the remaining regions into the categories of trees, grass, and roads (what they are more like, depending on tortuosity and color).

The results of rule execution are organized as a decision tree, the general structure of which is shown in Fig. 2. Each color image region has its own decision tree. Of all the classifications derived, the one with the highest reliability is chosen as the result. Similarly, when interpreting rules of the second type, the neighbors are substituted in descending order of the degree of compliance with the specified requirements.

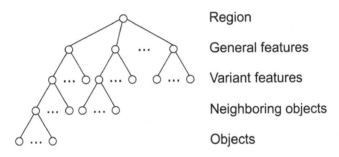

Fig. 2. Decision tree structure

4   Experiment

An experiment on the automatic classification of objects was conducted on an urban area aerial image taken from Inria Aerial Image Labeling Dataset [14]. The dataset contains the building ground truth, providing an opportunity to assess the quality of building identification using the *Intersection over Union (IoU)* and *Accuracy* [15, 16] metrics. These measures are calculated as follows:

$$IoU = |A \cap G|/|A \cup G|, Accuracy = |A \cap G|/|A|,$$

where A is the set of pixels that the program has classified as pixels of target objects; G is the set of pixels that are related to target objects in the ground truth.

As a result of automatic analysis of the image that has the size 5000×5000 and contains a total of 793 buildings, the following performance values were obtained:

$$IoU = 0.56, Accuracy = 0.83.$$

The values obtained can be considered satisfactory. It should be noted that the applied metrics work at the pixel level and require the most accurate determination of building boundaries. In this paper, the desire for accurate detection of objects was not put at the forefront. The most difficult to classify were small buildings partially covered with trees, since their visible parts often do not have any distinctive elements of geometric shape. Such situations require special analysis strategies. Neural network approaches [14] also experience some difficulties on this dataset (the average value of *IoU* does not exceed 0.6), leaving considerable room for improvement.

Figure 3 shows examples of the work of our approach and two other approaches in the literature.

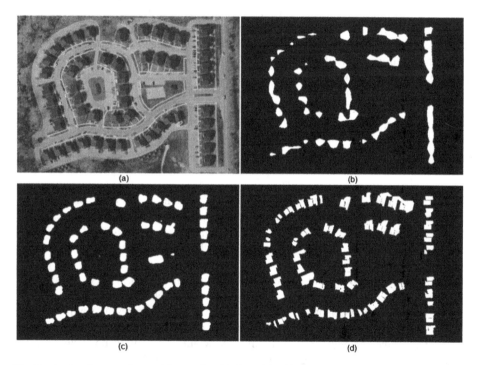

Fig. 3. A visual comparison of the results: (a) the original image; (b) FCN results [14]; (c) MLP results [14]; (d) our results

Practice shows that manual creation of the ground truth labeling for a single large aerospace image takes more than an hour. And additionally it is necessary to prepare a set of test images. The obtained estimate *IoU* = 56% indicates the possibility of reducing labor costs by half. The important point is that the developed system does not require training and can be relatively easily reconfigured to other images. Thus, the system can be useful for automating the creation of training datasets to expand the scope of application of artificial neural networks.

The Labor Costs for Setting Up the System. The setting up is carried out on one of the most representative images and consists in formation of decision rules. Each rule is designed to recognize one category of objects by checking the values of the features specified in it. Fine-tuning the color image segmentation involves determining the optimal combination of values of 3 parameters and takes no more than 30 min. The current version of the system uses 12 shape features. At the stage of preprocessing, quantitative values of features are calculated. For the rules to work, they are translated into qualitative ones. To this end, the user requests a histogram of a feature, sets the number of ranges and specifies their boundaries. Setting the value ranges of one feature takes a maximum of 15 min. The formation of a decision rule for the desired category of objects consists in choosing the necessary features from the set of possible ones and specifying identifiers of qualitative values. In our experiments, the development of an object detection strategy and formation of decision rules took one full working day. At the same time, the action of the well-known Pareto principle was clearly felt: a small share of the efforts (formulated rules) gave the main share of the result (recognized objects), and the remaining efforts were associated with the struggle for improving the detection quality within 10–20%. Given this fact, in the future it is advisable to limit the rules development process to 4 h. Then the total labor costs for setting up the system are 7.5 man-hours.

5 Conclusion

Thus, the proposed approach to the analysis of aerospace images is based on structural-spatial analysis and iterative reasoning with the use of fuzzy logic and expert rules of inference. During iterations, the decision tree is built, the transition to local (contextual) rules and additional features is carried out, and the ranges of acceptable values are adjusted.

Particular attention is paid to geometric features of objects. The set of standard geometric characteristics (perimeter, area, squareness, circleness, elongation, etc.) of objects has been supplemented with such more complex features as significant elements, straightness, presence of three sides of a rectangle, presence of significant perpendicular line segments, tortuosity, average width, and contour point density.

The advantages of the logical approach to image analysis are the following: (a) argumentation of the decision; (b) the possibility of context-sensitive analysis; (c) automatic generation of descriptions of objects and scenes; (d) there is no need for training on labeled datasets; (e) relatively simple adjustment to the required type of images and shooting conditions.

Based on the classification results, it is possible to form a training dataset for neural network type recognition systems. This may require some manual adjustment of the results: removal of false objects and refinement of the edges of true objects. If necessary, two-stage training can be organized. In this case, at the second level, with the help of additional features, "specialization" is carried out according to the seasons (winter, summer, autumn), types of terrain (agricultural grounds, highland), and other parameters of shooting.

Further enhancement of the system is seen in the organization of flexible search strategies, for example, specific techniques for large/extended/small objects. Due to context-sensitive strategies, the system will automatically, depending on the content of a particular area, adapt to the shooting conditions, the texture of objects, combinations of objects of different categories, the nature of the edges between them, etc.

Acknowledgment. This work is supported by the Russian Science Foundation under grant No. 18-71-00109.

References

1. Blaschke, T., et al.: Geographic object-based image analysis – towards a new paradigm. ISPRS J. Photogramm. Remote Sens. **87**, 180–191 (2014). https://doi.org/10.1016/j.isprsjprs.2013.09.014
2. Souza-Filho, P.W.M., Nascimento, W.R., Santos, D.C., Weber, E.J., Silva, R.O., Siqueira, J.O.: A GEOBIA approach for multitemporal land-cover and land-use change analysis in a tropical watershed in the southeastern Amazon. Remote Sens. **10**(11), 1683 (2018). https://doi.org/10.3390/rs10111683
3. Baker, F., Smith, C.: A GIS and object based image analysis approach to mapping the greenspace composition of domestic gardens in Leicester, UK. Landsc. Urban Plan. **183**, 133–146 (2019). https://doi.org/10.1016/j.landurbplan.2018.12.002
4. Lehner, A., Naeimi, V., Steinnocher, K.: Sentinel-1 for object-based delineation of built-up land within urban areas. In: Ragia, L., Laurini, R., Rocha, J.G. (eds.) GISTAM 2017. CCIS, vol. 936, pp. 19–35. Springer, Cham (2019). https://doi.org/10.1007/978-3-030-06010-7_2
5. Najafi, P., Navid, H., Feizizadeh, B., Eskandari, I.: Object-based satellite image analysis applied for crop residue estimating using Landsat OLI imagery. Int. J. Remote Sens. **39**(19), 6117–6136 (2018). https://doi.org/10.1080/01431161.2018.1454621
6. Antunes, R.R., Bias, E.S., Costa, G.A.O.P., Brites, R.S.: Object-based analysis for urban land cover mapping using the InterIMAGE And The SIPINA free software packages. Bull. Geod. Sci. **24**(1), 1–17 (2018). https://doi.org/10.1590/s1982-21702018000100001
7. Belgiu, M., Hofer, B., Hofmann, P.: Coupling formalized knowledge bases with object-based image analysis. Remote Sens. Lett. **5**(6), 530–538 (2014). https://doi.org/10.1080/2150704X.2014.930563
8. Kasimov, D.R., Kuchuganov, A.V., Kuchuganov, V.N., Oskolkov, P.P.: Approximation of color images based on the clusterization of the color palette and smoothing boundaries by splines and arcs. Program. Comput. Softw. **44**(5), 295–302 (2018). https://doi.org/10.1134/S0361768818050043
9. Lhomme, S., He, D.C., Weber, C., Morin, D.: A new approach to building identification from very-high-spatial-resolution images. Int. J. Remote Sens. **30**, 1341–1354 (2009). https://doi.org/10.1080/01431160802509017
10. You, Y., et al.: Building detection from VHR remote sensing imagery based on the morphological building index. Remote Sens. **10**(8), 1288 (2018). https://doi.org/10.3390/rs10081287
11. Zadeh, L.A.: The concept of a linguistic variable and its application to approximate reasoning—I. Inf. Sci. **8**(3), 199–249 (1975). https://doi.org/10.1016/0020-0255(75)90036-5
12. Liao, T.W.: A procedure for the generation of interval type-2 membership functions from data. Appl. Soft Comput. **52**, 925–936 (2017). https://doi.org/10.1016/j.asoc.2016.09.034

13. Dhar, S., Kundu, M.K.: A novel method for image thresholding using interval type-2 fuzzy set and Bat algorithm. Appl. Soft Comput. **63**, 154–166 (2018). https://doi.org/10.1016/j.asoc.2017.11.032

14. Maggiori, E., Tarabalka, Y., Charpiat, G., Alliez, P.: Can semantic labeling methods generalize to any city? The Inria aerial image labeling benchmark. In: IEEE International Geoscience and Remote Sensing Symposium, IGARSS 2017 (2017). https://doi.org/10.1109/igarss.2017.8127684

15. Sokolova, M., Lapalme, G.: A systematic analysis of performance measures for classification tasks. Inf. Process. Manag. **45**(4), 427–437 (2009). https://doi.org/10.1016/j.ipm.2009.03.002

16. Fernandez-Moral, E., Martins, R., Wolf, D., Rives, P.: A new metric for evaluating semantic segmentation: leveraging global and contour accuracy. In: Workshop on Planning, Perception and Navigation for Intelligent Vehicles, PPNIV17 2017 (2017). https://doi.org/10.1109/ivs.2018.8500497

Data Compression Algorithms in Analysis of UI Layouts Visual Complexity

Maxim Bakaev$^{(\boxtimes)}$ ⓘ, Ekaterina Goltsova, Vladimir Khvorostov, and Olga Razumnikova ⓘ

Novosibirsk State Technical University, Novosibirsk, Russia
{bakaev,xvorostov,razumnikova}@corp.nstu.ru

Abstract. Measuring visual complexity (VC) of human-computer user interfaces (UIs) sees increasing development, as VC has been found to affect users' cognitive load, aesthetical impressions and overall performance. Spatial allocation and ordering of UI elements is the major feature manipulated by an interface designer, and in our paper we focus on perceived complexity of layouts. Algorithmic Information Theory has justified the use of data compression algorithms for generating metrics of VC as lengths of coded representations, so we consider two established algorithms: RLE and Deflate. First, we propose the method for obtaining coded representations of UI layouts based on decreasing of visual fidelity that roughly corresponds to the "squint test" widely used in practical usability engineering. To confirm applicability of the method and the predictive power of the compression algorithms, we ran two experimental surveys with over 4700 layout configurations, 21 real websites, and 149 participants overall. We found that the compression algorithms' metrics were significant in VC models, but the classical purely informational Hick's law metric was even more influential. Unexpectedly, algorithms with higher compression ratios that presumably come closer to the "real" Kolmogorov complexity did not explain layouts' VC perception better. The proposed novel UI coding method and the analysis of the compression algorithms' metrics can contribute to user behavior modeling in HCI and static testing of software UIs.

Keywords: Algorithmic complexity · Static UI analysis · Human-Computer interaction · Information processing

1 Introduction

1.1 Visual Complexity in Human-Computer Interaction

A few decades ago, with the increasing ubiquity of computers and the growing number of users, visual complexity (VC) started becoming a research field of its own, detaching itself from the general studies of complex systems [1]. Nowadays it is well-known in human-computer interaction (HCI) that perceived user interface VC significantly affects not just cognitive load, but also user preferences, aesthetical and other affective impressions [2–5]. The general guideline in HCI is that all other things being equal, VC

© Springer Nature Switzerland AG 2019
N. Bjørner et al. (Eds.): PSI 2019, LNCS 11964, pp. 167–184, 2019.
https://doi.org/10.1007/978-3-030-37487-7_14

should be decreased (in some cases, a certain level of complexity should be maintained, due to reasons of aesthetic perception). However, we so far lack universally accepted quantitative measure and the respective techniques for automated assessment of user interface VC, although their development is largely seen as desirable [6].

One of the obstacles in tackling this problem is that VC is not universal and the factors and features affecting it depend of the object being perceived. For instance, for certain signs (hieroglyphs) these factors included area and, correspondingly, the number of lines and strokes, while for shapes of familiar objects it was the number of turns [7]. Most current research works seem to focus on images (even more often, on photos), while publications related to complexity in data visualization and user interfaces (UIs) are relatively scarce. As some examples, we can note [8] and [9], where the authors proposed the formulas and developed software tools for calculating the UI complexity values, as well as [10].

1.2   Complexity and Data Compression

Still, there are universal approaches in VC research and quantification, and they are based on Shannon's Information Theory and on Gestalt principles of perception [11]. The former provides robust quantitative apparatus for measuring information content (calculating entropy), but it has been repeatedly shown that information-theoretic complexity does not correspond to human visual perception well, particularly since it does not consider spatial structures [12]. The latter has the concept of "visual simplicity" as the foundational principle, and has been shown to match the humans' "top-down" perception of objects well. However, it used to suffer from lack of quantitative methods, at least until the emergence of Algorithmic Information Theory (AIT), which linked this approach to Kolmogorov algorithmic complexity [13].

With AIT it became possible to directly link the concepts of "simplicity" and "probability" and unite the two corresponding approaches. The complexity of a percept is the length of the string that generates the percept and at the same time expressed through Kolmogorov probability of the percept. The compression algorithm acts as a practical substitute of the universal Turing machine, taking the compressed string (previously produced with the same algorithm) to reproduce the original string. Kolmogorov complexity is defined as the length of the shortest program needed to produce a string – hence, the length of the compressed string can stand for the pseudo-Kolmogorov complexity of the original string [11]. Higher compression ratios presumably allow the compressed string's length to approach the "real" Kolmogorov complexity.

1.3   Related Work and Research Question

The compression algorithm probably seeing the widest use for producing VC is JPEG (as specified e.g. in ISO/IEC 10918-1:1994 standard), which was specifically designed to consider particulars of images perception by humans. In relation to complexity, this mainstream compression algorithm is a subset of spatial-frequency analysis, of which some more advanced versions are sometimes utilized, such as discrete Fourier analysis with varying window size and number of harmonics [7]. Some alternatives include calculating Subband Entropy [14] or Fractal Dimension of the image, using Zipf's Law, preliminary edge detection filters application, etc. [15].

In HCI and UI analysis, the above approaches have been successfully applied to images (JPEG compression algorithm, frequency-based entropy measures, image types [15], etc.), textual content (characters recognition in fonts, graphic complexity [16], etc.), high-order UI design measures (e.g. amount of whitespace in [2]) and so on. Meanwhile, UI layouts have not been in the focus of quantitative VC research, even though they are known to have significant impact on users' perception of UIs and are important for preserving their attained experience with a computer system [17]. To the best of our knowledge, [18] was the only work to propose a layout complexity metric, based on spatial allocation and diversity of UI elements, but this research direction seemingly failed to gain momentum.

One possible reason why studies of UI layouts have been relatively scarce is that the spatial regularity component in perception is hard to isolate. Indeed, the widely accepted neurological model is that the "what" and "where" information processing is rather detached and performed in ventral and dorsal streams of the brain respectively. Also it was noted that the three basic factors in information complexity metrics: numeric size, variety, and relation are evaluated in different stages of brain information processing: perception, cognition, and action. However, in practical UI engineering these factors are interlinked, and the effect of spatial allocation of UI elements is barely distinguishable from the others. We in our work, however, propose the method potentially capable of negating the superfluous effects, perform a model experiment first, where UI layouts were represented as uniform cells in a 2D grid. Then we validate the approach with the real web UIs, which are nowadays most often designed as vertically or horizontally aligned blocks, each consisting of several logically connected UI elements.

So, the goal of our paper is finding out if humans' perception of UI layouts complexity can be well explained with the measures supplied by data compression algorithms. In Methods, we briefly reiterate on the Hick's law, acting as the baseline information-theoretic measure, and describe the compression algorithms used in our study: RLE-based one and classical Deflate. We further introduce our method for coding the considered visual objects – UI layouts. Since cases were reported when vertical or horizontal alignment of the same UI elements mattered in terms of visual search time [19], we also investigate the different ways to convert two-dimensional layouts into bit string representations. We conclude the Sect. 2 with the hypotheses detailing the research question of our work. In Sect. 3, we describe experimental research we performed with the model layouts and analyze the data we obtained from 78 participants. In Sect. 4, we verify our findings with real UIs of 21 operating websites, assessed by 63 subjective evaluators and coded according to the proposed method. In Conclusions, we summarize our results, note limitations of our study and outline prospects for further research.

2 Methods

2.1 Entropy and Human Perception

Almost immediately after its emergence, the Shannon's Information Theory was applied to psychological and perception problems. The prerequisite for using information concepts in visual perception was measuring the information content of stimuli [11]. Arguably the most influential undertaking with regard to the cognitive aspect was the one by W.E. Hick (1952), who postulated that reaction time (RT) when choosing from equally probable alternatives is proportional to the logarithm of their number (N_H):

$$RT \sim \log_2(N_H + 1) \tag{1}$$

Naturally, (1) is a particular case – with the equiprobable alternatives – of the more fundamental relation between RT and the entropy of the stimuli set (H_T), which was later noted by Ray Hyman:

$$RT = a_H + b_H H_T, \tag{2}$$

where a_H and b_H are empirically defined coefficients.

Some of the popular UI design guidelines are in fact based on the related entropy minimization principle: grouping of interface elements and aligning them by grid, importance of consistency and standards, aesthetics of minimalism, etc. However, despite the demonstrated applicability of the Hick's law for certain aspects related to UI design, it currently has little use in HCI [20]. First, calculating the informational content of stimuli in practice is generally more problematic. Second, it is believed that since the information-theoretic approach is analytical by nature, it is fundamentally limited in explaining human perception, which is mostly top-down: that is, focused on higher-order images and structures. As we mentioned before, AIT made it possible to bond Information Theory with Gestalt principles of perception, which are concerned exactly with how visual sensory input is organized into a percept. Within this school, it was empirically shown that the coded string lengths, the complexity measures, and performance measures in experiments are highly correlated [11].

The process of obtaining the complexity measure is as follows. The pre-requisite of AIT application to perception of a visual form, including a GUI, is translating the form into a string of symbols. Although there are many ways to convert 2D grid representations that we use in our study into 1D strings, we need to do that considering human perception of regularity. Both theory (see in [17]) and practical UI design agree that vertical and horizontal alignment best correspond to perceived regularity in UI, so we will consider both these ways. AIT equate the complexity of the visual form with the length of the code required to represent the form, and data compression algorithms can act as practical analogue of the AIT definition of complexity (length of the bit string required to generate the initial string) [11]. Correspondingly, after processing the representative string with a compression algorithm, we obtain a complexity measure (approximated, as the real one is incomputable). Presumably, the complexity measures for UI layouts will be well correlated with perception of complexity, as is the case for other types of visual objects.

2.2   The Compression Algorithms

In our work we rely on two algorithms that are classical in lossless image compression, even though they may well provide worse compression than more advanced methods, such as based on k-th order entropy. We deliberately use one rather basic method (RLE), seeking to have significant difference in the compression ratios. The two employed methods also allow more natural application on rather small 2D grids that we use in our model experiment and comparison with JPEG-based compression measure, which we use in the experiment with the real web UIs.

Run-Length Encoding (RLE). RLE is one of the oldest and simplest algorithms for lossless data compression, which was already in use for handling images in the 1960s. The idea of the algorithm is relatively straightforward: *runs* of data are replaced with a single data value and the count of how many times it's repeated. Runs are sequences in which the same data value occurs several times, and these are quite common in icons, line drawings and other imagery with large mono-colored areas. The algorithm doesn't deal with 2D images, but can work with the linear string of bytes containing serialized rows of the image. In the best case, a string of some 64 repeating value would be compressed into 2 bits, i.e. providing *compression ratio* of 32 or *data rate saving* of 0.96875. It should be noted that for some kinds of files, such as high-quality photographic images, the RLE algorithm compression may even increase the volume, due to lack of runs. Based on RLE encoding principle, a number of more sophisticated algorithms and compressed data file formats were developed (.TGA, .PCX, etc.), but in our work we are going to employ a simple and straightforward RLE implementation.

The *encode* function implements simple RLE algorithm compression. The input variable for the function is binary string.

```
function encode($input)
{
  if (!$input) {
    return '';
  }

  $output = '';
  $prev = $letter = null;
  $count = 1;
  foreach (str_split($input) as $letter) {
      if ($letter === $prev) {
        $count++;
      } else {
        if ($count > 1) {
          $output .= $count;
        }
        $output .= $prev;
        $count = 1;
      }
      $prev = $letter;
  }

  if ($count > 1) {
    $output .= $count;
  }

  $output .= $letter;
  return $output;
}
```

Deflate. Deflate is a lossless data compression algorithm that is based on combination of *LZ77* algorithm and *Huffman coding*. It was developed by P. Katz, who used it in PKZIP archiving software, and was later defined in RFC 1951 specification. It is free from patent protections, so many compressed data formats (e.g. .PNG images) rely on Deflate. Today's popular implementation of the algorithm is in widely used *zlib* software library, which is also capable of compressing data according to the somewhat adjusted RFC 1950 and RFC 1952 *(gzip)* variations.

In the first stage of Deflate, LZ77-based "sliding window" approach is used to replace duplicate series of data (strings) with back-references to a single copy of that data. In the second stage, commonly used symbols are replaced with shorted representations and less common symbols – with longer ones, based on Huffman coding method. The Huffman algorithm (which doesn't guarantee optimal result, but has very reasonable time complexity) produces a variable-length code table for encoding source symbols. The Huffman codes are "prefix-free", i.e. an encoding bit string is never a prefix for another encoding bit string. The Huffman coding is now widespread, being used in compression of many kinds of data, especially photos (JPEG) and multimedia, as well as in data transmission protocols. At the same time, it does provide good data compression ratio for small alphabet sizes.

For the purposes of current research work, we relied on PHP's standard *zlib_encode* function, called with ZLIB_ENCODING_RAW parameter (corresponding to the RFC 1951 specification), to obtain the compressed string.

2.3   The "Squint" Coarsening Method

To turn layouts (as visual objects) into string representation, in our study we propose a novel method, which is based on decrease of UI visual fidelity (coarsening) – overlaying 2D grid. Layout grids with blocks aligned vertically and/or horizontally, are de-facto standard in modern interface design, and they are implemented in Bootstrap, Axure and many other tools. Each cells of the overlaid grid contain either 1 (the area has interface elements) or 0 (few or no perceived interface elements). Such uniformity allows focusing on layout and eliminating other factors, such as perception of colors, diversity of elements, etc. Naturally, it makes the method inadequate for UI studies that involve user tasks and actual interactions, textual content, etc.

At the same time, the aforementioned coarse model still reflects most layout-related aspects of real UIs: visual organization (hierarchy), elements' weights and forms, edges, whitespace, etc. Perception-wise, Gestalt principles (particularly proximity and continuation) remain legitimate, while most UI grid quality/layout metrics can be calculated on the model: balance, symmetry, alignment points, etc. The grid model also supports scanning (thus matching the users' prevalent way of interacting with new web pages), during which the quick but persistent impressions of the UI are known to be made.

Overall, the method can be said to correspond to the informal "squint test" popular in practical UI design, which allows estimating the quality of interface elements' visual organization (see software implementation of the coarsening e.g. in [21]). The approach also starts seeing methodological use in research – for instance, in [22] they used similar method in studying user attention distribution in interaction with 2D graphic UIs.

2.4   Hypotheses and the Experimental Material

Based on the research objectives and the related work, we formulated the following hypotheses for our experimental investigation:

1. Lengths of strings output by the data compression algorithms should explain layouts' complexity perception in humans better than the baseline measure. For the latter we are using the purely informational Hick's law, lacking the spatial allocation consideration.
2. The algorithm providing higher data compression ratio better explains the layout complexity perception, since its output is closer to the algorithmic complexity.

3. The conversion of two-dimensional layout into bit string sent to a compression algorithm is uniform for vertical and horizontal dimensions (as said before, we consider only these two types of the filling curve) – i.e. it does not consistently affect the measure's explanatory power.

Layouts (Experiment 1). For the model testing of the hypotheses and assessment of the coarsening method's applicability, we used two-dimensional grids (all square, to better align with the hypothesis #3). In the grid, square cells of the same sizes were allocated, most of which were white, corresponding to zeros, while a varying number of them were filled with blue color, corresponding to ones. In Fig. 1 we show example of the grid, with the corresponding numerical values overlaying the cells (in the experiment they did not show to participants). The two-dimension matrix corresponding to the example is: [[0, 0, 1, 0, 0], [1, 0, 0, 0, 1], [0, 0, 1, 0, 0], [0, 1, 0, 1, 1], [0, 1, 0, 0, 0]].

Websites (Experiment 2). The goals were to check if our model results generalize to real UIs and if the coarsening method can be feasible in practice. Since there are many interfering factors, not just layouts, we should expect to find smaller statistical effects (this is why our first experiment was with models). We chose to focus on web interfaces, so that the popular JPEG algorithm could be more dependable in producing the additional baseline measure. So, we employed 21 operating websites of 11 German universities and 10 Russian ones – in all cases, English versions were used. The websites for the experiment were manually selected, with the requirements that (1) the universities are not too well-known, so that their reputations do not bias the evaluations; (2) the designs are sufficiently diverse in terms of layout, colors, images, etc.

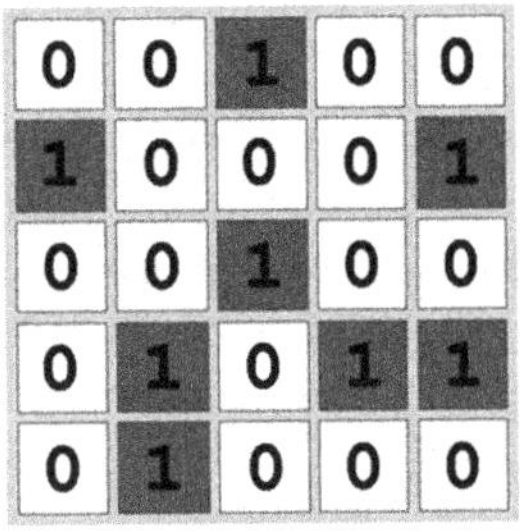

Fig. 1. Example of the grid with explanation of the numerical values corresponding to the cells.

3   Experiment 1: Layouts

3.1   Experiment Description

Participants. The overall number of valid subjects in our experimental sessions undertaken within one month was 78 (57 females, 20 males, 1 undefined). Most of them were Bachelor and Master students of Novosibirsk State Technical University, who took part in the experiment voluntary (no random selection was performed).

The subjects' age ranged from 17 to 65, mean 21.7 (SD = 2.03). All the participants had normal or corrected to normal vision and reasonable experience in IT usage. Most of the participants worked from desktop computers installed in the university computer rooms. There were also 17 other registrations with the online surveying system, but none of those subjects completed the assignment (on average, each of them completed only 4.4% of the assigned evaluations), so they were discarded from the experiment.

Design. The experiment used within-subjects design. The main independent variables were:

- Number of filled cells in the grid (the "ones" in the matrix), ranging from 4 to 13: N;
- Number of all cells in the grid (elements in the matrix). We used two levels, 25 (5*5 grid) and 36 (6*6 grid): S_0;
- Layout configuration – i.e. allocation of filled cells in the grid, which was performed randomly.

For the purposes of the compression algorithms application, the layout configurations needed to be converted into bit string. We used two ways to do that: by rows (matrix [[1, 1], [0, 0]] becomes [1100] string) and by columns (the same matrix becomes [1010]), in both cases starting from the top left element. So, we also got several "derived" independent variables in the experiment:

- Lengths of the row- and column-based bit strings compressed with the RLE-based algorithm: L_{RLE-R} and L_{RLE-C};
- Lengths of the row- and column-based bit strings compressed with the Deflate algorithm: L_{D-R} and L_{D-C};
- The corresponding data compression ratios for the algorithms: C_{RLE-R}, C_{RLE-C}, C_{D-R}, C_{D-C}.

The dependent variable was Complexity – the subjects' subjective evaluations of presented layouts complexity, ranging from 1 (lowest complexity) to 5 (highest complexity).

Procedure. To support the experimental procedure, we used our specially developed web-based software. Before the experiment, we used it to collect data on the participants (gender, age, university major, etc.). In each trial, the subject was shown a layout with random allocation of the colored cells (configuration) and varying N and S_0 and asked to evaluate it per the Complexity scale. The values of all the variables would be saved be the software, and the participant moved to the next trial. The configurations were independent between the trials, and the overall number of layouts to be evaluated by each subject was set to 100. The interface of the software could be either in Russian or in English, with the scale also dubbed in German.

3.2   Descriptive Statistics

The total number of layouts used in the experiment was 4734. The subjects submitted 7800 evaluations in total, and averaged evaluations for 4702 layouts (99.3%) were considered valid. Save for outliers, completing each trial on average took a participant 13.69 s, so the average time spent on an experimental session was 22.82 min.

The averaged value for Complexity in the experiment was 2.58 (SD = 0.96)[1]. The Pearson correlation between S_0 and N was significant, but quite low (r = 0.096, p < 0.001).

To test the hypothesis #3 (differences for row- and column-based strings compression) we used t-tests, which found no statistically significant differences for L_{RLE-R} and L_{RLE-C} (t_{4701} = −0.808, p = 0.419, r = 0.708) or L_{D-R} and L_{D-C} (t_{4701} = −1.035, p = 0.301, r = 0.590). So, in the further analysis we used the "best" values, equal to the minimal length or maximal compression ratio for each string:

$$L_{RLE} = \min\{L_{RLE-R}; L_{RLE-C}\} \tag{3}$$

$$L_D = \min\{L_{D-R}; L_{D-C}\} \tag{4}$$

$$C_{RLE} = \max\{C_{RLE-R}; C_{RLE-C}\} \tag{5}$$

$$C_D = \max\{C_{D-R}; C_{D-C}\} \tag{6}$$

Ranges, means and standard deviations for the considered independent variables are shown in Table 1. We found statistically significant Pearson's correlations for L_{RLE} with L_D (r = 0.718, p < 0.001), $\log_2 N$ with L_{RLE} (r = 0.736, p < 0.001), and $\log_2 N$ with L_D (r = 0.702, p < 0.001). At the same time, t-test suggested statistically significant difference between C_{RLE} and C_D (t_{4701} = −87.5, p < 0.001, r = 0.734). Since the compression ratios for the two algorithms in the experiment were different, the testing of our hypothesis #2 would be possible.

3.3   Effects of Independent Variables

In Table 1 we also show Pearson correlations between Complexity and the respective independent variables, all of which were significant (p < 0.001).

With respect to the hypothesis #1, we can note that the strongest correlation (r = 0.539) was found for $\log_2 N$, which suggests Hick's law is rather applicable for explaining the perception of layouts' complexity. However, the differences in correlations are marginal compared to the ones found for N and L_{RLE}, which implies the need for further analysis.

With respect to the hypothesis #2, while Deflate algorithm provided significantly better compression ratio (mean of 2.23 vs. 1.85 for RLE), thus finding more regularities in the layouts. However, its correlation with the perceived complexity was notably weaker than for RLE algorithm. We will further elaborate on this in the regression analysis.

---

[1] We are aware about the controversy existing in the research community about treating Likert and other ordinal scales as rational ones for some methods. In our analysis we tried to use methods appropriate for ordinal scales when possible, but nevertheless were not restricted to them, if more robust analysis could be performed. We ask the readers to judge for themselves whether the potential bias in the results overweighs their usefulness.

Table 1. Descriptive statistics and the correlations for the independent variables (experiment 1).

Variable	Range	Mean (SD)	r (Complexity)
S_0	25; 36	–	0.163
N	4–13	7.46 (2.01)	0.535
$\log_2 N$	2.00–3.70	2.84 (0.42)	**0.539**
L_{RLE}	8–30	17.14 (3.54)	0.531
L_D	8–20	13.95 (1.99)	0.440
C_{RLE}	1.09–4.50	1.85 (0.40)	−0.400
C_D	1.39–4.00	2.23 (0.42)	−0.199

3.4   Regression Analysis

To explore whether the variables considered in the paper could explain layout complexity perception, we performed regression analysis for Complexity with two groups of factors. The informational component was $\log_2 N$, as having the highest correlation with Complexity and being best theoretically justified by the Hick's law. The regression model with this single factor was significant ($F_{1,4700} = 1926$, $p < 0.001$), but had relatively low $R^2 = 0.291$:

$$Complexity = -0.95 + 1.24 \log_2 N. \tag{7}$$

Further, we attempted regression with all 7 independent variables (see in Table 1) as factors. We used Backwards variable selection method, which led to the model with just two significant factors: $\log_2 N$ (Beta = 0.323, $p < 0.001$) and L_{RLE} (Beta = 0.294, $p < 0.001$). With respect to the hypothesis #2, we should specially note that the L_D factor was not significant ($p = 0.552$). The model had somehow improved $R^2 = 0.330$ ($F_{2,4699} = 1158$, $R^2_{adj} = 0.330$):

$$Complexity = -0.9 + 0.74 \log_2 N + 0.08 L_{RLE}. \tag{8}$$

To evaluate the quality of the two models that had different number of factors (k), we also calculated Akaike Information Criterion (AIC) using the following formulation for the linear regression:

$$AIC = 2k + n \ln(RSS), \tag{9}$$

where n is sample size (in our case, n = 4702), RSS are the respective residual sums of squares. AIC for (7) amounted to 37758, while AIC for (8) was 37490, which suggests that the "information loss" of the second model is lower and it should be preferred over the first one.

4 Experiment 2: Websites

The first stage was experimental survey in which we collected subjective evaluations for website homepages, per dimensions related to visual complexity (see [23] for more detail). In the second stage, the web UIs were processed by annotators to be converted into coded representations.

4.1 Experiment Description (Subjective Complexity)

Participants. In total, 63 participants (30 male, 33 female) provided their evaluations of the websites' complexity. The convenience sampling method was applied, with most of the participants being students or universities staff members. The self-denoted age ranged from 19 to 72, mean 27.6, SD = 8.07. The self-denoted nationalities were Russian (65.1%), German (17.5%), Argentinian (4.8%), and others (including Bulgarian, Vietnamese, Korean, etc.). Submissions by another 13 participants were discarded as being incomplete (none of them had at least 50% of websites evaluated).

Design. Since providing the evaluations in absolute numbers would be unattainable for the participants who were not web design professionals, we chose to rely on ordinal values. For each of the following statements, 7-point Likert scale was used (1 being "completely disagree", 7 – "completely agree"), resulting in the respective ordinal variables:

- "This webpage has many elements." SElements
- "The elements in the webpage are very diverse." SVocab
- "The elements in the webpage are well-ordered." SOrder
- "The webpage has a lot of text." SText
- "The webpage has a lot of graphics." SImg
- "The webpage has a lot of whitespace." SWhite
- "The webpage appears very complex." SComplex

In the current work, we only used SComplex as the dependent variable in the experiment 2. We also employed SElements and SWhite to extra check the applicability of the proposed coarsening method implementation, which we describe further.

Since for web UIs we can use the JPEG algorithm measure, we introduced two additional independent variables:

- The size of JPEG-100 compressed file, measured in MB: L_{JPEG};
- The corresponding compression ratio, calculated as the area S (in pixels) of the screenshot divided by the JPEG file size (in bytes): C_{JPEG}.

Procedure. The survey to collect data was implemented using LimeSurvey, and the participants used a web browser to interact with it. Some of them worked in university computer rooms, while the others used their own computer equipment with varying screen resolutions, to better represent the real context of use. Each subject was asked to evaluate the screenshots of the 21 websites' homepages (presented one by one in random order) per the 7 subjective scales. On average, it took each participant 30.3 min to complete the survey, and the data collection session lasted 19 days overall. We used screenshots, not the actual websites, to ensure uniformity of the experimental material between the participants.

4.2   Experiment Description (Layout Annotation)

Participants. In the second stage of the experiment, we employed 8 annotators (4 male, 4 female), whose ages ranged from 18 to 21 (mean 19.0, SD = 1.0). They were students of Novosibirsk State Technical University who volunteered to participate in this study as part of their practical training course. All the participants worked simultaneously in a same room, under instructor's supervision.

Design. The independent variables resulted from the annotation of the UIs:

- Number of rows in the overlaid grid: W_S_R;
- Number of columns in the overlaid grid: W_S_C;
- "Configuration" – the placement of 0s and 1s in the grid cells.

From these, we got the "derived" independent variables:

- Number of cells containing 1s: W_N;
- Number of all cells in the grid (W_S_R multiplied by W_S_C): W_S_0;
- Lengths of the row- and column-based bit strings compressed with the RLE-based algorithm: W_L_{RLE-R} and W_L_{RLE-C};
- Lengths of the row- and column-based bit strings compressed with the Deflate algorithm: W_L_{D-R} and W_L_{D-C};
- The corresponding data compression ratios for the algorithms: W_C_{RLE-R}, W_C_{RLE-C}, W_C_{D-R}, W_C_{D-C}.

Procedure. The screenshots of the websites were printed out in color on A4 format paper sheets (since the two websites were not found to be valid, the total number of annotated websites was 19). The participants were instructed to put the provided tracing paper A4 format sheets over the printed out screenshots and use the pencils to draw grid layouts marking 0 or 1 in each cell. The numbers of rows and columns in the grid were to be chosen individually by each annotator and each screenshot, depending on their impression of the layout design grid. However, the participants were told that more rows and columns are generally preferred over less. In the grid cells, 0s and 1s were also to be assigned subjectively, depending if the cell's interior was mostly whitespace (0) or interface elements/content (1). The order in which each of the 8 annotators processed the 19 screenshots was randomized.

4.3   Descriptive Statistics

In the first stage of the experiment, we collected 1323 complexity evaluations for the 21 websites. Websites #9 and #14 were removed from further study due to technical problems with the screenshots (90.5% valid). In the second stage, we collected 152 annotations for the remaining 19 website screenshots. On overall, it took the annotators about 1 h to finish their job.

The averaged value for SComplex (the complexity scale in this experiment ranged from 1 to 7) was 3.61 (SD = 0.77). The Pearson correlation between W_S_0 and W_N was highly significant (r = 0.929, p < 0.001).

We used t-tests to check statistical significance of differences in compression for row- and column-based strings. We found no statistically significant difference between W_L_{RLE-R} and W_L_{RLE-C} (t_{151} = 1.222, p = 0.224, r = 0.807). However, the difference between W_L_{D-R} and W_L_{D-C} was significant (t_{4701} = −3.873, p < 0.001, r = 0.951), the mean lengths being 13.37 and 13.97 respectively. Still, we decided to use the "best" values for both algorithms (W_L_{RLE} and W_L_D), in correspondence with the experiment 1.

Again, we found statistically significant Pearson's correlations for W_L_{RLE} with W_L_D (r = 0.941, p < 0.001), $\log_2$W_N with W_L_{RLE} (r = 0.735, p < 0.001), and $\log_2$W_N with W_L_D (r = 0.657, p < 0.001). L_{JPEG} had no significant correlations (at α = 0.05) with either of these three variables, but its positive correlation with W_S_0 was found to be significant (r = 0.486, p = 0.035), which suggests validity of this "screenshot length" measure provided by the annotators.

In this experiment, t-test showed no statistically significant difference between W_C_{RLE} and W_C_D (p = 0.983). However, C_{JPEG} was found to be significantly different (at α = 0.08) from both W_C_{RLE} (t_{18} = −1.86, p = 0.08) and W_C_D (t_{18} = −2.1, p = 0.05).

4.4   Effects of Independent Variables

In Table 2 we show Pearson correlations between SComplex and the respective independent variables, but in this experiment none of the correlations were significant at α = 0.05, which is explained in particular by the small sample size.

Table 2. Descriptive statistics and the correlations for the independent variables (experiment 2).

Variable	Range	Mean (SD)	r (SComplex)
W_S_0	22.25–54.75	34.22 (9.53)	0.245
W_N	12.5–32.00	21.82 (6.04)	0.343
$\log_2$W_N	3.64–5.0	4.39 (0.42)	**0.349**
W_L_{RLE}	6.75–22.5	15.14 (4.06)	0.149
W_L_D	8.25–17.38	12.94 (2.23)	0.269
L_{JPEG}	0.56–9.11	1.68 (1.95)	0.332
W_C_{RLE}	1.80–3.74	2.58 (0.57)	0.058
W_C_D	1.82–3.56	2.58 (0.48)	0.126
C_{JPEG}	1.19–3.18	2.22 (0.57)	−0.262

Just like in the first experiment, the strongest correlation with complexity (r = 0.349) was found for $\log_2$W_N. The correlation for L_{JPEG} that we considered as the baseline was somehow weaker (r = 0.332).

Hypothesis #2 couldn't be validated by strict analogy with the first experiment, since in the second one there was no significant difference between the compression ratios provided by RLE and Deflate algorithms. But we should note that while JPEG algorithm compression ratio was significantly lower on average, C_{JPEG} had stronger correlation ($r = -0.262$) with SComplex, in comparison with W_C_{RLE} and W_C_D.

Additional analysis was performed to explore relations between the number of elements specified by participants of the subjective complexity evaluation stage and the annotators' results. We found significant correlations between SElements and W_N ($r = 0.719$, $p = 0.001$), which was stronger than the one between SElements and W_S_0 ($r = 0.562$, $p = 0.012$). The correlation between SWhite and the calculated whitespace measure ($1 - W\_N/W\_S_0$) was also significant ($r = 0.531$, $p = 0.019$). These results suggest that whitespace was mostly annotated as grid cells with 0s, while the interface elements visible to the complexity evaluators were annotated as grid cells with 1s.

4.5   Regression Analysis

Again, first we performed regression analysis with the baseline factors. The model with $\log_2 W\_N$ was not significant ($p = 0.143$) and had $R^2 = 0.122$. The model with L_{JPEG} had lower significance ($p = 0.164$) and $R^2 = 0.110$. Notably, the regression models for the other factors we considered (W_S_0, W_N, W_L_{RLE}, W_L_D) had even lower significances and R^2 values.

Further, we attempted regression with all 9 independent variables (see in Table 2) as factors. We used Backwards variable selection method, which now led to the model with three significant factors (at $\alpha = 0.07$): $\log_2 W\_N$ (Beta = 0.619, $p = 0.067$), W_L_{RLE} (Beta = -1.534, $p = 0.043$), W_L_D (Beta = 1.306, $p = 0.054$). This model had $R^2 = 0.339$ ($F_{3,15} = 2.57$, $R^2_{adj} = 0.207$, AIC = 43.2):

$$SComplex = -2.85 + 1.15 \log_2 W\_N - 0.29 W\_L_{RLE} + 0.45 W\_L_D \qquad (10)$$

However, among the intermediate models considered within the Backwards selection, there was a model with higher $R^2_{adj} = 0.263$ and lower AIC = 42.5. The factors in this model ($F_{4,14} = 2.61$, $R^2 = 0.427$) were $\log_2 W\_N$ (Beta = 0.498, $p = 0.134$), W_L_{RLE} (Beta = -1.694, $p = 0.026$), W_L_D (Beta = 1.471, $p = 0.031$), and L_{JPEG} (Beta = 0.328, $p = 0.165$):

$$SComplex = -2.37 + 0.92 \log_2 W\_N - 0.32 W\_L_{RLE} + \\ 0.51 W\_L_D + 0.13 L_{JPEG} \qquad (11)$$

5   Conclusion

In our paper we examined perceived visual complexity of UI layouts, which are a major controlled feature for every human-computer interface designer. Particularly, we sought to introduce data compression algorithms, which with respect to complexity have both solid theoretical justification (AIT) and wide practical application

(JPEG-based metrics). So, we proposed the UI layouts coding method and employed the RLE and Deflate algorithms to produce compressed strings. In Experiment 1, Deflate provided better compression ratio, which was expected from it as the more advanced algorithm. In Experiment 2, no significant difference in the compression ratios could be found, probably due to very limited sample size.

Our analysis of the experimental data suggests the following conclusions per the hypotheses formulated in the study:

Hypothesis #1. The compressed strings' lengths do explain layouts' complexity perception in humans, as the corresponding factors were significant in regressions for the model (8) and real UIs (10). However, the correlations (Tables 1 and 2) suggest that the Hick's law factor is even stronger connected to the perceived layout complexity.

Hypothesis #2. Unexpectedly, algorithms that showed higher compression ratios had weaker connection to the perceived complexity (Tables 1 and 2). LD was not significant in regression (8), unlike LRLE, while LJPEG had the lowest significance in (11).

Hypothesis #3. Generally, matrix conversion to string representation was no different by rows or by columns, with the only exception of the 4.4% difference for Deflate algorithm in experiment 2, where the sample size was relatively small.

Hence, we see the main contributions of our paper as the following:

1. We proposed the **novel "squint" coarsening method for coding UI layouts** into binary strings and demonstrated its use with real web interfaces. Practical applicability of the method is supported by highly significant correlation (r = 0.719) between the subjectively assessed number of interface elements and the number of annotated cells containing 1s, as well as significant correlation (r = 0.531) between the subjective amount of whitespace and the share of annotated cells containing 0s.
2. We demonstrated that compression algorithms can provide metrics that improve prediction of perceived VC of UI layouts. At the same time, we found that the classical Hick's law informational metric is well applicable as the main factor, which may imply its certain "revival" in HCI.
3. We found that better compression algorithms, which presumably come closer to the "real" Kolmogorov complexity, do not explain layouts VC perception better. It may mean that layouts are a specific type of visual objects [24], whereas human perception of them doesn't rely on optimal coding.
4. We found that the way two-dimensional matrix representing the modelled UI layout is converted into bit string (by rows or by columns) does not affect the compression measure's explaining power with regard to layouts VC.

We see the main limitation of our study in employment of ordinal scales to measure VC of both model representation and web UIs. We plan to develop the approach for using interval scale, presumably based on tasks performance time. Also, the sample size in the websites experiment was relatively small, so the found statistical effects were not always convincing. Finally, the proposed coarsening method was inspired by UI design practice, and in our study it was applied to web UI layouts only. At the current point we cannot surmise if it will adequately work for UI on other platforms (mobile, desktop) or images in general.

Our further prospects include software implementation of the proposed coarsening method, so that coded representations for web UI screenshots could be collected automatically. We also plan to explore whether the coarsening method that we proposed and applied for WUI layouts only, could be suitable for producing coded representations for other types of visual objects.

Acknowledgement. The reported study was funded by Russian Ministry of Education and Science, according to the research project No. 2.2327.2017/4.6.

References

1. Castellani, B.: Brian castellani on the complexity sciences. Theory Cult. Soc. **October, 9** (2014). https://www.theoryculturesociety.org/brian-castellani-on-the-complexity-sciences/
2. Reinecke, K., et al.: Predicting users' first impressions of website aesthetics with a quantification of perceived visual complexity and colorfulness. In: Proceedings of the ACM SIGCHI Conference on Human Factors in Computing Systems, pp. 2049–2058 (2013)
3. Machado, P., et al.: Computerized measures of visual complexity. Acta Physiol. **160**, 43–57 (2015)
4. Michailidou, E., Harper, S., Bechhofer, S.: Visual complexity and aesthetic perception of web pages. In: Proceedings of the 26th ACM International Conference on Design of Communication, pp. 215–224 (2008)
5. Taba, S.E.S., Keivanloo, I., Zou, Y., Ng, J., Ng, T.: An exploratory study on the relation between user interface complexity and the perceived quality. In: Casteleyn, S., Rossi, G., Winckler, M. (eds.) ICWE 2014. LNCS, vol. 8541, pp. 370–379. Springer, Cham (2014). https://doi.org/10.1007/978-3-319-08245-5_22
6. Wu, O., Hu, W., Shi, L.: Measuring the visual complexities of web pages. ACM Trans. Web (TWEB) **7**(1), 1 (2013)
7. Chikhman, V., et al.: Complexity of images: experimental and computational estimates compared. Perception **41**(6), 631–647 (2012)
8. Alemerien, K., Magel, K.: GUIEvaluator: a Metric-tool for evaluating the complexity of graphical user interfaces. In: SEKE, pp. 13–18 (2014)
9. Stickel, C., Ebner, M., Holzinger, A.: The XAOS metric – understanding visual complexity as measure of usability. In: Leitner, G., Hitz, M., Holzinger, A. (eds.) USAB 2010. LNCS, vol. 6389, pp. 278–290. Springer, Heidelberg (2010). https://doi.org/10.1007/978-3-642-16607-5_18
10. Miniukovich, A., De Angeli, A.: Quantification of interface visual complexity. In Proceedings of the 2014 ACM International Working Conference on Advanced Visual Interfaces, pp. 153–160 (2014)
11. Donderi, D.C.: Visual complexity: a review. Psychol. Bull. **132**(1), 73 (2006)
12. Yu, H., Winkler, S.: Image complexity and spatial information. In: IEEE Fifth International Workshop on Quality of Multimedia Experience (QoMEX), pp. 12–17 (2013)
13. Solomonoff, R.: The application of algorithmic probability to problems in artificial intelligence. Mach. Intell. Pattern Recognit. **4**, 473–491 (1986)
14. Rosenholtz, R., Li, Y., Nakano, L.: Measuring visual clutter. J. Vis. **7**(2), 1–22 (2007)
15. Carballal, A., et al.: Distinguishing paintings from photographs by complexity estimates. Neural Comput. Appl. **30**(6), 1–13 (2016)
16. Chang, L.Y., Chen, Y.C., Perfetti, C.A.: GraphCom: a multidimensional measure of graphic complexity applied to 131 written languages. Behav. Res. Methods **50**(1), 427–449 (2018)

17. Heil, S., Bakaev, M., Gaedke, M.: Measuring and ensuring similarity of user interfaces: the impact of web layout. In: Cellary, W., Mokbel, M.F., Wang, J., Wang, H., Zhou, R., Zhang, Y. (eds.) WISE 2016. LNCS, vol. 10041, pp. 252–260. Springer, Cham (2016). https://doi.org/10.1007/978-3-319-48740-3_18

18. Comber, T., Maltby, J.R.: Layout complexity: does it measure usability? In: Howard, S., Hammond, J., Lindgaard, G. (eds.) Human-Computer Interaction INTERACT '97. ITIFIP, pp. 623–626. Springer, Boston, MA (1997). https://doi.org/10.1007/978-0-387-35175-9_109

19. Michalski, R., Grobelny, J., Karwowski, W.: The effects of graphical interface design characteristics on human–computer interaction task efficiency. Int. J. Ind. Ergon. 36(11), 959–977 (2006)

20. Seow, S.C.: Information theoretic models of HCI: a comparison of the Hick-Hyman law and Fitts' law. Hum.-Comput. Interact. 20(3), 315–352 (2005)

21. Kim, N.W., et al.: BubbleView: an interface for crowdsourcing image importance maps and tracking visual attention. ACM Trans. Comput.-Hum. Interact. (TOCHI), 24(5) (2017). Article no. 36

22. Xu, P., Sugano, Y., Bulling, A.: Spatio-temporal modeling and prediction of visual attention in graphical user interfaces. In: Proceedings of the ACM CHI Conference on Human Factors in Computing Systems, pp. 3299–3310 (2016)

23. Bakaev, M., Heil, S., Khvorostov, V., Gaedke, M.: HCI vision for automated analysis and mining of web user interfaces. In: Mikkonen, T., Klamma, R., Hernández, J. (eds.) ICWE 2018. LNCS, vol. 10845, pp. 136–144. Springer, Cham (2018). https://doi.org/10.1007/978-3-319-91662-0_10

24. Simon, H.A.: Complexity and the representation of patterned sequences of symbols. Psychol. Rev. 79(5), 369 (1972)

Computable Topology for Reliable Computations

Margarita Korovina[1(✉)] and Oleg Kudinov[2]

[1] A.P. Ershov Institute of Informatics Systems, SbRAS, Novosibirsk, Russia
`rita.korovina@gmail.com`
[2] Sobolev Institute of Mathematics, SbRAS, Novosibirsk State University,
Novosibirsk, Russia
`kud@math.nsc.ru`

Abstract. Using the framework of computable topology we investigate computable minimality of lifted domain presentations of computable Polish spaces, in particular the real numbers, the Cantor and Baire spaces, the continuous functions on a compact interval, which are widely used in theoretical computer science, e.g., automata theory, computable analysis and reliable computations. We prove that all lifted domain presentations for computable Polish spaces are computably and topologically minimal. Then we show that a naive adaptation of the notion of stability from computable model theory does not work in this framework. Instead of stability we propose another approach based on principal translators and prove that in the case of the real numbers we can effectively construct a principal computable translator from the lifted domain presentation to any other effective domain presentation.

Keywords: Computable topology · Reliable computation · Computable analysis · Lifted domain presentation

1 Introduction

Computations over continuous data are central in scientific computing and engineering. This motivates research in investigating properties of different frameworks for representing computable objects and computations over them. One of such frameworks is the well established domain theory approach proposed by Scott [17] and Ershov [3], where computational processes and data types are modelled using appropriate algebraic or continuous domains.

The research leading to these results has received funding from the DFG grants WERA MU 1801/5-1 and CAVER BE 1267/14-1 and RFBR grant A-17-01-00247. O. V. Kudinov was supported by the Program of Basic Scientific Research of the Siberian Branch of the Russian Academy of Sciences (Grant No. I.1.1, Project 0314-2019-0001). M. V. Korovina was supported by the Program of Basic Scientific Research of the Siberian Branch of the Russian Academy of Sciences (Grant No. IV.39.1.3, Project 0317-2017-0003).

N. Bjørner et al. (Eds.): PSI 2019, LNCS 11964, pp. 185–198, 2019.
https://doi.org/10.1007/978-3-030-37487-7_15

Informally, any representation of a space X is the factorisation of a part $\tilde{\mathbb{D}}$ of an appropriate algebraic domain $\mathbb{D}$ up to homeomorphism. The existence and uniqueness of representations of spaces by (algebraic) Scott-Ershov domains have been investigated in [4,5], where some canonical representations have been introduced. However the uniform characterisations of such representations have not been proposed in details. In this paper, we address similar problems in the setting of continuous domains which are more suitable, in practice, for continuous data computations [2,17]. We aim at uniting independently developed concepts of computability on computable metric spaces and on weakly effective ω-continuous domains [7,12,20].

In particular, following ideas from [1,9,22], we propose homeomorphic embeddings of computable Polish spaces into the lifted domains that endow the original spaces with computational structures and investigate the following natural problems. One of them whether lifted domain presentations of computable Polish spaces are computably and/or topologically minimal. Another one concerns a characterisation of translators from lifted domain presentations to other effective domain presentations of computable Polish spaces. The last problem is originated in computable model theory [14,16] and is related to stability of structures and spaces. In particular, we show cases when computable and continuous translations between different presentations of spaces exist and/or unique.

In this paper we introduce the key notion of a computably minimal domain presentation and show that the canonical lifted domain presentations are computably minimal. Moreover, since there are infinitely many computable translators from any computably minimal domain presentation to any computable one (see Sect. 3.3), using the idea of a principal (maximal) computable numbering from recursion theory [18] we introduce the notion of a principal computable (continuous) translator and prove that in the case of the real numbers we can effectively construct a principal computable translator from the lifted domain presentation to any other effective domain presentation.

The paper is organised as follows. In Sect. 2 we give some basic concepts from domain theory, computable Polish spaces and effectively enumerable topological spaces. We use effectively enumerable T_0-spaces as a uniform framework to represent computability on domains and computable Polish spaces. Section 3 contains the main contributions of the paper. We first computably embed a computable Polish space $\mathbb{P}$ into a lifted domain $\mathbb{D}^{\mathbb{P}}$ that is a weakly effective ω-continuous domain such that the Scott topology on $\mathbb{D}^{\mathbb{P}}$ agrees with the standard topology on $\mathbb{P}$ and the proposed embedding is a homeomorphism between the set of maximal elements and the original space. We prove that lifted domain presentations are computably and topologically minimal. Then we show that while all topologically minimal presentations of computable Polish spaces are not stable there exist principal translators in the case of the lifted domain presentation of the reals.

2   Preliminaries

We refer the reader to [7,9,10,19–21] for basic definitions and fundamental concepts of computable topology and to [1,2] for basic definitions and fundamental concepts of domain representations of reliable computations. A numbering of a set Y is a total surjective map $\gamma : \omega \to Y$. We use the standard notations for the real numbers $\mathbb{R}$ and $C([a,b])$ for the set of continuous real-valued functions defined on a compact interval $[a,b]$.

2.1   Weakly Effective ω-continuous Domains

In this section we present a background on domain theory. The reader can find more details in [2,6]. Let $(D; \perp, \leq)$ be a partial order with a least element $\perp$. A subset $A \subseteq D$ is *directed* if $A \neq \emptyset$ and $(\forall x, y \in A)(\exists z \in A)(x \leq z \wedge y \leq z)$. We say that D is a *directed complete partial order*, denoted dcpo, if any directed set $A \subseteq D$ has a supremum in D, denoted $\bigsqcup A$. For two elements $x, y \in D$ we say x is *way-below* y, denoted $x \ll y$, if whenever $y \leq \bigsqcup A$ for a directed set A, then there exists $a \in A$ such that $x \leq a$. A function $f : \mathbb{D} \to \widetilde{\mathbb{D}}$ between cpos is continuous if f is monotone and for each directed set $A \subseteq D$ we have $F(\bigsqcup A) = \bigsqcup \{f(x) \mid x \in A\}$. We say that $\mathbf{B} \subseteq D$ is a *basis* (base) for D if for every $x \in D$ the set $approx_{\mathbf{B}}(x) = \{y \in \mathbf{B} \mid y \ll x\}$ is directed and $x = \bigsqcup approx_{\mathbf{B}}(x)$. We say that D is *continuous* if it has a basis; it is $\omega-continuous$ if it has a countable basis. We denote the predicate $Cons(a,b) \leftrightharpoons (\exists c \in D)(a \leq c) \wedge (b \leq c)$.

Definition 1 *[6]. Let* $\mathbb{D} = (D; \mathbf{B}, \beta, \leq, \perp)$ *be an* $\omega-continuous$ *domain with a basis* $\mathbf{B}$, *the least element* $\perp \in \mathbf{B}$ *and its numbering* $\beta : \omega \to B$ *such that* $\beta(0) = \perp$. *We say that* $\mathbb{D}$ *is weakly effective if the relation* $\beta(i) \ll \beta(j)$ *is computably enumerable.*

One of the well-known examples of weakly effective ω–continuous domains is the interval domain $\mathcal{I}_{\mathbb{R}} = \{[a,b] \mid a, b \in \mathbb{R}, a \leq b\} \cup \perp$ with the inverse order and the countable basis that is the collection of all compact intervals with rational endpoints together with the least element $\perp$ (see e.g. [2]).

Proposition 1 (Interpolation Property) *[6]. Let* $\mathbb{D}$ *be a continuous domain and let* $M \subseteq D$ *be a finite set that* $(\forall a \in M)\, a \ll y$. *Then there exists* $x \in D$ *such that* $M \ll x \ll y$ *holds. If* $\mathbb{D}$ *is* $\omega-continuous$ *then* x *may be chosen from the basis.*

Definition 2. *We say that* $\mathbb{D} = (D; \mathbf{B}, \beta, \leq, \perp)$ *is a weakly effective consistently complete* $\omega-continuous$ *domain if the following requirements hold:*

1. $\mathbb{D} = (D; \mathbf{B}, \beta, \leq, \perp)$ *is a weakly effective* $\omega-continuous$ *domain.*
2. $\mathbb{D} = (D; \leq)$ *is consistently complete, i.e., for all* $a, b \in D$ *if* $Cons(a,b)$ *holds then there exists* $d \leftrightharpoons a \sqcup b$ *such that* $\forall (c \in D)(a \leq c \wedge b \leq c) \to d \leq c$.
3. *The predicate* $Cons(a,b)$ *is computable enumerable on* $\mathbf{B}$, *i.e., the set* $\{(k,l) \mid Cons(\beta(k), \beta(l))\}$ *is c.e.*

4. *The operator $\cup$ is partially computable on* **B**, *i.e., for some partial computable function* $p : \omega^2 \to \omega$:
   (a) $(k,l) \in \mathrm{dom}(p) \leftrightarrow Cons(\beta(k), \beta(l))$;
   (b) $Cons(\beta(k), \beta(l)) \to \beta(k) \cup \beta(l) = \beta(p(k,l))$.

2.2 Perfect Computable Polish Spaces

In this paper we work with the following notion of a computable Polish space abbreviated as *CPS*. A *perfect computable Polish space*, simply *computable Polish space*, is a complete separable metric space $\mathbb{P}$ without isolated points and with a metric $d : P \times P \to \mathbb{R}$ such that there is a countable dense subset $\mathcal{B}$ called a *basis of* $\mathbb{P}$ with the numbering $\alpha : \omega \to \mathcal{B}$ that makes the following two relations: $\{(n,m,i) \mid d(\alpha(n), \alpha(m)) < q_i,\ q_i \in \mathbb{Q}\}$ and $\{(n,m,i) \mid d(\alpha(n), \alpha(m)) > q_i,\ q_i \in \mathbb{Q}\}$ computably enumerable (c.f. [22] see also [15]).

The standard notations $B(a,r)$ and $\overline{B}(a,r)$ are used for open and closed balls with the center a and the radius r. We also use the notation $\alpha(n) = b_n$ for a numbering $\alpha : \omega \to \mathcal{B}$.

2.3 Effectively Enumerable Topological Spaces

Let (X, τ, α) be a topological space, where X is a non-empty set, $B_\tau \subseteq 2^X$ is a base of the topology τ and $\alpha : \omega \to B_\tau$ is a numbering. In notations we skip τ since it can be recovered by α. Further on we will often abbreviate (X, α) by $\mathbb{X}$ if α is clear from a context.

Definition 3 *[12]. A topological space (X, α) is effectively enumerable if there exists a computable function $g : \omega \times \omega \times \omega \to \omega$ such that*

$$\alpha(i) \cap \alpha(j) = \bigcup_{n \in \omega} \alpha(g(i,j,n)) \text{ and}$$

$$\{i \mid \alpha(i) \neq \emptyset\} \text{ is computably enumerable.}$$

Definition 4. *Let (X, α) be an effectively enumerable topological space.*

1. *A set $\mathcal{O} \subseteq X$ is effectively open if there exists a computably enumerable set $V \subseteq \omega$ such that $\mathcal{O} = \bigcup_{n \in V} \alpha(n)$.*
2. *A sequence $\{\mathcal{O}_n\}_{n \in \omega}$ of effectively open sets is called computable if there exists a computable sequence $\{V_n\}_{n \in \omega}$ of computably enumerable sets such that $\mathcal{O}_n = \bigcup_{k \in V_n} \alpha(k)$.*

Definition 5 *[10]. Let $\mathbb{X} = (X, \alpha)$ be an effectively enumerable topological space and $\mathbb{Y} = (Y, \beta)$ be an effectively enumerable T_0–space. A function $f : \mathbb{X} \to \mathbb{Y}$ is called* partial computable *(pcf) if the following properties hold. There exist a* *computable sequence of effectively open sets* $\{\mathcal{O}_n\}_{n\in\omega}$ *and a computable function* $H : \omega^2 \to \omega$ *such that*

$$\mathrm{dom}(f) = \bigcap_{n\in\omega} \mathcal{O}_n \ and$$

$$f^{-1}(\beta(m)) = \bigcup_{i\in\omega} \alpha(H(m,i)) \cap \mathrm{dom}(f).$$

In the following if a partial computable function f is everywhere defined we say f is a *computable function*. It is easy to see that computable functions are effectively continuous and map a computable element to a computable element (c.g. [21]).

Remark 1. It is worth noting that the weakly effective ω–continuous domains and computable Polish spaces with induced topologies are proper subclasses of effectively enumerable T_0–spaces [12]. Therefore for uniformity we consider all those spaces in the settings of the effectively enumerable T_0–spaces.

3   Main Results

In this section we first computably embed a computable Polish space $\mathbb{P}$ into a lifted domain $\mathbb{D}^{\mathbb{P}}$ that is a weakly effective ω–continuous domain such that the Scott topology on $\mathbb{D}^{\mathbb{P}}$ agrees with the standard topology on $\mathbb{P}$ and the proposed embedding is a homeomorphism between the set of maximal elements and the original space. We prove that lifted domain presentations are computably and topologically minimal. Then we show that while all topologically minimal presentations of computable Polish spaces are not stable there exist principal translators in the case of the lifted domain presentation of the reals.

3.1   Effective Domain Presentations for *CPS*

Definition 6. *Let* $\mathbb{P}$ *be a computable Polish space. A triple* $(\mathbb{P}, \mathbb{D}, \varphi)$ *is called an effective domain presentation if*

1. $\mathbb{D} = (D; \mathbf{B}, \beta, \leq, \bot)$ *is a weakly effective consistently complete* ω–*continuous domain;*
2. *The function* $\varphi : \mathbb{P} \to \mathbb{D}$ *is a computable homeomorphic embedding such that* $\mathrm{im}(\varphi) = \bigcap_{n\in\omega} \mathcal{O}_n$ *for some computable sequence of effectively open sets* $\{\mathcal{O}_n\}_{n\in\omega};$

The definition has been motivated by observations and examples in [1,13,23]. Thus in [13] we proposed a computable homeomorphic embedding $\varphi : C[0,1] \to \mathbb{D}$, where $\mathbb{D}$ is a weakly effective consistently complete ω–continuous domain consisting of all continuous functions from the compact $[0,1]$ to $\mathcal{I}_{\mathbb{R}}$. Remarkably it turns out that $(C[0,1], \mathbb{D}, \varphi)$ is an effective domain presentation.

We recall from [9] the construction and properties of lifted domains for computable Polish spaces. Let $\mathbb{P} = (P, d, \mathcal{B}) \in CPS$. Then the lifted domain $(\mathbb{D}^{\mathbb{P}}, \psi)$ for $\mathbb{P} \in CPS$ is defined as follows:

1. $D^{\mathbb{P}} \leftrightharpoons P \times \mathbb{R}^{+} = \{(a, r) \mid a \in P \text{ and } r \in \mathbb{R}^{+}\}$;
2. $(b, q) \leq (a, r) \leftrightharpoons d(a, b) + r \leq q$;
3. $\mathbf{B} \leftrightharpoons \{(a, q) \mid a \in \mathcal{B} \text{ and } q \in \mathbb{Q}^{>0}\}$;
4. The numbering $\beta : \omega \to \mathbf{B}$ is induced by $\alpha : \omega \to \mathcal{B}$ and the standard numbering of $\mathbb{Q}^{>0}$.

It is easy to see that the way-below relation $\ll$ has the property $(b, q) \ll (a, r) \leftrightarrow d(a, b) + r < q$ and the sub-basis of the Scott topology $\tau_{D^{\mathbb{P}}}$ is the set of open sets $\mathcal{U}_{n,q} = \{(b, r) \mid (b, r) \gg (\alpha(n), q)\}$, where $\alpha(n) \in \mathcal{B}$ and $q \in \mathbb{Q}^{>0}\}$. The function ψ is defined as follows $\psi(a) = (a, 0)$.

Proposition 2. *The lifted domain $(\mathbb{D}^{\mathbb{P}}, \psi)$ for $\mathbb{P} \in CPS$ has the following properties:*

1. $\mathbb{D}^{\mathbb{P}} = (D^{\mathbb{P}}; \mathbf{B}, \beta, \leq, \bot)$ *is a weakly effective ω–continuous domain;*
2. $\psi : \mathbb{P} \to \mathbb{D}^{\mathbb{P}}$ *is a computable canonical homeomorphic embedding;*
3. $\mathrm{im}(\psi)$ *is dense in $D^{\mathbb{P}}$ and coincides with the set of maximal elements;*
4. $\mathrm{im}(\psi)$ *is an effective intersection of effectively open sets;*
5. $\mathbf{B} \cap \mathrm{im}(\psi) = \emptyset$.

Proof. The claims follow from [9,10].

Corollary 1. *Let $(\mathbb{D}^{\mathbb{P}}, \psi)$ be the lifted domain for $\mathbb{P} \in CPS$. If $(\mathbb{P}, \mathbb{D}^{\mathbb{P}}, \psi)$ is a weakly effective consistently complete ω–continuous domain then it is an effective domain presentation.*

Further on we call such lifted domains $(\mathbb{P}, \mathbb{D}^{\mathbb{P}}, \psi)$ as lifted domain presentations.

Proposition 3. *The interval domain $\mathcal{I}_{\mathbb{R}}$ with the standard embedding is computationally isomorphic to the lifted domain presentation $(\mathbb{R}, \mathbb{D}^{\mathbb{R}}, \psi)$.*

3.2 Computable and Topological Minimality

In this section we assume that $\mathbb{P} = (P, d, \mathcal{B}) \in CPS$, $(\mathbb{P}, \mathbb{D}^{\mathbb{P}}, \psi)$ is the corresponding lifted domain presentation for $\mathbb{P}$. For the basic elements of a weakly effective ω–continuous domain $\mathbb{D} = (D; \mathbf{B}, \beta, \leq, \bot)$ we use the following notation $\mathbf{B} = \{\beta_1, \ldots, \beta_n, \ldots\}$ and $\beta_0 = \bot$.

Definition 7. *Let $(\mathbb{P}, \mathbb{D}_1, \varphi_1)$ and $(\mathbb{P}, \mathbb{D}_2, \varphi_2)$ be effective domain presentations. A function $F : \mathbb{D}_1 \to \mathbb{D}_2$ is called a computable (continuous) translator if the following diagram is commutative:*

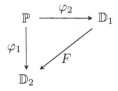

Definition 8. *An effective domain presentation* $(\mathbb{P}, \mathbb{D}, \psi)$ *is called computably (topologically) minimal if for any effective domain presentation* $(\mathbb{P}, \widetilde{\mathbb{D}}, \widetilde{\psi})$ *there exists a computable (continuous) translator* $G : \mathbb{D} \to \widetilde{\mathbb{D}}$.

Theorem 1. *For any computable Polish space* $\mathbb{P}$ *the lifted domain presentation* $(\mathbb{P}, \mathbb{D}^{\mathbb{P}}, \psi)$ *is computably minimal.*

The proof is based on the following propositions.

Lemma 1. *Let* $\mathbb{D} = (D; \mathbf{B}, \beta, \leq, \perp)$ *be a weakly effective* ω-*continuous domain and* $\mathbb{X}$ *be an effectively enumerable topological space. If a function* $f : \mathbb{X} \to \mathbb{D}$ *is computable then the following accessions hold.*

1. *Let* $A_\beta = f^{-1}(\mathcal{U}_\beta)$, *where* $\mathcal{U}_\beta = \{d \in D \mid d \gg \beta\}$. *Then* $\{A_\beta\}_{\beta \in \mathbf{B}}$ *is a computable sequence of effectively open subsets of* X *such that, for all* $\beta, \gamma \in \mathbf{B}$, $A_\beta = \bigcup_{\beta' \gg \beta} A_{\beta'}$, $A_\beta \cap A_\gamma = \bigcup_{\beta' \gg \beta \wedge \beta' \gg \gamma} A_{\beta'}$ *and if* $\beta \leq \gamma$ *then* $A_\beta \supseteq A_\gamma$.
2. $f(x) = \bigsqcup\{\beta \in \mathbf{B} \mid x \in A_\beta\}$.

Proof. Let us show the first accession. Computability of the sequence $\{A_\beta\}_{\beta \in \mathbf{B}}$ follows from computability of f. The relation $A_\beta \supseteq \bigcup_{\beta' \gg \beta} A_{\beta'}$ is straightforward. Assume now that $x \in A_\beta$. By definition, $f(x) \in \mathcal{U}_\beta$, i.e., $f(x) \gg \beta$. By the interpolation property there exists $\beta' \in \mathbf{B}$ such that $f(x) \gg \beta' \gg \beta$. So $x \in A_{\beta'}$, $x \in \bigcup_{\beta' \gg \beta} A_{\beta'}$. The relation $A_\beta \cap A_\gamma \supseteq \bigcup_{\beta' \gg \beta \wedge \beta' \gg \gamma} A_{\beta'}$ is straightforward. In order to show $A_\beta \cap A_\gamma \subseteq \bigcup_{\beta' \gg \beta \wedge \beta' \gg \gamma} A_{\beta'}$ we assume $x \in A_\beta \cap A_\gamma$. By definition, $f(x) \gg \beta$ and $f(x) \gg \gamma$. By the interpolation property and computability of f there exists $\beta' \in \mathbf{B}$ such that $f(x) \gg \beta'$ and $\beta' \gg \beta \wedge \beta' \gg \gamma$. So $x \in A_{\beta'}$.

The second assertion follows from the following observation. On the one hand, if $x \in A_\beta$ then $f(x) \gg \beta$, so $f(x) \geq \bigsqcup\{\beta \in \mathbf{B} \mid x \in A_\beta\}$. On the other hand, if $f(x) \gg \beta'$ then $x \in A_{\beta'}$, so $\beta' \leq \bigsqcup\{\beta \in \mathbf{B} \mid x \in A_\beta\}$. Since $f(x) = \bigsqcup\{\beta' \mid \beta' \ll f(x)\}$ we have $f(x) \leq \bigsqcup\{\beta \in \mathbf{B} \mid x \in A_\beta\}$.

Lemma 2. *Let* $\mathbb{D} = (D; \mathbf{B}, \beta, \leq, \perp)$ *be a weakly effective* ω-*continuous domain,* $\mathbb{X}$ *be an effectively enumerable topological space and* $\{A_\beta\}_{\beta \in \mathbf{B}}$ *be a computable sequence of effectively open sets of* X *such that*

1. *If* $\beta_1 \leq \beta_2$ *then* $A_{\beta_1} \supseteq A_{\beta_2}$.
2. *For all* $\beta, \gamma \in \mathbf{B}$, $A_\beta = \bigcup_{\beta' \gg \beta} A_{\beta'}$ *and* $A_\beta \cap A_\gamma = \bigcup_{\beta' \gg \beta \wedge \beta' \gg \gamma} A_{\beta'}$. *Then the function* $F : \mathbb{X} \to \mathbb{D}$ *defined as follows* $F(x) = \bigsqcup\{\beta \in \mathbf{B} \mid x \in A_\beta\}$ *is computable. Moreover,* $A_\beta = F^{-1}(\mathcal{U}_\beta)$.

Proof. It is sufficient to show that $x \in F^{-1}(\mathcal{U}_\beta) \leftrightarrow F(x) \gg \beta$. If $x \in A_\beta$ then there exists $\beta' \gg \beta$ such that $x \in A_{\beta'}$ and $F(x) \gg \beta' \gg \beta$, i.e., $F(x) \gg \beta$. If $F(x) \gg \beta$ then there exists $\beta' \gg \beta$ such that $x \in A_{\beta'}$ and $\beta' \geq \beta$, so $x \in A_\beta$.

Lemma 3. *Let* $\mathbb{D}_1 = (D_1; \mathbf{B}_1, \beta^1, \leq, \perp_1)$ *and* $\mathbb{D}_2 = (D_2; \mathbf{B}_2, \beta^2, \leq, \perp_2)$ *be weakly effective* ω-*continuous domains and a function* $F^* : \mathbb{D}_1 \to \mathbb{D}_2$ *be pcf such that* $\operatorname{dom}(F^*)$ *is effectively open in* D_1. *Then one can effectively construct a total computable extension* $F : \mathbb{D}_1 \to \mathbb{D}_2$.

Proof. Put

$$F(a) = \begin{cases} F^*(a) & \text{if } a \in \mathrm{dom}(F^*) \\ \bot_2 & \text{otherwise.} \end{cases}$$

Monotonicity of F is straightforward. To show limit preservation we assume that $\{a_i \mid i \in I\}$ is directed and $\bigsqcup_{i \in I} a_i = a$. If $a \in \mathrm{dom}(F^*)$ then, by the definition of Scott topology, there exists $j \in I$ such that $a_j \in \mathrm{dom}(F^*)$ and $\bigsqcup_{i \geq j} a_i = a$. So $F(a) = F^*(a) = \bigsqcup_{i > j} F^*(a_i) = \bigsqcup_{i \geq j} F(a_i) = \bigsqcup_{i \in I} F(a_i)$ If $a \notin \mathrm{dom}(F^*)$ then, for all $i \in I$, $a_i \notin \mathrm{dom}(F^*)$. So $F(a_i) = \bot_2$ and $F(a) = \bigsqcup_{i \in I} F(a_i)$. Hence F is continuous. For computability let us show that $F(\beta_n^1) \ll \beta_k^2$ is computably enumerable. Indeed, $F(\beta_n^1) \ll \beta_k^2 \leftrightarrow (\beta_n^1 \in \mathrm{dom}(F^*) \wedge F^*(\beta_n^1) \ll \beta_m^2) \vee \beta_m^2 \ll \bot_2$. Hence F is computable.

Theorem 2. *Let $\mathbb{D} = (D; \mathbf{B}, \beta, \leq, \bot)$ be a weakly effective consistently complete ω-continuous domain, $\mathbb{P}$ be a computable Polish space and $(\mathbb{P}, \mathbb{D}^\mathbb{P}, \psi)$ be its lifted domain presentation. Then for any computable function $f : \mathbb{P} \to \mathbb{D}$ one can effectively construct a computable extension $F : \mathbb{D}^\mathbb{P} \to \mathbb{D}$ such that $F(\psi(x)) = f(x)$, i.e., the following diagram is commutative:*

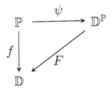

Proof. Let us fix the numbering $\beta^\mathbb{P}$ of the basic elements of $\mathbb{D}^\mathbb{P}$ such that $\beta_0^\mathbb{P} = \beta^\mathbb{P}(0) = \bot$. This induces the numbering of basic open balls in $\mathbb{P}$ such that if $\beta_k^\mathbb{P} = (a_i, r_i)$ then $B_k \leftrightharpoons B(a_i, r_i)$ for the corresponding ball.

By definition, $f^{-1}(\mathcal{U}_{\beta_i}) = \bigcup_{k \in W_{\nu(i)}} B_k$ for a computable function $\nu : \omega \to \omega$, where $\mathcal{U}_{\beta_i} = \{d \in D \mid d \gg \beta_i\}$. Then for any $x = (a, r) \in \mathbb{D}^\mathbb{P}$ such that $x \neq \bot$ we define

$$C_x = \{\beta_k \mid (\exists l \in W_{\nu(k)}) \beta_l^\mathbb{P} \ll x\}.$$

It is worth noting that any finite nonempty $A = \{\beta_{k_1}, \ldots, \beta_{k_s}\} \subseteq C_x$ is consistent in D. Indeed, we could take any $y \in B(a, r)$. Then, by the definition of ν, $y \in f^{-1}(\mathcal{U}_{\beta_{k_i}})$ for $i = 1, \ldots, s$. So, $f(y) \gg \beta_{k_i}$ for $i = 1, \ldots, s$ and hence A is consistent. Therefore, the set $\tilde{C}_x = \{\bigsqcup A \mid A \subseteq C_x$ is finite and consistent$\}$ is directed and we put

$$F(x) = \begin{cases} \bigsqcup \tilde{C}_x & \text{if } C_x \neq \emptyset \\ \bot & \text{otherwise.} \end{cases}$$

In terms of the corresponding sets $A_\beta \leftrightharpoons \{x \in D^\mathbb{P} \mid F(x) \gg \beta\}$, where $\beta \in \mathbf{B}_\mathbb{D}$, this means that $A_\beta = \{x \in D^\mathbb{P} \mid (\exists a \in D^\mathbb{P}) a \gg \beta\}$. By Lemmas 1–3 the function F is continuous.

For $k, l \in \omega$, $\beta_l \ll F(\beta_k^{\mathbb{P}})$ if and only if there exists a finite consistent set $A \subseteq C_x$ such that $\beta_l \ll \bigcup A$. This relation is computably enumerable since one can compute the index of the basic element $\bigcup A$. So, F is computable. Let us show that $F(\psi(x)) = f(x)$. From the one hand, by construction, for $x \in P$, from $\beta_k \in C_{\psi(x)}$ it follows that $f(x) \in \mathcal{U}_{\beta_k}$. So $F(\psi(x)) \leq f(x)$. From the other hand, if $\beta_k \ll f(x)$ then $f(x) \in \mathcal{U}_{\beta_k}$ so $\beta_k \in C_{\psi(x)}$ and $F(\psi(x)) \geq \beta_k$. As corollary, $F(\psi(x)) = f(x)$.

Remark 2. It is worth noting that the statement of the previous theorem holds not only for any lifted domain presentation but also for any effective domain presentation $\varphi : \mathbb{P} \to \mathbb{D}_0$ with the following conditions: the function φ^{-1} is pcf and for all $d \in D_0$ there exists $x \in P$ such that $\varphi(x) \geq d$.

Corollary 2. *For any computable Polish space $\mathbb{P}$ the lifted domain presentation $(\mathbb{P}, \mathbb{D}^{\mathbb{P}}, \psi)$ is topologically minimal.*

Proof. The claim follows from the relativization of Theorem 1 to an oracle making a lifted domain presentation computably minimal.

Our considerations above revel the following properties of the interval domain for real numbers that widely used in domain theory and interval computations.

Theorem 3. *Let $(\mathbb{P}_1, \mathbb{D}^{\mathbb{P}_1}, \psi_1)$ be a lifted domain presentation and $(\mathbb{R}, \mathcal{I}_{\mathbb{R}}, \psi_2)$ be the standard interval domain presentation for the reals. For any pcf $f : \mathbb{P}_1 \to \mathbb{R}$ one can effectively construct a total computable function $F : \mathbb{D}^{\mathbb{P}_1} \to \mathcal{I}_{\mathbb{R}}$ such that*

1. $f(x) = y \leftrightarrow F(\psi_1(x)) = \psi_2(y) \wedge (x \in \mathrm{dom}(f))$;
2. *if $x \notin \mathrm{dom}(f)$ then $F(\psi_1(x)) \notin max(\mathcal{I}_{\mathbb{R}})$.*

Proof. Let $f : \mathbb{P}_1 \to \mathbb{R}$ be pcf. In [8] we have shown that for the class of real-valued functions from computable metric spaces the notion of pcf coincides with majorant-computability. That means that we can effectively construct effectively open sets $U(x, y)$ and $V(x, y)$ such that $V(x, \cdot) < U(x, \cdot)$ and

$$f(x) = y \leftrightarrow \forall z_1 \forall z_2 \, (V(x, z_1) < y < U(x, z_2)) \wedge$$
$$\{z \mid V(a, z)\} \cup \{z \mid U(a, z)\} = \mathbb{R} \setminus \{y\}.$$

Now we define $H : \mathbb{P}_1 \to \mathcal{I}_{\mathbb{R}}$ as follows: Put

$$H(x) = \begin{cases} [\sup\{y \mid V(x, y), \inf\{z \mid U(x, z)\}] & \text{if } V(x, \cdot), U(x, \cdot) \neq \emptyset \\ \bot & \text{otherwise.} \end{cases}$$

It is easy to see that H is a computable function and, for all $x \in \mathbb{P}$, $H([x]) = f(x)$. Then the existence of F follows from Theorem 2.

3.3   Principal Translators

In this section we introduce the notion of a principal computable (continuous) translator and prove that in the case of the real numbers we can effectively construct a principal computable translator from the lifted domain presentation to any other domain presentation.

Definition 9. *For a computable Polish space $\mathbb{P}$, let $(\mathbb{P}, \mathbb{D}_1, \varphi_1)$ and $(\mathbb{P}, \mathbb{D}_2, \varphi_2)$ be its effective domain presentations. We call a computable (continuous) translator $G : \mathbb{D}_1 \to \mathbb{D}_2$ principal if $F \leq G$ for any computable (continuous) translator $F : \mathbb{D}_1 \to \mathbb{D}_2$.*

Definition 10. *An effective domain presentation $(\mathbb{P}, \mathbb{D}, \varphi)$ is called (computably) stable if for any effective domain presentation $(\mathbb{P}, \widetilde{\mathbb{D}}, \widetilde{\psi})$ there exists a unique continuous (computable) translator $G : \mathbb{D} \to \widetilde{\mathbb{D}}$.*

Proposition 4. *For any computable Polish space the lifted domain presentation is neither computably stable nor stable.*

Proof. It is sufficient to show that there are infinitely many continuous even computable translators for $\widetilde{\mathbb{D}} \equiv \mathbb{D}^{\mathbb{P}}$. Put

$$G \equiv \mathrm{id} \ \text{and}\ \varphi_q\big((a, r)\big) = (a, q * r), \ \text{where}\ q \in \mathbb{Q}^+ \ \text{and}\ q > 1.$$

We have:

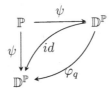

All of these translators are computable and different from each other.

Proposition 5. *If an effective domain presentation $(\mathbb{P}, \mathbb{D}, \theta)$ is topologically (computably) minimal then it is not (computably) stable.*

Proof. Let $\mathbb{D} = (D; \mathbf{B}, \beta, \leq, \perp)$. It is enough to observe topological part, the rest is just an analog. Assume $F : \mathbb{D} \to \mathbb{D}^{\mathbb{P}}$ is a continuous translator. We have the following commutative diagram:

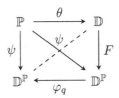

Since $F(\mathbf{B}) \not\subseteq max(D^{\mathbb{P}})$, there exists $a \in \mathbf{B}$ such that $F(a) \notin max(\mathbb{D}^{\mathbb{P}})$. Then $\varphi_q(F(a)) \neq F(a)$, where φ is defined in Proposition 4. We have $\varphi_q \circ F : \mathbb{D} \to \mathbb{D}^{\mathbb{P}}$ is a continuous translator and $\varphi_q \circ F \neq F$.

Theorem 4. *Let $(\mathbb{P}, \mathbb{D}^{\mathbb{P}}, \psi)$ be the lifted domain presentation and $(\mathbb{P}, \widetilde{\mathbb{D}}, \widetilde{\psi})$ be an effective domain presentation. Then there exists a principal continuous translator $G : \mathbb{D}^{\mathbb{P}} \to \widetilde{\mathbb{D}}$.*

Proof. Let us define

$$G((a,r)) = \bigsqcup \{g((a, r + \tfrac{1}{n}))\}_{n \in \omega}, \text{ where } g((a,r)) = \inf\{\widetilde{\psi}(x) \mid (a,r) \leq \psi(x)\}.$$

From the definition of ψ it is easy to see that $g((a,r)) = \inf\{\widetilde{\psi}(x) \mid (a,r) \leq (x,0)\} = \inf\{\widetilde{\psi}(x) \mid x \in \overline{B}(a,r)\}$. In order to show that G is a required we prove that G is total and monotone, preserves limits and makes the corresponding diagram commutative.

Totality. It is worth noting that for any $Y \subseteq \widetilde{D}$ there exists $\inf(Y)$. Indeed, since $\widetilde{\mathbb{D}}$ is consistently complete the set $\{z \mid z \leq Y\}$ is directed. Therefore $\inf(Y) = \bigsqcup\{z \mid z \leq Y\}$ for $Y \neq \emptyset$ and $\inf(\emptyset) = \bot$ by the definition of dcpo.

Monotonicity. By definition it is clear that g is monotone Assume $(b, R) \leq (a, r)$, i.e., $d(a, b) + r \leq R$. By definition, $G((a, r)) = \bigsqcup \inf\{\widetilde{\psi}(x) \mid x \in \overline{B}(a, r + \tfrac{1}{n})\}_{n \in \omega}$, $G((b, R)) = \bigsqcup \inf\{\widetilde{\psi}(x) \mid x \in \overline{B}(b, R + \tfrac{1}{n})\}_{n \in \omega}$ and, by assumption, $(b, R + \tfrac{1}{n}) \leq (a, r + \tfrac{1}{n})$. Therefore $G((b, R)) \leq G((a, r))$.

Limit Preservation. Since $\widetilde{\mathbb{D}}$ is a weakly effective ω–continuous domain to prove that G preserves limits it is sufficient to consider countable directed sets. We show first that for any directed sets $\mathcal{A}, \mathcal{B} \subseteq D$, if $\bigsqcup \mathcal{A} = \bigsqcup \mathcal{B} = (a, r)$ and $\mathcal{A} \ll (a, r)$, $\mathcal{B} \ll (a, r)$ then $\bigsqcup\{g((a, r)) \mid (a, r) \in \mathcal{A}\} = \bigsqcup\{g((b, R)) \mid (b, R) \in \mathcal{B}\}$ that looks as the low semi-continuity condition. Let us pick a basic elements $\beta \in \widetilde{\mathbf{B}}$ such that $\beta \ll \bigsqcup\{g((a, r)) \mid (a, r) \in \mathcal{A}\}$. By the definition of the way-below relation, there exists $(a, r) \in \mathcal{A}$ such that $\beta \ll g((a, r))$ so for all $x \in \overline{B}(a, r)$ we have $\beta \ll \widetilde{\psi}(x)$. Since $\bigsqcup \mathcal{A} = \bigsqcup \mathcal{B}$ there exists $(b, R) \geq (a, r)$ so for all $x \in \overline{B}(b, R)$ we have $\beta \ll \widetilde{\psi}(x)$. This means $\beta \ll \bigsqcup\{g((b, R)) \mid (b, R) \in \mathcal{B}\}$. Since β is arbitrary chosen $\bigsqcup\{g((a, r)) \mid (a, r) \in \mathcal{A}\} \geq \bigsqcup\{g((b, R)) \mid (b, R) \in \mathcal{B}\}$. By symmetry, $\bigsqcup\{g((a, r)) \mid (a, r) \in \mathcal{A}\} = \bigsqcup\{g((b, R)) \mid (b, R) \in \mathcal{B}\}$.

Now assume that, for a countable directed set $\mathcal{A} \subseteq D$, $\bigsqcup \mathcal{A} = (a, r)$. It is well-known that we can extract some monotone sequence $\{(a_n, r_n)\}_{n \in \omega}$ of elements of $\mathcal{A}$ such that $\bigsqcup\{(a_n, r_n)\}_{n \in \omega} = (a, r)$. Therefore it is sufficient to prove that $\bigsqcup\{G((a_n, r_n))\}_{n \in \omega} = G(a, r)$. By definition $G((a_n, r_n)) = \bigsqcup\{(a_n, r_n + \tfrac{1}{k}\}_{k \in \omega}$. It is easy to see that $\bigsqcup\{(a_n, r_n + \tfrac{1}{k})\}_{n, k \in \omega} = (a, r)$ and $(a_n, r_n + \tfrac{1}{k}) \ll (a, r)$ for all $n, k \in \omega$. By the property of g which we proved above $\bigsqcup\{g((a_n, r_n + \tfrac{1}{k}))\}_{n, k \in \omega} = \bigsqcup\{g(a, r + \tfrac{1}{m})\}_{m \in \omega}$ so $\bigsqcup G((a_n, r_n)) = G((a, r))$. Therefore G is a continuous function.

Commutativity of the Diagram. We show that $\widetilde{\psi}(x) = G(\psi(x))$, i.e, $\widetilde{\psi}(x) = G((x, 0))$ since $\psi(x) = (x, 0)$. By definition, $G((x, 0)) = \bigsqcup\{g((x, \tfrac{1}{n}))\}$ and, for all $n \in \omega$, $g(x, \frac{1}{n}) \leq \widetilde{\psi}(x)$. Therefore $\widetilde{\psi}(x) \geq G((x, 0))$. Since $\widetilde{\psi}$ is continuous in x for all $\widetilde{\beta} \in \widetilde{\mathbf{B}}$ such that $\widetilde{\beta} \ll \widetilde{\psi}(x)$ there exist $\sigma > 0$ such that for all $y \in P$ if $d(y, x) < \sigma$ then $\widetilde{b} \ll \widetilde{\psi}(y)$. It is worth noting that if $\frac{1}{n} < \sigma$ then $g(x, \frac{1}{n}) \leq \widetilde{\beta}$. So we have $G((x, 0)) \geq \widetilde{\beta}$. By continuity, $\widetilde{\psi}(x) = \bigsqcup\{\widetilde{\beta} \mid \widetilde{\beta} \ll \widetilde{\psi}(x)\}$ so $\widetilde{\psi}(x) \leq G((x, 0))$.

Maximality. Let us show that for any continuous translator $F : \mathbb{D}^{\mathbb{R}} \to \widetilde{\mathbb{D}}$ we have $F \leq G$. First we observe that if $x \in max(\mathbb{D}^{\mathbb{P}})$ then $F(x) = G(x)$. By monotonicity of F, $F((a, r)) \leq \inf\{\widetilde{\psi}(x) \mid (a, r) \leq \psi(x)\} = g((a, r))$. Similarly, $F((a, r + \frac{1}{n})) \leq g((a, r + \frac{1}{n}))$. Since $G((a, r)) = \bigsqcup\{g((a, r + \frac{1}{n}))\}_{n \in \omega}$ and $F((a, r)) = \bigsqcup\{F((a, r + \frac{1}{n}))\}_{n \in \omega}$ we have $F((a, r)) \leq G((a, r))$. As a corollary G is a required function.

Theorem 5. *Let $(\mathbb{R}, \mathbb{D}^{\mathbb{R}}, \psi)$ be the lifted domain presentation and $(\mathbb{R}, \widetilde{\mathbb{D}}, \widetilde{\psi})$ be an effective domain presentation. Then there exists a principal computable translator $G : \mathbb{D}^{\mathbb{R}} \to \widetilde{\mathbb{D}}$.*

Proof. Let us show that in the case of $\mathbb{P} = \mathbb{R}$, the continuous function G from the previous proof is computable under the assumption that $\widetilde{\psi}$ is computable.

Computability. In order to show that G is computable it is sufficient to show that $F(\beta_k) \gg \widetilde{\beta}_m$ is computably enumerable. First we assume that $\beta_k = (a_k, r_k)$ and observe that the relation $g((a_k, r_k)) \gg \widetilde{\beta}_m$ is computable enumerable. It follows from the following formula and the uniformity principle [11].

$$g((a_k, r_k)) \gg \widetilde{\beta}_m \leftrightarrow (\forall x \in \overline{B}(a_k, r_k)) \, \widetilde{\psi}(x) \gg \widetilde{\beta}_m \leftrightarrow$$
$$(\forall x \in \overline{B}(a_k, r_k)) \, x \in \widetilde{\psi}^{-1}(\mathcal{U}_{\widetilde{\beta}_m}).$$

Since, by definition, $G((a_k, r_k)) = \bigsqcup\{g((a_k, r_k + \frac{1}{n}))\}_{n \in \omega}$ we have

$$G((a_k, r_k)) \gg \widetilde{\beta}_m \leftrightarrow (\exists n \in \omega) \, g((a_k, r_k + \frac{1}{n})) \gg \widetilde{\beta}_m.$$

Therefore the required relation is computably enumerable and G is computable.

4 Conclusion and Future Work

In this paper we characterised computably minimal presentations of computable Polish spaces. We showed that between any computably minimal presentations one can effectively construct a translator. This gives a technique to convert one computably minimal presentation to another. Therefore a user can chose any preferable computably minimal presentation and then if necessary convert to canonical one. For the lifted domain of the real numbers we provided a principal computable translator. This highlighted a direction of how to approach a formalisation of higher type computations over the reals.

References

1. Edalat, A., Heckmann, R.: A computational model for metric spaces. Theoret. Comput. Sci. **193**(1–2), 53–73 (1998)
2. Edalat, A.: Domains for computation in mathematics, physics and exact real arithmetic. Bull. Symb. Log. **3**(4), 401–452 (1997)
3. Ershov, Yu.L.: Computable functionals of finite types. Algebra Log. **11**(4), 367–437 (1996)
4. Blanck, J.: Interval domains and computable sequences: a case study of domain reductions. Comput. J. **56**(1), 45–52 (2013)
5. Blanck, J.: Domain representability of metric spaces. Ann. Pure Appl. Log. **83**(3), 225–247 (1997)
6. Gierz, G., Heinrich Hofmann, K., Keime, lK., Lawson, J.D., Mislove, M.W.: Continuous Lattices and Domain. Encyclopedia of Mathematics and its Applications 93. Cambridge University Press, Cambridge (2003)
7. Grubba, T., Weihrauch, K.: Elementary computable topology. J. UCS. **15**(6), 1381–1422 (2009)
8. Korovina, M., Kudinov, O.: Weak reduction principle and computable metric spaces. In: Manea, F., Miller, R.G., Nowotka, D. (eds.) CiE 2018. LNCS, vol. 10936, pp. 234–243. Springer, Cham (2018). https://doi.org/10.1007/978-3-319-94418-0_24
9. Korovina, M., Kudinov, O.: Highlights of the Rice-Shapiro theorem in computable topology. In: Petrenko, A.K., Voronkov, A. (eds.) PSI 2017. LNCS, vol. 10742, pp. 241–255. Springer, Cham (2018). https://doi.org/10.1007/978-3-319-74313-4_18
10. Korovina, M., Kudinov, O.: Outline of partial computability in computable topology. In: Kari, J., Manea, F., Petre, I. (eds.) CiE 2017. LNCS, vol. 10307, pp. 64–76. Springer, Cham (2017). https://doi.org/10.1007/978-3-319-58741-7_7
11. Korovina, M., Kudinov, O.: The uniformity principle for Σ-definability. J. Log. Comput. **19**(1), 159–174 (2009)
12. Korovina, M., Kudinov, O.: Towards computability over effectively enumerable topological spaces. Electron. Notes Theoret. Comput. Sci. **221**, 115–125 (2008)
13. Korovina, M.V., Kudinov, O.V.: Formalisation of computability of operators and real-valued functionals via domain theory. In: Blanck, J., Brattka, V., Hertling, P. (eds.) CCA 2000. LNCS, vol. 2064, pp. 146–168. Springer, Heidelberg (2001). https://doi.org/10.1007/3-540-45335-0_10
14. Mal'Cev, A.: Constructive algebras. Uspehi Math Nauk **16**(3), 3–60 (1961)
15. Moschovakis, Y.N.: Recursive metric spaces. Fund. Math. **55**, 215–238 (1964)
16. Rabin, M.: Computable algebra, general theory and theory of computable fields. Trans. Am. Math. Soc. **95**, 341–360 (1960)
17. Scott, D.: Lectures on a mathematical theory of computation. In: Broy, M., Schmidt, G. (eds.) Theoretical Foundations of Programming Methodology. NATO Advanced Study Institutes Series (Series C – Mathematical and Physical Sciences), vol. 91, pp. 145–292. Springer, Dordrecht (1982). https://doi.org/10.1007/978-94-009-7893-5_9
18. Soare, R.I.: Recursively Enumerable Sets and Degrees: A Study of Computable Functions and Computably Generated Sets. Springer, Heidelberg (1987)
19. Spreen, D.: On some decision problems in programming. Inf. Comput. **122**(1), 120–139 (1995)
20. Spreen, D.: On effective topological spaces. J. Symb. Log. **63**(1), 185–221 (1998)

21. Weihrauch, K.: Computable Analysis. Springer, Heidelberg (2000). https://doi. org/10.1007/978-3-642-56999-9
22. Weihrauch, K.: Computability on computable metric spaces. Theoret. Comput. Sci. **113**(1), 191–210 (1993)
23. Weihrauch, K., Schreiber, U.: Embedding metric spaces into CPO's. Theoret. Comput. Sci. **16**, 5–24 (1981)

About Leaks of Confidential Data in the Process of Indexing Sites by Search Crawlers

Sergey Kratov[(✉)]

Institute of Computational Mathematics and Mathematical Geophysics SB RAS,
Novosibirsk, Russia
kratov@sscc.ru

Abstract. The large number of sites for very different purposes (online stores, ticketing systems, hotel reservations, etc.) collect and store personal information of their users, as well as other confidential data, such as history and results of user interaction with these sites. Some of such data, not intended for open access, nevertheless falls into the search output and may be available to unauthorized persons when specific requests are made. This article describes the reasons for such incidents occurrence and the basic recommendations for technical specialists (developers and administrators) that will help prevent leaks.

Keywords: Data leaks · Site indexing · Search crawlers · Robots.txt · Noindex · X-Robots-Tag · Htaccess

1 The Possible Sources of Data Leaks

One of the factors determining the effectiveness of the search is the completeness of the index. So the search engines try to index as many pages as possible to select those that most closely match the users' requests. Therefore, in addition to going through the links on the pages, the search engines also resort to other methods that allow it to discover the appearance of new pages on the Internet. Very often sites generate individualized pages for each user. So that search engines cannot get to seemingly public pages from links on the main page of the site. Accordingly, it is logical for search engines to obtain page addresses for indexing from as many sources as possible. In particular, for example, users agree by default with possible analysis and collection of browsers anonymous data on page visits and other actions, when installing browsers, often developed by search engines (Yandex, Google). This is the legal way for search engines to collect most of the pages ever viewed by users. For example, Yandex. Browser collects anonymized statistical information, which includes, in addition, the addresses of the pages visited. This happens in all cases when the user clearly did not forbid doing this in the browser settings (the option "Send usage statistics to Yandex"). At the same time, thematic forums for developers described situations when, due to a

The research has been supported by the ICMMG SB RAS budget project N 0315-2016-0006.

N. Bjørner et al. (Eds.): PSI 2019, LNCS 11964, pp. 199–204, 2019.
https://doi.org/10.1007/978-3-030-37487-7_16

technical error of Yandex employees, information about individual pages viewed in the browser came to the list of indexing for Yandex crawlers [1].

Another source of data for the search engines index replenishment can be the counters of analytical systems (the most common ones in Russia are Yandex.Metrica and Google Analytics) placed in the page source code. For example, as specified in the Yandex.Metrica user agreement [2] if site administrators do not forbid sending site pages to indexing, the addresses of the pages on which the counter is installed are passed to Yandex indexing (and it is possible subsequently to the search output). By default, such option is enabled. That is how a few years ago SMS from the mobile operator Megafon's site fells in the search output [3]. There was the possibility of anonymous sending SMS on the operator's site to its clients. This did not require registration on the site. At the same time, the site developers, for the convenience of users, generated for each sending a page with a random address, which displayed the SMS text and the status of its delivery. These pages got into Yandex's search output and became available to any user of the search engine.

Only the couple of data leakage cases were listed above on the example of the one of the search engines services. Nevertheless, there is no reason to suppose that the rest of the search engines are fundamentally different. The issues of search engines legality and their crawlers «ethical» nature in the data collection process have already been repeatedly discussed in the other researchers' works [4–6].

2 The Informing Developers and Users About the Possibility of Leaks

Search crawlers cannot access and indexing information from pages that require authorization. At the same time, modern sites often require complex passwords, which are not always convenient for users to remember. For the convenience of users, developers often generate and send to users in emails (in plain text) links to pages with unique long addresses from a random character set that cannot be guessed or enumerated. So users can grant direct access to sites without entering a username and password. Users navigate through such link, their browser or analytics counter tells the search engine that an unknown page has appeared, the search crawler indexes it. In this case, the crawler has no information about whether the personal data is placed on the page, whether confidential information is contained in tables (for example, financial indicators) or the content of the page is publicly available. Useful recommendations for developers who are forced to generate and send pages with automatic login are available in the corresponding W3C manual [7].

Confidential data periodically fell into search indexes during the entire existence of search engines. The number of such leaks, increased in recent years, is associated with the growing popularity of the Internet and, accordingly, the number of users of the network. More and more people are entering the network, now they are not only IT specialists, but also users far from information technologies. Most users believe that a document accessible via a unique link is securely protected and will never get into the index. The main changes to minimize the number of similar incidents in the future should be done by site developers to ensure their quality work. Search engines, in turn, should also fully cover their indexing mechanisms for both developers and site users. In particular, to inform developers that any page that is available to users without authorization can sooner or later get into the index and search output. The last such large-scale data leak in the Russian-speaking Internet segment occurred in early July 2018. The search engine Yandex indexed and included in its search output a large array of documents from the Google Docs service [8]. The documents were publicly available and, accordingly, were available for indexing, but at the same time, many of them contained confidential information not intended for unauthorized persons. Moreover, some of the documents were not only available for viewing, but also for editing to any user who passed them by link from the index. Formally, both Yandex and Google in this situation acted within the law. The documents were excluded from the search output in identifying the problem. The problem arose primarily because of the lack of users' awareness about the specifics of the access differentiation to their documents in the service. But this fact does not cancel the presence of the problem itself.

3 The Prohibition of Confidential Data Indexing. Directives for Search Crawlers

The most effective way to deny access to confidential information is to use authorization to access it. However, in those cases when it is impossible or impractical for not to complicate the work of users with the site, developers can use other methods that will prevent search crawlers from indexing the contents of the pages and in many ways will reduce the probability of their getting into the search output. For example, it is possible to use the robots.txt file [9–11] or corresponding tags in the HTML markup and page headers.

The de-facto standard of exclusions for crawlers Robots.txt has been open for discussion on the Technical World Wide Web mailing list. It represents a consensus on 30 June 1994 between the majority of robot authors and has since been supported by most search engines. Robots.txt is the text file describing the limitations of the search crawlers' access to the web server's content. This file should be uploaded to the site's root directory. The file consists of separate records, the Disallow field is used to prevent indexing. With this field, developers can deny access to individual directories/ pages for all or individual search crawlers. The example of the appropriate entry completely closing access to the site for search crawlers is shown in (1).

$$
\begin{aligned}
&\texttt{User-agent: *}\\
&\texttt{Disallow: /}
\end{aligned}
\tag{1}
$$

In the User-agent field, individual search crawlers can be enumerated, for example, Yandex or Googlebot. In the Disallow field, you can specify both the name of the individual file and the directory as a whole. More details about the syntax of robots.txt and practical recommendations for its use can be read in the original description [12] and earlier studies on this topic [13, 14]. It is also recommended after creating or editing the file to check its syntax correctness by using search engines special services [15, 16].

In cases where site administrators do not have access to the site root directory to host the robots.txt file, or site administrators do not want to advertise the individual directories/files addresses, the noindex tag can be used anywhere in the HTML code of the page, as shown in (2).

$$
\texttt{<noindex> the text that does not need to be indexed </ noindex>} \tag{2}
$$

The noindex tag is only valid for the search engine Yandex and it is not included in the official HTML specification so, if it is used in the code of the pages, they may fail to validate the html code correctness. In such cases the noindex tag can be used in the format shown in (3).

$$
\texttt{<! - noindex -> the text that does not need to be indexed <! - / noindex ->} \tag{3}
$$

The noindex tag can also be used as the metatag, in which case its action will extend to the entire text of the page as a whole, as shown in (4).

$$
\texttt{<meta name = "robots" content = "noindex" />} \tag{4}
$$

In addition, although Google does not index the contents of pages blocked in the robots.txt file, such pages URLs found on other pages on the Internet can still be indexed [17]. In this case, the use of noindex in the metatag form in the page header will further prohibit its indexing when a search crawler hits it.

The separate metatag can be requested to delete the previously indexed page copy from the search engine cache, as shown in (5).

$$
\texttt{<meta name = "robots" content = "noarchive" />} \tag{5}
$$

The noindex metatag can be used only in the code of html-pages. If developers want to deny access to other types of documents, they can use the X-Robots-Tag metatag contained in the HTTP header. An example of the HTTP header that prohibits crawlers from indexing the page is shown in (6).

$$
\begin{array}{l}
\texttt{HTTP / 1.1 200 OK} \\
\texttt{...} \\
\texttt{X-Robots-Tag: noindex} \\
\texttt{...}
\end{array} \tag{6}
$$

If site works on the Apache web server, its administrators can insert the appropriate headers using directives in the .htaccess file. For example, the directives prohibit search crawlers from indexing all pdf-files of the site are shown in (7).

```
<Files ~ "\.pdf$">
Header set X-Robots-Tag "noindex, nofollow"     (7)
</ Files>
```

For more details about syntax and usage examples, see the appropriate Google manual [18].

4   Conclusion

Unfortunately, using the above methods does not guarantee that the site pages and individual files will not be indexed. These methods are recommendatory for search crawlers and the implementation or non-implementation of recommendations depends only on the particular crawler. The problem is that different search engines differently interpret the web servers' directives, their recommendations for improving the sites' indexing also often contradict each other. That is, the developers, having done everything according to the Google's instructions, can create a situation in which the Yandex will index a lot of documents that should not have been indexed, and vice versa. For example, Google does not handle noindex tags in the text of the pages, and Yandex - X-Robots-Tag in HTTP headers.

Therefore, administrators of already working sites need to conduct their basic audit for the leaking confidential data possibility to search engines:

- Carry out the entire tree of the site's links analysis - scan search output and other sources (Yandex.Metrics, Google Analytics, Yandex.Webmaster and Google Search Console). Identify the site's pages containing confidential data. Finding the reasons and determining how to hide these pages from indexing and from the publicly available part of the site.
- Analyze files, links to which are not present on the site pages - identify confidential files accessible via direct links, including those that are not yet in the search output. Search for the reasons for such files availability and determine how to hide them from public access.

In addition to the above actions to prohibit the confidential data's indexing, developers can also strongly encourage to take the following actions when creating new sites:

- Exclude any of the confidential data from sharing with authorization using.
- Identify search crawlers and block them from accessing any private information. And developers should not only use one of the methods recommended by any search engine, but duplicate, using all protection methods. Verify that the protection methods used are universal and workable for all search engines.
- Maximally inform users about all available privacy settings within each site.

References

1. YandexBot crawls the links that the user views (in Russian). https://habr.com/en/post/262695/. Accessed 27 Apr 2019
2. Terms of Use of Yandex.Metrica service. https://yandex.ru/legal/metrica_termsofuse/. Accessed 29 Aug 2018
3. FAQ on the SMS texts leakage from Megafon site (in Russian). https://habr.com/en/post/124387/. Accessed 27 Apr 2019
4. Schellekens, M.H.M.: Are internet robots adequately regulated? Comput. Law Secur. Rev. **29**(6), 666–675 (2013). https://doi.org/10.1016/j.clsr.2013.09.003
5. Sun, Y., Councill, I.G., Giles, C.L.: The ethicality of web crawlers. In: Proceedings of 2010 IEEE/WIC/ACM International Conference on Web Intelligence, WI 2010, pp. 668–675 (2010). https://doi.org/10.1109/wi-iat.2010.316
6. Giles, C.L., Sun, Y., Councill, I.G.: Measuring the web crawler ethics. In: Proceedings of the 19th International Conference on World Wide Web, WWW 2010, pp. 1101–1102 (2010). https://doi.org/10.1145/1772690.1772824
7. Good Practices for Capability URLs. https://www.w3.org/TR/capability-urls/. Accessed 29 Aug 2018
8. Yandex began to index Google Docs with passwords (in Russian). https://habr.com/en/post/416219/. Accessed 27 Apr 2019
9. Martin-Galan, B., Hernandez-Perez, T., Rodriguez-Mateos, D., et al.: The use of robots.txt and sitemaps in the Spanish public administration. PROFESIONAL DE LA INFORMACION **18**(6), 625–630 (2009). https://doi.org/10.3145/epi.2009.nov.05
10. Kolay, S., D'Alberto, P., Dasdan, A., Bhattacharjee, A.: A larger scale study of robots.txt. In: Proceeding of the 17th International Conference on World Wide Web 2008, WWW 2008, pp. 1171–1172 (2008). https://doi.org/10.1145/1367497.1367711
11. Sun, Y., Zhuang, Z., Councill, I.G., Giles, C.L.: Determining bias to search engines from robots.txt. In: Proceedings of the IEEE/WIC/ACM International Conference on Web Intelligence, WI 2007, pp. 149–155 (2007). https://doi.org/10.1109/wi.2007.98
12. A Standard for Robot Exclusion. http://www.robotstxt.org/orig.html. Accessed 29 Aug 2018
13. Tong, W., Xie, X.: A research on a defending policy against the Webcrawler's attack. In: 2009 3rd International Conference on Anti-counterfeiting, Security, and Identification in Communication, ASID 2009 (2009). https://doi.org/10.1109/icasid.2009.5276948
14. Bates, M.E.: What makes information "public"? Online (Wilton, Connecticut) **28**(6), 64 (2004)
15. Robots.txt analysis. https://webmaster.yandex.ru/tools/robotstxt/. Accessed 29 Aug 2018
16. robots.txt Tester. https://www.google.com/webmasters/tools/robots-testing-tool. Accessed 29 Aug 2018
17. Blocking URLs with a robots.txt file. https://support.google.com/webmasters/answer/6062608. Accessed 29 Aug 2018
18. Robots meta tag and X-Robots-Tag HTTP header specifications. https://developers.google.com/search/reference/robots_meta_tag. Accessed 29 Aug 2018

An Ontology-Based Approach to the Agile Requirements Engineering

Marina Murtazina$^{(\boxtimes)}$ and Tatiana Avdeenko

Novosibirsk State Technical University, 630073 Novosibirsk, Russia
murtazina@corp.nstu.ru

Abstract. The paper presents an approach to the agile requirements engineering based on the OWL ontologies. A brief overview of the benefits of an ontology-based approach to requirements engineering is given. Attention is focused on agile engineering requirements process. The proposed approach uses three ontologies. The first ontology is used to represent knowledge about the agile requirements engineering process. The second ontology is designed to match natural language sentences with the requirements in order to identify conflicts. The third ontology is used to accumulate the knowledge about the domain of the software product. The first ontology is core. This ontology consists of classes corresponding to events, roles and artefacts of agile development. Object properties established between the individuals of class can be used to identify directly or indirectly linked requirements and requirements artefacts. This enables maintaining requirements traceability. Also the ontology takes into account particular qualities of working with the requirements in agile development processes including knowledge about the criteria for assessing the quality of user stories that is the most common form to record the requirements in agile methods. The ontologies are implemented in the Protégé environment.

Keywords: Requirements engineering · Ontology · Agile environment

1 Introduction

The success of software products depends on the extent to which they, as tools, can be effectively used in the implementation of the end user tasks. That is why requirements engineering plays a key role in the software development. The requirements engineering as a field of knowledge includes elicitation, analysis, specification and validation of the requirements [1]. By their nature, the software requirements represent complex knowledge that is extracted in the process of requirements engineering from various sources, including many stakeholders, whose views on the developed product can be diametrically opposed. In this regard, the requirements can be considered as a result of alternative solutions in the field of determining functional and qualitative characteristics of the software.

The decision making process in requirements engineering depends greatly on the experience and intuition of the development team. In particular, the team members use their experience in analyzing feasibility and determining complexity of the requirements, identifying inconsistencies and incompleteness in the requirements sets,

© Springer Nature Switzerland AG 2019
N. Bjørner et al. (Eds.): PSI 2019, LNCS 11964, pp. 205–213, 2019.
https://doi.org/10.1007/978-3-030-37487-7_17

forecasting implementation deadlines, assessing implementation risks, etc. Frequent modifications of the requirements inherent to the agile development methodologies as a reaction to changes in the business environment, requires permanent monitoring on the consistency of the requirements specification and the actual priority of the software product functions. Therefore, the ability to quickly identify and resolve conflicting requirements, and also revise priorities to meet new requirements, is critical to the development of the software development project.

The scientific discourse of recent years is characterized by a focus on the application of ontological models to the software development process. Ontologies provide a formal representation of knowledge and relationships between the concepts used in the software development. Ontologies can be used for requirements analysis and specification phases [2]. Ontologies allow to expand the possibilities of model-driven requirements engineering (MDRE) through the use of machine reasoning. Over the past few years ontology-driven requirements engineering (ODRE) has become a leading trend [3].

The success of the ontological approach in the requirements engineering is determined by its capabilities, such as availability of the domain vocabulary, formulating knowledge about the application area and its reuse, understanding the problem area, improving communication between specialists from different fields [4]. Ontologies in the requirements engineering are used to formalize the structure of documents for working with the requirements, to represent the types of the requirements and knowledge about the domain of the software product [5]. Ontologies also allow formulating the rules (axioms) for reasoning about traceability, consistency and completeness of the requirements [6]. The ontological approach is useful for comparing stakeholders' points of view on different subsystems of a single information system [7].

Ontologies can be used to improve the requirements development [8] and requirements management [9] in agile software development process. Ontological approach to the requirements engineering allows to improve the process of user story formulation [10], to facilitate verification of compliance with the quality characteristics of individual user stories and sets of user stories [11], as well as to obtain more accurate assessments of the efforts required to implement user stories [12]. Summarizing the above, it should be noted that most studies of the possibilities of using ontologies in requirements engineering do not take into account the specifics of the project management life cycle or the software development life cycle. To the best of our knowledge, very few papers apply ontology-based approach to the agile project development. However, it seems that the application of the ontology-base approach can be especially valuable for agile development. It is precisely under conditions of permanent changes in the requirements and their priorities inherent to the agile development that knowledge engineering methods prove to be especially useful. Representation of knowledge about the project requirements in the form of ontologies allows the use of machine reasoning methods that can be used for discovering logical inconsistencies.

In the present paper we propose an ontology-based approach to the agile requirements engineering using a system of three ontologies. The first ontology is needed to represent knowledge about the agile requirements engineering process, the second one is designed to match natural language sentences with the requirements in order to identify conflicts, the third ontology is used to accumulate the knowledge about the domain of the software product. The paper is organized as follows. In Sect. 2 we provide a review of the research topic and the terminology used. In Sect. 3 we define the ontology for agile requirements engineering process. In Sect. 4, we give conclusions about the prospects of using this approach in agile software development.

2   Theoretical Background

2.1   Requirements Engineering in Agile Software Development

In agile development, the software requirements specification (SRS) is an integrated requirements package which is maintained up to date. This package is not a single physical document, but a logical structure filled with requirements for a software product.

To date, the Scrum framework is the most popular among the agile project management framework. The basis of Scrum is the theory of empirical control. According to this theory, the source of knowledge is experience, and the source of solutions is real data. The basic scheme of the Scrum framework works is presented in Fig. 1.

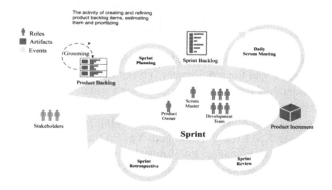

Fig. 1. The basic scheme of the Scrum framework works

According to Agile Manifesto [13], agile development encourages the creation of the minimum amount of documentation necessary to manage and coordinate the project participants work in developing a software product. When a software project is launched, it is not necessary to create a comprehensive requirements document. First, the document "Vision and Scope" is developed. This document determines the stakeholders vision on the software being developed in terms of the key needs and constraints under which the project will be implemented.

Next, work begins on filling the Product Backlog, which is a prioritized list of currently existing product requirements, which is never complete. Product backlog items can be divided into product features, defect, technical work, knowledge acquisition by type of work [14]. Product feature is a unit of functionality of a software product that satisfies a requirement. The remaining three types of product backlog items are needed to plan work on eliminating defects, refactoring, database migration, research necessary to implement the requirements of any type, etc.

Before a feature is scheduled for a sprint, it is necessary to decompose it into small user stories, develop basic behavior scenarios, evaluate implementation efforts, identify dependences on other user stories, and determine the priority. It is also necessary to analyze low priority user stories. Perhaps these product backlog items became important, or, on the contrary, so unimportant that they should be removed. This work is done by the Product Owner together with the development team as part of the Backlog grooming.

Backlog grooming (Product backlog refinement or grooming) is an activity throughout the sprint aimed at revising the backlog of the product to prepare its product for the next sprint planning. Backlog grooming helps ensure that the requirements will be clarified, and user stories will be prepared for work in advance of planning for the sprint. As a result of Backlog grooming, the top of the Product Backlog should include user stories prepared for sprint. In this case, such user stories should be enough for 2–3 sprints. User stories should be clear to all team members, evaluated by the team, and acceptance criteria should be indicated for the stories. The acceptance criteria can be written in the form of simple sentences or behavior scenarios, in particular, in the form of Gherkin scenarios.

2.2 User Stories

Initially, user stories were recorded on cards of small sizes. The card is not intended to collect all information about the requirement. The card must contain several sentences that reflect the essence of the requirement. The card usually indicates the identifier, name, text, acceptance criteria and its assessment (priority, risk, evaluation of the efforts, etc.). The user story should follow the following pattern:

As a <type of user X>, I want <some goal Y>, So that <some reason Z>

Nevertheless, it is easy to make a lot of mistakes when writing a user story. In this connection, writing the user story text is one of the cornerstones of agile engineering requirements. Suppose it is necessary to describe the functionality that will allow the social network users to sell stickers sets that they can add to messages. In this case, the user has a standard free stickers set. Suppose the story was formulated as follows: "As a user, I want to add sticker sets from the paid collection, So that I can see new stickers in my sticker sets". In this user story, the type of user is not specified, there is no understanding of what problem the user solves, what is his motive. If the system users are divided into logged users and visitors, then it is probably a logged in user. And, most likely, the developer will immediately understand this and without losing time on figuring out the type of user will be able to implement the feature correctly. But if logged-in users are in turn subdivided (for example, there are users with a premium account that this service should already be included in the payment), the feature may be implemented incorrectly, or the developer will spend time clarifying out who the user is. In order to avoid mistakes in the first part of the user story, it is necessary to build a user roles model and accept an agreement that if this is not about any user, but about a certain group of users, this should be reflected in the user story. Further, the user story inaccurately defined user action and absolutely not indicated his motivation. This user story is better stated in the following wording: "As a logged-in user, I want to buy new stickers sets, So that I can decorate my messages with non-standard stickers". Another important point when writing stories is the use of possessive pronouns, the omission of which can drastically change the meaning of the requirement.

Despite the huge popularity, the number of ways to assess the quality of user stories is small. Many existing approaches use the INVEST model proposed in 2003 by Bill Wake. According to this model, user history should be: Independent, Negotiable, Valuable, Estimable, Small, Testable [15].

The aim of using the Independent criterion is to keep the number of dependencies on other user stories to a minimum. The presence of dependencies makes it difficult to prioritize and, accordingly, planning a sprint. The details of user stories should also be negotiable. According to the Negotiable criterion, the user story text should contain information only about what it needs to be implemented for. A typical example of a breach of Negotiable criterion is when a Product Owner tells a team how to implement a user story. According to the Valuable criterion, user stories should be valuable to the customer or end user, or both. According to the Estimable criterion, the user story must be clear to the development team so that the team can determine the necessary effort. If a team cannot estimate user story, then the user story is either too large, or ambiguously formulated, or the team does not have enough knowledge, for example, about some technology. In the first case, it is necessary to decompose the user story, in the second - to eliminate the ambiguity of the wording, in the third - to conduct research in order to obtain the necessary knowledge. When sprint planning, it is necessary that the user stories that are considered to be candidates for implementation have a small size so that several user stories can be planned for the sprint. Testable criterion means that each acceptance criteria must have a clear pass or fail result.

The development of a user stories list for the project can be preceded by the construction of the Feature tree [16]. Function trees are a good way to organize project information. The Product Owner begins building the Feature tree in Sprint 0. The start of the Feature tree can be generated based on information from the document "Vision and Scope". Since all product features are usually undefined during sprint 0, the Feature tree is constantly evolving. Further, the items of the Feature tree are added to the Product backlog, where they are supplemented with user stories.

3   OWL Ontology for Agile Requirements Engineering

In this paper, it is proposed to use the OWL ontology system to support the requirements engineering. The first ontology contains knowledge of requirements engineering within the framework of an agile approach including knowledge about types of requirements. The second ontology is a model for identifying conflicting requirements. The third is a model that includes a software product feature tree, a user roles model and the connections between them.

In Fig. 2 shows the taxonomy of the upper level classes for ontology "Guide", and also object properties reflecting the relations between ontology classes.

Fig. 2. The taxonomy of the upper level classes for ontology "Guide" and object properties

The ontology "Guide" consists of classes corresponding to events, roles and arte-facts of agile development. The instances (individuals) of the ontology classes are the software requirements and their artefacts, as well as information about the development team and stakeholders. Object properties reflect relations that can be established between individuals. For example, to specify the relationship "the requirement refines another requirement" the object properties "refines" are used. This object property, in turn, includes as subproperties that can be established between different classes (or individuals) of requirements artefacts which are also requirements by their nature (for example, the behavior scenario refines user story). Object property "traceFrom" is intended to define of bottom-up tracing links. For the object property "traceFrom" and its subproperties, inverse properties are given through the "Inverse Of" relation-ship. This allows the top-down tracing of the "traceTo" relationship. Object property "conflicts" enables specifying that the requirements conflict with each other. This can be done directly in this ontology or transferred from the additional ontology "Detection of conflicts in the requirements". In Fig. 3 lists the objects properties for this ontology and their domains and ranges.

Individuals of the ontology "Detection of conflicts in the requirements" are elements extracted from the requirements text. The sentence that expresses a requirement, regardless of the technique used for recording requirements, can be divided into main parts: the subject, the action, and the object to which the action of the subject is directed. To identify conflicts between user stories need to extract from user story text the func-tional user role, the action and the object on which the action is directed. Object properties "sameAsActor", "sameAsAction" and "sameAsObject" are set between instances of the corresponding classes if same name is used for the elements of two requirements or the full name in one and an abbreviation in the second. Object properties "isaActor" and "isaObject" are used to establish hierarchical relations. For example, a senior manager is a manager. Object properties "antonymsAction" and "antonymsObject" are set between instances of the corresponding classes if they have the opposite value (for example, "my comment about the product" and "someone else's comment about the product"). Object properties "partOfAction" and "partOfObject" are set between instances of the respective classes if one is part of the other. Object properties "synonymsActor", "synonymsAction" and "synonymsObject" are set if the values of the corresponding requirements elements have a synonymous value. In all other cases it is considered that the corresponding elements of the requirements are bound by object property "no-relationActor", "no-relationAction" or "no-relationObject".

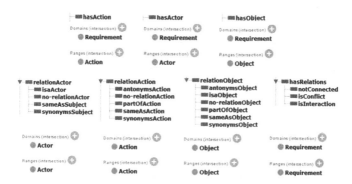

Fig. 3. Classes and object properties for ontology «Detection of conflicts in the requirements»

The following production rules are used to determine the type of relations between the two requirements:

If ObjectProperty_between_class_instances (Actor1, Actor2)
AND ObjectProperty_between_class_instances (Action1, Action2)
AND ObjectProperty_between_class_instances (Object1, Object2)
Then Object properties_between_class_instances (Requirement1, Requirement2).

Relations between actors, actions and objects can be established on the basis of information from the domain ontology as well as using linguistic ontologies, such as WordNet.

To illustrate the idea of the proposed approach to the formation of a software product domain model in the form of an OWL ontology consider a fragment of ontology for an online store (см. Fig. 4).

When building the software product domain ontology it is necessary to analyze the user roles (class "User") and also which software product sections users can work with (class "Office") and build a Feature tree (class "Features"). Further, it should be determined which sections can be used by certain users, and also indicate which features are associated with these sections. Instances of the class "Object" are objects that the user works with (for example, a sales report or a search string). Instances of the class "Action" are verbs that are used to describe user actions. Actions, respectively, can be divided into four operations: reading, adding, editing, deleting. In this example, users are divided into groups depending on the two properties "isLogin" and "isRegistered". The knowledge of which user office is owned is also used to assign a user to a class.

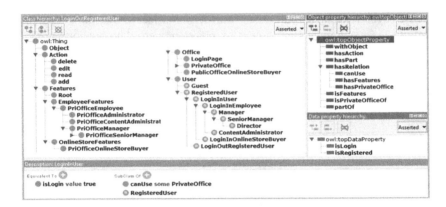

Fig. 4. Ontology «OnlineStore»

A list of the features available in office is indicated for each class of the corresponding office. Subclasses of personal offices automatically inherit features set for the classes in which they belong.

4   Conclusion and Future Work

The OWL ontology system containing three ontologies was developed based on the analysis of the results of ontology application in requirements engineering. The first ontology accumulates knowledge about the development of software products in a agile environment. The second one contains knowledge about the relations between the elements of sentence with a requirement (role, action, object). This allows analyzing pairs of requirements in order to identify conflicts. The third one contains knowledge of the software product domain.

We have developed a model through which enables solving typical problems for requirements engineering in agile software development. These include the formation and refinement of the Product backlog, requirements tracing and the conflicting requirements identification. The next stage of our research will include the development of the algorithm for prioritizing and re-prioritizing requirements based on the business value of the product backlog item, assessment of the efforts to requirements implement and risks, as well as the dependencies between product backlog items that are recorded in the ontology.

Acknowledgments. The reported study was funded by Russian Ministry of Education and Science, according to the research project No. 2.2327.2017/4.6.

References

1. ISO/IEC. Software Engineering - Guide to the software engineering body of knowledge (SWEBOK). 2nd edn. ISO/IEC TR 19759 (2015)
2. Bhatia, M.P.S., Kumar, A., Beniwal R.: Ontologies for software engineering: past, present and future. Ind. J. Sci. Technol. **9**(9). http://www.indjst.org/index.php/indjst/article/view/71384/67982. Accessed 02 Feb 2019
3. Siegemund, K.: Contributions to ontology-driven requirements engineering: dissertation to obtain the academic degree doctoral engineer (Dr.-Ing.). Technischen Universität Dresden, Dresden (2014)
4. Valaski, J., Reinehr, S., Malucelli A.: Which roles ontologies play on software requirements engineering. In: International Conference on Software Engineering Research and Practice, pp. 24–30. CSREA Press (2016)
5. Castañeda, V., Ballejos, L., Caliusco, M.L., Galli, M.R.: The use of ontologies in requirements engineering. Glob. J. Res. Eng. **10**(6), 2–8 (2010)
6. Goknil, A., Kurtev, I., van den Berg, K.: A metamodeling approach for reasoning about requirements. In: Schieferdecker, I., Hartman, A. (eds.) ECMDA-FA 2008. LNCS, vol. 5095, pp. 310–325. Springer, Heidelberg (2008). https://doi.org/10.1007/978-3-540-69100-6_21
7. Assawamekin, N., Sunetnanta, T., Pluempitiwiriyawej, C.: Ontology-based multi perspective requirements traceability framework. Knowl. Inf. Syst. **25**(3), 493–522 (2010)
8. Sitthithanasakul, S., Choosri, N.: Using ontology to enhance requirement engineering in agile software process. In: 2016 10th International Conference on Software, Knowledge, Information Management and Applications, pp. 181–186. IEEE (2017)
9. Avdeenko, T., Murtazina, M.: Intelligent support of requirements management in agile environment. In: Borangiu, T., Trentesaux, D., Thomas, A., Cavalieri, S. (eds.) SOHOMA 2018. SCI, vol. 803, pp. 97–108. Springer, Cham (2019). https://doi.org/10.1007/978-3-030-03003-2_7
10. Thamrongchote, C., Vatanawood, W.: Business process ontology for defining user story. In: 15th International Conference on Computer and Information Science. IEEE, Okayama (2016)
11. Murtazina, M.S., Avdeenko, T.V.: Ontology-based approach to the requirements engineering in agile environment. In: 2018 XIV International Scientific-Technical Conference on Actual Problems of Electronics Instrument Engineering (APEIE), pp. 496–501. IEEE, Novosibirsk (2018)
12. Adnan, M., Afzal, M.: Ontology based multiagent effort estimation system for scrum agile method. IEEE Access **5**, 25993–26005 (2017)
13. Agile Manifesto. https://agilemanifesto.org/. Accessed 02 Feb 2019
14. Rubin, K.S.: Essential Scrum: A Practical Guide to the Most Popular Agile Process. Addison-Wesley, Boston (2013)
15. Wake, B.: INVEST in Good Stories, and SMART Tasks. https://xp123.com/articles/invest-in-good-stories-and-smart-tasks/. Accessed 02 Feb 2019
16. Babar, M.A., Brown, A.W., Mistrik, I.: Agile Software Architecture: Aligning Agile Processes and Software Architectures, 1st edn. Elsevier, Waltham (2013)

Effective Scheduling of Strict Periodic Task Sets with Given Permissible Periods in RTOS

Sophia A. Zelenova[1] and Sergey V. Zelenov[1,2(✉)] (iD)

[1] Ivannikov Institute for System Programming of the Russian Academy of Sciences (ISP RAS), 25, Alexander Solzhenitsyn st., Moscow 109004, Russia
{sophia,zelenov}@ispras.ru
[2] National Research University Higher School of Economics (HSE), 20, Myasnitskaya Ulitsa, Moscow 101000, Russia
szelenov@hse.ru
http://www.ispras.ru/, https://www.hse.ru/

Abstract. In the paper, we suggest new approach to schedulability problem for strict periodic tasks (a periodic task is strict if it must be started in equal intervals of time – task's period). Given permissible tasks' periods, our approach allows to obtain quickly all schedulable sets of tasks with such periods and to build immediately a conflict-free schedule for each obtained set. The approach is based on mathematical methods of graph theory and number theory. We illustrate the approach by a number of examples and present current practical results.

Keywords: Scheduling · Real-time system · Strict periodic task

1 Introduction

Real-time systems are complex and promising area of research. The such kind of system requires distributed computing for real relation representation. Thus it becomes necessary to have different kind of scheduling of task processing.

Now we recall some terms.

Suppose processor time is divided into minimal parts (scheduler quantums) that are numerated. We refer to such a part as a *point*.

A point number t is called *starting* for a task if the task processing starts at this point. The processing points different from the starting point are called *additional*. A task duration is the number of all processing points for the task.

A task is called *periodic*, if its processing is repeated at equal time intervals. Length of time of one such interval is called a *period p* of the task. A periodic task is called *strict periodic*, if its adjacent starting points are at a distance exactly equal to the task period. Besides, additional points related to the same processing must be processed during the period following the corresponding starting point.

N. Bjørner et al. (Eds.): PSI 2019, LNCS 11964, pp. 214–222, 2019.
https://doi.org/10.1007/978-3-030-37487-7_18

In this paper, we discuss static[1] scheduling of strictly periodic preemptive[2] tasks.

There are two simple considerations used to find conflict-free schedules.

The first is *CPU usage*. Let $p_1, ..., p_k$ be periods of periodic tasks executed on a processor. Let l_i be the worst case execution time for one instance of the task with period p_i. Then CPU usage should not be more than 100% [1]:

$$\frac{l_1}{p_1} + ... + \frac{l_k}{p_k} \leq 1. \tag{1}$$

The second is the *necessary condition for conflict-free scheduling*. Let p_1 and p_2 be periods of two tasks. And let t_1 and t_2 be starting points of the tasks. If $t_1 - t_2$ is divisible by the greatest common divisor (GCD) of p_1 and p_2 without remainder, then the schedule has conflict [2].

The standard way to find a schedule for a task system consists of two steps. the *first step* is to place the starting points. The *second step* is to place the additional points. These two actions have to be considered separately, because it is not clear how to distribute the starting and additional points at the same time, and whether it is possible in principle.

In the existing works, scheduling algorithms are based on the exhaustive search of suitable points [3–5]. But exhaustive search evokes the problem of combinatorial explosion. The available methods of limiting the search are unsatisfactory, therefore, it is not uncommon when a scheduling algorithm fails to find a solution even though it exists.

We propose a different approach to the problem described above. This approach is based on our study of numerical properties of period systems [6].

Our research concerns only the first step of scheduling, namely, the distribution of starting points. Therefore, in the rest of the paper, the term "schedule" means only the location of starting points (thus, we mean all durations $l_i = 1$ for all tasks). In the paper, we propose an effective algorithm that enumerates all schedulable task sets and builds starting points for them in an acceptable time. We describe an outline of this algorithm and present some experimental results.

2   Preliminaries

Recall that $G[S]$ denotes the induced subgraph of a graph G for vertex subset S.

Let D be a set of GCD of task period pairs. And let H be a closure of D with respect to the operation of taking the greatest common divisor. Denote by G_H a directed graph constructed as follows. Vertices of G_H are elements of H and there is an edge from a vertice d_1 to a vertice d_2 if d_2 is divisible by d_1 and there is no any d_3 such, that d_3 is divisible by d_1 and d_2 is divisible by d_3. The vertice d_1 is called a *parent* and d_2 is called a *child*.

---

[1] Scheduling is called *static*, if the schedule is built before running the system.
[2] Task is called *preemptive*, if it may be interrupted by another task.

Now, for all $d \in H$, denote by G_d an undirected graph constructed as follows. Vertices of G_d are all task periods and there is an edge between two vertices if the periods have GCD equal to d.

In [6] we prove the following criterion for the existence of a conflict-free schedule:

Theorem 1. *The system of tasks with periods p_1, p_2, ..., p_k has a conflict-free schedule if and only if*

1. *For all $d \in G_H$, graph G_d have the proper coloring involving at most of d colors.*
2. *Colors in different G_d graphs are "inherited" with respect to G_H. This means that two vertices having different colors in G_{parent} for a parent node from G_H cannot have the same color in G_{child} for a child node from G_H.*
3. *For any $d \in G_H$ with parents $d_i \in G_H$, any period subset, which is colored by the same color in each G_{d_i}, is colored by at most $m(d) = \frac{d}{LCM(d_i)}$ colors in G_d. The number $m(d)$ is called multiplier for a divider d.*

If graph G_H is a tree, then the condition 3 of Theorem 1 is much simpler, and all conditions of Theorem 1 may be presented briefly—see the Table 1.

Table 1. Conditions of Theorem 1 when graph G_H is a tree

	G_{parent}		G_{child}
1.	Properly colored with $\leqslant parent$ colors		Properly colored with $\leqslant child$ colors
2.	Some vertices u and v are assigned to **different** colors	$\Rightarrow$	u and v are assigned to **different** colors
3.	A subset S of vertices is assigned to the **same** color	$\Rightarrow$	S is colored with $\leqslant m(child) = \frac{child}{parent}$ colors

Consider two examples of application of Theorem 1.

Example 1. This example (Fig. 1) shows the case when the construction of a conflict-free schedule is impossible due to a violation of the third condition of Theorem 1.

Let 6, 12, 14, 18, and 30 be periods of tasks.

Graph G_H consists of two vertices: 2 and 6 (Fig. 1a).

In order to properly color G_2, the set $S = \{6, 12, 18, 30\}$ must be assigned to the same color in G_2 (Fig. 1b). Since $G_6[S]$ is complete subgraph, then in order to properly color G_6, all vertices of the set S must be assigned to different colors in G_6 (Fig. 1c). But $m(6) = \frac{6}{2} = 3$, thus, by the condition 3 of Theorem 1, there are only three colors for coloring four elements of S.

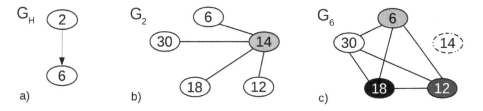

Fig. 1. A violation of the third condition of Theorem 1.

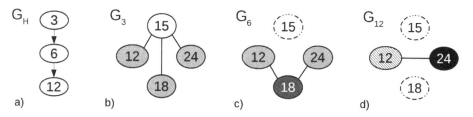

Fig. 2. Conflict-free scheduling using Theorem 1.

Example 2. This example (Fig. 2) shows a "positive" application of Theorem 1.
Let 12, 15, 18, and 24 be periods of tasks.

Graph G_H consists of three vertices: 3, 6, and 12 (Fig. 2.a).

Graph G_3 may be properly colored as follows: we assign vertex 15 a color $c_{3,1}$, and we assign vertices 12, 18, and 24 a color $c_{3,2}$ (Fig. 2b). Thus, start point for 15 has some reminder (for example, 1) modulo 3, while start points for 12, 18, and 24 have some another reminder (for example, 0) modulo 3 (Table 2, second column).

Table 2. Reminders and start points

Period	Reminder modulo ...			Start point
	3	6	12	
12	0	0	0	0
15	1	1	1	1
18	0	3	3	3
24	0	0	6	6

Consider graph G_6. Since $m(6) = \frac{6}{3} = 2$, then there are two colors for coloring 12, 18, and 24 in graph G_6. Thus, we assign vertex 18 a color $c_{6,1}$, and we assign vertices 12 and 24 a color $c_{6,2}$ (Fig. 2c). Corresponding reminders modulo 6 are shown in Table 2, third column. Note that each chosen reminder modulo 6 has the reminder modulo 3 previously chosen during analysis of graph G_3.

Consider graph G_{12}. Since $m(12) = \frac{12}{6} = 2$, then there are two colors for coloring two vertices 12 and 24 in graph G_{12} (Fig. 2d). Corresponding reminders modulo 12 are shown in Table 2, fourth column. Again, note that each chosen reminder modulo 12 has the reminder modulo 6 previously chosen during analysis of graph G_6.

As a result, for all chosen reminders, one can find corresponding start points for all tasks (Table 2, last column).

Other examples of application of Theorem 1 may be found in [7].

3   Motivation and Problem Statement

In real conditions, the task period depends on technical characteristics of devices used. For example, it may correspond to the frequency of signals that are sent or received by the task. And these characteristics are not diverse. Table 3 shows examples of widely used task periods in industrial RTOS.

So, if the number of different permissible periods is not so large, is it possible to generate all good task period sets? ("Good" means that there is a conflict-free location of the starting points.)

Table 3. Frequencies and periods. One second contains 2000 points.

Hz	Period	Hz	Period	Hz	Period
400	5	60	32–35	30	60–65
200	10	50	40	20	100
100	20	40	50	10	200

Let $p_1 < p_2 < ... < p_k$ be all permissible periods. Suppose there are n_1 tasks with period p_1, n_2 tasks with period p_2, ..., n_k tasks with period p_k. The tuple $(n_1, n_2, ..., n_k)$ is called *correct* if it satisfies the condition (1) of the CPU usage. We say that the correct tuple $(n_1, n_2, ..., n_k)$ is a *solution* if there is a conflict-free location of starting points for tasks with such periods. The solutions can be partially ordered as follows. We say that $(n_1^{(1)}, ..., n_k^{(1)}) \leq (n_1^{(1)}, ..., n_k^{(1)})$ if $n_i^{(1)} \leq n_i^{(2)}$ for all $i = 1, ..., k$.

It turns out that Theorem 1 provides means to construct an algorithm for generating all maximal solutions. ("Maximal" means maximal with respect to the introduced order.) Obviously, for any solution τ, there exists a maximal solution $\tilde{\tau}$, such that $\tau \leq \tilde{\tau}$. So, if we have all maximal solutions, then we can construct all solutions.

4   Algorithm Sketch

In the most general form, the generation algorithm is as follows.

Loop: divider d in G_H
   If d is root **Then**
      Loop: iterate valid assignments of colors to periods p_i
         Color set contains d elements, which should be assigned to the periods
         (i.e. vertices of the graph G_d) taking into account the conditions of
         Theorem 1. Important: several periods can be assigned to the same
         color if such assignment does not violate the proper coloring condition.
      End of loop: iterate valid assignments of colors to periods p_i
   Else
      Loop: iterate valid assignments of colors to periods p_i
         In this case, it is necessary to take into account the assignment of col-
         ors constructed for all parents of the divider d. Colors must be inher-
         itors (w.r.t condition 2 of Theorem 1) of the parent colors. If there
         are several parents, the inheritance must be agreed with all parents.
         Other conditions of Theorem 1 must be satisfied as well.
      End of loop: iterate valid assignments of colors to periods p_i
End of loop: divider d in G_H

Note that the generator assignes all colors, so we do get the maximal solutions. In addition, the information obtained during the construction of the maximal tuple makes it possible to build immediately a conflict-free schedule for this tuple.

Illustrate presented algorithm by the following example.

Example 3. Let 8 and 12 be all permissible periods of tasks.
   Given a period p, denote by $S^{(p)}$ a set of all vertices for p in G_d.
   Graph G_H consists of three vertices: 4, 8, and 12 (Fig. 3a).

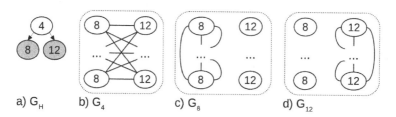

Fig. 3. Graphs G_H and G_d for generation algorithm when periods are 8 and 12

   Graph G_4 is complete bipartite with two disjoint sets of vertices $S^{(8)}$ and $S^{(12)}$ (Fig. 3b). By condition 1 of Theorem 1, graph G_4 must be properly colored with at most 4 colors. Suppose that $S^{(8)}$ is colored using k colors. Then $S^{(12)}$ is colored using other $4 - k$ colors.

   Consider graph G_8. Subgraph $G_8[S^{(8)}]$ is complete, and all vertices of $S^{(12)}$ are isolated (Fig. 3c). Thus, all vertices of $S^{(8)}$ must be assigned to different colors, and all vertices of $S^{(12)}$ may be assigned to $4 - k$ colors used during coloring of G_4 (we can not assign all vertices of $S^{(12)}$ to the same color, since condition 2 of Theorem 1). Since $m(8) = \frac{8}{4} = 2$, then, by condition 3 of Theorem 1, there are at most $2k$ colors for coloring $S^{(8)}$. So, we have $\max |S^{(8)}| = 2k$.

Consider graph G_{12}. Subgraph $G_{12}[S^{(12)}]$ is complete, and all vertices of $S^{(8)}$ are isolated (Fig. 3d). Similarly, since $m(12) = \frac{12}{4} = 3$, then we have $\max |S^{(12)}| = 3(4 - k)$.

In this simple example, loops "iterate valid assignments of colors to periods p_i" work as follows. For $d = 4$ (root), our algorithm iterates valid values of k. For $d = 8$ and $d = 12$, we have trivial iteration of the only assignment.

On the basis of the presented algorithm scheme, we have developed a generator of the solution set. Our implementation generates the desired set of maximal solutions in an acceptable time. The results of the experiments are given below in Sect. 6.

5   Application of the Generator

Now let's discuss how to use such a generator in practice.

A generated set of solutions gives an answer to the first question of scheduling: is it possible to build a conflict-free starting points for a given set of tasks. In addition, we can get a schedule for starting points.

Complete information about available solutions allows, for example, to automatically assign some given tasks to several processors without any risk of choosing a non-schedulable combination of periods for each processor.

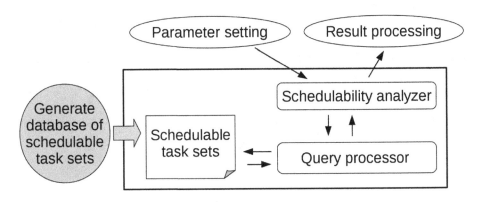

Fig. 4. A possible architecture of the automatic scheduler.

An automatic scheduler may include the following components (see Fig. 4):

- Database which includes all generated solutions for the given period set and the schedules for these solutions.
- A query processor for standard database queries.
- Analyzer that builds a task processing schedule, in accordance with the user-specified parameters.

Table 4. The number of maximal solutions for experimental period sets

Period set	G_H	Time	The number of maximal solutions	The number of maximal correct tuples
10, 20, 35, 40, 80	5a	0,5 s	656	7 456
10, 20, 40, 50, 100, 200	5b	32 min 17 s	176 604	188 844
10, 64, 20, 32, 40, 50, 100, 200	5c	42 min 34 s	552 610	6 108 197
10, 65, 20, 35, 40, 100, 200, 400, 1000	5d	16 min 5 s	702 264	1 263 391 852

6   Experimental Results

We conducted several experiments to generate sets of solutions for different period sets taken from realistic scenarios. Corresponding graphs G_H have different structural complexity (see Fig. 5): Fig. 5a and b shows graphs G_H with simple structure, while Fig. 5c and d shows graphs G_H with more complicated structure. For all produced solutions, schedules were generated and tested for compliance with the necessary condition for conflict-free schedules (see Sect. 1).

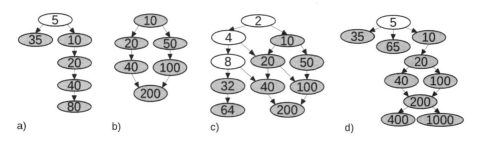

Fig. 5. Graphs G_H for experimental period sets.

Table 4 shows the number of maximal solutions for experimental period sets. The last column contains the number of maximal correct tuples for each period set. This characteristic shows that the structure of the graph G_H is more important, then quantitative indicators of period set is. For example, consider two last period sets. One can see that two large periods (400 and 1000) dramatically increase the number of maximal correct tuples, but have little effect on the number of solutions.

Table 4 shows also that the presence of additional cross-links in G_H increases the generation time, apparently complicating generation process, while the tree structure of the graph G_H simplifies and speeds up the generation.

7   Conclusion

In this paper, we studied the problem of effective finding the starting execution points for scheduling strictly periodic tasks with given permissible periods. The main innovation is: instead of solving partial schedulability problem for each set of tasks, we suggest to enumerate all schedulable sets of tasks with given permissible periods. Based on previously obtained theoretical results, we propose a corresponding algorithm. Our implementation of the algorithm completes in an acceptable time. The algorithm allows to build a database of schedulable sets of tasks with all data necessary for schedule construction. Then one can use this database to check any set of tasks against schedulability condition and to obtain schedule immediately.

References

1. Liu, C.L., Layland, J.W.: Scheduling algorithms for multiprogramming in a hard-real-time environment. J. ACM **20**, 46–61 (1973)
2. Yomsi, P.M., Sorel, Y.: Non-schedulability conditions for off-line scheduling of real-time systems subject to precedence and strict periodicity constraints. In: Proceedings of the 11th IEEE International Conference on Emerging Technologies and Factory Automation, ETFA 2006, Prague (2006)
3. Yomsi, P.M., Sorel, Y.: Schedulability analysis for non necessarily harmonic real-time systems with precedence and strict periodicity constraints using the exact number of preemptions and no idle time. In: Proceedings of the 4th Multidisciplinary International Scheduling Conference, MISTA 2009, Dublin, Ireland (2009)
4. Zelenov, S.V.: Scheduling of strictly periodic tasks in real-time systems. Trudy ISP RAN. Proc. ISP RAS **20**, 113–122 (2011). (in Russian)
5. Tretyakov, A.V.: Automation of scheduling for periodic real-time systems. Trudy ISP RAN. Proc. ISP RAS **22**, 375–400 (2012). (in Russian)
6. Zelenova, S.A., Zelenov, S.V.: Non-conflict scheduling criterion for strict periodic tasks. Trudy ISP RAN. Proc. ISP RAS **29**(6), 183–202 (2017). https://doi.org/10.15514/ISPRAS-2017-29(6)-10. (in Russian)
7. Zelenova, S.A., Zelenov, S.V.: Schedulability analysis for strictly periodic tasks in RTOS. Program. Comput. Softw. **44**(3), 159–169 (2018). https://doi.org/10.1134/S0361768818030076

Verification and Validation of Semantic Annotations

Oleksandra Panasiuk$^{(\boxtimes)}$, Omar Holzknecht$^{(\boxtimes)}$, Umutcan Şimşek$^{(\boxtimes)}$,
Elias Kärle, and Dieter Fensel

University of Innsbruck, Technikerstrasse 21a, 6020 Innsbruck, Austria
{oleksandra.panasiuk,omar.holzknecht,umutcan.simsek,elias.karle,
dieter.fensel}@sti2.at

Abstract. In this paper, we propose a framework to perform verification and validation of semantically annotated data. The annotations, extracted from websites, are verified against the schema.org vocabulary and Domain Specifications to ensure the syntactic correctness and completeness of the annotations. The Domain Specifications allow for checking of the compliance of annotations against corresponding domain-specific constraints. The validation mechanism will detect errors and inconsistencies between the content of the analyzed schema.org annotations and the content of the web pages where the annotations were found.

Keywords: Verification · Validation · Semantic annotation · Schema.org

1 Introduction

The introduction of the Semantic Web [3] changed the way content, data and services are published and consumed online fundamentally. For the first time, data in websites becomes not only machine-readable, but also machine understandable and interpretable. The semantic description of resources is driving the development of a new generation of applications, like intelligent personal assistants and chatbots, and the development of knowledge graphs and artificial intelligence applications. The use of semantic annotations was accelerated by the introduction of schema.org [8]. Schema.org was launched by the search engines Bing, Google, Yahoo! and Yandex in 2011. It has since become a de-facto standard for annotating data on the web [15]. The schema.org vocabulary, serialized with Microdata, RDFa, or JSON-LD, is used to mark up website content. Schema.org is the most widespread vocabulary on the web, and is used on more than a quarter of web pages [9,14].

Even though studies have shown that the amount of semantically annotated websites are growing rapidly, there are still shortcomings when it comes to the quality of annotations [12,17]. Also the analyses in [1,10] underline the inconsistencies and syntactic and semantic errors in semantic annotations. The lack

© Springer Nature Switzerland AG 2019
N. Bjørner et al. (Eds.): PSI 2019, LNCS 11964, pp. 223–231, 2019.
https://doi.org/10.1007/978-3-030-37487-7_19

of completeness and correctness of the semantic annotations makes content unreachable for automated agents, causes incorrect appearances in knowledge graphs and search results, or makes crawling and reasoning less effective for building applications on top of semantic annotations. These errors may be caused by missing guidelines, insufficient expertise and technical or human errors. Data quality is a critical aspect for efficient knowledge representation and processing. Therefore, it is important to define methods and techniques for semantic data verification and validation, and to develop tools which will make this process efficient, tangible and understandable, also for non-technical users.

In this paper, we extend our previous work [21], where we introduced a Domain Specification, and present an approach for verification and validation of semantic annotations. A Domain Specification (DS) is a design pattern for semantic annotations; an extended subset of types, properties, and ranges from schema.org. The semantify.it Evaluator[1] is a developed tool that allows the verification and validation of schema.org annotations which are collected from web pages. Those annotations can be verified against the schema.org vocabulary and Domain Specifications. The verification against Domain Specifications allows for the checking of the compliance of annotations against corresponding domain-specific constraints. The validation approach extends the functionality of the tool by detecting the consistency errors between semantic annotations and annotated content.

The remainder of this paper is structured as follows: Sect. 2 describes the verification approach of semantic annotations. Section 3 describes the validation approach. Section 4 concludes our work and describes future work.

2   Verification

In this section we discuss the verification process of semantic annotations according to schema.org and Domain Specifications. The section is structured as follows: Sect. 2.1 gives the definition of the semantic annotation verification, Sect. 2.2 describes related work, Sect. 2.3 discusses our approach, and Sect. 2.4 describes the evaluation method.

2.1   Definition

The verification process of semantic annotations consists of two parts, namely, (I) checking the conformance with the schema.org vocabulary, and (II) checking the compliance with an appropriate Domain Specification. While the first verification step ensures that the annotation uses proper vocabulary terms defined in schema.org and its extensions, the second step ensures that the annotation is in compliance with the domain-specific constraints defined in a corresponding DS.

---

[1] https://semantify.it/evaluator.

2.2   Related Work

In this section, we refer to the existing approaches and tools to verify structured data. There are tools for verifying schema.org annotations, such as the Google Structured Data Testing tool[2], the Google Email Markup Tester[3], the Yandex Structured Data Validator[4], and the Bing Markup Validator[5]. They verify annotations of web pages that use Microdata, Microformats, RDFa, or JSON-LD as markup formats against schema.org. But these tools do not provide the check of completeness and correctness. For example, they can allow one to have empty range values, redundancy of information, or semantic consistency issues (e.g. the end day of the event is earlier than the start day). In [7] SPARQL and SPIN are used for constraint formulation and data quality check. The use of SPARQL and SPIN query template sets allows the identification of syntax errors, missing values, unique value violations, out of range values, and functional dependency violations. The Shape Expression (ShEx) definition language [20] allows RDF verification[6] through the declaration of constraints. In [4] the authors define a schema formalism for describing the topology of an RDF graph that uses regular bag expressions (RBEs) to define constraints. In [5] the authors described the semantics of Shapes Schemas for RDF, and presented two algorithms for the verification of an RDF graph against a Shapes Schema. The Shapes Constraint Language[7] (SHACL) is a language for formulating structural constraints on RDF graphs. SHACL allows us to define constraints targeting specific nodes in a data graph based on their type, identifier, or a SPARQL query. The existing approaches can be adapted for our needs but not fully, as they are developed for RDF graph verification and not for schema.org annotations in particular.

2.3   Our Approach

To enable the verification of semantic annotations according to the schema.org vocabulary and to Domain Specifications, we developed a tool that executes a corresponding verification algorithm. This tool takes as inputs the schema.org annotation to verify and a DS that corresponds to the domain of the annotation. The outcome of this verification process is provided in a formalized, structured format, to enable the further machine processing of the verification result.

The verification algorithm consists of two parts, the first checks the general compliance of the input annotation with the schema.org vocabulary, while the latter checks the domain-specific compliance of the input annotation with the given Domain Specification. The following objectives are given for the conformity verification of the input annotation according to the schema.org vocabulary:

---

[2] https://search.google.com/structured-data/testing-tool/.
[3] https://www.google.com/webmasters/markup-tester/.
[4] https://webmaster.yandex.com/tools/microtest/.
[5] https://www.bing.com/toolbox/markup-validator.
[6] Authors use term "validation" in their paper due to content definition.
[7] https://www.w3.org/TR/shacl-ucr/.

1. The correct usage of serialization formats allowed by schema.org, hence RDFa, Microdata, or JSON-LD.
2. The correct usage of vocabulary terms from schema.org in the annotations, including types, properties, enumerations, and literals (data types).
3. The correct usage of vocabulary relationships from schema.org in the annotations, hence, the compliance with domain and range definitions for properties.

The domain-specific verification of the input annotation is enabled through the use of Domain Specifications[8], e.g. DSs for annotation of tourism domain and GeoData [18,19]. DSs have a standardized data model. This data model consists of the possible specification nodes with corresponding attributes that can be used to create a DS document (e.g. specification nodes for types, properties, ranges, etc.). A DS document is constructed by the recursive selection of these grammar nodes, which, as a result, form a specific syntax (structure) that has to be satisfied by the verified annotations [11]. Keywords in these specification nodes allow the definition of additional constraints (e.g. "multipleValuesAllowed" or "isOptional" for property nodes). In our approach, the verification algorithm has to ensure that the input annotation is in compliance with the domain-specific constraints defined by the input DS. In order to achieve this, the verification tool has to be able to understand the DS data model, the possible constraint definitions, and to check if verified annotations are in compliance with them.

2.4   Evaluation

We implement our approach in the semantify.it Evaluator[9]. The tool provides a verification report with detailed information about detected errors according to the schema.org vocabulary (see Fig. 1) and Domain Specifications (see Fig. 2).

Nr.	Type	Markup	View	SDO-Valid
1	MusicEvent	jsonld	🔍	Valid with Warnings 🅑
2	WebSite	jsonld	🔍	Valid with Warnings 🅑
3	BreadcrumbList	jsonld	🔍	Not Valid 🅑
4	BreadcrumbList	microdata	🔍	Valid ✅
5	PostalAddress	microdata	🔍	Valid ✅

Fig. 1. Schema.org verification

Besides the verification result itself, the report includes details about the detected errors, e.g. error codes (ID of the error type), error titles, error severity

---

[8] List of available Domain Specifications: https://semantify.it/domainSpecifications/public.

[9] https://semantify.it/evaluator.

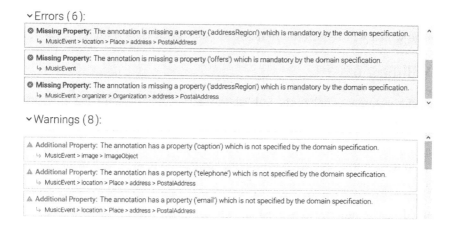

Fig. 2. Domain specification verification. Verification report

levels, error paths (where within the annotation the error occurred), and textual descriptions of the errors. The implementation itself can be evaluated through unit tests in terms of a correct functionality (correctness) and the implementation of all possible constraint possibilities of the Domain Specification vocabulary (completeness). This can be achieved by comparing the structured representation of the result, namely the JSON file produced by the verification algorithm, which is used to generate a human-readable verification report for the user (see Fig. 3), with the expected verification report outcome specified in the test cases for predefined annotation-Domain Specification pairs.

		https://www.mayrhofen.at/			

Evaluation Settings		Crawling Settings			
Schema.org verification:	Yes	Timeout:	10000	Use sitemap:	Yes
Domain-specific verification:	Yes	WaitFor:	3000	Crawl Sub-domains:	No
Annotation validation:	Yes	Max. crawled Links:	100	Respect Robots.txt:	Yes

EDIT SETTINGS   START EVALUATION

Status	Start date	Crawling	Schema.org Verification	Domain-specific Verification	Annotation Validation
✔	16. Apr 19, 12:07	159 ⅄ 239 📄	238	1 ⊗	0	39	99	100

Fig. 3. semantify.it Evaluator. Verification and validation report

A formal proof of the correctness and completeness of our implemented algorithm is rather straightforward given the simplicity of our current knowledge representation formalism. In our ongoing work[10], we develop a richer constraint language which will require more detailed analysis of these issues.

3   Validation

Search engines may penalize the publisher of structured data if their annotations include content that is invisible to users, and/or markup irrelevant or misleading content. These penalties may have negative effects on a website (e.g. bad position of the website in search results) or even lead to non-integration of the structured data (e.g. no generation of rich snippets). For example, annotations of the Destination Management Organizations (DMOs) usually include a list of offers. These offers must comply with offers which are described on the website, and all URLs contained in the annotations must match with the URLs in the content. Such issues can be detected through the validation of semantic annotations.

In this section, we discuss the validation process of semantic annotations and the proposed approach. The section is structured as follows: Sect. 3.1 gives the definition of the semantic annotation validation, Sect. 3.2 describes some related work, Sect. 3.3 discusses our approach, and Sect. 3.4 describes the evaluation method.

3.1   Definition

The validation of semantic annotations is the process of checking whether the content of a semantic annotation corresponds to the content of the web page that it represents, and if it is consistent with it. Semantic annotations should include the actual information of the web page, correct links, images and literal values without overlapping or redundancy.

3.2   Related Work

The incorrect representation of the structured data can make data unreachable for automated engines, cause an incorrect appearance in the search results, or make crawling and reasoning less effective for building applications on top of semantic data. The errors may be caused by not following recommended guidelines, e.g. structured data guidelines[11], insufficient expertise, technical or human errors (some of the issues can be detected by Google search console[12]), and/or annotations not being in accordance with the content of web pages, so-called "spammy structured markup"[13]. There is no direct literature related to the methods of detecting inconsistency between semantic annotations and content of web pages, but the problem of the content conformity restriction is also mentioned in [13].

---

[10] The paper is under double blind review and can't be revealed.

[11] https://developers.google.com/search/docs/guides/sd-policies.

[12] https://search.google.com/search-console/about.

[13] https://support.google.com/webmasters/answer/9044175?hl=en&visit_id=6368625 21420978682-2839371720&rd=1#spammy-structured-markup.

3.3   Our Approach

Since semantic annotations are created and published by different data providers or agencies in varying quantity and quality and using different assumptions, the validity of data should be prioritized to increase the quality of structured data. To solve the problem of detecting errors caused by inconsistencies between analyzed schema.org annotations and the content of the web pages where the annotations were found, we propose a validation framework. The framework consists of the following objectives:

1. Detect the main inconsistencies between the content of schema.org annotations and the content of their corresponding web pages.
2. Develop an algorithm for the consistency check between a web page and corresponding semantic annotations. The information from web pages can be extracted from the source of a web page by tracking the appropriate HTML tags, keywords, lists, images, URLs, paragraph tags and the associated full text. Some natural language processing and machine learning techniques can be applied to extract important information from the textual description, e.g price, email, telephone number and so on. There exist some approaches to extract information from a text, such as named entity recognition [16] to locate and categorize important nouns and proper nouns in a text, web information extraction systems [6], and text mining techniques [2].
3. Define metrics to evaluate the consistencies of the semantic annotations according to the annotated content. In this step, we analyze existing data quality metrics that can be applied on the structured data and define metrics that can be useful to evaluate the consistency between a web page content and semantic annotation. We measure the consistency for different types of values, such as URL, string, boolean, enumeration, rating value, date and time formats.
4. Provide a validation tool to present the overall score for a web page and detailed insights about the evaluated consistency scores on a per value level.

3.4   Evaluation

To ensure the validity of the report results, we will organize a user study of semantic annotations and annotated web pages to prove the performance of our framework. The questionnaire will be structured in a way to get quantitative and qualitative feedback about the consistencies between a web page and annotation content (see Fig. 4) according to the results provided by the framework (see Fig. 3). As our use case, we will use annotated data and websites of Destination Management Organizations, such as Best of Zillertal Fügen[14], Mayrhofen[15], Seefeld[16], and Zillertal Arena[17].

---

[14] https://www.best-of-zillertal.at.
[15] https://www.mayrhofen.at.
[16] https://www.seefeld.com/.
[17] https://www.zillertalarena.com.

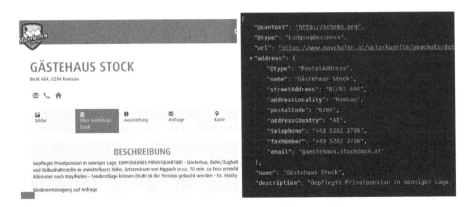

Fig. 4. Web page content and annotation content

4 Conclusion and Future Work

Semantic annotations will be used for improved search results by search engines or as building blocks of knowledge graphs. Therefore, the quality issues in terms of structure and consistency can have an impact on where the annotations are utilized and lead, for instance, to false representation in the search results or to low-quality knowledge graphs. In this paper, we described our ongoing work for an approach to verify and validate semantic annotations and the tool that is evolving as the implementation of this approach.

For the future work, we will define Domain Specifications with SHACL in order to comply with the recent W3C Recommendation for RDF validation. We will develop an abstract syntax and formal semantics for Domain Specifications and map it to SHACL notions, for instance by aligning the concept of Domain Specifications with SHACL node shapes.

References

1. Akbar, Z., Kärle, E., Panasiuk, O., Şimşek, U., Toma, I., Fensel, D.: Complete semantics to empower touristic service providers. In: Panetto, H., et al. (eds.) OTM 2017 Conferences. LNCS, vol. 10574, pp. 353–370. Springer, Cham (2017). https://doi.org/10.1007/978-3-319-69459-7_24
2. Allahyari, M., et al.: A brief survey of text mining: classification, clustering and extraction techniques. arXiv preprint arXiv:1707.02919 (2017)
3. Berners-Lee, T., Hendler, J., Lassila, O.: The semantic web. Sci. Am. **284**(5), 34–43 (2001)
4. Boneva, I., Gayo, J.E.L., Hym, S., Prud'hommeau, E.G., Solbrig, H.R., Staworko, S.: Validating RDF with shape expressions. CoRR, abs/1404.1270 (2014)
5. Boneva, I., Labra Gayo, J.E., Prud'hommeaux, E.G.: Semantics and validation of shapes schemas for RDF. In: d'Amato, C., et al. (eds.) ISWC 2017. LNCS, vol. 10587, pp. 104–120. Springer, Cham (2017). https://doi.org/10.1007/978-3-319-68288-4_7

6. Chang, C.H., Kayed, M., Girgis, M.R., Shaalan, K.F.: A survey of web information extraction systems. IEEE Trans. Knowl. Data Eng. **18**(10), 1411–1428 (2006)
7. Fürber, C., Hepp, M.: Using SPARQL and SPIN for data quality management on the semantic web. In: Abramowicz, W., Tolksdorf, R. (eds.) BIS 2010. LNBIP, vol. 47, pp. 35–46. Springer, Heidelberg (2010). https://doi.org/10.1007/978-3-642-12814-1_4
8. Guha, R.: Introducing schema.org: search engines come together for a richer web. Google Official Blog (2011)
9. Guha, R.V., Brickley, D., Macbeth, S.: Schema.org: evolution of structured data on the web. Commun. ACM **59**(2), 44–51 (2016)
10. Hollenstein, N., Schneider, N., Webber, B.L.: Inconsistency detection in semantic annotation. In: LREC (2016)
11. Holzknecht, O.: Enabling domain-specific validation of schema.org annotations. Master's thesis, Innsbruck University, Innrain 52, 6020 Innsbruck, Austria, November 2018
12. Kärle, E., Fensel, A., Toma, I., Fensel, D.: Why are there more hotels in tyrol than in Austria? Analyzing schema.org usage in the hotel domain. In: Inversini, A., Schegg, R. (eds.) Information and Communication Technologies in Tourism 2016, pp. 99–112. Springer, Cham (2016). https://doi.org/10.1007/978-3-319-28231-2_8
13. Kärle, E., Fensel, D.: Heuristics for publishing dynamic content as structured data with schema.org. arXiv preprint arXiv:1808.06012 (2018)
14. Meusel, R., Petrovski, P., Bizer, C.: The WebDataCommons Microdata, RDFa and microformat dataset series. In: Mika, P., et al. (eds.) ISWC 2014. LNCS, vol. 8796, pp. 277–292. Springer, Cham (2014). https://doi.org/10.1007/978-3-319-11964-9_18
15. Mika, P.: On schema.org and why it matters for the web. IEEE Internet Comput. **19**(4), 52–55 (2015)
16. Mohit, B.: Named entity recognition. In: Zitouni, I. (ed.) Natural Language Processing of Semitic Languages. TANLP, pp. 221–245. Springer, Heidelberg (2014). https://doi.org/10.1007/978-3-642-45358-8_7
17. Mühleisen, H., Bizer, C.: Web data commons-extracting structured data from two large web corpora. LDOW **937**, 133–145 (2012)
18. Panasiuk, O., Kärle, E., Şimşek, U., Fensel, D.: Defining tourism domains for semantic annotation of web content. e-Rev. Tour. Res. **9** (2018). Research notes from the ENTER 2018 Conference on ICT in Tourism
19. Panasiuk, O., Akbar, Z., Gerrier, T., Fensel, D.: Representing geodata for tourism with schema.org. In: Proceedings of the 4th International Conference on Geographical Information Systems Theory, Applications and Management - Volume 1: GISTAM, pp. 239–246. INSTICC, SciTePress (2018)
20. Prud'hommeaux, E., Labra Gayo, J.E., Solbrig, H.: Shape expressions: an RDF validation and transformation language. In: Proceedings of the 10th International Conference on Semantic Systems, pp. 32–40. ACM (2014)
21. Şimşek, U., Kärle, E., Holzknecht, O., Fensel, D.: Domain specific semantic validation of schema.org annotations. In: Petrenko, A.K., Voronkov, A. (eds.) PSI 2017. LNCS, vol. 10742, pp. 417–429. Springer, Cham (2018). https://doi.org/10.1007/978-3-319-74313-4_31

Towards Automatic Deductive Verification of C Programs over Linear Arrays

Dmitry Kondratyev$^{(\boxtimes)}$ ⓘ, Ilya Maryasov ⓘ, and Valery Nepomniaschy ⓘ

A. P. Ershov Institute of Informatics Systems,
Siberian Branch of the Russian Academy of Sciences,
6, Acad. Lavrentjev pr., Novosibirsk 630090, Russia
apple-66@mail.ru, {ivm,vnep}@iis.nsk.su
http://www.iis.nsk.su

Abstract. The generation and proving of verification conditions, which correspond to loops, may cause difficulties during deductive verification because the construction of required invariants is a challenge, especially for nested loops. The methods of invariant synthesis are often heuristic ones. Another way is the symbolic method of loop invariant elimination. Its idea is to represent a loop body in a form of special replacement operation under certain constraints. This operation expresses loop effect with possible **break** statement in a symbolic form and allows introducing an inference rule, which uses no invariants in axiomatic semantics. This work represents the further development of this method. The inner loops are interesting because of the higher nesting level, the more complicated loop invariant. A good example for this case to verify is a class of linear array sorting programs, which iteratively increase the sorted part. In this paper, we consider the insertion sort program. A special algorithm was developed and implemented to prove verification conditions automatically in ACL2. It generates automatically auxiliary lemmas, which allow to prove obtained verification conditions in ACL2 in automatic mode.

Keywords: C-light · Loop invariant elimination · Mixed axiomatic semantics · Definite iteration · C-lightVer · Array sorting program · ACL2 prover · Deductive verification · Lemma discovery · Proof strategy

1 Introduction

C program verification is an urgent problem today. Some projects (e.g. [2,4]) suggests different solutions. But none of them contains any methods for automatic verification of loop-containing programs without invariants. As it is known, in

This research is partially supported by RFBR grant 17-01-00789.

N. Bjørner et al. (Eds.): PSI 2019, LNCS 11964, pp. 232–242, 2019.
https://doi.org/10.1007/978-3-030-37487-7_20

order to verify loops we need invariants whose construction is a challenge. Therefore, the user has to provide these invariants. For many cases, it is a difficult task.

Tuerk [19] suggested to use pre- and post-conditions for while-loops, but the user still has to construct them himself. Li et al. [11] developed a learning algorithm of loop invariants generation, but their method does not support array operations and the **break** statement in the loop body. Galeotti et al. [5] improved a well-known method of post-condition mutation by a combination of test case generation and dynamic invariant detection. However, this approach failed to infer full invariant for sorting programs. Srivastava et al. [17] proposed a method, which is based on user-provided invariant templates. This method also is not able to perform a full verification of sorting programs. Kovács [10] developed the method of the automatic invariant generation for the P-solvable loops, where right operands of assignment statements in the loop body must have a form of polynomial expression and the **break** statement is not considered.

We consider loops with certain restrictions [16]. We extend our mixed axiomatic semantics of the C-light language [1] with a new rule for verification of such loops, based on the replacement operation [16]. The verification conditions are generated by C-lightVer system [9] using this rule.

In our previous paper [8], we considered the strategy of automatic proving of verification conditions. It can be applied, if a program loop includes the **break** statement. This strategy belongs to the class based on auxiliary lemma discovering [6].

The new goal is the verification of the insertion sort program, which has different specification. Sorting programs are programs over changeable arrays with loop exit. Suzuki et al. [18] described decidability of verification conditions with the permutation predicates, if such conditions are representable in the Presburger arithmetic. But verification conditions are not representable in presburger arithmetic in our case due to replacement operation. Sorting programs can contain downward loops and can use the value of loop counter after iterations are finished. Thus, we had to change our algorithm of replacement operation generation. Also, we overcame the difficulties in proving verification conditions by developing new strategies of proof. This paper describes the solution of these problems.

2   Preliminary Concepts

We develop a two-level system of deductive verification of the C-light programs [14]. The C-light language is a powerful subset of C language. To prove obtained in our system verification conditions, we use the theorem prover ACL2 [15]. The input language of ACL2 is an applicative dialect of Common Lisp language, which supports only functional paradigm and does not support imperative one.

Since Common Lisp language focuses on list processing, arrays of the C-light language we simulate by lists. Consider list operations in ACL2. If *expr* is an expression of ACL2 language, then (*update-nth i expr l*) is a new list, which coincides with a list l except for i-th element, whose value is *expr*. The function *len* returns the length of a list.

To verify programs without invariants, we implemented the method of loop invariants elimination for definite iteration [16] in our system. Our previous works [12,13] dealt with definite iteration over unchangeable data structures with/without loop exit. In this paper, we moved to changeable data structures with possible **break** statement in the loop body.

Consider the statement `for x in S do v := body(v, x) end`, where S is a structure, x is the variable of the type "an element S", v is a vector of loop variables, which does not contain x and *body* represents the loop body computation, which does not modify x and which terminates for each $x \in S$. The structure S can be modified as described below. The loop body can contain only the assignment statements, the **if** statements, possibly nested, and the **break** statements. Such **for** statement is named a definite iteration. Let v_0 be the vector of values of variables from v just before the loop. To express the effect of the iteration let us define a replacement operation $rep(v, S, body, n)$, where $rep(v, S, body, 0) = v_0$, $rep(v, S, body, i) = body(rep(v, S, body, i-1), s_i)$ for all $i = 1, 2, \ldots, n$. A number of theorems, which express important properties of the replacement operation, were proved in [16].

The inference rule for definite iterations has the form:

$$\frac{\{P\}\ \mathbf{A};\ \{Q(v \leftarrow rep(v, S, body, n))\}}{\{P\}\ \mathbf{A};\ \textbf{for x in S do v := body(v, x) end}\ \{Q\}}$$

Here A are program statements before the loop. We find the weakest precondition applying the mixed axiomatic semantics [1] of the C-light language.

3 Generation of Replacement Operation

In this paper, we extend the class of definite iterations by downward iteration

$$\texttt{for (i = n - 1; i >= 0; i--) v := body(v, i) end,}$$

where n is the number of elements of array. The definition of *rep* is generated by a special translator [8]. The statements of the loop body are translated to the constructions of the ACL2 language. The fields of the structure of the type *frame* correspond to the variables of v and the function *frame-init* creates the object of the type *frame* with given field values.

For downward iteration, the generator of *rep* was modified. Firstly, it has to generate not only the structure *frame* but the structure *envir*. It stores the values of variables, which are used but are not modified inside the loop. Moreover, the generator makes a definition of the function *envir-init*, which creates an object of the type *envir* with given field values. The structure *envir* has also a dedicated field *upper-bound*, whose value is an inaccessible upper bound of the loop counter, which is equal to $(n-1)+1$.

Secondly, in the case of downward iteration, the value of loop counter is not equal to the number of iteration. In order to distinguish from loop counter i, the first argument of *rep* is called *iteration*. Therefore, the generator has to include not only the elements of the vector v, but also the loop counter to the fields of the structure *frame*. This allows using the value of the loop counter after loop execution.

One of the restrictions of the symbolic method [16] is that the loop counter is not modified by the loop body. So the third change of the generator is the usage of the difference between the upper bound and iteration number as the value of loop counter in the body of *rep*. In the case of iteration continuation, the loop counter is initialized by the difference between the same value and 1. In the case of the loop exit, the loop counter is not modified. Note that such approach can simplify the proof because it expresses the value of the loop counter explicitly.

4   Verification of Insertion Sort Program

Let us demonstrate the motivating example. Consider the following insertion sort program, which orders a given linear array a of the length n:

```
/* P */ void insertion_sort(int a[], int n) {int k, i, j;
        /* INV */ for (i = 1; i < n; i++) {
                  k = a[i];
                  for (j = i - 1; j >= 0; j--) {
                      if (a[j] <= k) break;
                      a[j + 1] = a[j];}
                  a[j + 1] = k;}}/* Q */
```

The program pre-condition, post-condition, and invariant have the form:

$$P \equiv 0 < n \wedge a = a_0 \wedge n \leq len(a_0), \ Q \equiv perm(0, n-1, a_0, a) \wedge ord(0, n-1, a),$$
$$INV \equiv i \leq n \wedge n \leq len(a) \wedge len(a_0) = len(a) \wedge$$
$$a_0[i : n-1] = a[i : n-1] \wedge perm(0, i-1, a_0, a) \wedge ord(0, i-1, a),$$

where $perm(i, j, a_0, a)$ means that array a is the permutation of array a_0 from i-th to j-th element, $ord(i, j, a)$ denotes that array a is ordered from i-th to j-th element. Note that Galeotti et al. [5] did not prove the permutation, and Srivastava et al. [17] used more weaker property $\forall i \exists j \ (0 \leq i < n) \Rightarrow (0 \leq j < n \wedge a_0[i] = a[j])$ then permutation.

Applying rules of the mixed axiomatic semantics [1] we obtain three verification conditions: the condition of loop entry, the condition of loop exit and the condition of iteration continuation.

The first and the second verification conditions were proved in ACL2 automatically. Consider the third verification condition, which is the most difficult.

$$i < n \wedge INV \Rightarrow ((((INV(i \leftarrow i+1))(a \leftarrow update\text{-}nth(j+1, k, a)))$$
$$(j \leftarrow rep(i, envir\text{-}init(i, k), frame\text{-}init(i-1, a)).j,$$
$$a \leftarrow rep(i, envir\text{-}init(i, k), frame\text{-}init(i-1, a)).a))(k \leftarrow a[i]))$$

Due to the symbolic method of definite iteration verification, we do not need to provide an invariant for inner loop. This verification condition can be found in [20] (in the syntax of ACL2). It was automatically generated and named vc-3 in the file vc-3.lisp. To prove this verification condition the strategies from Sect. 5 were applied.

5   Method of Automation of Verification Conditions Proving

During this research, four strategies of verification conditions proving were developed. They are based on the automatic generation of lemmas. Their proof can help to prove a verification condition. Automatically generated formulas can be not theorems, therefore only successful proving of them in ACL2 allows adding them into the underlying theory. In ACL2, such formulas can be given to the user for proving them in interactive mode or can be proved automatically. We will give here key lemmas, which were added to the underlying theory in our example. These lemmas allowed ACL2 to prove the verification condition.

Let us introduce common notions for all strategies. Each of them gets a finite downward iteration over array a. We will define strategies using notions from Sect. 3.

Let us consider the verification condition of a form $(X_1 \wedge X_2 \wedge \ldots \wedge X_w) \Rightarrow (C_1 \wedge C_2 \wedge \ldots \wedge C_m)$, where X_1, X_2, ..., X_w are hypotheses and C_1, C_2, ..., C_m are goals. If the verification is not of that form, let us bring it to such form. We will consider each goal separately: $(X_1 \wedge X_2 \wedge \ldots \wedge X_w) \Rightarrow C_i$, where $1 \leq i \leq m$. Let $Y = \{C_1, C_2, \ldots, C_m\}$.

Let us make a correspondence between parameters of strategies and our finite iteration with its continuation condition from our example. In our case, the parameter a stands for array a, parameter n stands for variable i, parameter i stands for variable j. Parameter $T \equiv INV \wedge (i < n)$. Let $a[i:j]$ be a subarray of array a from i-th to j-th element inclusively.

5.1   The Strategy of Premises Choice

The condition of the applicability of this strategy is the form of considered finite iteration (with possible loop exit). This strategy is applied, if during verification condition proving, we try to prove a statement about the property of rep. Let R be such a statement. Thereby, the first argument of our strategy is the finite iteration, the second one is the definition of rep, the third argument is R.

The strategy is oriented to solving a problem of transformation of R to lemma, which has the form of implication. R becomes the conclusion of such implication. Therefore, the problem is reduced to a generation of the premise, which should allow to prove the lemma and the verification condition.

To overcome this difficulty we use more generalized statements as premises than T. For example, the statement $L_1 \equiv (iteration \in N) \wedge (iteration \leq$

$env.upper\text{-}bound) \wedge (env.upper\text{-}bound < (len(fr.a))) \wedge (fr.j = (env.upper\text{-}bound -1))$ or the statement $L_2 \equiv (env.upper\text{-}bound \in N) \wedge (env.upper\text{-}bound < (len(fr.a))) \wedge (fr.j = (env.upper\text{-}bound - 1)) \wedge \neg fr.loop\text{-}break.$

We plan to extend the set of premises. The choice is determined by one, which helps ACL2 to prove the lemma. For each $L \in \{L_1, L_2\}$, we try to prove formula $lm \equiv L \Rightarrow P$ in ACL2. All such lemmas start with the prefix rep-lemma- in [20].

Let us generate auxiliary formula lm' in a form of implication. Its premise is T and its conclusion is constructed from R by replacing n, env, and fr by iteration parameters. Let us substitute the iteration parameters into lm to prove lm'. Because of the same premises, it is more convenient to use lm' for verification condition proving. In [20] the names of all such lemmas start with prefix vc-3-lemma-.

For example, consider the statement about equality of two subarrays as $R \equiv a[0 : rep(iteration, env, fr).j] = (rep(iteration, env, fr).a)[0 : rep(iteration, env, fr).j]$. Applying our strategy to R, we add a lemma $L_1 \Rightarrow P$ to the underlying theory, which can be found in [20] under the name rep-lemma-76.

5.2   The Strategy for Finite Iteration over Changeable Array

The condition of the applicability of this strategy is the form of considered finite iteration and the presence of assignment statement a[expr-index] = expr-value; in a loop body. Let an iteration consists of w assignment statements. With the help of the function $c\_kernel\_translator$, we will translate each expression $expr\text{-}index_i$ to the expression $expr\text{-}ind_i$ of ACL2 language for each $i\colon 1 \leq i \leq w$.

Let us generate and try to prove by the strategy from Sect. 5.1 the following statement: $(index \neq expr\text{-}ind_1) \wedge \ldots \wedge (index \neq expr\text{-}ind_w) \Rightarrow rep(iteration - 1, env, fr).a[index] = rep(iteration, env, fr).a[index]$. In case of a successful proof of such formula, the corresponding lemma is added to the underlying theory. It states, that an array element, whose index is not in the set of indices of left operands of assignment statements, is not changed at the next iteration.

Consider the application of this strategy to our example. Note that the loop contains the assignment statement a[j + 1] = a[j];. Since the value of loop counter is $env.upper\text{-}bound - iteration$, the generated lemma rep-lemma-22 [20] has the following form: $L_1 \wedge (index \neq (env.upper\text{-}bound - iteration) + 1) \Rightarrow rep(iteration - 1, env, fr).a[index] = rep(iteration, env, fr). a[index]$.

5.3   The Strategy for Finite Iteration with break Statement

The condition of the applicability of this strategy is the form of considered finite iteration and the presence of break statement. Let break-condition be a conjunction of controlling expressions of the if statements on the path to break statement (we make all necessary substitutions in case of assignment statements). In fact, break-condition is a function $br\text{-}cond(iteration, env, fr)$.

The value of the field *loop-break* of the structure *frame* is the detector for certain iteration, whether **break** statement occurred earlier. Note that the number of iteration, which led to loop exit, is $br\text{-}iter = env.upper\text{-}bound - rep(env.upper\text{-}bound, env, fr).i$. This strategy attempts to prove the set of auxiliary lemmas obtained from the following statements about **break**:

1. If $rep(iteration, env, fr).loop\text{-}break$ then $rep(iteration, env, fr).i = rep(iteration - 1, env, fr).i$.
2. If $\neg rep(iteration, env, fr).loop\text{-}break$ then $rep(iteration, env, fr).i = env.upper\text{-}bound - iteration - 1$.
3. If $rep(iter, env, fr).loop\text{-}break$ and $iter \leq iteration$ then $rep(iteration, env, fr).loop\text{-}break$.
4. If $rep(iter, env, fr).loop\text{-}break$ and $iter \leq iteration$ then $rep(iter, env, fr) = rep(iteration, env, fr)$.
5. If $\neg rep(iteration, env, fr).loop\text{-}break$ and $iter \leq iteration$ then $\neg rep(iter, env, fr).loop\text{-}break$.
6. $\neg(br\text{-}iter - 1, fr, env).loop\text{-}break$ and $rep(br\text{-}iter - 1, fr, env).loop\text{-}break$.
7. If $iter \in [br\text{-}iter : env.upper\text{-}bound]$ then $rep(env, iter, fr).loop\text{-}break$.
8. If $iteration \in [0 : br\text{-}iter - 1]$ then $\neg rep(iteration, env, fr).loop\text{-}break$.
9. If $iteration \in [0 : br\text{-}iter - 1]$ then $\neg br\text{-}cond(iteration, env, fr)$.
10. $iteration \in [br\text{-}iter : env.upper\text{-}bound] \Rightarrow br\text{-}cond(iteration, env, fr)$.
11. $\neg br\text{-}cond(br\text{-}iter - 1, env, fr)$ and $br\text{-}cond(br\text{-}iter, env, fr)$.

These statements are based on the fact, that the property "whether a loop exit occurred" is monotonic relative to the number of iteration. The strategy from Sect. 5.1 is applied to these statements.

Consider the application of this strategy to our example. As the loop contains **break** statement the break-condition is $(a[rep(iteration-1, env, fr).j]) \leq env.k$. In our case the statement 11 has the form: $a[rep(br\text{-}iter - 1, env, fr).j] > env.k$ and $a[rep(br\text{-}iter, env, fr).j, env, fr)] \leq env.k$. Using obtained by the strategy statements 1 and 2 we have the equivalent break-condition: $a[rep(env.upper\text{-}bound, env, fr).j + 2] > env.k$ and $a[rep(env.upper\text{-}bound, env, fr).j] \leq env.k$. By the strategy from Sect. 5.1 these statements are transformed to lemmas [20] **rep-lemma-83**: $L_2 \Rightarrow env.k < a[rep(env.upper\text{-}bound, env, fr).j + 2]$ and **rep-lemma- 108**: $L_2 \Rightarrow a[rep(env.upper\text{-}bound, env, fr).j] \leq env.k$.

5.4   The Strategy for Functions with Concatenation Property

The strategy for functions with concatenation property generates statements of equality between subarrays of array a and subarrays of array $rep(n, env, fr).a$. These subarrays are chosen using analysis of loop body. These statements are converted to lemmas using the strategy from Sect. 5.1. These lemmas are proved using the strategy from Sect. 5.3 and the strategy from Sect. 5.2. The set D of pairs of equivalent subarrays is obtained as the result. The first item of each pair from D is a subarray of array a and a second item is a subarray of array $rep(n, env, fr).a$.

The predicate V has the concatenation property if $(V(i,k,u_1,\ldots,u_r) \wedge V(k,j, u_1,\ldots,u_r) \wedge (i \leq k) \wedge (k < j)) \Rightarrow V(i,j,u_1,\ldots,u_r)$. The predicate V has the concatenation with the splice at bounds property by condition f if $(V(i,k,u_1,\ldots, u_r) \wedge V(k,j,u_1,\ldots,u_r) \wedge (i \leq k) \wedge (k < j) \wedge f(u_1[k], u_1[k + 1])\ldots \wedge f(u_r[k], u_r[k+1])) \Rightarrow V(i,j,u_1,\ldots,u_r)$.

These patterns of the properties are used in check whether this strategy is applicable. To do this, loop and post-condition analysis are performed. For all predicates in post-condition, we search theorems satisfying given property patterns in all used theories. Analysis of loop allows ascertaining whether the loop corresponds to the form of considering definite iteration.

The strategy starts at an analysis of the elements of the set Y. Let Z be a set of goals from Y, which are the applications of a predicate satisfying concatenation property or concatenation with a splice at bounds property.

For each goal $U(\ldots) \in Z$ the following steps are performed:

1. The iteration does not cover items from the segment $[0 : rep(n, env, fr).i]$. Therefore, we can suppose that the segment is not modified by rep. If we succeeded in proving the statement about equality $a[0 : rep(n, env, fr).i]$ and $(rep(n, env, fr).a)[0 : rep(n, env, fr).i]$ then the pair $([0 : rep(n, env, fr).i], [0 : rep(n, env, fr).i])$ is added to set D.

2. In case of presence of statements `a[i + expr] = a[i];`, where $expr$ is a C-light expression, the hypothesis about array shift arises. With the help of $c\_kernel\_translator$ from [8] we obtain $expression$, which is $expr$ in ACL2 language. If we succeeded in proving the statement about equality $a[(rep(n, env, fr).i + 1) : (n - expression)]$ and $(rep(n, env, fr).a)[(rep(n, env, fr).i + 1 + expression) : n]$ then the pair $([(rep(n, env, fr).i + 1) : (n - expression)], [(rep(n, env, fr).i + 1 + expression) : n])$ is added to set D.

3. In case of presence of **break** statement, we apply the strategy from Sect. 5.3 if predicate U satisfies the property of concatenation with a splice at bounds by condition f. Note that break-condition can contain f and depends on $br\text{-}iter$ defined in Sect. 5.3. If we proved the formula obtained from the statement 11 from the Sect. 5.3, then such lemma can help to prove the range splice. If we succeeded in proving $T \wedge \neg br\text{-}cond(br\text{-}iter - 1, env, fr) \wedge br\text{-}cond(br\text{-}iter, env, fr) \Rightarrow f((rep(n, env, fr).a)[rep(n, env, fr).i], (rep(n, env, fr).a)[rep(n, env, fr).i + 1])$ then this lemma is added to underlying theory. This lemma states about the range splice between $rep(n, env, fr).i$ and $rep(n, env, fr).i + 1$, i. e. in the point of loop exit. In case of successful proof, we add this lemma to the underlying theory.

   For statements of the form `a[i + expr] = a[i];` we generate and check the formula about range splice of $rep(n, env, fr).i + expression$ and $rep(n, env, fr).i + expression + 1$.

4. The strategy generates lemmas about truth of U for second items of pairs from D starting from truth of U for first items of pairs from D. These lemmas allow ACL2 to prove truth of U for subarrays obtained by concatenation of second items of pairs from D. Let ACL2 prove $T \Rightarrow U(\ldots)$ using these lemmas.

Let us apply this strategy to our example. All lemmas mentioned above can be found in [20]. After post-condition analysis, the theorems `permutation-7` and `ordered-3` were detected in the underlying theory. Since `permutation-7` satisfies the pattern, the predicate *perm* satisfies concatenation property. The theorem `ordered-3` satisfies the pattern with a splice at bounds, where $\leq$ is used as a relation f. Therefore, the predicate *ord* satisfies the concatenation property with a splice at bounds with respect to $\leq$.

Consider lemmas appeared at proving two goals. Let A be the goal containing predicate *perm*. Let B be the goal containing predicate *ord*. Thus, $A, B \in Z$. Then, let $G \equiv T \Rightarrow A$ and let $H \equiv T \Rightarrow B$. Let $e = update\text{-}nth(rep(i, env, fr).j + 1, k, rep(i, env, fr).a)$.

Consider first the application of strategy steps to formula A. The application of strategy to $a[0 : rep(n, env, fr).j] = (rep(i, env, fr).a)[0 : rep(i, env, fr).j]$ is described in Sect. 5.1. After that, the permutation of a and e in the range $[0 : rep(i, env, fr).j]$ was proved.

During analysis, the statement `a[j + 1] = a[j];` was detected, which is a potential array shift. Thus, the constant 1 corresponds to *expression*. With the help of `rep-lemma-22` and the strategy from Sect. 5.1, `rep-lemma-55` was obtained from $a[rep(i, env, fr).j+1 : i-1] = (rep(i, env, fr).a[rep(i, env, fr).j + 2 : i]$. It allowed to prove permutation of $a[rep(i, env, fr).j + 1 : i - 1]$ and $e[rep(i, env, fr).j + 2 : i]$.

The statement $e[rep(i, env, fr).j + 1 : rep(i, env, fr).j + 1] = a[i : i]$ was proved automatically. It allowed to prove the permutation of $a[i : i]$ and $e[rep(i, env, fr).j + 1 : rep(i, env, fr).j + 1]$. As permutation satisfies concatenation property, the permutation of a and e in the range $[rep(i, env, fr).j + 1 : i]$ was proved. Finally, using concatenation property we get permutation of a and e in the range $[0 : i]$.

Consider the application of strategy steps to formula B. The predicate *ord* satisfies the property of concatenation with a splice at bounds, so it is necessary to check that the relation $\leq$ holds at bounds. This property was successfully checked in Sect. 5.3.

The full proof can be found in [20].

6   Conclusion

This paper represents the method for the automation of the C-light program verification. In case of definite iteration over changeable arrays with loop exit, this method allows generating verification conditions without loop invariants.

This generation is based on the new inference rule for the C-light `for` statement which uses the replacement operation. This operation is generated automatically by the special algorithm [8], which translates loop body statements to ACL2 constructs. In this paper, we described changes to this algorithm, which extends the application of our method to downward iterations.

To prove obtained verification conditions, we apply special strategies based on lemma discovering. The successful proving of such lemmas allows us to prove the verification conditions. We developed four strategies. Their application was illustrated by the verification of insertion sort program. They supplement the symbolic method of definite iterations and allow automatizing the process of deductive verification.

Also, the verification of the functions implementing BLAS interface [3] is an actual problem. Earlier we performed such experiments successfully [7]. Our methods allowed us to verify the function $asum$, which implements the corresponding function from BLAS interface: it calculates the sum of absolute values of a vector.

References

1. Anureev, I.S., Maryasov, I.V., Nepomniaschy, V.A.: C-programs verification based on mixed axiomatic semantics. Autom. Control Comput. Sci. **45**(7), 485–500 (2011)
2. Cohen, E., et al.: VCC: a practical system for verifying concurrent C. In: Berghofer, S., Nipkow, T., Urban, C., Wenzel, M. (eds.) TPHOLs 2009. LNCS, vol. 5674, pp. 23–42. Springer, Heidelberg (2009). https://doi.org/10.1007/978-3-642-03359-9_2
3. Dongarra, J.J., van der Steen, A.J.: High-performance computing systems: status and outlook. Acta Numerica **21**, 379–474 (2012)
4. Filliâtre, J.-C., Marché, C.: Multi-prover verification of C programs. In: Davies, J., Schulte, W., Barnett, M. (eds.) ICFEM 2004. LNCS, vol. 3308, pp. 15–29. Springer, Heidelberg (2004). https://doi.org/10.1007/978-3-540-30482-1_10
5. Galeotti, J.P., Furia, C.A., May, E., Fraser, G., Zeller, A.: Inferring loop invariants by mutation, dynamic analysis, and static checking. IEEE Trans. Softw. Eng. **41**(10), 1019–1037 (2015)
6. Johansson, M.: Lemma discovery for induction. In: Kaliszyk, C., Brady, E., Kohlhase, A., Sacerdoti Coen, C. (eds.) CICM 2019. LNCS (LNAI), vol. 11617, pp. 125–139. Springer, Cham (2019). https://doi.org/10.1007/978-3-030-23250-4_9
7. Kondratyev, D.: Implementing the symbolic method of verification in the C-light project. In: Petrenko, A.K., Voronkov, A. (eds.) PSI 2017. LNCS, vol. 10742, pp. 227–240. Springer, Cham (2018). https://doi.org/10.1007/978-3-319-74313-4_17
8. Kondratyev, D.A., Maryasov, I.V., Nepomniaschy, V.A.: The automation of C program verification by symbolic method of loop invariants elimination. Autom. Control Comput. Sci. **53**(7) (2019, to appear)
9. Kondratyev, D.A., Promsky, A.V.: Towards automated error localization in C programs with loops. Syst. Inform. **14**, 31–44 (2019)
10. Kovács, L.: Symbolic computation and automated reasoning for program analysis. In: Ábrahám, E., Huisman, M. (eds.) IFM 2016. LNCS, vol. 9681, pp. 20–27. Springer, Cham (2016). https://doi.org/10.1007/978-3-319-33693-0_2
11. Li, J., Sun, J., Li, L., Le, Q. L., Lin, S.-W.: Automatic loop invariant generation and refinement through selective sampling. In: Proceedings on ASE 2017, pp. 782–792. Conference Publishing Consulting, Passau (2017)
12. Maryasov, I.V., Nepomniaschy, V.A.: Loop invariants elimination for definite iterations over unchangeable data structures in C programs. Model. Anal. Inform. Syst. **22**(6), 773–782 (2015)
13. Maryasov, I.V., Nepomniaschy, V.A., Kondratyev, D.A.: Invariant elimination of definite iterations over arrays in C programs verification. Model. Anal. Inf. Syst. **24**(6), 743–754 (2017)

14. Maryasov, I.V., Nepomniaschy, V.A., Promsky, A.V., Kondratyev, D.A.: Automatic C program verification based on mixed axiomatic semantics. Autom. Control Comput. Sci. **48**(7), 407–414 (2014)

15. Moore, J.S.: Milestones from the Pure Lisp theorem prover to ACL2. Formal Aspects of Computing, pp. 1–34 (2019)

16. Nepomniaschy, V.A.: Symbolic method of verification of definite iterations over altered data structures. Program. Comput. Softw. **31**(1), 1–9 (2005)

17. Srivastava, S., Gulwani, S., Foster, J.S.: Template-based program verification and program synthesis. Int. J. Softw. Tools Technol. Transf. **15**(5–6), 497–518 (2012)

18. Suzuki, N., Jefferson, D.: Verification decidability of Presburger array programs. J. ACM **27**(1), 191–205 (1980)

19. Tuerk, T.: Local reasoning about while-loops. In: Theory Workshop Proceedings on VSTTE 2010, pp. 29–39. Heriot-Watt University, Edinburgh (2010)

20. Verification of Insertion Sorting Program. https://bitbucket.org/Kondratyev/sorting. Accessed 26 Apr 2019

Hermes: A Reversible Language for Writing Encryption Algorithms (Work in Progress)

Torben Ægidius Mogensen[✉]

DIKU, University of Copenhagen,
Universitetsparken 5, 2100 Copenhagen, Denmark
torbenm@di.ku.dk

Abstract. We describe the programming language Hermes, which is designed for writing private-key encryption algorithms. Specifically, every program written in Hermes is reversible: It can run equally well forwards and backwards. This means that you only write the encryption algorithm and get the decryption algorithm for free. Hermes also ensures that all variables are cleared after use, so the memory will not contain data that can be used for side-channel attacks. Additionally, to prevent side-channel attacks that extract information from running times, control structures that may give data-dependent execution times are avoided.

1 Introduction

Recent work [7] have investigated using the reversible language Janus [3,14] for writing encryption algorithms. Janus is a structured imperative language where all statements are reversible. A requirement for reversibility is that no information is ever discarded: No variable is destructively overwritten in such a way that the original value is lost. Instead, it must be updated in a reversible manner or swapped with another variable. Since encryption is by nature reversible, it seems natural to write these in a reversible programming language. Additionally, reversible languages requires that all intermediate variables are cleared to 0 before they are discarded, which ensures that no information that could potentially be used for side-channel attacks is left in memory. But non-cleared variables is not the only side-channel attack used against encryption: If the time used to encrypt data can depend on the values of the data and the encryption key, attackers can gain (some) information about the data or the key simply by measuring the time used for encryption. Janus has control structures the timing of which depend on the values of variables, so it does not protect against timing-based attacks.

So we propose a language, Hermes, specifically designed for encryption. What Hermes has in common with Janus is reversible update statements, swap statements, and procedures that can be called both forwards and backwards. The main differences to Janus are that Hermes operates on integers of specified sizes,

© Springer Nature Switzerland AG 2019
N. Bjørner et al. (Eds.): PSI 2019, LNCS 11964, pp. 243–251, 2019.
https://doi.org/10.1007/978-3-030-37487-7_21

specifically 32 and 64-bit signed and unsigned integers, and there are no time-sensitive control structures. The syntax of Hermes resembles C, so programs will be readily readable by C programmers.

Figure 1 shows a Hermes implementation of TEA, a Tiny Encryption Algorithm [9] corresponding to the C code in Fig. 2, which is taken from the Wikipedia page for TEA [13]. While the Hermes code resembles the C code, this does not mean that we can automatically convert C programs to Hermes: In general, C statements are not reversible, and their timing may depend on data. But if an encryption algorithm is designed to be reversible and immune to timing attacks, it will usually be simple to (manually) port to Hermes. But the purpose is not to port existing C implementations of cyphers to Hermes, but to allow cypher designers to develop their cyphers in a language that ensures both reversibility and immunity to timing attacks.

```
encrypt (u32 v[2], u32 k[4])
{
    u32 v0, v1, sum, k0, k1, k2, k3;
    const u32 delta = 0x9E3779B9;           /* key schedule constant */
    v0 <-> v[0]; v1 <-> v[1];                       /* set up */
    k0 += k[0]; k1 += k[1]; k2 += k[2]; k3 += k[3]; /* cache key */
    for (i=0; 32) {                         /* basic cycle start */
        sum += delta;
        v0 += ((v1<<4) + k0) ^ (v1 + sum) ^ ((v1>>5) + k1);
        v1 += ((v0<<4) + k2) ^ (v0 + sum) ^ ((v0>>5) + k3);
        i++;
    }                                       /* end cycle */
    k0 -= k[0]; k1 -= k[1]; k2 -= k[2]; k3 -= k[3]; /* clear locals */
    sum -= delta << 5;      /* alternatively, sum -= 0xC6EF3720 */
    v[0] <-> v0; v[1] <-> v1;               /* return coded values */
}
```

Fig. 1. TEA in Hermes

Note that while the C version needs a separate decryption procedure, this is not required in Hermes, as decryption is achieved by running the encryption procedure backwards. Apart from often using the swap operator <->, the Hermes code is very similar to the encryption part of the C code, except that the local variables are explicitly cleared. If they were not, an error would be reported when running the program. Note that constants do not need to be cleared.

2   Hermes

The Syntax of Hermes is shown in Fig. 3. A program consists of one or more procedures, where the procedure called **main** is the entry point of the program. Unlike in C, the **main** procedure has no arguments. Arguments to procedures are passed by reference and to avoid aliasing, no variable or array may be passed several times in the same call.

```
void encrypt (uint32_t v[2], uint32_t k[4]) {
    uint32_t v0=v[0], v1=v[1], sum=0, i;     /* set up */
    uint32_t delta=0x9E3779B9;                /* key schedule constant */
    uint32_t k0=k[0], k1=k[1], k2=k[2], k3=k[3];   /* cache key */
    for (i=0; i<32; i++) {                    /* basic cycle start */
        sum += delta;
        v0 += ((v1<<4) + k0) ^ (v1 + sum) ^ ((v1>>5) + k1);
        v1 += ((v0<<4) + k2) ^ (v0 + sum) ^ ((v0>>5) + k3);
    }                                         /* end cycle */
    v[0]=v0; v[1]=v1;
}

void decrypt (uint32_t v[2], uint32_t k[4]) {
    uint32_t v0=v[0], v1=v[1], sum=0xC6EF3720, i;   /* sum=32*delta */
    uint32_t delta=0x9E3779B9;                /* key schedule constant */
    uint32_t k0=k[0], k1=k[1], k2=k[2], k3=k[3];   /* cache key */
    for (i=0; i<32; i++) {                    /* basic cycle start */
        v1 -= ((v0<<4) + k2) ^ (v0 + sum) ^ ((v0>>5) + k3);
        v0 -= ((v1<<4) + k0) ^ (v1 + sum) ^ ((v1>>5) + k1);
        sum -= delta;
    }                                         /* end cycle */
    v[0]=v0; v[1]=v1;
}
```

Fig. 2. TEA in C

The values used in Hermes are variables or one-dimensional arrays the elements of which are of the types u8, u16, u32, or u64, representing unsigned two's complement numbers corresponding to the C types uint8_t, uint16_t, uint32_t, and uint64_t. Sizes of arrays must be specified when they are declared. All variables are local to procedures, and must be cleared to zero before the end of the procedure. If not, a run-time error is reported.

Constants are initialised with a value and can not be modified. Constants do not need to be zeroed before procedure exit.

The body of a procedure is a statement. This can be

- The empty statement (;),
- An update using one of the update operators +=, -=, ^=, <<=, or >>=, where the last two operators are rotate-left and rotate-right. The root variable on the left-hand side is not allowed to occur elsewhere on the update statement (neither left-hand side nor right-hand side). For example, the statements i += a[i]; and a[a[i]] += 1; are not allowed, but a[i] += i; is allowed, as i is not the root variable on the left-hand side. Additionally, if the variable on the left-hand side is a loop variable (see later), the right-hand side expression must be a constant expression. Rotates are done on the word size of the variable on the left-hand side. For example, if x is an 8-bit number, x <<= 11 will rotate the 8-bit number 3 positions left. Rotates are not found as operators in C, but they are commonly used in cryptology, and they are reversible, so it is natural to include them in Hermes.

- Increment or decrement of a variable or array element. These are special cases of updates.
- A conditional update. In addition to the restrictions for unconditional updates, the root variable on the left-hand side may not occur in the condition, nor may it be a loop variable. To avoid value-dependent timing, the right-hand side is always evaluated and afterwards logically ANDed with the condition before using the result in an update. As such, the conditional update does not any power to the language, it just aids readability of otherwise somewhat cryptic code.
- A swap of two variables or array elements, using the swap operator `<->`. The root variables on either side may not occur in any index expression, nor may they be loop variables. For example, the statements `i <-> a[i];` and `a[a[i]] <-> j;` are not allowed, but `a[i] <-> a[j];` is allowed. A swap is implemented as three updates (using `^=`) to avoid introducing a temporary variable that might leak information.
- A conditional swap. In addition to the restrictions of the normal swap, neither root variable may occur in the condition. Conditional swap is commonly used in elliptic-curve cryptography to avoid time-variant conditionals.
- A block in curly braces, consisting of a number of declarations and a number of statements. Variables and array elements are initialised to 0 and they must be returned to 0 at the end of the block (otherwise a run-time error is issued).
- A for loop. This specifies the initial and final values for a counter variable and a body that will be executed until the counter variable reaches its final value. Updating the counter variable is, unlike in C, done in the body of the loop. The final value must be reached exactly, otherwise the loop continues. The counter variable is local to the for loop and need not be declared (it is always of type `u32`). The expressions for initial and final values for the loop counter must be constant expressions. Also, the loop counter may only be unconditionally updated with constant expressions, but it may be updated multiple times and with any update operator (`+=`, `-=`, `^=`, `<<=`, and `>>=`).
- An assertion. If the condition evaluates to false, a run-time error is issued. This is included for testing purposes.
- A procedure call. Arguments are passed by reference. No variable may be repeated in the argument list, so the statements `call f(i, i);`, `call f(i, a[i]);`, and `call f(a, a[i]);` are illegal. To avoid potential modification, loop variables can not be passed as arguments to procedures.
- An inverse procedure call. This executes the procedure in backwards order, so the sequence `call f(x); uncall f(x);` has no net effect.
- Print and scan statements. These use format strings like in C, except that the formats are `%u8`, `%u16`, etc. Before reading a variable or array element, this must have the value 0, otherwise, a run-time error is issued. After printing a variable or array element, this is set to 0. Loop variables and constants can not be printed or scanned.

Expressions are variables, array elements, constants, operators applied to expressions, or conditions. Constants are numbers in decimal or hexadecimal form,

$$Program \;\; \rightarrow Procedure^{+}$$

$$Procedure \rightarrow \textbf{id} \; (\; Decls2^{?} \;) \; Stat$$

$$
\begin{array}{ll}
Stat & \rightarrow \; ; \\
& | \; Lval \; \textbf{update} \; Exp \; ; \\
& | \; Lval \; \texttt{++}; \\
& | \; Lval \; \texttt{--}; \\
& | \; \textbf{if} \; (\; Exp \;) \; Lval \; \textbf{update} \; Exp \; ; \\
& | \; Lval \; \texttt{<->} Lval \\
& | \; \textbf{if} \; (\; Exp \;) \; Lval \; \texttt{<->} Lval \\
& | \; \textbf{for} \; (\; \textbf{id} \; \texttt{=} Exp \; ; \; Exp \;) \; Stat \\
& | \; \textbf{assert} \; (\; Exp \;); \\
& | \; \textbf{call} \; \textbf{id} \; (\; Lvals) \\
& | \; \textbf{uncall} \; \textbf{id} \; (\; Lvals) \\
& | \; \textbf{printf} \; (\; \textbf{stringConst} \; , \; Lvals \;); \\
& | \; \textbf{scanf} \; (\; \textbf{stringConst} \; , \; Lvals \;); \\
& | \; \{ \; Decls1 \; Stat^{*} \}
\end{array}
$$

$$
\begin{array}{ll}
Exp & \rightarrow Lval \\
& | \; \textbf{numConst} \\
& | \; Exp \; \textbf{binOp} \; Exp \\
& | \; \textbf{unOp} \; Exp \\
& | \; (\; Exp \;)
\end{array}
$$

$$
\begin{array}{ll}
Lval & \rightarrow \textbf{id} \\
& | \; \textbf{id} \; [\; Exp \;]
\end{array}
$$

$$
\begin{array}{ll}
Lvals & \rightarrow Lval \\
& | \; Lval \; , \; Lvals
\end{array}
$$

$$
\begin{array}{ll}
VarSpec & \rightarrow \textbf{id} \\
& | \; \textbf{id} \; [\; \textbf{numConst} \;]
\end{array}
$$

$$
\begin{array}{ll}
VarSpecs & \rightarrow VarSpec \\
& | \; VarSpec \; , \; VarSpecs
\end{array}
$$

$$
\begin{array}{ll}
Decls1 & \rightarrow \\
& | \; \textbf{type} \; VarSpecs \; ; \; Decls1 \\
& | \; \textbf{const type} \; \textbf{id} \; \texttt{=} \; \textbf{numConst} \; ; \; Decls1
\end{array}
$$

$$
\begin{array}{ll}
Decls2 & \rightarrow \textbf{type} \; VarSpec \\
& | \; \textbf{type} \; VarSpec \; , \; Decls2
\end{array}
$$

Fig. 3. Syntax of Hermes

using C notation. Binary operators are +, -, *, /, %, &, |, ==, !=, <, >, <=, >=, <<, and >>. Unary operators are - and ~. All operators have the same meaning as in C, and like in C, there is no separate Boolean type – 0 is treated as logical falsehood and all non-zero values as falsehood. Note that we do not include sequential logical operators &&, ||, and !, as their timing may depend on the values of their arguments. Bitwise logical operators should be used instead.

3   More Examples

An implementation of the speck128 cipher [1,12] in C and Hermes is shown in
Fig. 4. Hermes has rotation built-in, so it does not need the ROR and ROL macros.
But since Hermes does not support macros, R must be defined as a procedure.
Since loop variables can not be modified, it is not allowed to pass them as
parameters to procedures, so we use a variable ii to hold a copy of the loop
variable i. The Hermes version does not use separate parameters for the original
and encrypted text, since we want to use the encryption function in reverse for
decryption. A complication compared to a normal C implementation is that the
round keys a and b must be restored (in the second for-loop) so they can be
reset to 0 before the procedure exits. Note the use of uncall to do R in reverse.
While the Hermes version is slightly larger than the C version, a C program
would have to define separate functions for encryption and decryption.

  To illustrate the use of conditional updates, Fig. 5 shows a simple shift-
register-based cipher. Note that, since the condition in a conditional update
may not involve the updated variable, the value of the condition is computed
in a variable c before the update. To ensure reversibility of the procedure, c is
returned (uncomputed) to 0 afterwards. We restrict K[0] to be even to make
this uncomputation possible.

  Figure 6 includes C and Hermes versions of the central part of the RC5
cipher [4,10], i.e., not including the key expansion part. Again, Hermes doesn't
need the ROL macro, and we use a single parameter for the original and encrypted
values (pt, ct), but we must pass the expanded keys (S[]) as a parameter since
we don't have global variables. As usual, Hermes doesn't need a separate decryption function. The updates to A and B must in Hermes be done as sequences of
reversible updates, which is slightly more verbose, but also makes it clearer that
the transformations are, in fact, reversible. The C version has two nearly identical lines for even and odd array entries. By swapping A and B, we avoid this in
the Hermes version at the cost of going through the loop twice as many times.

  We have implemented also Red Pike [11] and Blowfish [5] in Hermes.

4   Compiling Hermes to C

We have implemented a prototype of Hermes by writing a compiler from Hermes
to C. Each Hermes procedure is compiled to two C functions: One for running
forwards and one for running backwards. The backwards version of a procedure
is compiled by first doing a source-level inversion of the Hermes procedure and
then compiling the inverted procedure to C. A command-line option allows the
whole program to be executed backwards. Since Hermes (like Janus) is designed
to be locally reversible, inversion of procedures is simple.

  Individual Hermes statements are fairly straightforward to compile to C.
The compiler inserts the checks and forced zeroing required for reversibility and
compiles statements to time-invariant C. An issue with using C as the target language is that the C compiler may optimise away the statements that clear local

```c
#include <stdint.h>

#define ROR(x,r) ((x >> r) | (x << (64 - r)))
#define ROL(x,r) ((x << r) | (x >> (64 - r)))
#define R(x,y,k) (x = ROR(x,8), x += y, x ^= k, y = ROL(y,3), y ^= x)
#define ROUNDS 32

void encrypt(uint64_t ct[2],
             uint64_t const pt[2],
             uint64_t const K[2])
{
    uint64_t y = pt[0], x = pt[1], b = K[0], a = K[1];

    R(x, y, b);
    for (int i = 0; i < ROUNDS - 1; i++) {
        R(a, b, i);
        R(x, y, b);
    }

    ct[0] = y;
    ct[1] = x;
}
```

```
R(u64 x, u64 y, u64 k)
{ x >>= 8; x += y; x ^= k; y <<= 3; y ^= x; }

speck128(u64 ct[2], u64 K[2])
{
    u64 y, x, b, a, ii;
    y <-> ct[0]; x <-> ct[1]; b += K[0]; a += K[1];

    call R(x, y, b);
    for (i=0; 32) {
        call R(a, b, ii);
        call R(x, y, b);
        ii++; i++;
    }
    for (i=32; 0) {   /* restore a and b */
        i--; ii--;
        uncall R(a, b, ii);
    }
    y <-> ct[0]; x <-> ct[1]; b -= K[0]; a -= K[1];
}
```

Fig. 4. Spec128 in C (top) and Hermes (bottom)

variables, hence allowing information to leak. Other optimisations may make timing depend on the actual data, leading to another form of information leak. As an option, you can use the Zerostack modification of the Clang/LLVM [6] compiler, which aims to avoid such compiler-introduced leaks.

```
shift (u64 v, u64 K[2])
{
    u64 a, b, c;
    a += K[0]; b += K[1];    /* K[0] must be even */
    for (i=0; 13) {
        c ^= v & 1; if (c) v += a; c ^= v & 1;
        v ^= b; v <<= 5; i++;
    }
    a -= K[0]; b -= K[1];
}
```

Fig. 5. Simple shift-register block cipher

```
void RC5_ENCRYPT(WORD *pt, WORD *ct)
{
    WORD i, A = pt[0] + S[0], B = pt[1] + S[1];

    for(i = 1; i <= 12; i++)
    {
        A = ROL(A ^ B, B) + S[2*i];
        B = ROL(B ^ A, A) + S[2*i + 1];
    }
    ct[0] = A; ct[1] = B;
}
```

```
rc5(u32 ct[2], u32 S[25])
{
    u32 A, B;
    A <-> ct[0]; B <-> ct[1];
    A += S[0]; B += S[1];

    for (i=2; 25) {
        A ^= B; A <<= B; A += S[i];
        B <-> A;
        i++;
    }
    ct[0] <-> A; ct[1] <-> B;
}
```

Fig. 6. RC5 in C (top) and Hermes (bottom)

5   Future Work

To ensure reversibility and avoid information leaks, a number of conditions are tested at run-time: That variables and arrays are zeroed before returning from a procedure, that variables are zero before a scan statement, as well as explicit assertions. We will investigate whether some of these conditions can be verified at compile time, both to reduce the size of the target code, to reduce the running time, and, if all conditions can be verified at compile time, to guarantee that programs will never fail these conditions at run-time.

Some of the restrictions for timing-sensitive control can be relaxed if we add variables that are declared to be non-secret. These can, for example, be used for the size of the key or data. Statements that are conditional only on non-secret variables need not be time invariant, as no secret is leaked by this variable timing. This will allow recursion based on, say, the size of data. Loop bound expressions and loop indices can use non-secret variables, and loop counter variables themselves can be categorised as non-secret. We plan to add public/secret types in future versions of Hermes.

Because if the issues with using C as a target language, we plan to make a compiler to CT-Wasm [8], which is a variant of WebAssembly [2] that has a public/secret type system as proposed above and which ensures that timing is invariant over secret values.

References

1. Beaulieu, R., Shors, D., Smith, J., Treatman-Clark, S., Weeks, B., Wingers, L.: The SIMON and SPECK families of lightweight block ciphers. Cryptology ePrint Archive, Report 2013/404 (2013). https://eprint.iacr.org/2013/404
2. Haas, A., et al.: Bringing the web up to speed with webAssembly. SIGPLAN Not. **52**(6), 185–200 (2017)
3. Lutz, C.: Janus: a time-reversible language. A letter to Landauer. http://www.tetsuo.jp/ref/janus.pdf (1986)
4. Rivest, R.L.: The RC5 encryption algorithm. Dr. Dobb's J. **20**(1), 146–148 (1995)
5. Schneier, B.: Description of a new variable-length key, 64-bit block cipher (Blowfish). In: Anderson, R. (ed.) FSE 1993. LNCS, vol. 809, pp. 191–204. Springer, Heidelberg (1994). https://doi.org/10.1007/3-540-58108-1_24
6. Simon, L., Chisnall, D., Anderson, R.: What you get is what you C: controlling side effects in mainstream C compilers. In: 2018 IEEE European Symposium on Security and Privacy (EuroS&P), pp. 1–15, April 2018
7. Táborský, D., Larsen, K.F., Thomsen, M.K.: Encryption and reversible computations - work-in-progress paper. In: Kari, J., Ulidowski, I. (eds.) RC 2018. LNCS, vol. 11106, pp. 331–338. Springer, Cham (2018). https://doi.org/10.1007/978-3-319-99498-7_23
8. Watt, C., Renner, J., Popescu, N., Cauligi, S., Stefan, D.: CT-Wasm: type-driven secure cryptography for the web ecosystem. CoRR, abs/1808.01348 (2018)
9. Wheeler, D.J., Needham, R.M.: TEA, a tiny encryption algorithm. In: Preneel, B. (ed.) FSE 1994. LNCS, vol. 1008, pp. 363–366. Springer, Heidelberg (1995). https://doi.org/10.1007/3-540-60590-8_29
10. Wikipedia. Rc5. https://en.wikipedia.org/wiki/RC5. Accessed Feb 2019
11. Wikipedia. Red pike (cipher). https://en.wikipedia.org/wiki/Red_Pike_(cipher). Accessed Feb 2019
12. Wikipedia. Speck (cipher). https://en.wikipedia.org/wiki/Speck_(cipher). Accessed Feb 2019
13. Wikipedia. Tiny encryption algorithm. https://en.wikipedia.org/wiki/Tiny_Encryption_Algorithm. Accessed Jan 2019
14. Yokoyama, T., Axelsen, H.B., Glück, R.: Principles of a reversible programming language. In: Proceedings of the 5th Conference on Computing Frontiers, CF 2008, pp. 43–54. ACM, New York (2008)

Causality-Based Testing in Time Petri Nets

Elena Bozhenkova[1]([envelope]), Irina Virbitskaite[1,2], and Louchka Popova-Zeugmann[3]

[1] A.P. Ershov Institute of Informatics Systems, SB RAS, 6, Acad. Lavrentiev avenue,
Novosibirsk 630090, Russia
`bozhenko@iis.nsk.su`
[2] Novosibirsk State University, 2, Pirogova st., Novosibirsk 630090, Russia
[3] Humboldt University of Berlin, Unter den Linden 6, 10099 Berlin, Germany

Abstract. The intention of the paper is towards a causality-based framework for developing, studying, and comparing testing equivalences with causal net and causal tree semantics in the setting of time Petri nets (elementary net systems whose transitions are labeled with time firing intervals, can fire only if their lower time bounds are attained, and are forced to fire when their upper time bounds are reached). We establish the relationships between the equivalences showing the similarity of the semantics under consideration. This allows studying in detail the timing behaviour in addition to the degrees of relative concurrency of processes generated during the functioning of time Petri nets.

1 Introduction

The concept of testing equivalence was put forward by Hennessy and de Nicola in [12]. Two processes are considered testing equivalent if there is no test that can distinguish them. A test is usually itself a process applied to a process by computing both together in parallel. A particular computation is considered to be successful if the test reaches a designated successful state, and the process guarantees the test if every computation is successful. This notion is intuitively appealing and has led to a well-developed mathematical theory of processes that ties together the equivalences and preorders. Testing equivalences were thoroughly investigated and well-understood in the setting of transition systems (see [7,11] among others) which are a representative of the interleaving approach where concurrency relation is reduced to nondeterminism by treating concurrent execution of actions as the choice between sequentializations of their atomic actions. To overcome the limits of interleaving semantics, concurrency is often modeled by absence of causal dependencies, represented by partial orders, between systems' events. Several well-known variants of partial order testing [2,14] appeared in the literature. Furthermore, testing equivalences based on causal tree semantics are actively treated as well. Here, the behaviour of a system is represented in the form of a tree with edges labeled by actions and their

This work is supported in part by DFG (project CAVER, grant BE 1267/14-1).

N. Bjørner et al. (Eds.): PSI 2019, LNCS 11964, pp. 252–261, 2019.
https://doi.org/10.1007/978-3-030-37487-7_22

predecessors. So, information about causality relation between actions is kept precisely. The relationships between causal tree and partial order semantics have been thoroughly studied in [1,10,14].

As safety-critical applications often require verification of real time characteristics, in addition to functional or qualitative temporal properties, testing equivalences are expanded in concurrent models with time. The papers [8] and [16] provided an alternative characterization of timed testing for discrete-time transition models, on the base of a notion similar to that of an acceptance set in the testing theory. In [18], decidability questions of interleaving time-sensitive testing are investigated. Semantic theories based on testing were developed for process algebras with timing constraints in the papers [15] and [9]. Both the papers provide alternative characterizations of testing preorders in terms of refusal traces. Also, the authors of [9] proved the possibility of discretization in the context of their algebra and, as a consequence, reduction of dense-timed testing to discrete-timed one. In [6], the testing relations and the results on their alternative characterizations and the possibility of discretization were extended to Petri nets with associating time intervals to arcs from places to transitions. At the same time, to the best of our knowledge, there are only few mentions of a fusion of timing and causality-based semantics, in testing scenario. In this regard, the work [17] is a welcome exception, where time-sensitive testing were treated in the setting of event structures with time characteristics. Also, our origin is the papers [4,5] which contribute to the classification of the wealth of observational equivalences of linear time – branching time spectrum, based on interleaving, causal tree and partial order semantics of dense-time event structures with and without internal actions.

The intention of the paper is towards a causality-based framework for developing, studying, and comparing testing equivalences with causal net and causal tree semantics in the setting of time Petri nets (elementary net systems whose transitions are labeled with time firing intervals, can fire only if their lower time bounds are attained, and are forced to fire when their upper time bounds are reached). We establish the relationships between the equivalences showing the similarity of the semantics under consideration. To do this, we heavily rely on the concept of causal net processes of a time Petri net, which were put forward in the paper [3]. The proofs of the results obtained can be found at www.iis.nsk.su/virb/proofsketches-PSI-2019.

2 Time Petri Nets: Syntax and Interleaving Semantics

In this section, some terminology concerning the model of Petri nets with timing constraints (time intervals on the firings of transitions) and its interleaving semantics in terms of firing sequences are defined.

We start with recalling the definitions of the structure and behavior of Petri nets (elementary net systems) [13]. We use Act to denote an alphabet of actions.

Definition 1. – A (labeled over Act) Petri net is a tuple $\mathcal{N} = (P, T, F, M_0, L)$, where P is a finite set of places and T is a finite set of transitions such that $P \cap T = \emptyset$ and $P \cup T \neq \emptyset$, $F \subseteq (P \times T) \cup (T \times P)$ is a flow relation, $\emptyset \neq M_0 \subseteq P$ is an initial marking, $L : T \to Act$ is a labeling function. For $x \in P \cup T$, let ${}^\bullet x = \{y \mid (y, x) \in F\}$ and $x^\bullet = \{y \mid (x, y) \in F\}$ be the preset and postset of x, respectively. For $X \subseteq P \cup T$, define ${}^\bullet X = \bigcup_{x \in X} {}^\bullet x$ and $X^\bullet = \bigcup_{x \in X} x^\bullet$.

- A marking M of a Petri net $\mathcal{N}$ is any subset of P. A transition $t \in T$ is enabled at a marking M if ${}^\bullet t \subseteq M^1$. Let $En(M)$ be the set of transitions enabled at M.

  The firing of a transition t enabled at a marking M leads to the new marking M' (denoted $M \xrightarrow{t} M'$) iff $M' = (M \setminus {}^\bullet t) \cup t^\bullet$. We write $M \xrightarrow{\vartheta} M'$ iff $\vartheta = t_1 \ldots t_k$ and $M = M^0 \xrightarrow{t_1} M^1 \ldots M^{k-1} \xrightarrow{t_k} M^k = M'$ $(k \geq 0)$. In this case, ϑ is a firing sequence of $\mathcal{N}$ from M (to M'), and M' is a reachable marking of $\mathcal{N}$ from M. Let $RM(\mathcal{N})$ be the set of all reachable markings of $\mathcal{N}$ from M_0.

  We call $\mathcal{N}$ T-restricted iff ${}^\bullet t \neq \emptyset \neq t^\bullet$, for all transitions $t \in T$; contact-free iff whenever t is a transition enabled at a marking M, then $M \cap t^\bullet = \emptyset$, for all $M \in RM(\mathcal{N})$.

Following the approach of [3], we extend the above model to time Petri nets. Let the domain $\mathbb{T}$ of time values be the set of rational numbers. We denote by $[\tau_1, \tau_2]$ the closed interval between two time values $\tau_1, \tau_2 \in \mathbb{T}$. Infinity is allowed at the upper bounds of intervals. Let $Interv$ be the set of all such intervals.

Definition 2. – A (labeled over Act) time Petri net is a pair $\mathcal{TN} = (\mathcal{N}, D)$, where $\mathcal{N}$ is the underlying (labeled over Act) Petri net and $D : T \to Interv$ is a static timing function associating with each transition a time interval. For a transition $t \in T$, the boundaries of the interval $D(t) \in Interv$ are called the earliest firing time Eft and latest firing time Lft of t.

- A state of $\mathcal{TN}$ is a pair (M, I), where M is a marking and $I : En(M) \longrightarrow \mathbb{T}$ is a dynamic timing function. The initial state of $\mathcal{TN}$ is a pair $S_0 = (M_0, I_0)$, where M_0 is the initial marking and $I_0(t) = 0$, for all $t \in En(M_0)$.

  A transition t enabled at a marking M is fireable from a state $S = (M, I)$ after a delay time $\theta \in \mathbb{T}$ if $(Eft(t) \leq I(t) + \theta)$ and $(I(t') + \theta \leq Lft(t')$, for all $t' \in En(M)))$.

  The firing of a transition t fireable from a state $S = (M, I)$ after a delay time θ leads to the new state $S' = (M', I')$ (denoted $S \xrightarrow{(t, \theta)} S'$) given as follows:

  (a) $M \xrightarrow{t} M'$,

  (b) $\forall t' \in T \diamond I'(t') = \begin{cases} I(t') + \theta, & \text{if } t' \in En(M \setminus {}^\bullet t), \\ 0, & \text{if } t' \in En(M') \setminus En(M \setminus {}^\bullet t), \\ undefined, & otherwise. \end{cases}$

  Then, we write $S \xrightarrow{(a, \theta)} S'$, if $a = L(t)$. We use the notation $S \xrightarrow{\sigma} S'$ iff $\sigma = (t_1, \theta_1) \ldots (t_k, \theta_k)$ and $S = S^0 \xrightarrow{(t_1, \theta_1)} S^1 \ldots S^{k-1} \xrightarrow{(t_k, \theta_k)} S^k = S'$ $(k \geq 0)$.

---

[1] For technical convenience, we do not use the classical definition: a transition $t \in T$ is enabled at a marking M if ${}^\bullet t \subseteq M$ and $M \cap t^\bullet = \emptyset$. We will require the second part in the definition of the contact-free property.

In this case, σ is a firing sequence of $\mathcal{TN}$ from S (to S'), and S' is a reachable state of $\mathcal{TN}$ from S. Let $\mathcal{FS}(\mathcal{TN})$ be the set of all firing sequences of $\mathcal{TN}$ from S_0, and $RS(\mathcal{TN})$ be the set of all reachable states of $\mathcal{TN}$ from S_0. We call $\mathcal{TN}$ T-restricted iff the underlying Petri net is T-restricted; contact-free iff whenever t is a transition fireable from the state $S = (M, I)$ after some delay time θ, then $(M \setminus {}^\bullet t) \cap t^\bullet = \emptyset$, for all $S \in RS(\mathcal{TN})^2$; time-progressive iff for all sets $\{t_1, t_2, \ldots, t_n\} \subseteq T$ such that $t_i^\bullet \cap {}^\bullet t_{i+1} \neq \emptyset$ $(1 \leq i < n)$ and $t_n^\bullet \cap {}^\bullet t_1 \neq \emptyset$, it holds that $\sum_{1 \leq i \leq n} Eft(t_i) > 0^3$. In what follows, we will consider only T-restricted, contact-free and time-progressive time Petri nets and denote their class as $\mathbb{TN}$.

Example 1. A (labeled over $Act = \{a, b, c\}$) time Petri net $\mathcal{TN}$ is shown in Fig. 1. Here, the names are depicted near the elements, the flow relation is drawn by the arcs, the initial marking is represented as the set of the places with tokens, and the values of the labeling and timing functions are printed next to the transitions. It is not difficult to check that t_1 and t_3 are transitions enabled at the initial marking M_0 and, moreover, transitions fireable from the initial state $S_0 = (M_0, I_0)$ after a time delay $\theta \in [2, 3]$, where $M_0 = \{p_1, p_2\}$, $I_0(t) = \begin{cases} 0, & \text{if } t \in \{t_1, t_3\}, \\ undefined, & \text{otherwise.} \end{cases}$ The sequence $\sigma = (t_1, 3)\ (t_3, 0)\ (t_2, 2)\ (t_3, 2)\ (t_1, 0)$ $(t_5, 2)\ (t_4, 0)$ is a firing sequences of $\mathcal{TN}$ from S_0. Furthermore, it is easy to see that $\mathcal{TN}$ is really T-restricted, contact-free and time-progressive.

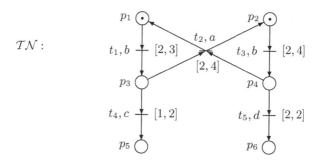

Fig. 1. An example of time Petri net.

3   Causality-Based Semantics of Time Petri Nets

3.1   Preliminaries

We start with considering definitions related to time causal nets.

---

[2] Clearly, if the underlying Petri net of $\mathcal{TN}$ is contact-free, then $\mathcal{TN}$ must be contact-free as well, but not vice versa.

[3] The time-progressive property shall guarantee the correctness of the modified definition of the contact-free property, for our purposes.

Definition 3. *A* (labeled over *Act*) time net *is a finite, acyclic net* $TN = (B, E, G, l, \tau)$ *with a set* B *of conditions, a set* E *of events, a flow relation* $G \subseteq (B \times E) \cup (E \times B)$ *such that* $\{e \mid (e, b) \in G\} = \{e \mid (b, e) \in G\} = E$, *a labeling function* $l : E \to Act$, *and a time function* $\tau : E \to \mathbb{T}$ *such that* $e \; G^+ \; e' \Rightarrow \tau(e) \leq \tau(e')$.

Introduce additional notions and notations for a time net $TN = (B, E, G, l, \tau)$. Let $\prec = G^+$, $\preceq = G^*$, and $\tau(TN) = \max\{\tau(e) \mid e \in E\}$. Specify $^\bullet x = \{y \mid (y, x) \in G\}$ and $x^\bullet = \{y \mid (x, y) \in G\}$, for $x \in B \cup E$, and, moreover, $^\bullet X = \bigcup_{x \in X} {}^\bullet x$ and $X^\bullet = \bigcup_{x \in X} x^\bullet$, for $X \subseteq B \cup E$. Furthermore, define the sets $^\bullet TN = \{b \in B \mid {}^\bullet b = \emptyset\}$ and $TN^\bullet = \{b \in B \mid b^\bullet = \emptyset\}$. TN is called a *time causal net*, if $|{}^\bullet b| \leq 1$ and $|b^\bullet| \leq 1$, for all $b \in B$. Notice that $\eta(TN) = (E_{TN}, \preceq_{TN} \cap (E_{TN} \times E_{TN}), l_{TN}, \tau_{TN})$ is a time poset[4]. Given a time causal net over Act, $TN = (B, E, G, l, \tau)$, $e, e' \in E$, $x, x' \in (B \cup E)$, and $E' \subseteq E$,

- $\downarrow e = \{x \mid x \preceq e\}$ (predecessors), $Earlier(e) = \{e' \in E \mid \tau(e') < \tau(e)\}$ (time predecessors), $x \smile x' \iff \neg((x \prec x') \vee (x' \prec x))$ (concurrency);
- E' is a *downward-closed subset* of E if $\downarrow e' \cap E \subseteq E'$, for all $e' \in E'$. In this case, $Cut(E') = (E'^\bullet \cup {}^\bullet TN) \setminus {}^\bullet E'$. Also, E' is called *timely sound subset* of E if $\tau(e') \leq \tau(e)$, for all $e' \in E'$ and $e \in E \setminus E'$;
- a sequence $\rho = e_1 \ldots e_k$ ($k \geq 0$) of events of TN is a *linearization of* TN if every event of TN appears in the sequence exactly once, and the following holds: $(e_i \preceq e_j \vee \tau(e_i) \leq \tau(e_j)) \Rightarrow i < j$, for all $1 \leq i, j \leq k$. For a linearization $\rho = e_1 \ldots e_k$ of TN, define $E_\rho^l = \bigcup_{1 \leq i \leq l} e_i$ ($0 \leq l \leq k$). Clearly, E_ρ^l is a downward-closed and timely sound subset of E, and, moreover, $\tau(e_k) = \tau(TN)$.

Lemma 1. *Every time causal net* TN *has a linearization* $\rho = e_1 \ldots e_k$. *Moreover,* $Cut(E_\rho^l) = \left(Cut(E_\rho^{l-1}) \setminus {}^\bullet e_l\right) \cup e^\bullet{}_l$, *and* $\left(Cut(E_\rho^{l-1}) \setminus {}^\bullet e_l\right) \cap e_l^\bullet = \emptyset$ ($1 \leq l \leq k$).

Time causal nets, $TN = (B, E, G, l, \tau)$ and $TN' = (B', E', G', l', \tau')$, are *isomorphic* (denoted $TN \simeq TN'$) iff there exists a bijective mapping $\beta : B \cup E \to B' \cup E'$ such that (i) $\beta(B) = B'$ and $\beta(E) = E'$; (ii) $x \, G \, y \iff \beta(x) \, G' \, \beta(y)$, for all $x, y \in B \cup E$; (iii) $l(e) = l'(\beta(e))$ and $\tau(e) = \tau'(\beta(e))$, for all $e \in E$. We say that TN is a *direct prefix of* TN' (denoted $TN \longrightarrow TN'$) if $B \subseteq B'$, E is a downward-closed and timely sound subset of E', $E' \setminus E = \{e\}$, $\downarrow e \cap E' \subseteq E$, $G = G' \cap (B \times E \cup E \times B)$, $l = l' \mid_E$, and $\tau = \tau' \mid_E$.

3.2   Time Causal Net Semantics

In this subsection, the concept of causality-based net processes of time Petri nets proposed in [3] is considered and studied.

---

[4] *A (labeled over Act) time poset (partially ordered set) is a tuple* $\eta = (X, \preceq, \lambda, \tau)$ *consisting of a finite set* X *of elements; a reflexive, antisymmetric and transitive relation* $\preceq$; *a labeling function* $\lambda : X \to Act$; *and a timing function* $\tau : X \to \mathbb{T}$ *such that* $e \preceq e' \Rightarrow \tau(e) \leq \tau(e')$. *Let* $\tau(\eta) = \max\{\tau(x) \mid x \in X\}$.

Definition 4. *Given a time Petri net* $\mathcal{TN} = ((P, T, F, M_0, L), D)$ *and a time causal net* $TN = (B, E, G, l, \tau)$,

- *a mapping* $\varphi : B \cup E \to P \cup T$ *is a* homomorphism *from* TN *to* $\mathcal{TN}$ *iff the following conditions hold:*
  - $\varphi(B) \subseteq P$, $\varphi(E) \subseteq T$;
  - *the restriction of* φ *to* $^{\bullet}e$ *is a bijection between* $^{\bullet}e$ *and* $^{\bullet}\varphi(e)$ *and the restriction of* φ *to* $e^{\bullet}$ *is a bijection between* $e^{\bullet}$ *and* $\varphi(e)^{\bullet}$, *for all* $e \in E$;
  - *the restriction of* φ *to* $^{\bullet}TN$ *is a bijection between* $^{\bullet}TN$ *and* M_0;
  - $l(e) = L(\varphi(e))$, *for all* $e \in E$.
- *a pair* $\pi = (TN, \varphi)$ *is a* time process *of a time Petri net* $\mathcal{TN}$ *iff* TN *is a time causal net and* φ *is a homomorphism from* TN *to* $\mathcal{TN}$.

Given a time process $\pi = (TN, \varphi)$ of $\mathcal{TN}$, a subset $B' \subseteq B_{TN}$, and a transition $t \in En(\varphi(B'))$, the time of enabling (TOE) of t, i.e. the latest global time moment when tokens appear in all input places of t, is defined in [3] as follows: $\mathbf{TOE}_\pi(B', t) = \max\left(\{\tau_{TN}(^{\bullet}b) \mid b \in B'_{[t]} \setminus {}^{\bullet}TN\} \cup \{0\}\right)$, where $B'_{[t]} = \{b \in B' \mid \varphi_{TN}(b) \in {}^{\bullet}t\}$.

Next, define the notion of a *correct time process of* $\mathcal{TN}$.

Definition 5. *A time process* $\pi = (TN, \varphi)$ *of* $\mathcal{TN}$ *is* correct *iff for all* $e \in E$ *it holds:*

(a) $\tau(e) \geq \mathbf{TOE}_\pi(^{\bullet}e, \varphi(e)) + Eft(\varphi(e))$,
(b) $\forall t \in En(\varphi(C_e)) \circ \tau(e) \leq \mathbf{TOE}_\pi(C_e, t) + Lft(t)$, *where* $C_e = Cut(Earlier(e))$.

Let $\mathcal{CP}(\mathcal{TN})$ *denote the set of correct time processes of* $\mathcal{TN}$.

Time processes $\pi = (TN, \varphi)$, $\pi' = (TN', \varphi') \in \mathcal{CP}(\mathcal{TN})$ are *isomorphic* (denoted $\pi \simeq \pi'$) iff there is an isomorphism $f : TN \simeq TN'$ such that $\varphi(x) = \varphi'(f(x))$, for all $x \in B \cup E$. From now on, for $\pi = (TN, \varphi)$, $\pi' = (TN', \varphi') \in \mathcal{CP}(\mathcal{TN})$, we write $\pi \longrightarrow \pi'$ in $\mathcal{TN}$ iff $TN \longrightarrow TN'$ and $\varphi = \varphi'|_{B \cup E}$.

We now intend to realize for a time Petri net the relationships between its firing sequences and its correct time processes. For $\pi = (TN, \varphi) \in \mathcal{CP}(\mathcal{TN})$, define the function FS_π that maps any linearization $\rho = e_1 \ldots e_k$ of TN to the sequence of the form: $FS_\pi(\rho) = (\varphi(e_1), \tau(e_1) - 0) \ldots (\varphi(e_k), \tau(e_k) - \tau(e_{k-1}))$. The following is a slight modification of Theorems 19, 21 and 22 from [3].

Proposition 1. *(i) Given* $\pi = (TN, \varphi) \in \mathcal{CP}(\mathcal{TN})$ *and a linearization* ρ *of* TN, *there is a unique firing sequence* $FS_\pi(\rho) \in \mathcal{FS}(\mathcal{TN})$.
(ii) Given $\sigma \in \mathcal{FS}(\mathcal{TN})$ *of* $\mathcal{TN}$, *there is a unique (up to an isomorphism) time process* $\pi_\sigma = (TN, \varphi) \in \mathcal{CP}(\mathcal{TN})$ *with a unique linearization* ρ_σ *of* TN *such that* $FS_{\pi_\sigma}(\rho_\sigma) = \sigma$.

Lemma 2. *Given* $\sigma \in \mathcal{FS}(\mathcal{TN})$ *and* $\pi \in \mathcal{CP}(\mathcal{TN})$ *such that* $\sigma = FS_\pi(\rho)$, *where* ρ *is a linearization of* TN_π,

(i) if $\sigma(t, \theta) \in \mathcal{FS}(\mathcal{TN})$, *there is* $\tilde{\pi} \in \mathcal{CP}(\mathcal{TN})$ *such that* $\pi \to \tilde{\pi}$ *in* $\mathcal{TN}$ *and* $\sigma(t, \theta) = FS_{\tilde{\pi}}(\rho e)$, *where* ρe *is a linearization of* $TN_{\tilde{\pi}}$;
(ii) if $\pi \to \tilde{\pi}$ *in* $\mathcal{TN}$, *then there is* $\sigma(t, \theta) \in \mathcal{FS}(\mathcal{TN})$ *such that* $\sigma(t, \theta) = FS_{\tilde{\pi}}(\rho e)$, *where* ρe *is a linearization of* $TN_{\tilde{\pi}}$.

3.3 Time Causal Tree Semantics

Causal trees [10] are synchronisation trees which carry in their labels additional information about causes of actions thus providing us with an interleaving description of concurrent processes which faithfully expresses causality. Time causal trees are an extension of causal trees by adding timing. In the time causal tree of $\mathcal{TN}$, the nodes are simply the firing sequences from $\mathcal{FS}(\mathcal{TN})$, and an arc exists between the two nodes if the second one is an extension of the first one. The causes in the labels of the arc have to be computed from the causality relation of the corresponding time processes of $\mathcal{TN}$.

Definition 6. *The* time causal tree *of* $\mathcal{TN}$, $TCT(\mathcal{TN})$, *is a tree* $(\mathcal{FS}(\mathcal{TN})$, A, $\phi)$, *where* $\mathcal{FS}(\mathcal{TN})$ *is the set of nodes with the root* ϵ; $A = \{(\sigma, \sigma(t, \theta)) \mid$ $\sigma, \sigma(t, \theta) \in \mathcal{FS}(\mathcal{TN})\}$ *is the set of arcs;* ϕ *is the labeling function such that* $\phi(\epsilon) = \epsilon$ *and* $\phi(\sigma, \sigma(t, \theta)) = (l_{\mathcal{TN}}(t), \theta, K)$, *where* $K = \{n - l + 1 \mid \sigma(t, \theta) = FS_{\pi_{\sigma(t,\theta)}}(e_1 \ \ldots \ e_n \ e)$, *for the linearization* $e_1 \ \ldots \ e_n \ e$ *of* $TN_{\pi_{\sigma(t,\theta)}}$, *and* $e_l \prec_{TN_{\sigma(t,\theta)}} e\}$. *Let* $path(\sigma)$ *be the path starting from the root and finishing in the node* σ *of* $TCT(\mathcal{TN})^5$.

Example 2. Consider the time Petri net $\mathcal{TN}$ (see Fig. 1) and its firing sequence $\sigma = (t_1, 3) \ (t_3, 0) \ (t_2, 2) \ (t_3, 2) \ (t_1, 0) \ (t_5, 2) \ (t_4, 0) \in \mathcal{FS}(\mathcal{TN})$. It is easy to get that $\phi(path(\sigma)) = (a, 3, \emptyset) \ (b, 0, \emptyset) \ (a, 2, \{1, 2\}) \ (b, 2, \{1, 2, 3\}) \ (a, 0, \{2, 3, 4\})$ $(d, 2, \{2, 3, 4, 5\}) \ (c, 0, \{2, 4, 5, 6\})$.

We finally establish some relationships between correct time processes and labeled paths in the time causal trees of two time Petri nets.

Proposition 2. *(i) Given* $\pi \in \mathcal{CP}(\mathcal{TN})$ *and* $\pi' \in \mathcal{CP}(\mathcal{TN}')$ *with an isomorphism* $f : \eta(TN_\pi) \to \eta(TN_{\pi'})$, $\phi(path(FS_\pi(\rho))) = \phi'(path(FS_{\pi'}(f(\rho))))$, *for any linearization* ρ *of* TN_π.
(ii) Given $\sigma \in \mathcal{FS}(\mathcal{TN})$ *and* $\sigma' \in \mathcal{FS}(\mathcal{TN}')$ *such that* $\phi(path(\sigma)) = \phi'(path(\sigma'))$, *there is an isomorphism* $f : \eta(TN_{\pi_\sigma}) \to \eta(TN_{\pi_{\sigma'}})$ *such that* $f(\rho_\sigma) = \rho_{\sigma'}$.

4 Testing Equivalences in Causality-Based Semantics

A kind of causal testing on event structure models has already been defined by Aceto, De Nicola and Fantechi in [2]. Their idea is that the experiments on event structures are pomsets instead of words and the behaviour which is tested for after the experiment consists of a set of actions. Instead of sets of actions, the authors of [14] have used sets of direct extensions of the executed pomsets, as tests. Also, in [14] a stronger version of causal testing has been put forward, based on posets rather than pomsets. Following this approach, we define poset testing equivalence on time Petri nets, relying on their correct time processes.

Definition 7. *Given time Petri nets* $\mathcal{TN}$ *and* $\mathcal{TN}'$,

---

^{5} We assume $path(\epsilon) = \epsilon$. Notice that in $TCT(\mathcal{TN})$, for any node $\sigma \in \mathcal{FS}(\mathcal{TN})$, there is a path starting from the root and finishing in σ.

- *for a time poset TP and a set $\mathbf{TP}$ of time posets, such that $TP \prec TP'$[6] for all $TP' \in \mathbf{TP}$, $\mathcal{TN}$ after TP $\mathbf{MUST}_{pos}$ $\mathbf{TP}$ iff for all $\pi = (TN, \varphi) \in \mathcal{CP}(\mathcal{TN})$ and for all isomorphisms $f : \eta(TN) \longrightarrow TP$[7], there exists $TP' \in \mathbf{TP}$, $\pi' = (TN', \varphi') \in \mathcal{CP}(\mathcal{TN})$, and an isomorphism $f' : \eta(TN') \longrightarrow TP'$ such that $\pi \to \pi'$ and $f \subseteq f'$;*
- *$\mathcal{TN}$ and $\mathcal{TN}'$ are poset testing equivalent (denoted $\mathcal{TN} \sim_{pos} TN'$) iff for all time posets TP and for all sets $\mathbf{TP}$ of time posets, such that $TP \prec TP'$ for all $TP' \in \mathbf{TP}$, it holds: $\mathcal{TN}$ after TP $\mathbf{MUST}_{pos}$ $\mathbf{TP}'$ $\iff$ $\mathcal{TN}'$ after TP $\mathbf{MUST}_{pos}$ $\mathbf{TP}'$.*

Example 3. Consider the time Petri nets $\mathcal{TN}_1$, $\mathcal{TN}_2$, and $\mathcal{TN}_3$ depicted in Fig. 2. It is easy to see that $\mathcal{TN}_1$ and $\mathcal{TN}_2$ are $\sim_{pos}$–equivalent whereas $\mathcal{TN}_2$ and $\mathcal{TN}_3$ are not. Let's make sure the latter. Define posets $TP = (\{x_1, x_2\}, \preceq, \lambda, \tau)$ and $TP' = (\{x_1, x_2, x_3\}, \preceq', \lambda', \tau')$, where $\preceq = \{(x_i, x_i) \mid 1 \leq i \leq 2\}$, $\lambda(x_1) =$

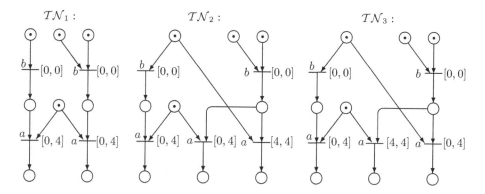

Fig. 2. $\sim_{pos}-$ and $\not\sim_{pos}$–equivalent time Petri nets.

$\lambda(x_2) = b$, $\tau(x_1) = \tau(x_2) = 0$; $\preceq' = \{(x_i, x_i) \mid 1 \leq i \leq 3\} \cup \{(x_2, x_3)\}$, $\lambda'(x_1) = \lambda'(x_2) = b$, $\lambda'(x_3) = a$, $\tau'(x_1) = \tau'(x_2) = 0$, and $\tau'(x_3) = 3.9$. For any time process $\pi_2 = (TN_2, \varphi_2) \in \mathcal{CP}(\mathcal{TN}_2)$ with E_{TN_2} consisting of two concurrent events with labels b and time values 0, and any isomorphism $f_2 : \eta(TN_2) \longrightarrow TP$, we can find $\pi_2' = (TN_2', \varphi_2') \in \mathcal{CP}(\mathcal{TN}_2)$ with $E_{TN_2'}$ consisting of two concurrent events with labels b and time values 0 and some third event with label a and time value 3.9, which is causally preceded by one of the b's, and an isomorphism $f_2' : \eta(TN_2') \longrightarrow TP'$ such that $\pi_2 \to \pi_2'$ and $f_2 \subset f_2'$. But this is not the case in $\mathcal{TN}_3$.

---

[6] A time poset η is a *direct prefix* of a time poset η' (denoted $\eta \prec \eta'$) iff $X \subseteq X'$, $X' \setminus X = \{x\}$, $\preceq = \preceq' \cap (X \times X)$, $\lambda = \lambda' \mid_X$, $\tau = \tau' \mid_X$, and x is a maximal w.r.t. $\preceq'$ element of X'.

[7] Time posets, $\eta = (X, \preceq, \lambda, \tau)$ and $\eta' = (X', \preceq', \lambda', \tau')$, are *isomorphic* (denoted $\eta \simeq \eta'$) iff there is a bijective mapping $\beta : X \to X'$ such that (i) $x \preceq y \iff \beta(x) \preceq' \beta(y)$, for all $x, y \in X$; (ii) $\lambda(x) = \lambda'(\beta(x))$ and $\tau(x) = \tau'(\beta(x))$, for all $x \in X$.

Second, the definition of testing equivalence on time causal trees is developed. For this we adapt the concept of causal tree testing on event structures from [14] to time Petri nets, in so doing the experiments and tests are constructed over the alphabet $Act \times \mathbb{T} \times 2^{\mathbb{N}}$ instead of over $Act \times 2^{\mathbb{N}}$.

Definition 8. *Given time Petri nets $\mathcal{TN}$ and $\mathcal{TN}'$ with their time causal trees $TCT(\mathcal{TN})$ and $TCT(\mathcal{TN}')$, respectively,*

- *for a sequence $w \in (Act \times \mathbb{T} \times 2^{\mathbb{N}})^*$ and a set $\mathbf{W} \subseteq (Act \times \mathbb{T} \times 2^{\mathbb{N}})$, $TCT(\mathcal{TN})$* **after** *w* **MUST W** *iff for all paths u in $TCT(\mathcal{TN})$ from its root to a node n such that $\phi(u) = w$, there exists a label $(a, d, K) \in \mathbf{W}$ and an arc r starting from n such that $\phi(r) = (a, d, K)$;*
- *$\mathcal{TN}$ and $\mathcal{TN}'$ are causal tree testing equivalent ($\mathcal{TN} \sim_{ct} \mathcal{TN}'$) iff for all $w \in (Act \times \mathbb{T} \times 2^{\mathbb{N}})^*$ and $\mathbf{W} \subseteq (Act \times \mathbb{T} \times 2^{\mathbb{N}})$, $TCT(\mathcal{TN})$* **after** *w* **MUST W** *$\Longleftrightarrow TCT(\mathcal{TN}')$* **after** *$w$* **MUST W**.

We finally establish the coincidence of poset and causal tree testing equivalences, in the setting of time Petri nets.

Theorem 1. *Given time Petri nets $\mathcal{TN}_1$ and $\mathcal{TN}_2$,*

$$\mathcal{TN}_1 \sim_{pos} \mathcal{TN}_2 \iff \mathcal{TN}_1 \sim_{ct} \mathcal{TN}_2.$$

5   Concluding Remarks

We have shown that some of the causality-based testing equivalences actively treated in the untimed and timed event structures literature may be lifted to the realm of time Petri nets. In particular, we have defined testing equivalences based on time causal trees and time causal nets, in the setting of safe Petri nets (elementary net systems) with strong timing (transitions are labeled with time firing intervals, enabled transitions are able to fire only if their lower time bounds are attained, and are forced to fire when their upper time bounds are reached). In doing so, we dealt with three behavioral representations of a time Petri net: firing sequences representing interleaving semantics, time causal net processes, from causal nets of which partial orders are derived, and the causal tree semantics constructed from the firing sequences and partial orders. We have realized for a time Petri net the relationships between its firing sequences and correct time processes, on the one hand, and the labeled paths in its time causal tree and correct time processes, on the other hand. As a main result, the coincidence between the testing equivalences in the semantics of time partial orders and time causal trees was established. It is worth noticing that the result also works for the untimed versions of the equivalences in the setting of untimed contact-free elementary net systems.

As for future work, we plan to see the place of the equivalences and semantics under consideration in the lattice of those in the linear-time—branching-time and interleaving—partial order spectra, constructed in the paper [19]. Also, we intend to extend the results obtained to time Petri nets with invisible actions.

References

1. Aceto, L.: History preserving, causal and mixed-ordering equivalence over stable event structures. Fundamenta Informaticae **17**(4), 319–331 (1992)
2. Aceto, L., De Nicola, R., Fantechi, A.: Testing equivalences for event structures. Lect. Notes Comput. Sci. **280**, 1–20 (1987)
3. Aura, T., Lilius, J.: A causal semantics for time Petri nets. Theor. Comput. Sci. **243**, 409–447 (2000)
4. Andreeva, M., Bozhenkova, E., Virbitskaite, I.: Analysis of timed concurrent models based on testing equivalenc. Fundamenta Informaticae **43**, 1–20 (2000)
5. Andreeva, M., Virbitskaite, I.: Observational equivalences for timed stable event structures. Fundamenta Informaticae **72**(1–3), 1–19 (2006)
6. Bihler, E., Vogler, W.: Timed Petri nets: efficiency of asynchronous systems. Lect. Notes Comput. Sci. **3185**, 25–58 (2004)
7. Cleaveland, R., Hennessy, M.: Testing equivalence as a bisimulation equivalence. Lect. Notes Comput. Sci. **407**, 11–23 (1989)
8. Cleaveland, R., Zwarico, A.E.: A theory of testing for real-time. In: Proceedings of 6th IEEE Symposium on Logic in Computer Science (LICS 1991), Amsterdam, The Netherlands, pp. 110–119 (1991)
9. Corradini, F., Vogler, W., Jenner, L.: Comparing the worst-case efficiency of asynchronous systems with PAFAS. Technical report, N 2000–6, Inst. fur Informatik of Univ. of Augsburg (2000)
10. Darondeau, P., Degano, P.: Refinement of actions in event structures and causal trees. Theor. Comput. Sci. **118**, 21–48 (1993)
11. De Nicola, R.: Extensional equivalences for transition systems. Acta Informatica **24**, 211–237 (1987)
12. De Nicola, R., Hennessy, M.: Testing equivalence for processes. Theor. Comput. Sci. **34**, 83–133 (1984)
13. Rozenberg, G., Engelfriet, J.: Elementary net systems. Lect. Notes Comput. Sci. **1491**, 12–121 (1998)
14. Goltz, U., Wehrheim, H.: Causal testing. Lect. Notes Comput. Sci. **1113**, 394–406 (1996)
15. Hennessy, M., Regan, T.: A process algebra for timed systems. Inf. Comput. **117**, 221–239 (1995)
16. Llana, L., de Frutos, D.: Denotational semantics for timed testing. Lect. Notes Comput. Sci. **1233**, 368–382 (1997)
17. Murphy, D.: Time and duration in noninterleaving concurrency. Fundamenta Informaticae **19**, 403–416 (1993)
18. Steffen, B., Weise, C.: Deciding testing equivalence for real-time processes with dense time. Lect. Notes Comput. Sci. **711**, 703–713 (1993)
19. Virbitskaite, I., Bushin, D., Best, E.: True concurrent equivalences in time Petri nets. Fundamenta Informaticae **149**(4), 401–418 (2016)

Author Index

Printed in the United States
By Bookmasters